A Suburb of Europe

A Suburb of Europe

Nineteenth-century Polish Approaches to Western Civilization

Jerzy Jedlicki

CEU PRESS

Central European University Press
Budapest

English edition published in 1999 by

Central European University Press
Október 6. utca 12
H–1051 Budapest
Hungary

400 West 59th Street
New York, NY 10019
USA

First published in Polish as *Jakiej cywilizacji Polacy potrzebują*
by Państwowe Wydawnictwo Naukowe
English edition published by arrangement with
Polish Scientific Publishers PWN
© Copyright by Państwowe Wydawnictwo Naukowe PWN, Warszawa 1988

Distributed by Plymbridge Distributors Ltd.
Estover Road, Plymouth PL6 7PZ, United Kingdom

ISBN 963-9116-27-0 Cloth
ISBN 963-9116-26-2 Paperback

Library of Congress Cataloging in Publication Data
A CIP catalog record for this book is available upon request

Printed in Hungary by Akadémiai Nyomda Kft.

Contents

Preface to the English Edition

The question of where modern civilization is heading and what can be expected of its progress dominated the social discourse of European intellectuals as early as the eighteenth century, before becoming a more ominous challenge to the world as a whole. As the most comprehensive of all the questions surrounding the fate of present and future generations, the question of the direction in which civilization is moving has become the core of many historiosophical systems. Although it has often been raised to the heights of abstract speculation, it draws its permanent significance from existential human experience.

The industrial revolution in England set in motion the profound changes that, two centuries later, affected the most distant territories of the globe and the most isolated social communities. An awareness of the world's instability no longer requires, as it did earlier, any historical knowledge since dramatic changes in environment and living conditions are taking place within the lifetime of the individual. And yet those people who introduce change, seldom aware themselves of its consequences, are but a handful in the midst of a conservative majority.[1]

Those who discovered the laws of nature and charted unknown lands, who invented new technologies, new sources of energy and new means of communication, who shaped new human needs and produced new objects with which to satisfy them, who designed new institutions, preached new religious and social creeds, who wrote laws and toppled old authorities—all these restless demiurges of the Great Transformation managed to impose upon the whole globe an incessant mutability of landscapes and ways of life.[2] Ancient human communities experienced civilizational change as something coming, or that had already come, from the outside, together with strangers from a distant city or from beyond the sea, who brought with them new objects and who espoused new morals. This invasion brought with it temptation and threat, promise and horror. It was, in the words of Arnold Toynbee, a challenge which could have been responded to with willing acquiescence, with bitter resistance, or with a mixture of trust and fear.[3] But whatever the initial emotional reaction, in one country after another the story usually ended with a gradual domestication of the new things, technologies and morals. The human race revealed again and again an unexpected adaptability that could not have been formed by slow natural evolution. The young familiarized themselves more rapidly with changing conditions and were more ready to seize new temptations and new opportunities, which meant that for the first time in history, the young could be more experienced than their elders. As a result, the authority of the elder generation and the regulative role of tradition began to weaken. Finally, the invasion broke into people's minds and souls, changing their desires and motivations, their value systems and cognitive attitudes.

This story was to repeat itself, more or less radically, in every village of the world, from Lancashire to New Guinea. In every intellectual center, dilettante and sophisticated social thought in turn absorbed the traumatic experiences of the human masses, their inarticulate hopes and fears, their gains and losses, and endeavored to express them in the language of mystical prophecy or rationalized doctrine. Every individual caught in the cogwheels of new civilization could choose from among several possible emotional attitudes and patterns of response. The same was true at the level of the local or ethnic community. And every response, once it emerged in the form of an elementary reflex, feeling, or mode of collective behavior, could then be transformed into an ideological, or even philosophical, proposition.

The mechanics of the impact of modernity appear to be more or less similar everywhere, in spite of the diversity of traditional cultures under siege. Thus, it is not hard to explain the striking typological similarities among responses formulated independently in various countries, however distant from each other, and at various times. "Westernizers" and "Slavophiles" can be found everywhere.

This, however, is not the whole story. Problems associated with the process of adaptation may last for as long as a few generations, but are then attenuated and disappear: having adopted a new system of concepts and values, people become accustomed to a new rhythm of work, to life in a landscape transformed by technological revolution. And yet, while its main emphasis may have shifted, the controversy over civilization has not been silenced. During the initial period of invasion it may have seemed that there was a choice: that the model of cosmopolitan industrial civilization could be accepted, rejected, or modified. Later, the direction of development seemed to be determined, less and less subject to any individual or collective will, while it remained unclear whether this path would lead to paradise or to hell, towards happiness or catastrophe for humankind. Would mastery of the forces of nature and the unrestrained increase of material goods lead to greater social justice, or would the reverse be true? Did it make people better or worse? Was it progress or decay? Social philosophy entered the age of futurology, the age of scientific, infallible predictions, of bright, or sinister, prophecy. In the chaos of events and processes, greater and lesser minds tried to discover a direction, an inevitable sequence of stages within human history, its moral sense and order. There was a common belief that the great stream of changes must be governed by some superior law, even if there was no agreement as to its character and content.

These two distinct phases in the attempt to understand and, if possible, steer the progress of civilization are, of course, idealized. In reality, the uneasy questions and cognitive conflicts, the controversial assessments and prognostics often appeared at the same time, creating a chaos from which one aspect of the controversy or another emerged to take precedence. The logical order of the problems was disturbed by the asynchronism of the stages of the economic and cultural development of various European and non-European countries. Social philosophy in the less advanced nations was able to make use not only of native experience, but also the knowledge acquired by more advanced stages of modern civilization and theories of development born on alien soil. Consciousness thus outpaced the transformation of living conditions so that in Poland for instance, intellectual reflection on modernity was almost abreast of that in the West, while industrial capitalism was advancing at a much slower pace.

This shortening of intellectual distance emerges most clearly if we compare the economic ideas propagated in countries located at different levels of modern civilization, such as Poland and France, in the first half of the nineteenth century. Judgments concerning the moral and aesthetic consequences of industrialism appear even less dependent on specific local points of view. Here the historian is in danger of falling into the trap of particularism: indeed, nothing is simpler than to see Slav indictment of the corrupt West as a symptom of a conservative fear of progress, typical of backward societies. In fact, all those antinomies of nature and civilization, country and town, spirit and matter, art and industry, organic and mechanical social bonds, etc., had previously been formulated and refined in British (or French or American) literature, but then, of course, both the blessings and curses of "material progress" were perceived inside, rather than outside the national culture.[4] Needless to say, it would be all too easy for the historian of Polish thought who is, by nature so to speak, inclined to overestimate its original character, to have such a narrowed field of vision.

While researching this book, however, I became increasingly strengthened in my conviction that particular traits of national ideologies are, in this respect, secondary. The more I read, the more aware I became that almost identical pro- and anti-modernization arguments occur in the documents and literary output of many nations and periods. There seemed to be a need for a comparative analysis which would take into account the universality, persistence and frequent recurrence of the same essential dilemmas, obsessions, fears and hopes emerging from the expansion of modern scientific and industrial civilization.

I did not, however, feel able to undertake such an ambitious task, and this book stops short of being a comparative study. True, I have tried not to lose sight of the universal aspect of the question under consideration and to remember that even national complexes and myths may be regarded as supranational phenomena. Indeed, I have stressed the ideological affinities of Polish and Western systems of social philosophy and brought into relief the impact on the Polish mind of such thinkers as Rousseau, Condorcet, Sismondi, Saint-Simon, or Marx, whose influence is undeniable. It seemed to me, however, that one must first of all present Polish approaches to Western civilization inasmuch as they were conditioned by specific historical circumstances, and were expressions of particular Polish viewpoints and complexes. After all, there is no denying that national history and cultural idiom played a role in shaping attitudes towards modernity and its literary precursors.

In Polish thought, the problem of a civilizational choice emerged in the middle of the eighteenth century and soon became—together with the question of constitutional reform—the most important subject of the political and cultural discourse of the Enlightenment. The question of whether the Polish–Lithuanian Commonwealth would participate in European progress, or hold itself aloof, cultivating its own individuality, became the main issue in the struggle between the "Enlightened" and the "Sarmatians." Among the intellectual elite of the nation—much as in the West—enthusiastic opinions about the "Enlightened Age" and the prospects for a new civilization collided with skepticism. Obviously, so prominent a subject found proper reflection in historical writing.[5]

After the fall of the Commonwealth, the hierarchy of interest in Polish social and political thought understandably changed. Questions surrounding the direction and merits of civilizational progress were now subordinated to the superior issue of the nation's right to an independent political existence. The question of Poland's relationship to Europe was colored by the claim that Western nations should help the Poles regain their freedom. As a consequence, the Polish controversy over the merits of European civilization, although never abated, was nonetheless often interrupted and overshadowed by the national question. Thus, while fragments of this discourse may be found in many monographs dealing with the history of the Polish national idea and the struggle against oppression, hardly anyone has tried to connect these fragments into a longer narrative. Only in the works of Andrzej Walicki devoted to Polish philosophy and the social thought of the romantic age, has the problem of civilizational choices been given its rightful place. One may suppose that this prominent historian of ideas owes his appreciation of this aspect of the Polish worldview to his extensive study of Russian thought.[6]

As is well known, it was in mid-century Russia that controversy over a model for future civilization defined the main line of ideological division. The same could not be true in Polish intellectual life, under partitions or in exile as it was. Here the organization of formal and informal, legal and clandestine parties was centered mainly around competing programs for the joint attainment of national liberation and long-awaited agrarian reform, and sometimes also, curiously enough, around literary programs, all of which, however, were only loosely correlated with the strategies of economic and civilizational development. In any event, despite conventional definitions, one can find positive occidentalists among Polish conservatives, ardent critics of bourgeois culture and ethics among liberals, or enthusiasts of modern technology among romanticists. Participation in the national and social revolutionary movement did not at all determine one's opinion about Western civilization and its suitability for Poland. Thus, in order to map positions in this dispute and to trace the outlines of Polish nineteenth-century images of a future world, the boundaries separating recognized ideological camps must frequently be crossed.

The reader should not expect to find here an integral description of anyone person's philosophical, social or economic views. From the texts analyzed, I have only drawn upon certain threads relevant to the main topic of this book. Its structure is subordinated to my intention to confront opposed attitudes and arguments as they in fact clashed in polemics. In the long nineteenth-century controversy over modern civilization one can distinguish several oppositions to which a name composed of two contrasting concepts may be given, such as "national idea and cosmopolitanism," "natural and artificial development," "moral and material progress" (or its equivalent, "Gospel and economics"), "Slavdom and the West," etc.[7] Such paired concepts have been used as titles for most chapters, and as the fulcra of the narrative.

The only definite chronological watershed I have introduced is 1863–64, the year of the tragic January Rising, but also of the final enfranchisement of the peasants in the Polish Kingdom. This was indeed a turning point in Polish political, social and intellectual history. Within the two parts of the book, the chapters are more or less synchronous.

I start with the 1760s, when the need to close the hiatus between Poland–Lithuania and Western Europe was raised for the first time. However, the main focus in part one is on the Polish intellectuals' encounter with Western experience in the first half of the nineteenth century, and on the "views of the future" that resulted from it.

The second part covers a shorter time span, the 1870s and 1880s, when all the existing assumptions of Polish social and political philosophy came to be re-evaluated in accordance with the new situation of the nation. It was a dark period in Polish history, for all but Galicia. In the West, the "ambiguities of progress" were exposed even earlier by critics of capitalism.

The narrative stops at the beginning of the 1890s, when modern political movements—nationalist, socialist and populist—began to emerge in the Polish lands. At the same time, Polish creative elites were rapidly absorbing the new currents in European intellectual, political and artistic life. They experienced all its vibrations and shared the typically modernist view of the decadence of Western civilization, as well as a foreboding of impending catastrophe. This period would require separate treatment within a wider, pan-European context.

This book covers more than a hundred years of the debate. It focuses on the writings of thinkers who lived, and published their work, in Central Poland, that is, in the Polish Kingdom after 1815. Only a few of the examples are drawn from the Lithuanian provinces of the former Commonwealth, incorporated in the Russian Empire, and from Galicia, annexed by the Habsburg Monarchy. Unfortunately, the Prussian partition zone, especially the province of Poznań, where social and political thought was, as a rule, more sober and down-to-earth is almost entirely absent from the book. The voluminous writings of the Polish political emigration, so important in the period between 1831 and 1870, are also given marginal treatment. As a result, the role of Warsaw as a cultural center, however dominant, may be given greater weight here than it had in reality.

However, I did not regard maintaining proportions, which are impossible to measure precisely, as a priority. When the Polish manuscript and, later, the Polish edition of this book were discussed during seminars, I was asked several times whether I had intended to describe and analyze the views of narrow intellectual elites, or the attitudes typical of the mentality of the Polish educated classes at large. My answer was that the only evidence I possessed concerned the views of the individual authors whose utterances—representing different levels of intellectual elaboration, from an esoteric philosophical system down to a newspaper column—I had read. With a rich dossier of texts as diverse as possible, I was able to go as far as reconstructing, for a given issue, a basic repertoire of standpoints. Taken together, these standpoints demarcate a field of choice, that is, the range of ideological options that were possible in a given period and place. We may realistically assume that someone well enough educated to be interested in a question of this kind and to form a judgment on it, was situated in such a field of influence of several systems of thought, and that they chose among them, or eclectically absorbed various divergent opinions.

We know little, of course, of the factors that strengthened the appeal and impact of particular ideological orientations, or those that weakened the social resonance of others. We can prove, more or less precisely, whose works and which periodicals were popular and widely read, and which were known only to a small group of sympathizers or were virtually unknown, often because they failed to get the censor's *imprimatur* or were not able to cross state borders. Information of this kind allows us to proceed cautiously from the history of ideas and doctrines to a more broadly conceived, but also less exact history of the intellectual life of the nation, or at least of its intelligentsia.

The intelligentsia, collectively, is one of the subjects of my story. It was a class, stratum, or milieu that succeeded in its aspiration to replace the nobility, or the educated elite of the former gentry, in its function as preserver of the historical sense of the nation under the most adverse circumstances, and as a guide towards a better future. Apart from the high nobility, the intelligentsia was—though in a quite different way—the most Westernized class of society and the one most interested in strengthening links with European scholarship and institutions. It saw itself as part of the world of European culture, but a somewhat underprivileged part, since its learning, development and social advancement were hampered in every possible way. It regarded its own country as a poor and neglected suburb of Europe, a suburb that looked at the Metropolis with contradictory feelings of envy, admiration and distrust—and sometimes with sincere or feigned contempt for the West's corrupt values and false glitter.

This curious combination of collective inferiority complex and national megalomania which was to compensate for it, seems typical of the educated strata of peripheral countries. It is difficult and painful to accept one's own country's peripheral status in the framework of a supranational civilization, and yet without such a recognition, no realistic program of development may be formulated.

I believe, therefore, that we need not be concerned with measuring the representativeness of individual opinions: in this respect the historian will never be able to match the methodological standards of contemporary social research. Be that as it may, describing the conflicts of values and explaining the dramatic splits within a national culture seems a more promising task for the history of ideas than computing the frequency of particular positions.

The first version of this book was written and discussed in the late 1970s. It came as a surprise to me when some of the people who attended my lectures and read the manuscript saw my subject and treatment as very timely, indeed contemporary. This was the time when Poles, able to travel abroad more easily than in previous decades, soon realized that, as a result of thirty-odd years of communist rule, the civilizational distance between Poland and the West had become huge once again. It was not only a question of economic indices, but of the whole infrastructure of everyday life. Comparisons with the West were devastating for the "actually existing socialism:" not only did the revolutionary promise to build a new civilization, an alternative to capitalism, completely fail, but communist party rule and the planned nationalized economy proved lamentably inefficient in every respect and finally appeared to be a conservative force of inertia and the main obstacle to progress. Yes, "progress"—this obsolete word, condemned by both social scientists and pessimist philosophers, reappeared in Polish discourse in response to the need for an antithesis of the acute sense of being once again on the periphery of Europe, a poor and humiliated relative of the happier, free and affluent nations.

This situation obviously brought with it a profound impression of *déjà vu*. Moreover, since a free discussion of the communist failure was still impossible in the legal press, the account of the nineteenth-century dispute in partly analogous circumstances seemed to serve as a convenient cloak, or a historical substitute, for a contemporary problem. So, for example, readers could not help comparing the story of the abortive industrialization stimulated by the government of the Polish Kingdom in the 1820s, with equally miscalculated overinvestment in heavy industry by the communist government: a policy that also warped proportions between the branches of the national economy, resulted in foreign debt exceeding the country's resources, and was partly responsible for the economic collapse in the 1970s.

Such unpleasant parallels may have been one of the reasons why the state quasi-monopolistic publisher was in no hurry to publish this book, which remained for four years "at the printers." When it finally appeared in 1988,[8] in the last year of the *ancien régime* (although we did not know at the time it was to be the last), the book got a very sympathetic reception, and not only in academic circles. Its reviewers were still speculating as to its actual meaning or message. Most of them understood the author's position as positively pro-Western (although with some appreciation of traditionalism), but, at the same time, deeply pessimistic as far as the fate of Poland was concerned. One critic even wrote about a historical *fatum* that condemns the countries of East-Central Europe to political dependence and economic backwardness and makes futile all efforts to break out of this vicious circle. Such a reading was in tune with the mood of that time, but it also expressed a conviction that, after all, the ill-conceived and failed communist attempt at modernization was only one episode in a much longer history of a peripheral location. No wonder that those discussing my book often compared Poland's lot to that of Latin American countries. All of them felt that the Polish controversy over the merits and faults of modern civilization, and over the ways of catching up with it, had not yet ended.

Soon after, the East-European scene underwent a radical change. In 1990, transformation in the direction of capitalism was already irreversible, and the resistance offered by both ex-communists and right-wing nationalist fundamentalists was surprisingly weak. And yet the controversy over paths of development has not, indeed, been closed—only its essence has changed. The question dividing public opinion in Poland is no longer whether capitalism will emerge, but what sort of capitalism, and how rapidly. The social costs of transformation are now at the crux of the matter: costs paid mainly by those who are unable to take part in the race. The arguments of those politicians and intellectuals who want to minimize the costs and seek a safer, middle road of development clash with the arguments of those who believe that fast privatization, the free market and low taxes will solve all the problems. The historian observing this keen debate cannot help noticing how striking a resemblance it bears to nineteenth-century arguments.

At the same time, the prospect of Poland joining the European Union has aroused, especially on the right, old fears of the loss of national identity and of being dissolved in a European melting-pot. More common is the anxiety that fascination with attractive patterns of American mass culture may prove detrimental to the core and idiomatic values of the domestic culture. Suspicions are voiced that the influx of foreign capital may be part of a Western plot to buy out for pennies and destroy Polish industry. These resentments, however marginal at present, could gain a stronger appeal in the event of economic stagnation or political crisis. They are also reminiscent of the past disputes that are the subject of this book.

In the preface to the Polish edition, written in 1984, I expressed my belief that the anxieties related in this book, although sometimes presented in archaic philosophical and linguistic garb, are by no means distant from our own concerns. Although the world of computers and satellites is a long way from the world of steam engines, people's attitudes towards civilizational change seem to persist, and indeed recur in every generation. I think that this statement is still valid even today, and that it applies to more than one country.

*

This book has been abridged and tailored for the English edition. Many historical details, and in particular numerous overt and covert references to Polish literature that would be incomprehensible for most Western readers, have been left out. Explanatory or encyclopaedic notes have been added where it seemed necessary. I assumed that certain historical and literary figures such as Tadeusz Kościuszko and Adam Mickiewicz are widely known, but did not make too many such assumptions, remembering that knowledge is usually diffused from the center to the peripheries and not the other way round. A chronology of the main events in the Polish history of the period is included for any interested readers.

Original French and German sources are cited, wherever possible, in their English translation. We used the editions available in Warsaw libraries. Since there was no available English edition of the two French authors, Say and Sismondi, we decided to leave the quotations in the original French, rather than translate them into English.

The author and translators had to make several arbitrary decisions as to geographical names. A common practice in British and American works is to write "Warsaw" and not "Warszawa," both in the text and in notes. We have followed this practice, although I regard putting "Warsaw" as the place of publication to be an example of Anglo-Saxon cultural imperialism (no Polish scholar would dare to use the Polonized name for London or New York in a bibliographical footnote). The practice is not uniform with respect to the names of other Polish towns, thus we decided on "Kraków" and not "Cracow," and "Gdańsk" rather than "Danzig." Similarly, in the text and on the enclosed maps, we use the Polish forms of "Lwów" (and not the German "Lemberg," Russian "L'vov" or Ukrainian "Lviv"), and "Wilno" (rather than the Russian or English "Vilna" and Lithuanian "Vilnius"), because I refer to those towns as vital centers of Polish culture in the nineteenth century. However, I am anxious that it should not be taken as proof of Polish cultural imperialism. On the other hand, "Wrocław" is mentioned here only as a place of publication after 1945; in the nineteenth century it was, of course, "Breslau."

Things are no simpler when it comes to the names of countries and provinces in Eastern Europe. I am rather reluctant to use the name "Poland" for the period when there was no Polish state, but it is difficult to be consistent. I carefully omitted the name "Wielkopolska," since its English equivalent is "Great Poland" while it was, in fact, very small at that time. I prefer to speak of "the province of Poznań." I also prefer "the Polish Kingdom" (i.e. after 1815) to the more frequent "Kingdom of Poland," because the latter name improperly suggests a sovereign monarchy. The Lithuanian part of the old Commonwealth plus the so-called Ruthenian lands were, after the partitions, called in the official Russian "Western gubernyas," and by many Poles *ziemie zabrane* ("lost" or "annexed lands"), while today they belong to the three independent states of Lithuania, Byelorussia and Ukraine. How should they be referred to in English? The decision is easier with respect to Eastern Galicia which became the Western Ukraine.

There were many exquisite quotations in the Polish edition of this book which should have been rendered in the contemporary English idiom. This was not possible to achieve, and while some flavor has inevitably been lost in translation, I can only hope that a little of that flavor has been saved.

J.J.

Notes to the Preface to the English Edition

1. See Robert A. Nisbet, *Social Change and History: Aspects of the Western Theory of Development* (New York, 1969).

2. Karl Polanyi, *The Great Transformation: The Political and Economic Origins of Our Time* (Boston, 1957).

3. A. J. Toynbee, *A Study of History*, especially vol. 12: *Reconsiderations* (London, 1964), pp. 254–63.

4. See, e.g., Alasdair Clayre (ed.), *Nature and Industrialization* (Oxford, 1977); Raymond Williams, *The Country and the City* (London, 1973) and *Culture and Society 1780–1950* (London, 1958); Herbert L. Sussman, *Victorians and the Machine: The Literary Response to Technology* (Cambridge, Mass., 1968), et al.

5. J. Michalski, "Sarmatyzm a europeizacja Polski w XVIII wieku", in Z. Stefanowska (ed.), *Swojskość i cudzoziemszczyzna w dziejach kultury polskiej* (Warsaw, 1973), pp. 113–68.

6. A. Walicki, *Philosophy and Romantic Nationalism: The Case of Poland* (Oxford, 1982); see also his *The Slavophile Controversy: History of a Conservative Utopia in Nineteenth-century Russian Thought* (Oxford, 1975) and *The Controversy over Capitalism: Studies in the Social Philosophy of the Russian Populists* (Oxford, 1969). I owe much to other books by Walicki and to our discussions.

7. I should add "innovation and routine", an opposition that was used as the title of a relevant book by my younger colleague, Tomasz Kizwalter, *"Nowatorstwo i rutyny:"*

Społeczeństwo Królestwa Polskiego wobec procesów modernizacji (1840–1862) (Warsaw, 1991).

8. *Jakiej cywilizacji Polacy potrzebują: Studia z dziejów idei i wyobraźni XIX wieku* (What kind of civilization the Poles need: Studies in the history of ideas and imagination of the nineteenth century) (Warsaw, 1988).

Chronology

1764 Stanisław Poniatowski elected King (Stanislaus Augustus)

1768 The Confederation of Bar and the beginning of civil war

1773 The first partition of Poland by Russia, Prussia and Austria

1788 The beginning of the Four Years Seym

1791 The Constitution of 3 May

1792 The Confederation of Targowica and Russian invasion

1793 The second partition of Poland by Russia and Prussia

1794 The Kościuszko insurrection

1795 The third and final partition by Russia, Prussia and Austria; the end of the Polish–Lithuanian Commonwealth

1796 Warsaw incorporated into Prussia

1806 Prussian army defeated at Jena: Emperor Napoleon creates the Duchy of Warsaw

1807 The Constitution of the Duchy of Warsaw; peasant serfdom abolished

1809 French and Polish war against Austria: a part of the Austrian partition zone incorporated in the Duchy

1812 Napoleon's invasion of Russia and his defeat: the retreat of the *Grande-Armée* (including Polish troops)

1813 Russian occupation of the Duchy of Warsaw

1815 The Congress of Vienna and the new partition of the Polish lands among three powers: an autonomous Polish Kingdom created under the scepter of the Russian Emperor; Kraków becomes a free republic; Emperor (Tsar) Alexander I grants a liberal constitution to the Kingdom

1816 Warsaw university founded

1822 First volume of Adam Mickiewicz's poetry, published in Wilno, marks the beginning of Polish romanticism

1824 Leaders of student fraternities (*Philomaths*) in Wilno imprisoned and/or deported to Russia

1825 Alexander I dies; Nicholas I, his successor on the Russian throne, crushes the Decembrist Rising in St. Petersburg

1826 Leaders of the clandestine Patriotic Society arrested

1830 The November Rising
1831 Polish–Russian war in the Kingdom and Lithuania; Polish defeat; beginnings of the Great Emigration
1832 The constitution of the Kingdom abrogated, Polish army disbanded, universities in Warsaw and Wilno closed down; Field Marshal Paskevitch appointed Nicholas I's viceroy in Warsaw; the Polish Democratic Society formed in France; Mickiewicz completes his drama *Forefathers–Part Three* in Dresden
1846 Anti-Austrian rising in Kraków; anti-gentry peasant rebellion in Galicia; the Republic of Kraków annexed by Austria
1848 Revolutions in Berlin and Vienna; patriotic movements in the Prussian and Austrian partition zones; anti-Prussian rising in the province of Poznań; emancipation of serfs in Galicia
1855 Russia defeated in the Crimean War; Nicholas I dies, succeeded by Alexander II
1856 Viceroy Paskevitch dies
1858 The Agrarian Society founded in the Kingdom, with the government's permission
1861 Serfdom abolished in Russia (including its Western provinces); big patriotic manifestations and tsarist reprisals in Warsaw; the Agrarian Society closed down; a clandestine organization, the "Reds," set up
1862 Tsarist "concessions" for the Kingdom: Margrave Wielopolski appointed Chairman of the Civil Government, reform of education undertaken, Warsaw university reopened as the Main School, the Jews granted equal rights; the underground Central Committee leads the irredentist movement
1863 The January Rising and guerrilla war against tsarism in the Kingdom and Lithuania
1864 The Rising suppressed, insurgents tried by military tribunals; enfranchisement of peasants in the Kingdom
1867 The Habsburg Monarchy transformed into Austria–Hungary; Galicia granted autonomy as a province, with Polish institutions; incorporation of the Kingdom in the Russian Empire: separate government institutions abolished
1869 The Warsaw Main School becomes a Russian university
1871 *Kulturkampf* (against the Catholic church) proclaimed in the unified German Reich; first manifestos of the "young press," or the Warsaw positivists
1872 Germanization of Polish schools intensified in the province of Poznań, Silesia and Pomerania

1880   Public trial of Polish socialists in Kraków
1881   Assassination of Tsar Alexander II organized by the *Narodnaya Vola*;
       Alexander III becomes his successor
1885   Final Russification of public schools in the former Kingdom; secret
       trial of 29 activists of the "Proletariat" party in Warsaw (six death
       sentences)
1887   The Polish League founded in exile
1892   Workers' unrest in Łódź; the Social-Democratic Party of Galicia
       founded
1893   Two rival clandestine Polish socialist parties founded in the Kingdom;
       the Polish League changed into the National League: the birth of a
       modern nationalist movement

Maps

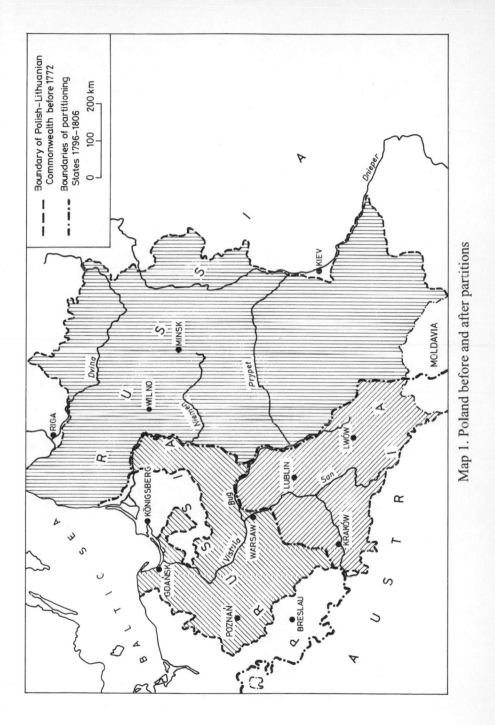

Map 1. Poland before and after partitions

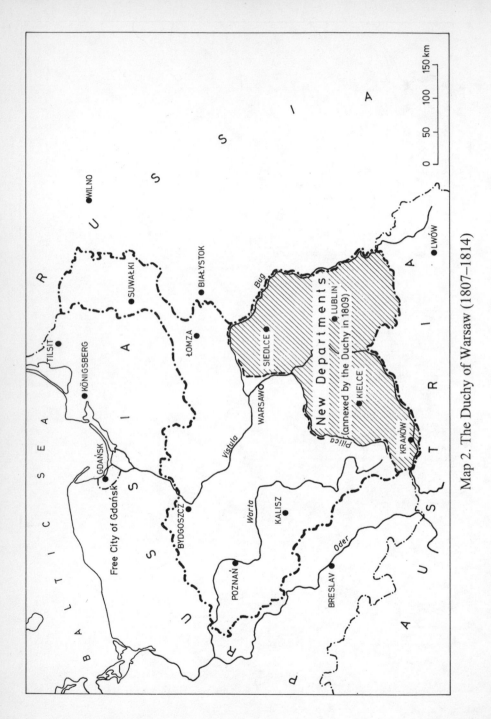

Map 2. The Duchy of Warsaw (1807–1814)

Map 3. Polish lands (1815–1914)

PART ONE

Images of the Future
from the 1780s to 1863

CHAPTER 1

National Identity
and Cosmopolitan Civilization

The intellectual upheaval which took place in the eighteenth century was introduced into Poland by a section of the hereditary, propertied aristocracy, supported by a small intellectual elite, most of whom were clerics. The qualities of both these elites were combined in the person of the new king and his closest associates from the *Monitor*[1] period.

The role played by these two groups was quite understandable. The traditional culture of the gentry, usually referred to as Sarmatian,[2] was by then so complacent and so mired in its own myths that it was incapable of producing any critique of its axioms. It could not break free of its own limitations since for generations it had been preoccupied with admiring itself in the flattering mirror of baroque eloquence. In order for this culture to realize that its fundamental beliefs could not be regarded as absolute, and in order for it to be able to relativize its values—an indispensable prerequisite of all criticism—its perspective had to be exteriorized in the most literal sense of the word: that is, it was necessary for members of the gentry to become temporary outsiders with respect to their own country.

Such an opportunity was only available to young magnates or learned young priests. Only they were given a chance to taste life in Rome, Paris or London. Familiar with foreign languages (mostly Latin and French) and armed with letters of recommendation, they usually confined their interests to the latest fashions and gambling, but some of them also read, studied, talked and drew comparisons with their own country.

The comparisons they drew were not to Poland's advantage. The scale of universal European values produced by the Enlightenment was almost the reverse of the criteria employed by Sarmatism. According to Sarmatian standards, Poland enjoyed all that was best in terms of government and traditions; according to the standards of the Enlightenment, they were the worst in Europe. Such radically differing opinions, combined with the ineffectually concealed contempt on the part of the enlightened elite for the political and traditional culture of the gentry, and the haughty, moralistic, didactic tone of the *Monitor,* meant that attempts at reform were given no social support and, as a result, met with little initial success.

Universalist and progressive ideas—including the concept of the natural rights of man—were not a product of social forces in Poland, but appeared in a courtly, aristocratic garb and were immediately regarded as a product of foreign philosophizing. The stigma of elitism and foreignness continued to surround them for a quarter of a century. Leaving aside the political events which provoked the armed rebellion of the gentry, referred to as the Confederation of Bar,[3] we can discern in its ideology and its hatred of the king the prototype of the many bloody rebellions, recurring from the eighteenth century to the present day, which aimed at protecting native traditions and religion against enlightened rulers who were too ready and eager to impose reforms and change the customs and institutions of their subjects. It is true that Stanislaus Augustus and his advisors never intended to bring Poles closer to Europe by employing such methods as those used by the Russian tsar Peter the Great. This was not simply because they did not have at their disposal anything like the means and resources available to the Russian despot. The main reason was that they represented a completely different culture. Nevertheless, the gentry, which constantly denounced the king for his alleged attempts at an *absolutum dominium*, reasoned and felt according to a certain logic: the gentry illuminati did not, and could not, understand the naive audacity of the rationalist reformers of the state, who imagined that by sheer subtle persuasion they would induce the people to rebuild the entire edifice of tradition and law. Considering the fact that this small group of people were dissatisfied with so many things in their own country, and enjoyed the protection of a powerful Russia and its army, it was only natural that they should be suspected of plans to use more effective means to achieve their goals.

The Polish followers of Montesquieu and Locke were not particularly keen on the use of force to bring about changes in the form of government. In their opinion, the new order of government and society, an order that would restore Poland's place among the European nations, should be based on a different set of traditions and views, although they had no idea how much patience, time and trust this would require. Work for the enlightenment of citizens' convictions—and thus for the improvement of government—and the rest, they believed, would improve as a matter of course. This "rest" included the economy.

The state of the economy was subject to the same radical criticism as the freedoms traditionally enjoyed by the gentry. While Sarmatian writers exulted in the years of plenty that Poland had enjoyed under the peaceful rule of Augustus III,[4] those writing for the *Monitor* seemed to be looking at a completely different country. This is how the wise Chinese observer, Yun-Nip, a creation of Ignacy Krasicki, described the country: "Poland is in a sorrier state than any other country in Europe, because she has neither an army of a size that would correspond to its vast territory, nor a treasury to maintain such an army, nor its own money. . . . Her agriculture . . . is not what it should be, her commerce is worth little, being in fact more harmful than profitable. There are few master craftsmen in the towns, and skills and education are not held in much esteem. . . . In trying to fathom the reasons for this, I did not have to search long for the source of all these evils, which is nothing more or less than exuberant, licentious freedom."[5] This assessment, and many others in the same tone, illustrate how the political rationalism of the Enlightenment was applied to the sphere of economics: towns would grow, the population would increase, and commerce and trade would develop as soon as governance replaced misgovernment and just laws were made for the population as a whole, not simply for one estate. The favorable development of the national economy would be simply a function of *bonus ordo*, that is, an honest and efficient administration and treasury. The straightforward one-way dependence of the economy on government and polity seemed obvious, at least in the early stages of the Enlightenment.

Changes in culture and in the basic orientation of society are always a dramatic process. By the very nature of things, the ideas of enthusiastic innovators inevitably encounter either passive or active resistance on the part of those, whose feelings, convictions and interests are closely bound to the long-established order and who therefore, when faced with plans for radical change, quite justifiably, react as if their world were being turned upside down. The more foreign the changes appear, the stronger the resistance. The guise in which the reform is presented also has a part to play, as do the tactics used by the reformers.

From this point of view, the Enlightenment, although it developed over several decades, can be seen as a dramatic breakthrough in the history of modern Polish culture. It meant a return to Europe for Poland. The impulses for the re-education of this "gentry nation" were generated locally, although such impulses had to be backed from outside by people familiar with contemporary European ideas in the areas of science, technology, law, philosophy and art. No wonder, then, that the admonitory exhortations of those men of the world tended, on the whole, to discourage the gentry and turn it against the program of reforms. As a result of numerous failures and only minor educational successes, the tone of the reformers was modified considerably. During the Four Years Seym[6] both the royal and the so-called patriotic factions became much more skilful in accommodating the ideas, style and wording of their programs and actions to the gentry-republican tradition, and even adopted, or affected to adopt, the gentry's dislike of all things foreign.

However, by the time this adjustment had taken place, certain unfortunate stereotypes had become fixed in the common consciousness. Everything Polish was now associated with the old days, and all that was novel, with the foreign ideas imposed on Poland by the unpopular king and the magnates, courtiers, libertines and fops who surrounded him. It is significant that the gentry, so jealous of all its freedoms, wished to be deprived of one of them—the freedom to travel. Instructions issued by local diets for Seym deputies contain numerous demands for the estates to make it unlawful for young gentry to go abroad, since those who returned to Poland after their foreign travels seemed to belong to a different nation. They altered their manner of dress, pursuits and way of thinking and showed a marked disrespect for everything in their own country and family home. Thus the dandy and the fashionable lady—popular targets of satire and comedy—made foreign ways so ridiculous that society's dislike became extended even to those who valued the development of science, the rights of man and principles of good govern-ment more than the manners of the salon and the boudoir. Defenders of the old tradition had an easy task; they did not have to ponder on what was worth imitating and what was not, since the very idea of imitating foreign models seemed ridiculous, perilous and irritatingly aristocratic, while the defense of the *status quo*—in the home and in the schools, in the manor and in the local diet—carried with it the sacredness of national tradition. The followers of the Enlightenment had to work hard to do away with such stereotypes and to show that progress could be more attractive in a Polish, rather than in a French guise, which they did by defending their ideas in the Seym and in the theater.

The dilemma of whether to follow foreign models or to uphold native tradition was not peculiar to Poland. Similar conflicts appeared everywhere with the arrival of Enlightenment ideas. After all, philosophers envisaged the future for the whole of humanity and not merely for individual peoples. Was not human nature the same the world over, irrespective of language and the way of life shaped by tradition? Did not all people wish for the same kind of happiness and freedom? The criteria and means towards progress varied, but all had a universal dimension: the development of science and learning, the triumph of invention and industry, religious tolerance, the social contract, the voluntary coming together of men enjoying equal rights to form nations, which in turn would form a world federation, lasting peace, the growth of morality—in other words, the growing liberation of humanity from the rule of backwardness, superstition and despotism.

For the time being, that part of mankind which was mature enough to enter the age of Reason and Light lived in Europe. On the whole, however, middle-class Europe, with its traditions of hard work and enterprise, played only a marginal role in the new movement. In general, this role was reserved for the polished, refined, educated Europe, that Europe which displayed a defiant and sacrilegious attitude towards the throne, the altar and the barbarian past. This Europe was cosmopolitan, and from the times of Louis XIV onwards, cosmopolitan implied French. Why was it France that managed to impose its style and its hegemony (unquestioned until the Revolution) on the intellectual elites of the entire continent? Undoubtedly this was due to its literature, philosophy, political thought, and also, at least up to a point, the power of this state which, while admittedly attacked by philosophers, at the same time lent to them the brilliance of its authority.

It remains a matter of dispute, as indeed it was at the time, whether, say, England in the eighteenth century did not produce more lasting values which would prove of greater significance to the world in the long run. (As a matter of fact, English models, so different from the French ones, played a considerable role in the Polish Enlightenment.) Still, whether it was justified or not, the fact remains that the tone was set by France. An authority on this epoch writes: "The authors who now brought honor to her name had the requisite quality for exciting emulation, they were in the ranks of modernity. There were none more eager, more daring or more prompt in formulating, defending and disseminating the ideas which were then so much engrossing the contemporary mind. Thus France still retained the literary supremacy which had come to her as a heritage, and she vindicated her title to the distinction by bringing a substantial contribution. Pretty well all the other races had an impression of being behind-hand when they compared themselves with her, and in their anxiety to catch up, the first thing that occurred to them was to take her for their guide."[7] An excellent exposé, with one reservation: intellectual historians are too quick to ascribe to nations the features of cultural elites. This may be merely a *façon de parler*, but still it remains very misleading. It was not nations (or "races") that read Voltaire and Diderot and "had an impression of being behind-hand." It was not nations but elites that, however small, held important positions and had influence; elites that were similar everywhere from St. Petersburg to Lisbon and which instead of communicating in Latin, as was once the case, now had no problem in exchanging ideas in polished, learned French.

These elites cannot be unambiguously defined in terms of the social position of their members. Among the "enlightened" one could meet kings and philosophers, undernourished men of letters and well-fed bishops, dip-

lomats and adventurers, bankers and courtesans. They may have differed
among themselves as to their education; they may have represented different
aspirations, views, and resources—in fact they could have differed in almost
every respect. But they were united and defined by style, and this style, once
again, was Parisian and, as such, European. It was above all the polished style
of social life—the art of repartee, wit, intrigue, love and dining, the style of
the salon in which the world's order was overturned.

The fusion of rationalist philosophy and politics with the salon and the
world of fashion was neither indispensable nor unbreakable. Nevertheless,
the two became bound together strongly enough to result in the emergence
of the popular stereotype of the blasé ironist who despised his native traditions, language and the faith of his forefathers. In all European countries it
was culturally foreign *afrancesados* who propagated eighteenth-century progress (although their support was often merely superficial). The Enlightenment aimed at being universal, but instead it acquired the stigma of foreignness. Those who had the enthusiasm and skills to become the spiritual leaders
of nations that were politically weak or fragmented, economically backward
because of their feudal legacy, and culturally peripheral—the Spanish, the
Germans, the Hungarians or the Poles—therefore faced a difficult dilemma.
They could, of course, adopt the ready-made intellectual accoutrements, the
contemporary European canon with its philosophy of the senses and reason,
the canon of constitutional thought (freedom, equality, natural law and the
rights of man), and the aesthetic canon of classicism, and, clad in this armor,
fight for the banishment of "the gross superstitions of the age," for the
abolition of serfdom and tyranny, for the reform of government, for a modern,
developing society. But to do so they had to pay the price of remaining for
long years a cultural satellite of Paris or, worse still, of provoking a rebellion
of the conservative gentry which was by no means eager to embrace the alien
gospel of progress. They could also do the reverse: they could shape the
cultural make-up of their own people and their political system by drawing
on the resources of their own petrified traditions, traditions which were
opposed to the intellectual supremacy of the West—but in this case the price
to be paid was the hampering of social change.

Of course, such widely different alternatives represented pure abstraction
rather than reality. Extreme means led nowhere. The first course could be
chosen only by those individuals whose education had made them men of the
world to such an extent that they had lost touch with local affairs and with
the grassroots of native culture and politics. In Polish literature an example
of such an attitude is provided by Jan Potocki, a Polish aristocrat who wrote
in French.[8] The second approach could be chosen only by staunch conserva-

tives. The true reformers of national culture had to opt for a middle course if they wanted to implant Western universalist ideas into minds that had been accustomed to different nourishment, and if they wanted to galvanize themselves and their compatriots into independent, creative action. The strategy of "nationalizing progress," so characteristic of the Late Enlightenment, meant a synthesis of the new and that which was native or had long been assimilated, a synthesis of the ideals of universal reason and the palpable reality of particular legacies, a synthesis which had to be constantly tested both in theory and social practice.

The mixing of such heterogeneous systems of values inevitably led to tension and inconsistencies. However, a definite pattern may be discerned among all these inconsistencies. Ideas and inventions were adopted, while the style that came with them was discarded whenever possible. Thus, from the time of Lessing, German culture and the German national consciousness, dominated as they were by French models, had to define a separate identity in opposition to those models. German culture had to create its own style of expression, adapted to national sentiments, before it could create a German literature and philosophy whose claim to be universal was no less justified than that of the Encyclopaedists.

During the Four Years Seym in Poland, the culture of the gentry nation was still a long way from assimilating the intellectual revolution, although the reform camp made efforts to lessen the gap between the two worlds and to weaken the alienating effect produced by the ideas of the Enlightenment. Hugo Kołłątaj[9] and Stanisław Staszic,[10] both of whom were fairly resilient to the charms of fine society, freely drew on the achievements of English and French science, philosophy and law. But they also displayed considerable pragmatism in their attempts to adapt these imports to existing Polish tastes and to the customs and mores of the Commonwealth.[11]

The French Revolution made this separation of idea and form easier. Part of European opinion saw in its unbridled radicalism and bravado the victory of the philosophical principles of progress and the rights of man, while the rest of Europe believed that it compromised these lofty ideals; whatever one's position, the relationship between political and intellectual revolution was undeniable. But what about French manners and style? These became the preserve of the emigrés, the refugees scattered all over the continent, the royalists, the governesses and the dancing-masters. In the late eighteenth century, imitating the "French example" meant being a Jacobin, while imitating "things French" meant being a snob.

It was only after the third partition of Poland (1795) that the word "civilization" appeared in the Polish language—and, in all probability, in other European languages as well—and began its extraordinary career. Coined in France before the Revolution, it soon spread all over the continent as yet another French export.[12] The meaning of the concept was never very precise. In fact, due to the very fluidity of its meaning, the word was to become indispensable, since it provided a synthesis of the vast complex of patterns which were Western European in their provenance but destined to be utilized by the whole of mankind. Civilization was something more than the sum of these patterns—it was a system. After all, this word "civilization" encapsulated the conviction that particular patterns were associated with each other in such a way that the adoption of one entailed the adoption of all. This meant that the mechanical methods of cotton spinning, the rotation of crops and the fertilization of soil, the abolition of serfdom, representative government, utilitarianist ethics, religious skepticism, hygiene and modern conveniences, the classical understanding of beauty as harmony, a knowledge of French and English, a faith in the power of the mind and in the future unification of mankind—all these and many other elements were mutually dependent and formed one inseparable whole. While one component could be omitted, neglected or disregarded, and another magnified into a supreme axiom, it remained a systematic, integral unity which lent itself to a general characterization, either positive or negative, and at the same time could be adapted to those grand historiosophical constructs which had so many followers among the representatives of European thought from the second half of the eighteenth century on.

For "civilization" was never viewed as static. It is true that it was ascribed certain permanent main features, but these developed in the course of history, indicating the direction of change and marking the successive stages of progress. The words "civilization" and "progress" became permanently united, although this union was quite soon questioned by some groups of conservative thinkers who sought symptoms of regression or even decadence in contemporary civilization. However, optimistic faith in the unhampered and boundless progress of civilization consistently differed from the utopias of the Enlightenment in that it never created *ex nihilo* ready-made worlds that were so perfect that they could never be changed. Instead, it allowed the worlds it created to emerge gradually from the real history of past ages, a history cleansed of accidental twists and turns and projected into future centuries by the designers' imagination, forming a continuous realization of the original ideals.

Antoine de Condorcet's *Esquisse d'un tableau historique des progrès de l'esprit humain*, written in 1793, constitutes an excellent illustration of this kind of unilinear synthesis of the progress of civilization. Of course, this progress was integral, covering all fields of human thought and activity: "It is the same with the entire system of the labors of men as with a well-composed work; of which the parts, though methodically distinct, must, nevertheless, be closely connected to form one single whole, and tend to one single objective."[13] From the beginnings of society the driving force of change was, and always will be, the never tiring curiosity and inquisitiveness of human beings. The last chapter of the *Esquisse*, concerned with "The Future Progress of Mankind," dazzles the present-day reader with the futurological imagination of its author. This French mathematician, philosopher and revolutionary politician of the eighteenth century was incredibly apt and perspicacious in his prognoses as to the main lines of development of the theoretical and applied sciences; he also underlined the significance of the popularization of learning. He thought it absolutely undeniable that progress in scientific cognition must entail a rationalization of the economic, social and political system. For the axiomatic premise of Enlightenment thought was that "all errors in politics and in morals are founded upon philosophical mistakes, which, themselves, are connected with physical errors." And if this were true, then it was obvious that the increasing understanding of the world would be accompanied by the perfection of individual and social morality, since "nature has connected, by a chain which cannot be broken, truth, happiness, and virtue."[14] The utopian element in the idea of civilization was not to be discerned in the trust in man's cognitive faculties or in prophecies of the boundless growth of technological power, but only in this mutual correlation of knowledge and virtue.

What is more, this correlation seemed to leave no room for the diversification of ideals and norms. After all, the rules of rational cognition were the same for all. And since it was on them that the world of ideas was based, then these ideas themselves had to be universal. From here it was just one step to the declaration that "in Europe the principles of the French Constitution are those of every enlightened mind," and that thanks to education, based on the knowledge of man's moral constitution, almost everybody would be guided by the same principles of justice, the same feelings and the same motivations.[15] Condorcet's ideological program, presented in the form of a historic prognosis, was built on the foundations of the idea of human dignity, the equality of the sexes, nations and races, universal peace and fraternity, and the reduction of inequality as regards access to education and welfare. The only thing it lacked was an allowance for the national separateness of cultures and traditions.

"Will not every nation one day arrive at the state of civilization attained by those people who are most enlightened, most free, most exempt from prejudices, as the French for instance, or the Anglo-Americans?" But of course, they were already drawing nearer to this point one by one: "Is there upon the face of the globe a single spot the inhabitants of which are condemned by nature never to enjoy liberty, never to exercise their reason?" Indeed: "The march of these people will be less slow and more sure than ours has been, because they will derive from us that light which we have been obliged to discover, and because for them to acquire the simple truths and infallible methods which we have obtained after long wandering in the mazes of error, it will be sufficient to seize upon their developments and proofs in our discourses and publications."[16]

This was the road to be taken by future generations. It was a road on which all real human values—freedom, virtue, respect for man's natural rights —"must necessarily amalgamate and become inseparable, the moment knowledge shall have arrived at a certain pitch in a great number of nations at once, the moment it shall have penetrated the whole mass of a great people, whose language shall have become universal, and whose commercial intercourse shall embrace the whole extent of the globe."[17]

Condorcet's *Esquisse* was a late echo from the French Age of Light. The author, an ideologue of the liberal stage of the Revolution, fell victim to its Jacobin stage, and the last work he wrote before he died only gained broad popularity thirty years later, when its message was taken over by Claude Henri Saint-Simon and Auguste Comte. I have used this text in order to convey the flavor of the Enlightenment doctrine of general civilization since Condorcet, more than anyone else, managed to unite its main components in a masterful, concise and consistent manner. It was truly a *summa* of the ardent feelings and dreams of the great Age of Reason, an age which would later be criticized for its cold rationalism and heartlessness.

This philosophical enthusiasm, this scientific faith in the brilliant future of mankind were just what the Poles needed in order to combat the general torpor which had overcome them after the partitions. The defeat of the Kościuszko insurrection[18] left the Poles with a feeling of painful loneliness and helplessness in the face of the united front of the partitioning powers. Europe looked with indifference at the downfall of the apparently anarchic republic of the gentry which was more or less generally seen as a relic of barbarism in comparison to Russia, the level of whose civilization was evidenced by the learned correspondence of Empress Catherine with Diderot. In any case, the other countries of Europe were occupied with the convulsions of the French Revolution, either trying to rescue the old order or to create a new one. Who cared about the independence of the Polish people?

However, in the global perspective of civilizational progress all of this constituted merely an episode. Poland, though torn asunder, was after all a member of the great family of nations striving towards fraternal unification. If only one could do away with the despotism of kings and emperors and with the tyranny of feudal, religious and intellectual superstitions! The objective was common, and the road to it well signposted by "the simple truths and infallible methods," fully developed and justified in French and English discourses. *Ex Occidente lux*. "Several nations are already in the vestibules of the Temple of Reason, but ours is not among them," lamented the Polish conspirators who had sworn allegiance to the Republican idea. "The immortal geniuses, Locke, Montesquieu, Rousseau, Mably . . . are the fathers of this philosophical light whose power has pierced the dark clouds of tyranny and fanaticism, but so far has failed to demolish all of its edifices whose spaciousness covers the whole earth. There are friends of mankind working in many countries to overturn these gothic structures covered with the dishonor of the human race. You will not find them in our country. Let us have the courage to join them in their endeavor."[19]

This is how Polish occidentalism was revived and given a new shape in the Prussian-occupied Warsaw of the latter years of the eighteenth century. Its basic conviction was that the West had created a better kind of civilization, the values of which would serve as the universal norm, radiating outwards and drawing into their orbit ever new, more distant countries. Poland was undoubtedly within the orbit of this civilization, but in comparison with the West was retarded and immature in its development. On the other hand, it was the most western of the Slavic peoples and for this reason had a mission to pass on the rays of Western light further to the East.

This new occidentalism was extremely serious, patriotic and didactic in style, and was in no way connected with the affected airs of the fashionable dandies of the day. It formed a common ideological platform for the elderly reformers of the Commonwealth and for the young republican conspirators, and also served as a guiding principle for liberal scholars and members of fraternal student associations. Taken together, they represented just a tiny group of different people who shared the conviction that the fate of the oppressed classes and peoples could be improved only through universal progress. It remains rather unclear whether the fulfilment of these hopes was meant to take centuries or months. In the late eighteenth century, thrones were being toppled and frontiers were changing from one day to the next. Europe was like a volcano, anything could happen.

Occidentalism was able to accommodate all kinds of ideologies. For the Warsaw Republicans it meant the rights of man and civic rights "from the

French constitution of the Third Year." Although these rights had only been proclaimed a few years previously, and had been immediately violated, they appeared to be "eternal, unshakeable, universal, and unchangeable for all times, places and countries."[20]

Ten years later Hugo Kołłątaj, seeing in Napoleon an instrument of providence with the mission of creating a federation of states in the form of a Western Empire, proclaimed that soon "an inhabitant of any part of the globe, wherever he will go . . . will find that every country is, as it were, a homeland for him: for everywhere [he will find] the same constitution, the same laws, the same weights and measures, and the same currency; no country's customs will be alien to him, only the language and the climate will be different."[21]

Likewise, Stanisław Staszic, looking both backwards and forwards, noticed "this incessant striving towards a fuller development of the conditions of civilization *ingrained in human nature*" and foresaw the happy finale of this process in the coming epoch in which all peoples would be united under one scepter and one law. The only problem was that by the time he came to finish his epic on the history of the *Human Race*, Napoleon was dying on St. Helena, so Staszic passed on the mission to Tsar Alexander I and his successors. According to Staszic, the main thread in the history of the world was the never ending battle of civilization against every manifestation of the spirit of exclusiveness: "the exclusiveness of land, birth, honor, gentility, superstitious faiths and . . . trade." This envious spirit was to be seen acknowledging defeat in almost every single nation: in the Duchy of Warsaw it had been defeated by the constitution of 1807 which abolished the privileges of the estates, thus putting an end to conflicts between groups of people. But still nations continued to compete and fight with one another; there was still the awful threat of war and hatred. It was only the coming of a European federation that would bring all quarrels to an end and crown the work "of socializing the human race,"[22] and this would be the true end of history.

With the downfall of Napoleon the cult of the God of War began to wane. In relations among states—according to Fryderyk Skarbek—politics had become the art of destruction, while the friends of mankind wanted it to be the science of peace. "This erroneous understanding of politics resulted in national selfishness, and since ugliness itself may sometimes be given a superficially alluring form, so was this disgusting selfishness beautified by giving it the holy name of the love of one's country. . . . It was not so much the love of man's rights under the shield of national freedom but rather hatred and the desire to humiliate the neighboring people that was seen as the aim of the love of one's country, while fraternity and unity in the great family of nations was . . . an unknown idea." After all, he went on, in each individual nation the supreme authority curbs and balances the pressure of private interests, but international relations still lack "this moral element, which is elevated above all local considerations, and which would cherish the peoples' common weal and oppose the pressure of national interests for the benefit of mankind."[23]

The spirit of the age of "enlightened liberalism" still reigned in Warsaw and Wilno several years after the Congress of Vienna,[24] before the Holy Alliance[25] stripped the whole country of its liberties. In this short period of vigor and optimism, the Polish intellectual elite felt a part of Europe like never after; it felt attuned to the rhythm of Europe's political and intellectual life. A Wilno liberal wrote in 1819: "It is a fine attribute of civilization that it immediately adopts all useful things, supports and popularizes national virtues and transplants good features of other peoples onto the native soil for the benefit of its own nation. In this way, all peoples draw closer to each other and become one enlightened community, receiving their laws from the human mind which is constantly perfecting itself."[26]

Among the "useful things" which were to be transplanted to the native country, education was given priority. It was seen as a system of rational social views rather than a collection of professional skills. The older proponents of the Enlightenment, such as Stanisław Potocki[27] and the brothers Śniadecki,[28] set out to brainwash the Sarmatian gentry and clergy, not hesitating to ridicule them mercilessly in their attempt to purge them as quickly as possible of prejudice and parochial backwardness. The young idealists of the Philomaths' Society[29] were beginning to discover Voltaire; in the following years they went through the whole of European thought, philosophy, law and poetry from the previous century, studying them feverishly, driven by their faith in progress and universal reason.

The verses of conventional style preceding Mickiewicz's *Ode to Youth*[30] deal harshly with the darkness and phantoms of superstition; shining with the light of freedom and of learning, they broke the fetters binding mankind, and ended with the Freemasons' chain of hands circling the entire globe. The imagination of these poets gave birth to a new, brave, open world, a world without frontiers and border guards, a Europe stretching from Philadelphia to Wilno and having one constitution encoding the freedom and sovereignty of the people, written by Benjamin Constant and translated into all languages.

The Polish brand of "civilization" was thus far only slightly concerned with the taming of nature by science and technology and the changing of human living conditions. It was above all a moral and political idea which included in its aims equal rights and the freedom of the individual and the nation. It conceived Poland as a country that would be intellectually modern, looking to the West and expecting from the West both inspiration and assistance in restoring independence; a Poland that was entitled to such assistance because it was, or wanted to be, a country like any other, participating in the same historical progress. Educated Polish liberals had no qualms about placing themselves and their country in one of the lower "grades" of the European school. In this school the Poles were supposed to take an exam in constitutional culture, political thought and the ability to introduce social reforms by legal means and in a spirit of freedom and moderation. The examining board was to be composed of European parliaments, universities, and last but not least, "public opinion," this new arbiter of justice. With the outbreak of the November Rising,[31] it was felt that the time had come for the liberals to sit this exam without the tutelage of St. Petersburg. This was the period when the eloquent Dominik Krysiński constantly repeated in his pamphlets and Seym speeches: "Europe is looking at us. Yes, Europe may admire us, but it will also judge us . . . European critics will observe, scrutinize and judge all our steps." He meant, above all, the steps taken by the Polish Parliament, the fact that it had the courage to call the government to account. "We are still novices," he said, "in constitutional education," but "the degree of our participation in the hierarchy of the civilized nations will depend on our statute on national representation."[32]

For civilization was to be classified in terms of stages, not types. A nation's task was to learn from its elders and to pass from one grade to the next. In the course of this education the nation became more like other nations, it matured and rid itself of the burden of its feudal past, its bad habits, and political gaucheness: "as perfection sets in and grows, these features will disappear, because sublimity is the same everywhere."[33]

How many misunderstandings have accumulated around this idealistic vision which was the product of naive faith rather than cool calculation, and which grew out of the conviction that the sublime qualities of the human spirit—prudence, justice, moderation and freedom—were accessible to all and the same for all. It was said repeatedly, then and later, that the Polish liberals, the last legion of the apostles of the Enlightenment, were narrow-minded advocates of rationalism who wished to elevate themselves immediately to a cosmopolitan position, failing to understand that their first duty was to their country and that it was only through the nation that they could play a part in the human community. Their cosmopolitan aims were seen by their critics as "the violation of the living truth of the heart." According to their critics, it was only with the advent of the spirit of romanticism that a response was evoked "on the part of the heart in favor of nationality and patriotism."[34]

This is an erroneous view. The National Freemasonry and the Patriotic Society[35] grew out of the spirit of the Enlightenment and its social thought. Although the gloomy fate of Walerian Łukasiński could serve as the model romantic biography of a conspirator and prisoner, the formative influences in his life were the liberal ideas of civilization and nationality. Łukasiński believed in simultaneous moral and material progress, and towards the end of his martyr's life called himself a cosmopolitan, although he dedicated "his last breath" to his home country.[36]

The axiom of serving the national community and the obligation to display an active and ardent patriotism, including the sacrificing of one's life, were, from the very beginning, inscribed in liberal ideology and were by no means at odds with the idea of the community of European civilization. After all, both these convictions were rooted in the same system of values. According to the liberals, "progress" meant a gradual extension of citizens' rights and the unchecked striving of peoples towards ever higher forms of unification. They gladly bid farewell to the decaying feudalism of their day with its division into estates and corporations and all its different local privileges, measures and laws. Feudalism was regarded as a system dominated by a "spirit of separateness," since hierarchical and obligatory dependencies, even if time-sanctioned, did not create mutual links. Such links, the liberals believed, were possible only among free people who enjoy equal rights. Therefore it was only with the abolition of serfdom, the acceptance of the Constitution of the Duchy of Warsaw (1807), and the introduction of the French Civil Code that one could talk of the creation of a total nation, a common country consisting of the gentry, the townspeople and the peasants. And if this were true, then participation in the national community and in the universal community went hand in hand; both were conditioned by the same revolution, and by the same social establishment. The *Orzeł Biały*, the mouthpiece of the young liberals, wrote in 1820: "True cosmopolitism is rooted in the principle of love of one's own country; it does not exclude the spirit of nationality. The man who is not an ardent citizen of his own nation cannot be a friend of mankind."[37] Had it only been a matter of reconciling friendship towards mankind with love of one's country, then everything would have been simple.

There were, however, many other elements that needed to be reconciled. Poland as it really was, with the entire detritus of its historical legacy, had to be reconciled with a Europe which had not yet come into being, a Europe that existed only in the world of ideas, in philosophical and learned treatises, in constitutional drafts of rights and of eternal peace. Admittedly, a look at recent history would have caused one's faith in the durability of man's decisions and habits to waver: in the twenty-five years following the Constitution of 3 May (1791) the system of government and the rulers of Warsaw changed eight times (five times as a result of war, and three times through diplomatic activity). Poland, like the rest of Europe, had taken a heavy battering from the various foreign armies that had marched to and from across her territories, and when peace finally prevailed, it might have seemed that the whole past had been completely uprooted. Half a century earlier, Stanislaus Augustus had envisaged for a short while a completely new "creation of the Polish world." Now, after 1815, similar sentiments dominated the thinking of the Enlightened Warsaw liberals, and the time itself seemed more favorable for such ideas. There was a new king,[38] a new state—though admittedly shrunken and no longer fully sovereign—new uniforms, a new constitution, new newspapers. The pre-partition past, with its moments of both glory and shame, seemed dead and buried, and the political statutes of the Commonwealth, including the Constitution of 3 May, now appeared impractical. "The experiences of the past mean nothing to us," the *Orzeł Biały* wrote. "Our present condition is . . . completely different. The power of the king augurs well for its durability, and his kind heart and the rights given us are a guarantee of the freedom of public life."[39]

With this complete change in the situation of the country a new order could be created, based on just and modern principles, without resorting to the axe of Peter the Great or the Jacobin guillotine. Curiously, in a contemporary Polish drama, Tsar Peter the Great appeared in the role of a liberal proselyte of the Enlightenment, his civilizational mission stemming from the conviction that "there is no better way to serve a nation than to give it wise laws and noble customs, even if these have been adopted from some other nation."[40] That is the point: to give the people not only wise laws, but also customs, to overcome the prejudices of the gentry, to change fundamentally the way of thinking and feeling by reforming the educational system, and to abolish estates in real life by abolishing them on paper—such was the rationalist *a priori* of the Wilno and Warsaw satirists, freemasons, and enthusiastic supporters of progress. This idealist design was also their weakest point, something which their critics were not slow to capitalize on.

Not all these critics were traditionalists who clung to every vestige of the past. Their opposition to the excessive demands of the modernizers was often a result of the fact that they were more conscious of the psychological tensions felt by people whose lot it was to live in a period of violent change. Wawrzyniec Surowiecki[41] cherished the idea of leading Poland onto the road of modern European development, but he was also aware of the strong resistance represented by traditional morals and attitudes.

Deeply rooted "superstitions," he argued as early as 1807, should not be eradicated by violence; they should be transformed gradually by "mixing old ingredients with new ones," in the adroit manner of the Christian missionaries. Mindful of both the methods of the Jacobins and the attempt by Napoleon in his own days to bring about unification, he insisted that "although the underlying intent and purpose of all legislation should be the same in all countries and should be consistent as regards the main outlines, nevertheless great prudence is necessary when it comes to its being applied locally to the character and needs of a people." Commands and prohibitions would remain ineffective unless they were in accordance with people's motivations for pursuing their interests, and motivations and habits could not be changed by decree. "We have, for instance, before our eyes the new example of France: inspired more by reason than prudence, its lawgivers entangled themselves and their people for a long time in a horrible state of disorder by hastily introducing new laws which, though often based on reason, were inappropri-ate; ... following the precepts of a newly-hatched theory, they tried to transform overnight a people living according to time-honored habits." Such excessive eagerness to "transform nations" might only cause upheavals; therefore, a prudent lawgiver did not strive for perfection, nor did he venture too far ahead of his time.[42]

Similar warnings were given by other authors, especially after 1815. The difference was that they did not refer to prejudice so often and were much more vocal about the need to consider national sentiments and traditions, thus addressing their remarks to Tsar Alexander rather than to the French or Polish radicals. Government and laws had to accommodate themselves to the character of the people, and not the other way round, argued Julian Czermiń-ski.[43] Fryderyk Skarbek warned against applying force in combating nation-alist passions, because this might only strengthen and inflame them; to attenuate such passions, it would be better to gratify them and in this way gradually win public opinion over to the side of moderation.[44]

This attitude may be regarded as practical conservatism; the methods it recommended could serve more efficiently than radical utopianism the aim of Europeanizing and democratizing Polish life. The problem was that the continuity of Polish national history had been brutally interrupted, and therefore the next generation saw continuity as something exceptionally precious. With all its revolutions, wars and partitions, the sudden rises and just as sudden falls in the fortunes of states, rulers and great families, this epoch paradoxically revealed the strength and durability of the attachment of Poles to their family home, native language and old customs. Inevitably, this gave rise to conservative impulses which were indispensable in the preservation of the sense of national identity.

The epithet "foreignness," which traditionally referred to the superficial phenomena of the language and manners of polite society, gradually came to encompass an ever larger set of manifestations of Western civilization in Poland. At the same time, there was a gradual tendency for the notion of nationality to be viewed as a counterbalance to everything that was new and alien. As a result, it broke free of the Enlightenment-liberal order of values and increasingly came to be associated with the idea of the characteristic features of the Slavic race which were confirmed by historical tradition. At first this shifting of semantic fields was only barely perceptible in contemporary writing, but it became consolidated in the pre-romantic philosophy of history which found particularly fertile soil in a country deprived of autonomous existence. Behind this philosophy was the feeling that a nation was an organic union of generations, and not a company whose rules might be changed at will, even with the best of intentions.[45] The glorious future of national freedom and the fraternity of peoples was an abstract promise, its final form was an enigma, and its realization was a gamble. The past, on the other hand, even for those who could not possibly know and remember it, was palpable; it could be told, relived and recovered as a treasure to be shared by all; it was possible for the nation to discover itself in this past. The romanticists were masters in exploiting and giving expression to this feeling and need; and the less they indulged in ideology, the more potent their psychology became.

Maurycy Mochnacki paid the following tribute to the political writers and scholars of the time of Stanislaus Augustus: "They restored its former brilliance to the Polish tongue, and its former popularity to learning, reintroducing the principle of truth with regard to history, and an abhorrence of prejudice and superstition. Their bold hand erected the edifice of contemporary civilization. They were great reformers in many ways and grafters of unknown notions. . . . And then you must agree, because we cannot conceal it from ourselves, that *these men created something completely new.*" The emphasis on these last words is his. And this is where the praise ends. The creation of "something completely new" was reprehensible, for it was the beginning of all evil—the loss of identity: "from foreign lands, from foreign climes, they took ideas and notions by the handful, which were like alien coins stamped with the mark of unknown minter, scattering them all over Poland. These coins circulated quickly. Together with alien ideas and an alien consciousness came alien feelings and customs. Almost nothing old was left... Our dress, our garments were changed. Most of us embraced this alien identity."[46]

This verdict became a prototype for numerous statements of a similar tone on the part of Polish romanticists, who regarded the civilizational activity of the Enlightenment as being anti-national: not because it was inherently evil, but because it was new and alien and was not organically produced on Polish soil. The critics disregarded the fact that, in the period before the Enlightenment, this soil was arid and the crops it produced were becoming poorer and poorer. Indeed, the whole point was not an evaluation of one cultural formation or another, be it Sarmatism or the Enlightenment. What was at stake was the very principle of the maturing of a nation which, in order to survive, had to understand its own separate identity. And this, according to Mochnacki, could be achieved only through the realization of its own tradition, its own biography.

The more frequent and commonplace the international contacts which helped diffuse cultural patterns became, and the easier it was for books, ideas, institutions and fashions to cross state borders, the more powerful the ideological defence of this original identity of individual peoples grew. It is natural for things to become more valuable when threatened. In Poland, Russia's political domination was the best breeding ground for occidental ideas, while the civilizational domination of the West, the influx of various attractive innovations, kindled the cult of national individuality. This cult and the resistance to foreign influences, which on the whole was instinctive and emotional, was elevated to the rank of the supreme aim of social philosophy by the conservatives and romanticists.

Józef Kalasanty Szaniawski, the first Polish theoretician to articulate this standpoint, wrote as early as 1808 that a nation needs its own natural foundations if it is to develop: "All other norms, derived from a different source, lead to the annihilation of this nation's inborn individuality and change it into a dead conglomerate with no character of its own." Those "who would like to apply models originating in some nation or another to all nations" are in error; the only universal truths are the truths of the Christian religion and metaphysics, while everything that has been hatched from the Enlightenment and revolution can only be French or English; it may be fine in its own place and time, but not anywhere else. Let each nation preserve its own separate history. The Poles in particular should "develop ... the original characteristics proper to our nationality and remove from them the destructive rust of foreign influence which has accumulated in the course of two centuries." At the same time, they should discard those opinions which have germinated under other skies and "so far have failed to acclimatize as it were to the local aura, and to get rid of all that which is useful only in a foreign system."[47]

This view became the motto of the defensive, ethnocentric camp and those who held the conviction that in culture and tradition native features defined the historical identity of a nation and constituted a supreme, autonomous value that did not have to be rationally justified. For a hundred or more years, this attitude would appear in the most diverse political currents, ranging from right to left; throughout the period of foreign domination, Polish ideologies would vie with one another trying to prove that each of them was more native and more deeply rooted in the national tradition than the others. This argument was very persuasive, and the vast tradition was capable of accommodating all kinds of opposites.

The idea of defending the national substance against the invasion of foreign concepts provoked a strong emotional response, but was in fact rather abstract in its content and often concealed disparate interests and objectives. The general thesis was readily applicable to legislation, industry, philosophy and art, but within each of these fields it remained ambiguous.

It was frequently referred to in legislation. During the November Rising, Aleksander Wielopolski demanded that the new constitution should not be "the fruit of abstract theoretical speculation," but "a live creation of our entire history:" "This constitution should not contain an *abstractum* of that which is common to all constitutional nations, but should give expression to national elements."[48] However, this "expression" of national elements could be understood in many different ways: after all, for some the Constitution of 3 May was national, while for others it formed a conglomeration of alien ideas which had nothing in common with the spirit of Polish law. The Napoleonic Code was at first regarded as an undoubted transplant with no attempt to adapt it to the edifice of Polish law, but twenty years later almost nobody regarded it as an imported product any longer. In any case, hardly anything in nineteenth-century law was indisputably national and organically associated with the lost past. It seems that when it came to the understanding of law as an expression of nationality, what mattered were not really the articles of the Constitution and the various codes, but a certain philosophical attitude, a word, a magic formula.

A magic formula was needed as a protection against civilization, which was at once "false" and merciless. "We all seem to draw now from one source; we all feel, think and write in the same way. Isn't this a visible result of the general mechanism of ideas, the mechanism of thought? How difficult it is to discover and to distinguish the essence of our people in its native environment in this monotonous civilization which blurs individual properties and all original features! . . . Ideas travel from country to country, and yet everywhere they adhere to the same order and frame. They are equally adequate and inadequate everywhere, equally valid and invalid."[49] This was the drama which dominated the epoch. It is, in fact, the same drama which even today is experienced without exception by all countries, nations, and tribes when they are confronted with the expansion of the Western type of civilization, with its ideological and political models, its science and technology, capitalist production and middle-class lifestyle. Everywhere, this expansion divides the national intelligentsia into "Slavophiles" and "Westernizers," that is, defenders of the native traditions and enthusiastic supporters of imported modernity. The task of both factions is to sharpen the opposition of principles up to the point where—in the exalted world of feelings and ideas —national culture and supranational civilization appear as *incompatibilia*.

In Poland the conflict could never take on a form as acute as in Russia or Turkey, or in some more distant Asian countries, for here the links with the West of Europe constituted an inherent element of native tradition. Therefore, opposition could only be relative. Whenever the principle of nationality was viewed as a bastion against "the aping of foreign models," this was never a result of a clash between two completely alien and independently developing cultures. Just as in Germany and Spain, it was rather a rebellion of a part against the whole, or better still, a resistance on the part of the urban periphery to the dictates of the "city." The role of pupil in the European school which had been imposed on the Polish people was not to everybody's liking. The romantics enjoined that "ideas, feelings and thoughts ought to and must be different in each nation, just as the history, religion, politics, jurisdiction and lifestyles of the various nations differ. This is the basis of their individual characteristics."[50]

Indeed, in this epoch, if not in the entire century, there was an almost universal conviction that scientific and technological civilization was, by the nature of things, "uniform," that it homogenized human thoughts and, within the orbit of its influence, leveled out all local cultural differences. However, while some saw it as beneficial, others regarded it as harmful. The liberals rejoiced that all nations would, one day, acquire the same truth, freedom and industry and could, as a result, become closer and communicate with each other; they had no regrets about the loss of the colorful mosaic of the archaic world. The romanticist, on the other hand, wanted each tribe to preserve its own truths and untruths, both drawn from the past. In the spirit of Herder they argued that "to each physical difference among peoples conforms a certain temperament, a certain way of thinking and feeling, a certain direction and an adequate power of the spirit, and only the whole of this disposition reveals to us the wealth and unfathomable nature of mankind. . . . Let us imagine all mankind shaped in the same way, let us imagine that all peoples are the same. How monotonous, bare and colorless this world would seem in comparison with the variegated garden of the peoples of the past. Were the philosophers capable of turning all the streams of peoples into one ocean of universal mankind, there would be nothing left for the poets to do but to follow the courses of the streams back to their sources and the mountains whose tips can be seen on the horizon of history."[51]

Perhaps, however, both the philosophers and the poets wcrc mistaken concerning this very point on which they agreed. True, the garden of the peoples of the past was variegated, but only for the rare traveller who in his wanderings across countries could admire the strangeness of exotic religions and rituals, the multiplicity of crops and the shapes of implements, the wealth of folktales and songs; later historians and poets could admire all these things. But this same medieval world was utterly monotonous to those who, from birth till death, never went beyond their own village, who were not aware of differences, and who, moreover, neither valued nor desired them.

Admittedly, the messengers of civilization—the merchant, teacher, land surveyor, and postmaster—intruded on this settled existence, bringing with them new, foreign forms of life and, in the process, destroying more than one ancient custom. But at the same time they obliterated the isolation of local communities and gave them access to other worlds. The development of modern means of transport, the interweaving of cultural influences, and mass migrations contributed to the emergence of a wealth of new forms and ideas, and, as a result, gave ever larger sections of people new, previously unknown possibilities of choice. Thus it was one of the paradoxes of modern civilization that while its mills worked without cease on creating a uniformity of ideas, feelings and thoughts, national cultures did not become impoverished, nor did the world become any less diversified than before.

In the early nineteenth century, both sides of the civilizational process could already be discerned: a growing uniformity in life, accompanied by a growing differentiation. However, it is understandable that the intelligentsia of a country which took more than it gave would be prone to succumb to a fearful obsession about the loss of their cultural identity; and that they would begin to fight the stereotype of a homogeneous civilization with the defensive stereotype of a homogeneous nation.

Ancient historians and geographers were the first to describe the character of tribes in the same terms as individuals, and this method of anthropomorphizing vast, differentiated communities survives even today. But it was the philosophers and political writers of the late eighteenth and early nineteenth centuries who showed a particular propensity for this method. They read the character of nations from their past, and their future from their alleged present qualities. Collective self-portraits became extremely popular in Polish writing in around 1815; almost every author described the "inherent disposition" of the Poles, listing their virtues and vices, though with a tendency to emphasize the former above the latter. Both the classicists and romanticists indulged in this kind of writing. Each image was slightly different and, taken together, form a long list of characteristics—a list that is fairly monotonous, though not without contradictions. It seems impossible to find a single author who would admit that the Poles actually differed among themselves.

Peoples were allowed to be different from other peoples, but not to display any internal differences. In terms of their morality, predilections and customs the Poles were supposed to stand apart from other nations, but among themselves they were expected to be more or less uniform in order to provide an effective obstacle both to the consequences of the partitions and to the plague of foreign influences. This task of defending and preserving the nation was, however, only one of the tasks which the Polish people had to tackle. A second task involved the exertion of genius and creative potential in thought, in art, and in the struggle for independence. Creativity and daring deeds called for individual greatness, for rivalry among individual ambitions and talents, that is, for variety. Therefore, right from the outset, the romanticists, to whom both of these tasks were dear, were embroiled in the chronic antinomy of elitist individualism and psychological collectivity: while they rebelled against the ties and conventions which put a check on their flights of fancy, they also wanted to believe that the world could be understood and transformed only—in the words of Mochnacki—by one "general national mind" which "must have the same powers and dispositions as the mind of each individual man."[52]

Popular collective psychology readily underlined regional differences, but viewed them as varieties of one collective pattern which was immune to the workings of time. No wonder, then, that more and more frequently it was not the character of the gentry that was taken as the hypothetical model for the true character of the nation, but that of the common people: the common people were closer to the original state of the nation, unaffected by the gloss of foreignness and completely lacking in individuality.

Obviously, the fact that the concept of the national character became associated with the tedious life of the people meant that it was more clearly opposed to the idea of accelerating civilizational change. It is equally obvious that the polarization of these two ideas could not bring in its wake any real program for the development of national culture. Apart from a handful of zealous Slavophiles, who dreamt of the revival of some form of proto-Slavic popular patriarchal system, no one really wanted Poland to be cut off from the West or from its thought and technology. At the same time, no one wanted the Poles to become Europeanized in such a way that would obscure the peculiar features of their historical heritage, including their language. By dedicating itself exclusively to European problems, Polish thought would condemn itself to a chronic aping of others and would not be able to adapt to the particular situation in which the enfettered nation lived. By dedicating itself exclusively to its own problems, it would condemn itself to parochial isolation and atrophy.

The history of European nations and cultures could be neither completely common, nor completely separate. Polish thought, which was engaged in an incessant struggle with the dilemma of "civilization and nationality," sought either a border separating the two realms, or a magic unifying formula. It was of no importance where the dividing line ran in these polemics—who was in favor of civilization, the imitation of the West and the landscape of the future, and who opted for nationality, a self-reliant culture and the landscape of the past—for the conflict was experienced by each individual mind which attempted to bring some order into the elusive course of the events and dreams of the epoch.

The simplest solution was to make a rigid distinction between the two spheres. The stronghold of nationality was beyond any doubt the language and national history. The two were mentioned together by Julian Niemcewicz in 1809 when he wrote that "now that the country is in a state of ruin, it is only the [native] tongue that rides the wave of the flood which has engulfed us, and together with the tongue remains the memory of our former existence."[53] A languishing classicism enlisted the help of a whole legion of guardians of the tongue, defenders of the old orthography, and translators of new philosophical, political and scientific terms, including in particular the brothers Śniadecki, Niemcewicz and Kajetan Koźmian. Accused by the romanticists of strict adherence to foreign poetics, they reciprocated by searching out the foreign words with which Mickiewicz had "littered" the Polish language.

In spite of all the warnings, the language used by the enlightened spheres underwent a process of rejuvenation. It adopted many new words, especially from French, and changed its phraseology and syntax, losing in the process many colorful Old Polish expressions. But it was never, not even for a moment, in danger of becoming extinct. Soon, thanks to Adam Mickiewicz, Juliusz Słowacki,[54] and Aleksander Fredro,[55] it would dazzle everyone with its robust flexibility and its charm.

Old customs fared much worse than the language. Peasant customs continued almost unchanged, but old gentry traditions survived only in out-of-the-way villages and hamlets, although even there—as Mickiewicz describes in *Pan Tadeusz*—new, foreign elements, portrayed, of course, in a ridiculous light, forced their way through the bulwarks of the Old Polish civilization. The changes were enormous in Warsaw, in the towns and the manors of the Kingdom, in the Prussian partition zone, and in Western Galicia. The long mustachio, the traditional coat with split sleeves, the karabela sabre, the patriarchal system of upbringing, all the accoutrements of the gentry gradually disappeared from everyday life; they ceased to be the norm and were turned into national symbols, remembered on special occasions or serving as theater props. The Europeanization of dress, customs, education and politics engulfed all and sundry, and the more headway it made, the more the disappearance of the national features was bemoaned.

However, not everyone lamented the demise of the old traditions. Those who particularly cherished the idea of progress (in whatever fashion they imagined it) tried to restrict the area set aside as a "national preserve" in such a way that it would not hamper social change. In his later years, when he was formulating his futuristic vision of united mankind, Staszic treated "nationality" with respect, but also with a measure of exasperation, as being all too handy a shield for the protection of "egotism." He believed that each people should protect its identity, the land of its forebears, its language and historic relics, but "governments, laws, arms, customs, education and sciences—together with reason and civilization—are shared by all nations. With the spreading of the light and the development of civilization . . . they must change and keep pace with progress."[56]

The liberals of the Society of Rogues in Wilno were just as cautious. They believed that to associate the old gentry's habits and notions of grandeur, with "the sacred name of nationality" was a "dishonor to the nation;" for "civilization presses us to shake off prejudice and to substitute virtues for local follies, using the example of other peoples and the universal experience of the centuries and nations."[57] Similar warnings had been voiced by the liberal press during the November Rising. Their polemical edge was directed against the conservative cult of nationality which "abuses this sacred word by fraudulently trying to introduce into our legal and political system principles which have long been superannuated:"[58] that is, the privileges of the gentry and the Church, peasant serfdom, and elitism in civil rights.

Thus, in the idiom of the liberals, nationality meant attachment to one's own country as long as it kept abreast of European progress, while for the traditionalists it was an inviolate preserve of culture and social structures.

Between these two opposites, there was no room for the precursors of
romanticism who wanted a new, democratic Poland, a country which would
generate new, previously unknown ideas and forms of life but which would
generate them on its own soil rather than copying them. They wanted a Poland
that would change its character without losing it, a Poland that would be at
once conservative and revolutionary; European, and yet clearly different from
all other nations.

In this light, the dispute about the borderlines between the domain of
civilization and the domain of nationality began to lose its relevance: the
problem was how to unify the two—how to nationalize civilization. In other
words, how to learn from it and use its discoveries and achievements, while
leaving on them a distinct Slavic mark.

For Mochnacki, the leading ideologue of Polish romanticism in its early
stage, the essence of national culture was not its "outer" manifestations, such
as language and customs, but the way of thinking and feeling. The civilization
which destroyed the individual features of this essence was a "false" civilization. For true civilization should respect the individual spirit of the nation:
"by civilization we should understand: *the power, courage and steady,
ceaseless manifestation and expression of this spirit in all interrelated skills,
in all products of the human mind*; in short, *in the general system of the actions
and the stirrings of thought of the entire nation*."[59] Hence, the European
civilization that really existed was false, and the real civilization was the one
that was yet to be born through "the expansion of the native, local *ego*" until
this ego embraced "all of mankind."[60]

Like no one before him and few after, Mochnacki took a keen interest in
originality, the key problem for all cultures whose development was strongly
dependent on foreign thought and on foreign norms. In no way did he want
Poland to be intellectually isolated, yet he felt that the great chance for Polish
culture was the fact that it was different, and not merely derivative. Creativity,
not imitation, was where its future lay. He kept repeating that it was not
enough to think with "someone else's head," cherish the fruit of "someone
else's labor," or see things with "someone else's eyes." Polish thought was
not yet self-sufficient; it was superficial, and hoped to become enriched
through the translations of foreign works, but in vain: "the ease with which
the best results can be attained in the intellectual field thanks to translations,
the excessive familiarity with foreign languages, and finally the vast space
which has separated the matters of our daily life from the world of serious
thinking, understanding and research—all of this augurs for us an epoch of
torpidity, or perhaps complete intellectual stagnation. For this reason, translations are harmful, since they are particularly conducive to stagnation, not

just in respect of the language, but also as regards the images and thoughts expressed in that language." After all, he argued, Montaigne, Montesquieu, Kant, Fichte and other authors wrote original things: they neither translated nor imitated anything.[61]

Regarding this question of the benefits or harmfulness of translations Mochnacki frequently contradicted himself, losing himself in his own arguments and constantly changing his mind. He wanted to liberate Polish literature and philosophy from the self-effacing consumption of ready-made ideas; he wanted them to give expression to the national genius and to act as partners in the European dialogue, but at the same time he condemned the attempts by Jan Śniadecki and the other empiricists to protect the Polish intellectual domain from the "plague" of German metaphysics, arguing that Polish literature, art and science owed almost all their recent achievements to this very influence. The fact is that the program of intellectual self-reliance had always been endangered by an inconsistency similar to that to which industrial protectionism is prone. Autarky and customs duties may facilitate the development of a country's own production, but they will never make it capable of competing on the international market. Mochnacki and his contemporaries dreamt of creating an originally national philosophy which would be the "science of our own judgment," arguing that "our cloudy sky, our rainy, drizzly air, our melancholy, sorrowful memories" all disposed the Poles to this aim.[62] However, if this philosophy was to investigate truths which were generally valid and significant, then the cloudy sky was not enough: discoveries are made only when one has reached the limits of cognition that have previously been attained by universal thought. Mickiewicz, before he developed into a thoroughly original poet, was one of the best educated and most open-minded Poles of his times, well-read in the leading works of European literature, which he imitated in his own early writings. Cultures condemn themselves to mediocrity not because of translations, but by surrounding themselves with walls.

In the writings of the epoch of the romantic breakthrough opinions on this problem are still confused and have not been thought through to the end. Mochnacki wanted to be able to detect a national note, a Polish mystique in literature, art, and philosophy. And what about physics? Physics was a different matter altogether, belonging as it does to the realm of reason which is governed by the laws of logic and progress common to all countries: "For this reason, sciences and skills are a common property of all ages and peoples, while the creations of the imagination and feelings . . . never bloom in a foreign age or on foreign soil."[63] The author of the treatise *On the Spirit and Sources of Poetry in Poland* thus attempted once again to separate the spheres of civilization and nationality. "The genius of Euclid, Newton and Kepler, when fittingly used, can be adopted and applied in any age and by any nation," he wrote, just like any representative of the Enlightenment. However, he was not completely sure of this, and worried lest an excessive reading of foreign works should restrain the flights of native thought. Thus he warned that "by translating people like Kepler, Galileo or Leibniz we shall never aspire to the supreme ideas of the human mind, we shall not expand its limits, we shall not fathom the eternal laws of nature. To reason means to live."[64]

The empiricists, who were held in contempt by the romanticists, knew well that reasoning bears fruit only when one reaches the final limits of objective knowledge, as Copernicus had once done. But for Mochnacki reasoning was above all a manifestation of the tribal genius. Therefore, in the statue of Copernicus carved in stone by Thorvaldsen, the Polish critic detected the "Sarmatian facial features of the Polish astronomer," seeing him as "a representative of the intellectual prowess of our entire nation and of all fraternal tribes."[65]

Nevertheless, it was more difficult to leave a national stamp on astronomy, physics or technology than on philosophy, history or poetry. By the same token, the idea of nationality as seen by the romanticists favored the formation of a model of Polish culture in which literature, history and philosophical speculation took first place, while the natural sciences, economics, technology and medicine were to all intents and purposes pushed into the background.

This had momentous consequences. A scientific and technological civilization is, by the nature of things, extrovert, that is, it aims at expanding cognitive and technical skills, irrespective of who makes use of them and where they are applied. It also tends to associate itself with existing authority, since it needs protection and support. On the other hand, a culture which is dominated by literature and the philosophy of history is independent and introvert. Hence, in Poland, culture came to concern itself mainly with probing the Polish soul, with helping the nation to understand itself, its destiny and mission. Such an understanding does not call for a perfecting of the tools of investigation, but rather of the powers of intuition; it does not require the growth of knowledge, which is always fragmentary and restricted to one specialization, but an overall view in a flash of spiritual illumination; it has no use for the techniques by which the natural and social landscape is gradually transformed, but looks instead for ways and means of creating, experiencing and sustaining the community, that collective national "we."

This contrast has of course been exaggerated, while in fact both orientations, the inward-looking approach and the technological approach, coexist in cultures. Everything is fine if they are evenly balanced. However, beginning in the 1820s, the balance was tipped in favor of self-reflection and national psychotherapy in the Polish cultural consciousness. And there was nothing strange in this. After all, the leading Polish authors operated under the supreme moral imperative of sustaining the collective sense of identity of a nation torn apart by three foreign powers and lacking any institution that could join together all its separate parts. What is more, this sense of common identity existed only among the gentry and the intelligentsia, and even then not among all of them. It was lacking among the common people who, as has been mentioned above, were seen by many as the mainstay of everything that was thoroughly native and Polish, the people who had yet to be taught the simple truth of the existence of national motherlands and whose legal, economic and intellectual emancipation had only just begun. This tragic paradox was to cast a shadow over the history of Poland for the entire nineteenth century. And that was not all. It was also necessary to foster contacts with the West, maintain an awareness of the common objective of freedom and social progress, ensure that these links were mutual and equal, continue learning from other peoples while casting off the complexes of an immature pupil.

Thus, Polish intellectual culture faced a formidable combination of tasks that no revolution could unravel; all that could be done was to maintain an awareness of their existence. Such a culture could not be merely empirical and utilitarian; it could not manage without myths. Historical myths, it seems, are a constructive part of any culture, but in nations which have experienced much humiliation myths gain supreme power over the minds of the inhabitants and determine the social consciousness.

The myth of "being the first" grew in popularity from the beginning of the nineteenth century onwards and was to fulfil an important function. This myth enabled the Poles to preserve their national pride by accepting some chosen elements from the program of contemporary European civilization, in the conviction that these elements had been known in Poland earlier. Although, through the fault of the gentry and various historical disasters this process of civilization had been interrupted and Poland relegated to an inferior position in Europe, it was, nevertheless, still possible to renew the links. Thus, it became the ambition of the pre-romantic faction of Polish liberal thought to prove that the Polish people could find sufficient strength within itself and enough appropriate models in its history to create a culture that would be modern but not imitative. The emergence from backwardness meant not so much the introduction of Western legal, economic or technological innovations as the reclaiming of valuable qualities present in native life in the period before the downfall.

In the post-partition period, Polish thinkers sought models in the sixteenth-century political and cultural renaissance and sometimes went back to pre-historic times. They explored the ancient history of the Slavs with great zeal and fervor. Since the available information about these times was scant and on the whole unreliable, the scope left to the imagination was vast, and everybody could shape the story of the past in a way that agreed with his own hierarchy of values. No wonder then that when Wawrzyniec Surowiecki, the champion of industrialization and civilizational work, looked back to the times preceding the foundation of the Polish state in the tenth century, he perceived there "a people who loved music, sculpture, and painting; who knew the difficult art of casting statues in precious metals; a people who dispatched numerous ships laden with the products of its own industry to Greece, Asia and the Hindus and who kept the whole of Northern Europe supplied with soft silks and gold; a people who had established powerful cities close to the ice-bound axes of the earth and held there fairs that attracted various tribes who lived within a radius of 500 miles and who knew neither the languages nor the names of their neighbors."[66]

A slightly different picture of the ancient Slavonic landscape was painted by Kazimierz Brodziński, an enthusiastic admirer of the pastoral way of life. He claimed that "our forebears left large cities and commerce to foreigners while they themselves, with no distinction as to estate, lived for agriculture;" this agriculture flourished because "they cherished a peaceful, industrious life more than treasures and luxury."[67]

All the currents in the existing study of Slavic cultures were inspired by Herder and accepted the same stereotypical features for the Slavic character: calm, peaceful, sensitive and democratic. Authors of modernized variants of this description of a pre-Slavic utopia stressed in addition the virtues of industry and inventiveness and the extraordinary creative powers of their forebears: for example, they had no doubt whatsoever that the Poles' ancestors knew runic writing and that they had committed to writing their legal codes, holy books and epics. This brilliant civilization, which once outshone its neighbors, had been destroyed, like many others in the history of the world, but it could be rebuilt from the native element hidden in the unchangeable nature of the tribe.

In the case of the reconstruction of the historic past of Poland, the mythical projection was somewhat contradicted by objective knowledge: as a result, it was difficult to sustain the thesis about Poland's priority in relation to the rest of Europe in the fields of science, art and industry. Hence, the conviction about her priority as regards the love and protection of freedom gained in strength. On this point, the pre-romantic liberals of 1820 ignored the political criticism of the Enlightenment and reverted directly to the self-idealization of the Sarmatian period. From such a perspective, the ancient freedoms and parliamentary system of Poland appeared completely in accord with the spirit of civil rights which had inspired Western Europe only shortly before, after centuries of feudalism and despotism. In this way, Poland won a leading position in human progress and now, in the years of the Congress Kingdom, she only had to develop those principles which "had been there in our people for centuries."[68]

We owe the most influential myth of "being the first" to Joachim Lelewel.[69] Himself the most sincere of democrats, he ascribed to his Polish ancestors his own attachment to the ideas of freedom and republican equality—ideas in which he perceived the foundations of European civilization. In the hypothetical ancient Slavic system of communes he saw the beginnings of contemporary democracy, and he regarded the republicanism and egalitarianism of the gentry as a further institutional development of the same trend. Admittedly, the democratic idea had been distorted because rights and liberties were restricted to one, privileged estate. Nevertheless, at least in this estate it had been preserved at a time when those nations which were oppressed by kings and Jesuits had completely forgotten it. This meant that Poland could claim priority over the English, the French and the Americans in proclaiming the rights of man and of citizens.

"When creating something new," wrote Lelewel in 1833, "one must accommodate and adapt what is old and national, and extract the new from the national. A structure which has no deep foundations is weak." Earlier, in 1831, he recommended that in introducing a new social order the Seym should "bring together the past and the future, and link the native Polish thing with the aspirations of the age."[70]

This concept represented a complete repudiation of the opposition between tradition and progress, or nationality and civilization. When "the native Polish thing" had been cleansed of the veneer of foreign feudalism, it became apparent that for centuries it had been convergent with the current program of European democracy: thanks to this, "the new" could easily be extracted from the "old and national."

This idea was put forward forcefully by a representative of the left wing in the rising of 1830–31: "While sharing the necessary European objectives, we must preserve our virtues, our character, our laws, our history, and our institutions, that is, our nationality and our individuality. . . . The dogma of the power of the people is a native historical monument. . . . The motherland of political freedom is our country, Poland. . . . As to liberal principles and institutions, we were ahead of all the nations of Europe . . . we need to revive the institutions, establish them everywhere and extend their influence to all citizens, and we do not need to copy anything."[71]

But who would have the will to revive institutions after forty years of historical twists and turns, in a completely new social setting? Who, especially on the left wing, really wanted to, and could, revive them in the event of the victory of a national revolution? And which institutions were worth reviving? The privileges of the gentry, local diets, the *liberum veto*, and corrupt courts? Or the system of the Constitution of 3 May, born out of the criticism of these "native historical monuments?" Still, the reintroduction of that constitution forty years later in a new reality would mean a step backwards. Under favorable circumstances it would be possible to restore the country within its shrunken borders, and to resuscitate names and symbols, but not institutions, laws, or even ideas. The idea of a revolution that would look backwards was an illusion and could not be contained in a realistic program—but it did become a feature of Polish sentimental history.

The ideas and aims of the struggle did not have their roots in the past, and the gentry–republican tradition, which was disowned by the reformers of the Enlightenment and discontinued following the partition of the country, was not the source of the values recognized by the Polish liberals and radicals. Their ideas and programs reflected entirely contemporary aims and grew out of an analysis of the existing situation of Poland and Europe. They had, however, to be sanctified and legitimized by the mythologized tradition; what was foreign had to be Polonized, and what was new had to don the old costume. An idealization of the past is usually a feature of a conservative attitude, but the Polish myths of "being the first" turned it into a handy tool for the adherents of social and civilizational progress.

The tailoring of Old Polish legacies to contemporary universal ideas performed an important psychological function. The Poles of the nineteenth century celebrated the freedom, equality, industry and civic attitude of their forebears so that the inherited glory could help them free themselves of the inferiority complex which inevitably resulted from a sober assessment of Poland's political and civilizational position. By resorting to a past whose genesis had been perpetuated in myths, the Polish intellectual elite could feel that they were still within the orbit of Western civilization without losing their sense of national continuity and dignity. In this way, the takers imagined themselves to be givers, and the wanderers of well-trodden paths felt like the direct descendants of the first pioneers.

The price to be paid for this complacency and for the denial of the very real conflict that existed between traditional values and the values of modernity was the further inflation of defensive mechanisms. In this respect, the myth of the exceptional nature of Polish history, which was meant to entitle the Poles to feel morally superior in relation to other European nations, had a lot to answer for. Revived in post-partition Poland, this myth was by no means new. It had originated in the sixteenth century, and was not even peculiarly Polish, but can probably be found in all nations. It expressed not so much the vainglory as the fears and claims of a once glorious tribe which now found itself in impoverished circumstances. It was ideologically far more adaptable than the theory of civilizational leadership, because it also suited the purposes of those who highlighted above all the chivalrous virtues of Polish tradition and contrasted them with the values of a civilization based on science, laws and industry: people like Jan Paweł Woronicz who invoked the old idea of Poland as the "bulwark of Christendom" and proclaimed that "Poland was drowning in blood for the sake of Europe, while Europe, safely hidden behind its back, was able to cultivate learning and reap the benefits."[72]

This myth of moral superiority, the idea of a special divine mission in relation to both the Polish people and the salvation of the world, bore ample fruit in the poetry, philosophy and political thought of the conquered nation. This myth was in keeping with the theory of the innocence of the civilization of the Slavic peoples who remained uncontaminated by the spirit of cold calculation and were therefore capable of sacrifice, and also with the theory of the seniority of their civilization. The two theories were compatible and interchangeable. Poland, seen as a chivalrous order of apostles of freedom who carried its gospel to the West and the East, was entrusted with this mission either by virtue of her tradition of armed struggle against infidel invaders or her tradition of free republican government, depending on the circumstances.

The romantic sanctification of tradition was practised by both the conservatives and the radical liberals, by the faithful sons of the Church and by those who saw the first signs of the obliteration of the original native traits in the Christianization of Poland. All of them, each according to their own purposes, credited the national past with principles cherished by themselves in order to prove that these principles carried the stamp of the highest authority. This trend would continue later, after the November Rising, when monarchism and republicanism, nobility and democracy, tolerance and intolerance would all claim that history proved them to constitute the core of the national heritage. And all of them would, in some way, be right, because each of these programs was indeed rooted in national history and each had its own antecedents. History alone did not provide any pointers as to what was good and what was disastrous for nineteenth-century Poland; nor did it indicate what was native and what was foreign since in the course of centuries the foreign had become native. Tradition did not endorse values; it only ratified them, unstintingly and indiscriminately. It did not specify objectives, but provided them with a justification.

From the early 1820s on, the writers of moralistic and satirical literature took great pleasure in pillorying the snobbery of high society, this attitude of humility before all things foreign, the influx of which was destroying or had already destroyed the true greatness of Poles. However, the very abundance of such stories and morality tales, as well as their contexts, proved that the national pride they apparently expressed was in fact defensive in character, and covering a deep complex of unrequited love. In these texts, France, the West and Europe emerge as a permanent reference system for the Polish enlightened classes: it was from there—as has been said before—that recognition and acceptance were expected. Unfortunately, the response was usually a disdainful lack of interest, occasionally contempt, which was immediately seen as an insult to the nation.

Polish culture did not know how to free itself of this psychological dependence, and it is doubtful whether under the existing political circumstances it could really do so. It continued to see itself through the mirror of European opinion and did not regard itself as an authority on these matters. The only cure for this complaint would have been a magic reversal of roles: that is, the development of the belief that everything that came from the West was of inferior quality. From here it would be just a step to maintaining that "home-made products" should always be favored before "foreign inventions."[73] So the aim of cultural autarky was not only to prove that native Polish culture was equally legitimate, but above all to demonstrate how lofty its tone was in comparison with the West, and how noble its simplicity.

The years of the Congress Kingdom were indeed a period of mass infiltration of Western science, technology, medicine, law, art, and ideology, and no one who held a place of importance in Polish culture remained completely immune to this influence. The charge of succumbing to foreign influence was therefore always double-edged: for example, it was used by the classicists against the romanticists, who reciprocated with equal justification. At the same time, even those who cherished the authenticity of national culture occasionally displayed a polemical inconsistency when they rebuked their opponents for not really caring about what was happening in European thought. Thus, Szaniawski's and Mochnacki's obsessive Francophobia, the result of their dislike of the legacy of the Enlightenment, was—up to a point—counterbalanced by their enthusiasm for German metaphysics. Many similar examples could be quoted. Each generalized attack against imitation proved to be, in the final analysis, merely a criticism of a certain choice of cultural patterns. Nevertheless, such generalizations had a purpose, though this purpose was psychological rather than pragmatic. The hopeless struggle against things foreign was indispensable for bolstering the vacillating national self-esteem: it authorized envy and disapproval at the same time, and allowed foreign inventions to be enjoyed even as they were condemned.

Many contemporary authors distinguished a low and a high sphere of culture, with the dividing line occupying different positions. The classicists took their cue from their normative poetics. The young patriotic conspirators put the supreme symbols and ideals of the epoch in the upper sphere: the White Eagle, Liberty, the Republic, the Constitution, and Education. The romantics elevated to the higher sphere national "subjectivity," everything in culture which led to "self-recognition," which allowed "tradition to actualize itself," and which contributed to the struggle for independence: poetry, philosophy and politics, the powerful emotions of faithfulness and treason, love and revenge, and the mysterious People, celebrated in ballad and song. They ascribed to the lower sphere everything which was "useful," ordinary and connected with everyday life.

This was a completely new hierarchy of values, bearing not the slightest resemblance to the old division, which though anachronistic had not completely vanished—the division which distinguished between the occupations of the gentry and the occupations of the common people. The romantic hierarchy was completely alien to the intellectual atmosphere of the Enlightenment, with its practical patriotism, its sense of empiricism and its faith in the formative power of good government and education. After the partitions, Staszic was the first to admit that in the final reckoning the fate of nations is resolved in the economic field, in the rivalry of civilizations. During his travels through Europe, he studied the productivity and wealth of the inhabitants of each country he visited. In his numerous educational projects for the Duchy of Warsaw and the Polish Kingdom, his main concern was utility: he stressed that young people should be taught applied sciences and learn how to work efficiently in agriculture, mining, industry, overland and water transportation, medicine and administration. "There is some unbreakable force, some supreme force in those peoples who, having developed their physical and moral capacities as widely as possible, have at their disposal a vast number of methods for using their manpower and natural resources," he argued on the eve of the war of 1812, and he warned young people against displaying excessive martial zeal since this, if abilities and means are lacking, "may result in the annihilation of nations."[74] But he also understood perfectly well this other, self-asserting function of culture. Addressing the Society of the Friends of Learning, he said that the sphere of literature "embraces those fields of learning that give nations immortality, that help preserve the nation's tongue . . . and that can link its past existence with its future." The purpose of history he expressed as follows: "by reading the works of his ancestors every young man should gain respect for them and for himself, and as a result feel proud of being a Pole."[75]

There was no contradiction here. Likewise, there was no contradiction in the ideas of the Wilno Philomaths who combined the principle of utilizing knowledge for social purposes in order to bring about civilizational transformations, with a love of poetry and nationality, and also with a passion for the philosophy of history. In the cultural trends of the twilight of the Enlightenment, *logos* and *praxis* still remained inseparably united.

However, younger and more feverish minds were scornful of those modes of thinking and working which failed to satisfy their impatient hunger for the ideal and which, moreover, provided an easy excuse for political opportunism. Seweryn Goszczyński would later recall how, having given up school in Podolia in 1819, he also abandoned the thought of studying in Wilno: "We had no warm feelings for Wilno. We thought this university to be the right place only for those for whom learning represented only the means of becoming a doctor or a professor. We did not find there a more lofty life which would suit our views of the future; and I, at any rate, was guided exclusively by political aims."[76]

The liberal alliance of a pragmatic attitude with a line of thinking which aspired to moral absolutes was drawing to an end; the polemical exchange between Mochnacki and Jan Śniadecki revealed the inability of the two sides to communicate. One side derided the new poetry, metaphysics and intuitive or speculative attempts at uncovering the mysteries of the existence of man and the nation. The other side attacked conformist literature which maintained a reprehensible alliance with the "social relations" of the epoch, and also launched assaults on the despotic rule of the "crude empiricism" which reigned in the sciences and arts, allowing them to dispense with a "systematic spirit" and philosophical self-knowledge.[77] This does not mean that Mochnacki failed to recognize the civilizational functions of the applied sciences. After all, every romanticist knew that someone had to plough, saw, harvest, cure people, produce soap, build bridges and teach arithmetic. But this was the lower, trivial side of culture, a culture which, through specialization and popularizing publications, led to the dissemination of "petty things, petty thoughts, petty imaginings."[78]

The critical writings of Mochnacki or Józef Gołuchowski reflected the conviction, fairly widespread among European intellectuals, that the Enlightenment had left behind it the legacy of a shattered world. Skeptical philosophy deprived both cognition and morality of a supernatural guarantee, and consequently of any authority or sense that could unite them. The sciences had gone their separate ways, each of them organizing its own individual, fragmented experiences in its own manner. That is why contemporary civilization was perceived as "false," as a "mechanism of notions." The romantic breakthrough fed on this sense of intellectual and axiological deficiency: attacks on empiricism, specialization, eclecticism, "intellectual shallowness," and the criterion of utility revealed an overwhelming desire for synthesis, a passionate search for a universal principle that would unite nature and restore meaning to history. Science could not provide such a principle, and for many its growing technical competence was not enough to compensate for the losses. The search for some unifying force took many different forms: dogmatic religion, initiation into mystical cults and the occult, metaphysical philosophies of nature, and evolutionist systems of the philosophy of history. Under the conditions prevailing in Poland, the philosopher's stone was obviously to be sought for in self-knowledge, which meant first of all national self-knowledge. When Mochnacki worried about the division between serious "thought and study" on the one hand and everyday matters on the other, he did not mean that "study" should be reduced to the level of the necessities of "life." What he did believe was that the life of the nation should become the object of integrating form of philosophical self-reflection.

In this way, self-understanding, the attempt to discover one's mission in the history of the world, and finally, in 1831, the attempt "to discover the aim of revolution," were to become the most important tasks for the intellectual activity of the nation, as expressed in its literature, philosophy and politics: in other words, in the activities of those who thought, experienced and suffered on behalf of the nation. For whole decades a part of the Polish intellectual elite would frantically search for answers to the questions: "who were we, who are we, who may we become?" And it was increasingly difficult for them to find a common language with those who would rather dedicate their knowledge and time to the extraction of coal, agrarian reform, and the combating of cholera epidemics.

Admittedly, from time to time, then as well as later, attempts were made to abolish this division of culture into a higher and lower sphere. For Jan Ludwik Żukowski, Mochnacki's friend, the opposition of man's moral and material aims, and that of the "aesthetic" and "utilitarian" functions of art, was a superstition which merely continued the ancient division between the liberal arts and slave crafts. He took a broad view of the "arts," meaning all fields of creativity and production: "The nineteenth century provides a theoretical explanation of the scientific principles of the arts, and by disseminating them tries in practice to include industry among their number."[79] In this extremely politicized epoch, Żukowski was one of the few Polish authors to be sensitive to social wrongs. An ardent spokesman for the abolition of corvée, he regarded this as a precondition for economic progress and prosperity in the countryside, which would make the peasants aware of their dignity as human beings and conscious of their being members of the nation. "Only this will contribute to the emergence of a truly national culture composed of our own, and not borrowed, elements; in this way, all the free springs of activity will be put in motion to speed up the country's general prosperity and bring it to the same level of power, happiness and culture which today is enjoyed by the peoples of England, France and North America."[80] This was an interesting attempt at reconciling that aspect of culture which seeks to understand the meaning of history with its more utilitarian aspect.

There would be many more, usually futile, attempts at reconciling the two orientations. In fact, the culture of self-knowledge and the technological culture would develop for half a century as it were independently, each of them ignoring the presence of the other. Each of them would be fostered by a different intelligentsia: the first by uprooted conspirators and exiles, by ideologues and poets, and the second by professionals.

This was not merely a division of tasks, but also a division of values and attitudes. The men whose approach to culture was professional did not burden their consciences with responsibility for the historic fate of the nation, and even less so for the fate of the world. They had little or no interest in ideological and messianic systems. They were practical and on the whole inclined to political and existential opportunism rather than rebellion against reality. They kept the reins of the imagination firmly in check and had no trust in lofty rhetoric and noble visions. They simply wanted to teach their fellow countrymen how to do well what it was possible and worthwhile to do without any great risk.

Their ideology was scientism, and for them the most honorable trade was "the vocation of a scholar and the position of a teacher." They believed that all the arts and industries had recognized the authority of science. In science, they argued, "men of all classes can find help, it has gained admittance to all social relations."[81]

From the point of view of the scholar—especially the naturalist or mathematician—and also from the point of view of the engineer, doctor, or even lawyer, the problem of the inherent values of the national culture appeared in a completely different light than in philosophical–literary reflections. Poland, after all, had every chance of producing truly original, inimitable works of literature and art, or of historical and social thought, inspired by the drama of the conquered but unbowed nation. But in the fields of mathematics, physics, chemistry and technology, agriculture and medicine, such claims could not be taken seriously.

The question concerning the originality of scientific work had two different dimensions. First, there was the question of whether a science which would have peculiarly national features was possible at all: for anybody competent in this field, the answer was obviously "no." The "nationalization" of science meant, in practice, that contemporary scholars spared no efforts in trying to coin and introduce Polish scientific and philosophical terms, many of which are still used. Second, there was the question of whether Polish scholars were working under suitable conditions for making discoveries and inventions of universal significance. The answer to this question was in principle also negative. As regards scientific facilities for empirical research Poland lagged behind the leading Western countries by fifty years or more, and the three Polish universities (in Kraków, Warsaw and Wilno) had only started to bridge this gap.

The main task of contemporary Polish scholars and researchers was thus not to produce new, original Polish ideas, but to study the contemporary methodology and objective knowledge of their Western masters and to disseminate this knowledge in their own country. This was what Mochnacki could not understand when he complained that in Copernicus' country "we copy other people's experiments in our own laboratories." Sometimes he admitted that scientific culture had to be governed by different rules than art and speculative thought; at other times, he insisted on extending his postulate for national autonomy to scientific culture. "History shows us," he argued, "that science is born out of uninterrupted research, perfected through our own work, our own inventions and discoveries. . . . Science has to be in us, in our very midst, and we must extract new skills from ourselves, out of our inner being."[82] This sounded fine, but such a program, if adopted, would have doomed Polish scientific culture to petrification and atrophy. It was to become atrophied anyway as a result of the defeat of the November Rising which was followed by the liquidation of the universities of Warsaw and Wilno and other Polish academic institutions by the tsarist authorities. Romanticism could not make up for this disaster; in the darkest hours of national oppression and exile it kept alive the flame of poetry and myth, but it failed to produce anything in the field of science.

As we have seen, at the twilight of the Enlightenment the philosophy of history solved the problem of the opposition between the national tradition and European civilization verbally—by finding a formula which allowed for compromise and by giving an appropriate account of history. Meanwhile, a practical problem which had to be faced was how an agricultural country, which was only just shedding the bonds of feudalism, should respond to the inevitable challenges of industrial civilization. This problem was dealt with in the seat of government and in the court, in the schoolroom and the home, on the land, on the road, and in the workshop. In the process of mutual adaptation—which is always difficult and beset by conflicts—both the national cultural heritage and the invading civilization underwent selection and modification. The daily life of the country did not conform to speculative systems and moral teachings: people adopted those foreign models that they thought useful or that they found attractive.

Obviously, the process of Europeanization did not proceed uniformly: it was more apparent in Warsaw than in the provinces, and exercised more the thoughts of professionals than the thoughts of country gentlemen. Skills such as architecture, civil engineering, mechanics, mining, banking, insurance, medicine and agronomy were still in their infancy and it was obvious that they had to be learnt in the West or, for those who could not go to foreign universities, from foreign specialists (not always the best ones) in Poland, or from imported books. The development of the applied sciences and the liberal arts, which was indispensable if the country was to join the train of civilizational progress, was supported by Adam Jerzy Czartoryski as curator of Wilno University,[83] and by the government of the Polish Kingdom which needed teachers for the Polytechnical Institute, the Agronomical Institute and the Mining School. The first Polish professional journals and magazines dedicated to the popularization of scientific and technological knowledge also helped in this work. Such ventures often lacked a consistent program and the results were sometimes fairly amateurish publications, but this is the usual way for scientific culture to begin and a high level of competence can be achieved only gradually.

It was important that the country remained open to the West. This was particularly true of the Kingdom until 1830—in spite of its political union with Russia and its very restricted autonomy, and the growing reaction and censorship in the government and in the Church. Apart from skills, ideas also seeped through from the West: faith in progress, the doctrine of representational government, more humane methods for punishing criminals, and a middle-class morality. These and other values, norms and political theories all reached Poland with the trademark of France, England or America, irrespective of how far they had materialized in their country of origin.

Imported skills and patterns thus began to transform the mentality of the Polish enlightened classes, leading to a form of progress which was verifiable in practice, and not merely metaphysical. At the same time, the resistance of tradition was tangible and by no means dignified, manifesting itself in the haughtiness of the nobility, their flaunting of lineage, their by now anachronistic customs and mores, the routine of farm life based on corvée, clerical resistance to secular learning and non-denominational schools. The moderate ideology of civilizational progress was harder to reconcile with this cumbersome legacy than the revolutionary–national rhetoric of the romanticists. For the moderates had to take up the interrupted work of the intellectual elite of Stanislaus Augustus' time and daily, step by step, uproot all sorts of prejudice and backwardness in social relations and sow the seeds of a new legacy of critical and inventive thought on this cleared ground. For the professors, economists and industrialists, the model was England which, unlike France, did not destroy its historic institutions, but likewise did not use them as an obstacle to modernization. For such people, national tradition did not form one sacred, indivisible whole. The abandonment of distinctions of rank among the gentry did not entail the abandonment of national dignity, and it was not necessary to do away with the Polish tongue along with feudal land laws. In the difficult years following the Congress of Vienna, Polish culture, despite all the fears on its behalf, showed an incredible ability to assimilate foreign products—words, ideas, inventions, styles and laws. By incorporating them into the most vital parts of the national heritage, it produced new alloys in the language, thought and scenery of the country, alloys that were more European and just as Polish as before.

In spite of this, even the most convinced supporters of modernization worried lest this progress should blur all marks of national separateness. Poland needed industry, and industry was developing under government protection in the Congress Kingdom. The desire was for this industry to be Polish, national. But it was easier to say what national art was, or what it was supposed to be, than what national industry was or how it should be created. The State Mining Corps could revive the ceremonials of the medieval miners' guilds—though these ceremonials belonged to the German rather than Polish tradition. But what traditions could be invoked by a cotton mill? Or a sugar mill? In order to give impetus to the manufacturing and building industries, Żukowski suggested the formation of a company which would erect new buildings in a Polish national style. But no one knew what this style was, or how it could be represented in modern buildings. Antonio Corazzi's classicism, which was the dominant style in monumental architecture, could hardly be called national. Should metal and textile factories be given the facades of country manors if a national style were to be applied in architecture.

The "nationalization of industry" was a popular slogan shortly before and during the November Rising, because industry was seen as the mainstay of

military power. The engineer Paweł Kaczyński, a professor at the Polytechnical Institute, saw the Polonization of industry as one of the conditions for
the liberation of the Polish nation. Giving vent to his feelings in a xenophobic
diatribe, he preached that in Poland "there will be no industry as long as it is
foreigners who bring it here, as long as it remains in the hands of foreigners."
This sentence is a logical contradiction: since foreigners did establish enterprises and did retain control of them, there was industry in Poland. This
industry, however, did not live up to the author's expectations. He further
argued: "As long as Polish hands are incapable of making what the Polish
nation needs, as long as Polish minds refuse to recognize that the produce of
Polish hands is superior to all other goods, we have no right to claim that we
have a Polish industry, we have no right to claim to be an independent
people."[84]

Poland did not have sufficient capital, credit, technological know-how or
machines, nor the industrialists and mechanics, or even an adequately qualified labor force, to create and manage industry independently. Kaczyński
himself, as indeed the majority of the more prominent technicians of that
generation, had learnt his trade in the West. Nevertheless, the wish for
industry and commerce to be strong without foreigners managing them and
drawing profits from them was to be one of the *leitmotifs* of Polish economic
nationalism throughout the nineteenth century. It should be remembered,
though, that this is the dream of the middle class and the intelligentsia of every
developing country.

If Poland was to catch up with more advanced countries or even simply
stop the gap from growing wider, it had first to admit the existence of such a
gap. However, the awareness of backwardness is always painful to national
pride, especially when this is combined with political disadvantage. Cultural
dependence is perceived as an extension of armed conquest, even if, as in
Poland, it comes from a different direction. Therefore, both kinds of dependence together seem to threaten the very existence of the national community
and this threat releases defensive mechanisms. The most effective of these
mechanisms is to subordinate measurable civilizational values—such as
natural resources, productivity, the nourishment of the people, the level of
education and hygiene, local government in towns and villages—to ideal
values which cannot be arranged on a scale. The possession of such ideal
values can give a sense of power and importance even to impoverished and
despised nations.

The Rising of 1830–31 confirmed the sense of such a hierarchy of values.
Had not the words of the prophets come true? Poland was once again the
bulwark of Europe. Insurrectionary papers, Seym oratory, and broadsheet

poetry all consolidated the conviction that Poland's challenge to Tsar Nicholas represented a watershed in world history in that it served as a shield for
the July Revolution in France, threatened with the Russian intervention. Even
if initially the White Eagle of Poland soared above the earth, attracted by the
"rainbow of the Franks" and "inspired with the Sun of July,"[85] soon the results
of the battles fought on the Mazovian plain were to determine the fate of the
freedom of nations: "A victory for us will be a victory for Mankind, but a
defeat means a regression of several centuries," one of the journalists wrote
at the time.[86] In February 1831, as the Russian army of Field Marshal Dibitch
was approaching Warsaw, an insurrectionary newspaper wrote: "We are
preventing civilization, freedom and all supreme human values from falling
over the brink of the precipice. We are defending the light, laws, and glory
for which the peoples of Western Europe have worked for centuries against
the sword of the northern barbarian. Never before has the destiny of a nation
been more sublime than ours."[87]

The dethronement of Nicholas I by the Warsaw Seym and the Polish–Russian war liberated Poland from the inferiority complex which had developed
as a result of the partitions. For so many years Poland had been merely an
object in the political games of the powers, and here it was, making its
comeback on the world scene voluntarily, and appearing in the role of a
subject, above all a moral subject. In Brodziński's famous speech *On the
Nationality of the Poles*, delivered on the fortieth anniversary of the Constitution of 3 May, the image of the messiah–victim came to the fore once again.
The antinomy of the national and the human found its resolution at the highest
level: the Poles had guarded their own freedoms and rights for centuries so
that they would be able to defend the freedom and solidarity of all peoples
when the time came. They had suffered doubly under the yoke of northern
despotism: "as a people participating in nineteenth-century civilization and
as a nation having the most sacred right to its own nationality."[88]

No one asked any longer what Poland owed to Western civilization,
because now the bleeding Poland was not the debtor but the moral creditor
of Europe: she was an apostle of the ethics of sacrifice in a world guided by
the policies of egotism and violence. What is more, this claim was recognized
as legitimate, for a short time at least, by liberal opinion in the West: never
before, and never again for the rest of the century, did Poland enjoy such
sympathy and admiration. Defeat could not sap this sublime feeling of moral
satisfaction. On the contrary: it increased the price of the sacrifice and the
debt which the world owed. A new bard prophesied that the peoples perishing
in slavery and hunger would be liberated through the sacrament of Polish

blood, and the book of Polish history would become their gospel: "And in our dark prisons the sins of mankind will be redeemed."[89]

Thus, under the pressure of events, the Polish national idea plunged into a state of narcissism where at long last it could admire itself in a mirror of its own making, not a French one. From this perspective the only hunger which could have any significance was the hunger for freedom and independence.

The gospel of Polish romanticism found its expression in the genius of its bards. They formulated these spiritual values and longings in such an enthralling way that it was possible completely to lose sight of the miserable condition of Polish society with its poor peasant farmsteads and Jewish stalls.

From this point on, we have two histories of culture. One is the sacred history of the nation, the history found in its songs, in its prisons, and on the battlefields. The other is the history of society, the history of sowing and reaping. And there is also the history of political thought, helplessly caught between the archangelic vision of the past and the future, and the harsh reality of Polish daily life.

Notes to Chapter 1

1. *Monitor* (1765–1785), a Warsaw journal, the idea for which came from Stanislaus Augustus, propagating the philosophical and moral ideas of the Enlightenment.
2. According to a sixteenth-century historical myth, the Polish gentry were descended from the ancient tribe of valiant Sarmatians mentioned by Roman geographers.
3. Confederation of Bar (1768–1772), a rising of the Catholic gentry, followed by a guerilla war against Stanislaus Augustus and his reforms, and the Russian army that supported him; the rebels objected to equal rights for dissenters.
4. Augustus III (1696–1763), Elector of Saxony, King of Poland from 1733; his reign coincided with a period of political inertia.
5. *Monitor* 1765, no. 60.
6. Four Years Seym (1788–1792), the permanent Diet that initiated political and legal reforms; its main achievement was the Constitution of 3 May of 1791. The partisans of State reform called themselves "patriots."
7. P. Hazard, *European Thought in the Eighteenth Century: from Montesquieu to Lessing*, trans. J. L. May (Cleveland and New York, 1963), p. 443.
8. Jan Potocki (1761–1815), a writer, archaeologist and traveler, the author of *Manuscrit trouvé à Saragosse (The Saragossa Manuscript)*.
9. Hugo Kołłątaj (1750–1812), a priest, philosopher, educational reformer and prominent political writer; co-author of the Constitution of 3 May.
10. Stanisław Staszic (1755–1826), a priest, influential political writer, and spokesman for burghers' rights and claims.

11. From the time of the Union of Lublin (1569), the gentry called their State (with an elected king) *Rzeczpospolita Obojga Narodów*, i.e., Commonwealth of the Two Nations, or the Polish–Lithuanian Commonwealth.

12. Cf. Lucien Febvre, "Civilisation: Evolution d'un mot et d'un groupe d'idées," in his *Pour une histoire à part entière* (Paris, 1962), pp. 481–528.

13. A. de Condorcet, *Outlines of an Historical View of the Progress of the Human Mind* (Dublin, 1796), p. 249.

14. Ibid., pp. 256, 287.

15. Ibid., pp. 259, 285–6.

16. Ibid., pp. 257, 264.

17. Ibid., p. 12.

18. The insurrection of 1794, a national rising which followed the second partition of Poland, and which aimed at removing Russian forces (aided by Prussia) from the much reduced Commonwealth; General Tadeusz Kościuszko was the Supreme Commander of the insurrection.

19. From manuscripts of the clandestine Republicans' Society (1798), quoted after M. Handelsman, *Rozwój narodowości nowoczesnej* (2nd ed., Warsaw, 1973), pp. 146–7.

20. Ibid., pp. 169, 174.

21. H. Kołłątaj, *Uwagi nad . . . Xięstwem Warszawskim* (Lwów, 1808), p. 127.

22. S. Staszic, *Ród ludzki* (draft version), ed. Z. Daszkowski, vol. 3 (Warsaw, 1959), pp. 228, 297 ff; also his *Pisma filozoficzne i społeczne*, ed. B. Suchodolski, vol. 2 (Warsaw, 1954), p. 321.

23. F. Skarbek, "O polityce" (1820), in W. Tatarkiewicz (ed.), *Jakiej filozofii Polacy potrzebują* (Warsaw, 1970), pp. 353–6.

24. The Congress of Vienna (1814–1815) instituted a new political division of the former Polish lands (see maps), and created from a part of the Duchy of Warsaw the autonomous "Polish Kingdom" (also called the Congress Kingdom) with the Russian Emperor as king.

25. The Holy Alliance, an antiliberal agreement concluded in 1815 by Russia, Prussia and Austria in defence of the existing order; later joined by some other European states.

26. Z. Skwarczyński (ed.), *"Wiadomości Brukowe": wybór artykułów* (Wrocław, 1962), p. LXII.

27. Stanisław Kostka Potocki (1752–1821), an aristocrat of liberal views, a freemason, minister of education in the Polish Kingdom, author of the satirical novel *Podróż do Ciemnogrodu* (A journey to Ignoranceville), 1820.

28. Jan Śniadecki (1756–1830), a mathematician, astronomer and philosopher–empiricist, professor of Cracow University and, from 1806, Wilno University. His brother Jędrzej Śniadecki (1768–1838), professor of chemistry in Wilno, president of the exclusive Society of Rogues, noted for its liberal satire.

29. The Philomaths' Society, a secret patriotic and educational organization, set up by a group of Wilno students in 1817 and crushed by the tsarist authorities in 1823–1824. The poet Adam Mickiewicz (1798–1855) was one of its founders and leaders.

30. "Oda do młodości" (1820), an early poem by Adam Mickiewicz, still classical in form, but extolling romantic elation and boldness in the service of high ideals.

31. The November Rising of 1830, a Polish rebellion against the tsarist autocracy, followed by the Polish–Russian war, ended in defeat in October 1831.

32. D. Krysiński, *Wybór pism* (Warsaw, 1956), pp. 117, 159 f, 179, 182–4, 187.

33. *Merkury* 1831, quoted after A. Zieliński, *Naród i narodowość w polskiej literaturze i publicystyce lat 1815–1831* (Wrocław, 1969), p. 267.

34. I. Chrzanowski, *Optymizm i pesymizm polski: studia z historii kultury* (Warsaw, 1971), p. 281.

35. Secret organizations active in the Congress Kingdom in 1819–1825; their aim was to rebuild an independent Poland.

36. Walerian Łukasiński (1786–1868), a major in the Polish army, the founder of the two societies mentioned above, arrested in 1822, court-martialled and imprisoned in the Kingdom until 1830; transported to St. Petersburg after the outbreak of the November Rising, he spent the remaining 38 years of his life unknown to anybody as a prisoner in the Schlüsselburg fortress. He left a diary which was not published until a hundred years later (Warsaw, 1960).

37. *Orzeł Biały* IV, 3 (1820), p. 41.

38. Alexander I, the autocratic Emperor of Russia, became the Polish King after the Congress of Vienna; in 1815 he bestowed a liberal constitution on the Kingdom.

39. *Orzeł Biały* II, 11 (1820), p. 207.

40. Quoted after Zieliński, *Naród i narodowość*, p. 31.

41. Wawrzyniec Surowiecki (1769–1827), a historian, economist, and publicist, an ardent advocate of industrial development in Poland.

42. W. Surowiecki, "Uwagi względem nowego prawodawstwa," in *Korrespondencya w materyach obraz kraiu i narodu roziaśniaiących*, ed. J. K. Szaniawski (Warsaw, 1807), pp. 186–9.

43. J. K. Czermiński, "O charakterze narodowym," in W. Tatarkiewicz (ed.), *Jakiej filozofii Polacy potrzebują*, pp. 371–2.

44. Skarbek, "O polityce," ibid., pp. 347–52.

45. See J. Szacki, *Ojczyzna, naród, rewolucja* (Warsaw, 1962), pp. 127–31.

46. Maurycy Mochnacki (1803–1834), an outstanding literary critic, a promoter of romanticism, a radical political writer during the November Rising, emigrated to France in 1831; the quotation (1830) is from his *Pisma po raz pierwszy edycją książkową objęte*, ed. A. Śliwiński (Lwów, 1910), p. 229.

47. Józef K. Szaniawski (1764–1843), a Jacobin in his youth, later an ultra-conservative philosopher and censor; the quotations date from 1808, cited after H. Hinz and A. Sikora (eds.), *Polska myśl filozoficzna: Oświecenie—Romantyzm* (Warsaw, 1964), pp. 258, 261.

48. Aleksander Wielopolski (1803–1877), a margrave, a prominent conservative and conciliatory politician, head of the civil government in the Polish Kingdom in 1862; here quoted after A. M. Skałkowski, *Aleksander Wielopolski w świetle archiwów rodzinnych*, vol. 2 (Poznań, 1947), p. 26.

49. M. Mochnacki, *O literaturze polskiej w wieku dziewiętnastym* (Kraków, 1923), p. 5.

50. An article by Mochnacki in *Gazeta Polska* 1827, quoted after A. Zieliński, *Naród i narodowość*, p. 47.

51. "Walter Scott i jego wiek współczesny," *Gazeta Polska* 1828, pp. 731–2.

52. Mochnacki, *O literaturze polskiej*, p. 45.

53. Julian Ursyn Niemcewicz (1758–1841), a poet, writer and politician, president of the Warsaw Society of the Friends of Learning in 1826–1831; here quoted after A. Kraushar, *Towarzystwo Warszawskie Przyjaciół Nauk, 1800–1832*, vol. II, 2 (Kraków, 1902), p. 229.

54. Juliusz Słowacki (1809–1849), together with Adam Mickiewicz, the most brilliant Polish romantic poet; lived in Paris from 1831.

55. Aleksander Fredro (1793–1876), a poet and the greatest Polish comedy writer; lived in Eastern Galicia from 1815.

56. S. Staszic, "Narodowość," in his *Pisma filozoficzne i społeczne*, vol. 2, p. 278.

57. Z. Skwarczyński (ed.), *"Wiadomości Brukowe,"* p. LXII.

58. *Merkury* 1831, quoted after A. Zieliński, *Naród i narodowość*, p. 267.

59. Mochnacki, *O literaturze polskiej*, p. 40.

60. Ibid., p. 51.

61. Mochnacki, *Pisma po raz pierwszy edycją książkową objęte*, pp. 49–51, 467.

62. Ibid., p. 468.

63. Ibid., p. 41.

64. Ibid., pp. 42, 51–2.

65. Ibid., p. 451.

66. W. Surowiecki, "Obraz dzieła o początkach, obyczajach, religii dawnych Słowian," in *Korrespondencya w materyach*, p. 204.

67. Kazimierz Brodziński (1791–1835), a poet, critic and historian of literature, a precursor of romanticism; the quotations are from his *Pisma estetyczno-krytyczne*, ed. Z. J. Nowak (Wrocław, 1964), pp. 83, 254.

68. K. Brodziński, *Wybór pism*, ed. A. Witkowska (Wrocław, 1966), p. 338.

69. Joachim Lelewel (1786–1861), the leading Polish historian in the period of romanticism, professor of Wilno and Warsaw universities, member of the National Government during the November Rising, later a political exile; in 1833 settled in Brussels.

70. J. Lelewel, *Dzieła*, vol. 2 (Warsaw, 1964), pp. 877–8; vol. 8 (Warsaw, 1961), p. 541.

71. *Nowa Polska* 1831, quoted after J. Szacki, *Ojczyzna, naród, rewolucja*, p. 244.

72. J. P. Woronicz, "Kazanie przy poświęceniu orłów polskich" (1807), quoted after I. Chrzanowski, *Optymizm i pesymizm*, p. 172.

73. A. Zieliński, *Naród i narodowość*, pp. 177–84.

74. Quoted after Kraushar, *Towarzystwo Warszawskie*, vol. II, 1, p. 274.

75. Ibid., vol. 1, pp. 376, 378.

76. Seweryn Goszczyński (1801–1876), a romantic poet, conspirator and insurgent; the quotation comes from his diary, *Podróż mojego życia* (Wilno, 1924), p. 27.

77. J. Śniadecki, *Wybór pism naukowych*, ed. Z. Libera and S. Drobot (Warsaw, 1954), pp. 11–35, 137–43, 165; Mochnacki, *Pisma po raz pierwszy*, pp. 60–70, 471–4.

78. Mochnacki, *Pisma po raz pierwszy*, p. 455.

79. J. L. Żukowski, "O sztuce," *Gazeta Polska* 1828, p. 400.

80. Żukowski, *O pansczyźnie* (Warsaw, 1830), p. 85.

81. *Pamiętnik Warszawski* 1829, quoted after J. Chałasiński, *Kultura i naród* (Warsaw, 1968), p. 352.

82. Mochnacki, *O literaturze polskiej*, pp. 77–9.

83. Wilno and the whole of Lithuania were not part of the Kingdom, but the university and the schools under its control remained Polish (until 1830). Prince Adam Czartoryski (1770–1861), a prominent politician and for some time Tsar Alexander I's advisor, was superintendent of the Wilno school region in 1803–1824.

84. P. J. Kaczyński, "Jak można usamowolnić cały naród polski?," *Gazeta Polska* 1831, quoted after A. Zieliński, *Naród i narodowość*, pp. 188, 248.

85. Phrases from Karol Kurpiński's song composed to the text of the French poet Casimir Delavigne, "La Varsovienne," written on hearing news of the insurrection in Warsaw.

86. L. Łętowski, *O sprawie narodu polskiego* (1831), p. 61.

87. Quoted after J. Ujejski, *Dzieje polskiego mesjanizmu do powstania listopadowego włącznie* (Lwów, 1931), p. 315.

88. Brodziński, *Wybór pism*, pp. 437, 446.

89. Wincenty Pol, *Pieśni Janusza i poezje wybrane*, ed. M. Romankówna (Kraków, 1949), pp. 34–5.

CHAPTER 2

"Natural" or "Artificial" Development

When exactly did it occur to Polish thinkers that the country's economy was in need of drastic reform, that it wasn't enough merely to lift the towns out of the state of decline in which they had been sunk for centuries, or to improve agriculture? When was it that circumstances called for a more profound structural transformation, that is, the need for the country to develóp in a definite direction, the direction which had been taken by the first industrialized countries of Europe—England, the Netherlands, and finally Prussia.

The Polish country gentleman was all in favor of limited economic and institutional changes. He was also familiar with terms such as decline and growth which were constantly in use in Seym debates and political writings in connection with such issues as the benefits of manufacturing, methods of improving river and overland transportation and commerce, and draft plans for reforming the treasury. But the dogma of change was alien to him. He did not regard economic development as an aim worth pursuing for its own sake. Was not Poland the granary of Europe, and would it not remain so forever? The complementary nature of the Polish economy in relation to countries which imported grain and exported manufactured products formed the basis of the gentry's economic ideology, and an industrial development which took its inspiration from mercantilist doctrine could undermine this foundation.

The foundation was, in fact, unexpectedly weakened by an external factor—the first partition of Poland in 1772. The annexation of Elbląg and the lower Vistula by Prussia, the severing of Gdańsk from its hinterland, and the imposition of customs on Polish grain transportation shook the gentry, showing them the fragility of a farm economy which was dependent on foreign trade. Soon afterwards Józef Wybicki demonstrated how "unjustifiable" it was to imagine that a country in which agriculture was in decline could remain "Europe's granary."[1] Staszic continued in the same vein, warning that the food deficit which had prevailed in the West for the last three hundred years was in fact coming to an end since the industrialized countries had increased their agricultural productivity, even though this productivity still fell short of the growth in population. In the final analysis, he wrote in 1785, "the new republic in America has fertile land, navigable rivers, good soils, in a word, everything needed to develop commerce. She will be able to supply grain to the Dutch and English far more cheaply."[2]

The adaptation of a national economy to the changing conditions of international exchange is a process which, by the nature of things, takes a long time. Nevertheless, as early as around 1785 it was possible to detect in Poland the first, unmistakable signs of change: the rapid growth in the size and turnover of the Warsaw banks, the first large-scale commercial–industrial ventures with the participation of the gentry, the formation of companies for trade in the Black Sea, intensive exploration for salt, the establishment of joint companies by merchants and gentry with the purpose of leasing state monopolies, and a new generation of private, royal and church factories which no longer exclusively produced luxury goods for the aristocracy, but also commodities for a wider range of consumers or for the army. Developments such as these proliferated in the 1780s: they were the manifestation of a new quality in the economic life of Poland, which had regained a relative political stability after the shock of the Confederation of Bar and the first partition.

This new spirit of enterprise was accompanied by a change in the economic orientation of a part of the enlightened gentry and the middle-class elite. In 1782 the *Pamiętnik Historyczno-Polityczny (The Historical–Political Diary)* first appeared, followed in 1786 by the *Dziennik Handlowy (The Commercial Daily)*. These two journals initiated a discussion on how the Polish economy could emerge from its state of stagnation. The "industrialist" publications made the gentry aware for the first time that the uniformly agrarian character of the Polish economy and its complementary nature in relation to the industrialized countries of the West was the main obstacle on the road to economic development.

On reading these publications today it is immediately obvious that they were pointing to what was then the only possible method of overcoming the economic stagnation of Poland and the state of ignorant bliss which doomed to failure all constitutional reforms, including the granting of rights to the townspeople and the peasants. Castellan Jezierski's notorious contempt for the townspeople[3] was, in his particular case, compounded by the haughtiness and competitiveness of the nouveau riche gentleman, but some of his arguments were rational, based as they were on his observations of an apathetic and unproductive class which, unlike in the West, made virtually no contribution to the improvement of the economy and culture of the country. At the same time, however, the landed gentry, though far wealthier than the townspeople, were mired in their culture of consumption and the routine of their feudal farms based on serf labor.

Meanwhile, the challenges posed by the new civilization called for at least as powerful an injection of energy and ingenuity as that which had accompanied the forcing through of political reforms. It was of no consequence that here and there a foundry had been built or a factory producing decorative kontush sashes. Bolder and more decisive steps were needed. But who was going to provide the initiative: the gentry, the townspeople, the Jews? The handful of ideologues who supported industrialization, as befitted representatives of the Enlightenment, addressed their demands and ideas to politicians, legislators, and the king. In his *Patriotic Letters* Wybicki argued that bad laws and an inefficient government had made Poland the poorest country in Europe, one reduced almost to a state of barbarity: hence the simple conclusion that good laws and "perfect government" would enable it to extract itself quickly from this sorry condition. A similar faith in the creative power of laws can be observed in the title of Piotr Świtkowski's treatise *The reasons why prudent legislation should increase domestic trade and circulation rather than foreign trade.*[4]

A tradition of mercantilist thought did exist in Poland, even if it was rather poor and inconsistent, but there was no official mercantilist policy. The idea of expecting the government to provide economic initiative was an unorthodox departure, dictated by the desire to break the vicious circle of stagnation.

The main problem in programs for economic growth in the Enlightenment period was how to discover the sources of accumulation. The promoters of development realized that there was no real chance for capital to flow spontaneously from agriculture to industry, and therefore, following the Prussian model, they thought the treasury should act as an instrument of transfer. They demanded that the treasury grant allowances and privileges and provide orders for entrepreneurs and companies which initiated new branches of industry. They drafted a major program for public works: the treasury was to build harbors, a merchant fleet, canals, roads and factories, finance prospecting for salt and minerals, and establish mines. Numerous projects were put forward for the establishment of a National Bank which would combine the functions of a bank of issue and a bank of credit and investment. The capital needed to carry these plans through was to come from the sale of royal estates.

It is hard to say whether the combined efforts of industrialists and ideologues would have brought about an economic breakthrough if history had given them more time. Following years of inertia, it would have taken decades for the gentry and the middle class to get used to the idea of investment and actually to adopt it as a policy. Nevertheless, it seemed possible to accelerate this process by political means. It is true that until 1786 the Seym did not show any interest in industrialization. However, a certain change in attitude became apparent during the Four Years Seym, manifesting itself not only in the raising of bankers and factory owners to the ranks of the nobility, but also, more importantly, in support for the formation of an armaments industry and in the appointment of "a deputation for drafting a law on the domestic economy of the country."[5] The first bill devised by this deputation (with the active participation of Jacek Jezierski) and presented to both chambers was given the name "The Establishment of Factories" (1791). It was fully committed to the idea of interventionism.[6] Although neither this scheme nor a similar program for the establishment of a National Bank was ever discussed by the Seym, busy as it was with the constitutional reform and preparations for the country's defense, nevertheless, the very fact that it was drafted justifies its being regarded as the first attempt at formulating a policy of induced growth for Poland.

Such a policy could only be introduced by a government with strong executive powers and one which could, at least to some degree, ignore the interests of the resolutely antifiscal landed gentry. The reform of the state was slowly proceeding in this direction, and it is possible that in stable conditions Poland would have been capable of setting in motion the process of development. Hence, the downfall of the state must be seen not only as a political catastrophe: it also meant that the first attempts at modernizing the economy were frustrated. The second partition (1793) brought about the dramatic collapse of the Warsaw banks. The majority of the recently initiated commercial and industrial ventures disappeared together with independence, and the short-lived career of the town patriciate came to an end.

This short period of interrupted growth left almost no trace in the rural landscape or the mentality of the gentry. However, it did leave its mark on the minds of the enlightened elite—or perhaps rather on their imaginations, since we are talking more about imagination than doctrine. Each epoch has its own myths in which its image is reflected in a particularly flattering light. Polish Sarmatism had its bards, and so did the Enlightenment. Reporting for the readers of the *Pamiętnik Historyczno-Polityczny* on the invention of the balloon, the lightning conductor and the steam engine, Piotr Świtkowski described, half jokingly, a vision of the future of human genius: "Oh, for the key to that inaccessible treasure-house which still hides thousands of similar things! Who knows, perhaps we will be able to prolong our life-span to several centuries, or to harness whales and be carried by a team of six of them from one pole to another both above and under water?"[7]

The *Siècle des lumières* fired the futurological longings of Poles, both naive and prophetic, and from this fairy-tale of an enchanted treasure-house of nature, geography and technology it wove a system of values in which the very impulse towards crossing the borders of the unknown became an aim in itself, the grand quest of the human spirit. The knights of these fairy-tales were the discoverers, inventors and industrialists, those who did not shy from the risk of experiment. Envious glances were cast at England where such knights were to be found in abundance. However, the enthusiasts realized that it was necessary to begin in small ways in their own backward country. The industrial ideology, which borrowed elements from various economic doctrines in order to increase the productive use of local resources, appealed alternately to the self-interest and the patriotism of both consumers and the holders of available capital. Of course, the idea of economic autarky was not lost from sight either. Staszic, with his usual tendency to formulate his theses in extreme language, warned against the hazards of "exterior commerce" and argued that "a country is unassailable when it produces its wealth in its own land and can fully rely on itself."[8]

To more sober-minded authors, economic self-sufficiency seemed a distant aim and one, moreover, that was not always desirable. Nevertheless, efforts to decrease Poland's dependence on foreign countries met with an enthusiastic response. "It's a shame that we don't cut our bread with our own knives!" fulminated Jacek Jezierski,[9] demanding that the government introduce not only protective customs duties, but also a ban on importing foreign products which could be produced from local raw materials, as well as a ban on exporting such raw materials (flax, wool, iron). But there was no unanimity on this matter. In the years 1786–87, the adherents of protectionism or prohibition clashed with the defenders of free trade in the pages of the *Dziennik Handlowy*, but this was a polemic about means rather than aims. No one questioned the need for industrialization in this journal: the problem was who would suffer and who would benefit from this policy. Those who were involved in larger industrial or commercial ventures complained that "Poland does not have a single law that favors manufacturing," or else demanded monopolistic privileges for companies to enable them to engage in trade in the Black Sea along the lines of the notorious colonial English and Dutch companies. On the other hand, their opponents, acting in the name of free competition as far as capital and goods were concerned, were against all *privilegia exclusiva* and advised the government "not to interfere in any particular industry or with the ways anyone wants to use his wealth," since as long as the security of people and property was guaranteed, "all the rest will materialize of its own accord."[10]

The participants in these disputes drew freely on the arguments of various schools of thought. Sometimes they adopted mercantilist doctrines, at other times they followed the physiocratic thinkers, or Smith—whatever suited them and their purses best at the time. They had little regard for purity of theory while propagating a new axiology of productive work, a new ethos of enterprise. Jan Ferdynand Nax sang the praises of the merchant–manufacturer: "it frequently happens that he single-handedly enriches some impoverished area in which even the profits from agriculture are subject to decay, in this way reviving all kinds of activity. ... As soon as a purchaser of agricultural produce or manufactured goods appears in an area, immediately both products begin to increase to the immense advantage of the country, and the inhabitants, awakened from their lazy stupor, will rush to compete with one another for a share in these profits."[11] Another author expressed his contempt for those merchants who "bring from abroad such goods as can just as well be produced locally," and who for this reason present a "hindrance to local factories;" in contrast to such merchants, true advantages are brought to the country by the "manufacturer who by his sweat increases local consumption and supplies goods which until now were brought from abroad for ready money."[12]

The heralds of the industrial epoch pronounced "idleness" to be the gravest sin and source of dishonor. Some even went as far as to suggest that not only all "loose" people should be sent to work in factories, but also included soldiers and even children, regarding this as the most suitable educational occupation for them. Any measure was good, provided that it helped "to revive the spirit of industrious ingenuity and to eradicate those superstitions which once viewed lazy indolence as some kind of privilege and dignity." Once this happened, there was no reason to doubt that Poland would equal "the most clever nations" in the field of arts and crafts.[13] No outlay or cost was to be spared in order to achieve this purpose. The consumption of luxury goods was to be restricted, and any surplus in the treasury, bank and demesne was to be invested in land, farm animals, tools and factories, and especially in roads, canals and navigable rivers.

In England, Nax wrote, "manufacturing is in such a state of perfection not because the English are more resourceful, ingenious or industrious than other peoples, but because the English, thrifty in all other things, are unstintingly openhanded when it comes to spending money on manufacturing. Right from the outset they plan their factories so as to produce the largest possible quantity of goods; in this way the costs of production are spread out and therefore lowered ... it does not matter how expensive the machines are, provided that time and labor is saved. The majority of those tasks which elsewhere are performed by hand are there carried out by machines driven by water, and where there is shortage of flowing water ... they usually employ this ingenious machine, the invention of which brings immense credit to the human mind."[14]

While Nax and Świtkowski were enthusing about James Watt's invention, Wybicki was wondering how he could turn his fellow members of the gentry away from their ancient prejudices and contempt for middle-class occupations, and encourage them to engage in new activities. At the very time that the Seym was debating *The Law on the Towns* (1791), Wybicki produced a didactic drama, *The Gentleman Turned Citizen* (1791), which was very different in tone from Molière's *Le Bourgeois Gentilhomme*. Its main character is an impoverished country gentleman who one day takes all the hides, wax, flax, hemp and looms he owns, loads them onto his cart and drives to the town with the intention of opening a factory. Perhaps one day he will hang up there his old sabre, the emblem and symbol of the noble estate.[15]

If we look at the situation in its proper perspective, the industrialist propaganda of the final years of the Commonwealth represented merely a small fraction of public opinion. Its voice was drowned out by the prevailing agrarianism of the gentry and the uproar surrounding the much more dramatic disputes concerning the political system of the state. However, it is worth remembering the presence of this handful of local economists whose futuristic projects were forged a quarter of a century before the militant French industrialism of the Restoration period. This current did not dry up with the collapse of the Commonwealth: it would rise once more to the surface of Polish intellectual life in the years of the Duchy of Warsaw, when an able, if somewhat despotic, government reawakened new hopes among those who vigorously supported the idea of bringing the country within the orbit of industrial civilization. The most outstanding spokesman of this movement was Wawrzyniec Surowiecki, an author with a brilliant gift for combining dry statistics with a visionary view of Poland's ancient past and its future.

We are not concerned here with the history of economic doctrines and the notions they employed, but rather with the axiological choices made by the economists and the workings of their imagination. We are interested in the vistas they perceived on the horizon, the kind of world they wanted to help create, and the type of culture and social organization which would result from the principles of economic calculus they preached. Such criteria seem particularly apt in relation to an epoch in which every Polish economist declared his dislike of abstract "speculation" and his desire to turn economics into a practical science, a science that would establish aims and means for the development of the national economy.

Surowiecki's work *O upadku przemysłu i miast w Polszcze* (*On the Decline of Industry and the Towns in Poland*, 1810), was, in terms of its message and rhetorical style, the last great didactic work of the Polish Enlightenment. In this final flowering of the movement, the author employs the classical Enlightenment-style contrast between the civilizational greatness of old Poland in the period from the fourteenth to the sixteenth century, and the horrifying state of decline into which she had sunk in the course of the following two hundred years. No one, not even Staszic, could equal Surowiecki in his evocation of the differences between the light of the sixteenth century and the darkness of the eighteenth. "Why are those vast fields, once boasting fine crops, covered today in gloomy woods? Why have flowering meadows, crystal-clear lakes and navigable rivers turned into quagmires and obnoxious bogs? Why have sadness, destitution and pale death crept into those once populous towns where life, joy and prosperity used to prevail? The fine mementoes of their former wealth lie today in hideous heaps covered with dirt and a permanent layer of growth. Hordes of noxious reptiles prepare their poison there, polluting the healthy air all around and killing the degenerate inhabitants of places which were seats of comfort and happiness in the times of their ancestors."[16] This passage illustrates the style, and also the axiology of this author. Surowiecki depicts a landscape after a cataclysm; he describes the horrifying condition of a nation which, having allowed the "enslavement" of its peasants, has brought itself to a state of collapse, first economic, then cultural and political also. "Industry" and "culture" go hand in hand here: one is not possible without the other.

The word that Surowiecki uses repeatedly whenever he diagnoses the condition of the country in the partition period is "numbness:" "In each of its parts a numbness could be observed which caused the most prolific sources of wealth and needs to dry up." The main reason for this numbness and weakness was the negligence of the gentry which, having deprived all other classes of their freedom and property, had begun to fear "any hint of novelty or change aimed at improving the country's condition."[17] He knew no mercy in his condemnation of the gentry: the squirearchy is shown as culturally sterile and obsolete. It is significant how little regard Surowiecki had for the epoch of national revival under Stanislaus Augustus: a few words of praise for "the monarch who undoubtedly deserved respect" and for a number of "enlightened lords" who established factories on their estates, and approval of the Commission for National Education[18] was all that the author of *On the Decline of Industry and the Towns in Poland* had to say about those years of intellectual revolution. This dismissal of the work of the older generation was probably dictated by a desire to throw into relief the black and white contrast between past stagnation and present development. It was only now, thanks to Napoleon's efforts to unite Europe, and to the abolition of serfdom in

Poland, that the process of rising from the depths of decline to attain a new position of glory could begin. This rise would be brought about by the efforts of young townspeople and local capitalists.

There are "ingenious" nations, and there are "sluggish" and lazy nations. The difference between them is not a result of the different character of the people in question; it is a consequence of good or bad principles of political government. "It is frequently to be observed that some nations do nothing to improve their lot in spite of the fact that they have abundant natural resources and all the necessary skills, and show a strong inclination to seek the good things of life."[19] These are "inactive" nations, because in general they restrict themselves to acquiring the "coarse nourishment of life" in order to satisfy their most basic needs. But human beings can only really be stimulated to work and exercise their ingenuity when they strive to live better and wealthier lives, when they develop an awareness of "luxury" needs and allow such needs to grow, that is, needs that have their source in culture and not in nature. Such needs are felt by those who have tasted them themselves, or who have seen them in others. "No one wants things that he has never seen, no one seeks treasures whose value he does not know." This is how Surowiecki describes the phenomenon which we know today as the "effect of demonstration." For him it is the psychological lever which facilitates the development of modern civilization. The example of countries which are more "ingenious" than others awakens new wishes and desires in "neglected" countries and therefore is the strongest stimulus to development.[20]

No limits should be placed on these desires. At this point Wawrzyniec Surowiecki departs from the line of thought of other writers—both the older generation of Staszic, and his juniors like Brodziński—who, regardless of the epoch, were fulsome in their praise of a simple and modest life. Surowiecki, on the other hand, opposes the laws of thrift and refuses to condemn "luxury." Indeed, who can really say where luxury begins? "What is luxury for one person, for another becomes an indispensable need" which he is no longer capable of renouncing. It is true that the knowledge of and satisfaction of more refined needs are not immediately attainable by all social classes, but they gradually filter down from the upper classes to the poorer and more backward strata, while the means used to restrict luxury are an outrage even to the common people: "Finally, who can say if what we call luxury is not one of the most powerful stimuli for enlivening industry and movement in a country? The free islander of India, the lazy African or the savage inhabitant of America were encouraged to redouble their efforts more by a shiny piece of glass and a cup of vodka than by hunger and primitive life."[21]

Human snobbery, fashion, competition in consumption and complete freedom of choice—all these are conducive to progress. All human needs together form one great chain of progress, and social classes "differ among themselves only inasmuch as the various kinds of employment in which they are engaged differ." The lot of the farmer is so closely associated with the lot of the craftsman that they both either attain the good life together or perish together. Both need wealthy consumers, and consumers need them in turn. All of them are served by scholars who, "by studying in depth the condition of agriculture and industry in a nation discover means of improving them or teach their fellow countrymen how to use foreign discoveries." It is to them first and foremost that those nations "which today surpass the others in perfection"[22] owe their superiority.

However, the main "hero" of Surowiecki's program for the future is the merchant. In fact, his treatise is perhaps the highest tribute ever paid to merchants in Polish. Because merchants had brought together the needs of all people, the interests of all classes, and the markets of all nations, they thus became the prime sponsors of culture and enlightenment: "Through his offices the Indian living thousands of miles away comes close to the inhabitant of the Vistula region; he supports the latter with his riches, labor and industry, and receives support in return. . . . By associating with various peoples, the merchant . . . familiarizes himself with their experiences which, transplanted onto his native soil, enable him partly to discover new sources of wealth, partly to save the costs of processing the produce, and partly to supply it more efficiently to those who need it. His calling encourages him in particular to associate with those nations where science and industry flower. . . . He brings his capital everywhere and scatters it around like a beneficent dew, enlivening and providing nourishment for all products of human industry." For this reason the merchant had more right than anyone else to ask his government for protection, justice and support.[23]

Logic demanded that this glorification of the stimulating role of international commerce be accompanied by the discarding of the vision of the world as an arena for ruthless rivalry among the states. As is well known, this post-mercantilist perspective was discarded by liberal economists from Quesnay to Say, the latter being particularly often quoted by Surowiecki. Nevertheless, there remained one dilemma: was equal exchange between unequal partners possible, and if so, to what extent? This question could not, and indeed still cannot, be answered unambiguously. The classical doctrine inclined Surowiecki and his contemporaries to answer in the affirmative: yes, it was not only possible, it was mutually profitable. Real life, however, proved otherwise, hence the obvious inconsistencies regarding this important subject.

Surowiecki argued that nature had not provided every country with all the necessary resources because it wanted the nations to "come closer and closer to one another and establish links of mutual assistance." In each individual society the well-being of all classes and trades is mutually dependent, and in the same way the well-being of one nation has an influence on the well-being of other peoples. This truth escapes those world rulers who base their false politics on the false assumption that "one nation can only build its own happiness on the ruins of another."[24] All goods, commodities and money flow where they are most desired and appreciated, and this movement must never be blocked: the merchant must have complete "freedom to trade" and the consumer must have complete freedom of choice between local and foreign products. If it happens sometimes that foreign competition harms local industry, then this is a sign that this industry has been either neglected or established in the wrong place. Free international exchange is therefore a natural regulator of the division of labor, in that it allots to each country the industrial specialization which is most profitable for it.

However, several pages further on in Surowiecki's treatise the author expresses completely different anxieties and warns against different dangers. It appears that "of all obstacles hampering industry, competition may prove the most dangerous;" more, it may become a horrible plague preventing all economic development. "In such a case, the weaker party, hamstrung by its neighbor's domination, can find no other rescue for itself but to align all its forces in order to breach the gap separating it from its neighbor or else, sadly watching the ruin of its own industry, throw itself on the mercy and submit to the yoke of this neighbor, paying him a perennial tribute out of funds which grow smaller day by day." It is not difficult to predict that this will be the lot of exclusively agricultural nations who can offer their own inhabitants and others only raw agricultural produce and who have to purchase all manufactured goods from others: "A nation which neglects to process the produce of its own soil loses its independence and must rely on those who can supply it with such processed goods."[25]

Free international exchange was thus seen as both a blessing and a curse. It was to be readily embraced and at the same time it had to be opposed. We are all too familiar with this knot of contradictions which has still not been resolved. For Surowiecki, writing at the threshold of the nineteenth century, this was the only dilemma that marred his bright vision of the future. However, he eventually solved the conflict by resorting to liberal doctrine: he strongly warned the governments of economically weak countries against applying trade barriers or high tariffs. In this way, he argued, one could cure the symptoms but not the causes of weaknesses in domestic industry, and although competition from stronger countries was harmful, it would prove even more harmful to keep it outside one's borders, because this would restrict consumption and commerce and would bring no advantages to industry. This did not mean that he advised the government of the Duchy of Warsaw to stand idly by and see whether Polish industry developed in a natural way, or perhaps failed to develop. "Watchful protection on the part of the government" formed a significant part of his program, but the instruments of this protection were not barriers, monopolies and customs duties, but constructive action aimed at stimulating accumulation and production. In this respect, Surowiecki followed the teachings of older Polish "industrialists" rather than Smith.

The call for the state to invest public funds in the construction and maintenance of vocational schools, roads and canals, and finally factories, was not, as we have seen, a new idea. However, it is worth observing how Surowiecki justified this idea. He expected the government to build large, modern factories which would "be provided with all kinds of time-saving inventions and which would reward the employees according to their merits." He was undoubtedly aware that a fiscal policy involving considerable expenditure might provoke the opposition of taxpayers; however, he believed that "the whole nation" could be easily persuaded of the need for sacrifices in order to ensure its future well-being. In order to encourage the government and the people to make such sacrifices, he presented the very modern thesis that there was a high multiplier involved in industrial investment: "The capital employed to create such funds in a country which has abundant natural resources can be regarded as capital lent at a usurious rate that brings profits to the treasury, the country and its individual inhabitants. A single model factory, apart from providing bread and employment for many people, has also an unusual advantage, namely, that through its beneficial influence it enlivens other kinds of industry within the radius of many miles in a very short time. There is not a single branch that it would not ask for help or to which it would not impart a higher value; it acts like a magnet: on the one hand, it attracts all other industries to itself, and on the other, it lends to them its own inestimable value. ... Therefore, the sacrificing of capital for such aims, even if for a while it is a burden to the nation, does not spell ruin and, moreover, in view of the uncountable advantages which it cannot fail to bring to the country, it should be voluntarily considered before all other expenditure."[26]

As has already been said, against the background of centuries of stagnation during the Commonwealth of the Gentry, the elites of the epoch of Stanislaus Augustus came to the conclusion that all reform must begin at the top. Political reform and the strengthening of the authority of the monarch and the government were understood as an indispensable condition for social revival and civilizational progress. The partitions did not immediately change this way of reasoning. At this point the opportunity arose for the government of the Duchy of Warsaw to take upon itself the duty of national leadership and become the catalyst for the country's development. Surowiecki was following a well-trodden path, and although he learnt a lot from his reading of Adam Smith and his disciples, it would have been inappropriate for him to suggest that for a "neglected country" the best government was the one which governed the least.

Poland had not yet reached the stage where the interests of private business were in conflict with dictatorial authority. It was still necessary to motivate people to engage in new forms of economic activity, to cultivate a spirit of accumulation and investment, to give direction and impetus to economic endeavor, and to ensure that rapid growth was accompanied by order and properly proportioned among the individual fields of production. Surowiecki, although a declared liberal, had no confidence in the proposition that economic equilibrium is created spontaneously in the free play of individual interests and expectations, because "by seeing things separately one is unable to gain a general view of the whole and consequently is unable to comprehend the mutual relations between things and maintain general harmony." For this purpose, one needs "a government of the internal economy" which will look after the needs of the country: "[this government] can best appreciate the skills and capabilities of each particular inhabitant and assign to him a proper role and occupation; it can best see where there is a shortage and where there is an excess of hands willing to work, what has been done and what still needs to be done, what brings more or less benefit to the country, what is in short supply in one place and what exists in abundance somewhere else, where work is being done properly and where it needs improvement and supervision."[27]

Here we have an early vision of a managed, almost planned economy, in which the government controlled the division of labor and decided on the allotment of resources. However, according to Surowiecki it was not the government that should establish the supreme aims of social endeavor, but rather "sages:" those who "ponder on behalf of others how people should live, how they should behave themselves, what they should do and what they should not do for their own advantage"—and for the common good. What distinguishes civilization is that it puts moral government under the control of scholars. "If we allow ourselves to become debased, or if we deprive society of this class of people, the results will be dire: the earth will shortly become the abode of wild *Canadians*, dangerous cannibals and cruel *tribes-*

men. Deluded by superstitions, prejudice, and license people will start to kill and devour each other. Then all the pleasures of social life will disappear, as well as arts, crafts, inventions, towns, imposing edifices, comfortable clothes, in fact everything which gratifies the senses and is good for the health and the reason."[28]

Fortunately, this would not happen, since it is inherent in human nature to strive ceaselessly for material well-being and for an ever higher degree of moral perfection. These are two facets of the same progress. In this striving, people's interests cannot be contradictory: occupational specialization and the division of labor call for increasingly harmonious cooperation between all classes of citizens. If some become richer than others, this is so because they have worked and saved longer or with greater ingenuity, and the fast growth of their capital is a lever for the development of national industries. "As the number of rich people multiplies, the amount of movement and work in the country multiplies; and the greater their wealth, the greater the competition for hands capable of work." There is a growth in production, employment, earnings, and in the general well-being. And the caring government, one that respects citizens' rights and is in turn respected by them, "maintains this harmonious movement in the nation, a movement that never ceases, that does not hamper anyone and that is constantly coming closer to a higher degree of perfection."[29]

Nothing but superstitions could prevent the impoverished state of Poland from following this straight road which had been signposted by the more gifted nations. The greatest hope for the future were the young townspeople who, provided they received the right education, would "change the physical and moral shape of the nation within one generation." All that was needed was daring energy, labor and funds for unearthing the inexhaustible resources of the land: "And then all poverty will disappear for good, villages will blossom, towns will be established, and the nation will again soar high to that glorious position which was once the boast of its forebears and to which its inborn virtues predispose it."[30]

The year was 1810, almost the last moment for issuing such a manifesto; the last moment for proclaiming such fervent, innocent faith, unmarred by any doubt, in the civilizational and morally transforming mission of managed capitalism *avant la lettre*, and in the spiritual community of the European nations united by the genius of Napoleon, whom Surowiecki saw as the herald of eternal peace.

It seems that a characteristic feature of many Enlightenment models of "progress" was this peculiar combination of a prudent, mature axiology and a simple, naive philosophy of history bound by the law of nature to implement constantly rational ideas. Both these elements are easily discernible in the writings of Surowiecki, a late follower of Enlightenment, who, towards the end of that epoch, used the assumptions of Enlightenment thought to construct the most farsighted and brilliantly optimistic program for civilizing Poland. It is another matter that his appeals were scarcely heard by his compatriots who were much more interested in the more urgent problems of war and politics.

A few years later Napoleon's Europe lay in ruins. This had many consequences, although one in particular, which was of momentous significance for economic thought, seldom receives the degree of notice and appreciation which it deserves. This was the rediscovery of England. The island which the continental traveler saw after years of war and blockade differed enormously from the England of his memories. The manufacturing industries had made great strides and the visible effect of this progress provoked both admiration and terror in observers. For in the richest and the most prosperous nation, the first to harness science and invention for everyday purposes, these observers found areas of dreadful poverty and degradation. It is true that Europe had long been accustomed to periods of hunger and unrelieved poverty, and that the sight of ragged beggars left people unmoved. But the wretchedness of the proletariat in the British towns was something completely different, in that it was a product of the brave new world envisaged by the prophets of industrialization. It was as if the curtains had been drawn aside to allow a glimpse of what awaited humanity. Just as the earthquake in 1755 which left Lisbon in ruins sowed the seeds of doubt in the minds of philosophers about the purposeful order of nature, and just as the bloody terror unleashed in 1793 in the name of humanity, equality and progress marred any faith in the noble ideals of political and social revolution, so the slums of Manchester and Leeds undermined the unreserved confidence in the new civilization.

And this was not all. The commercial crisis which swept Western Europe immediately after the continental blockade was lifted was a bad omen. All that was needed was for cheap English commodities to flood the market and wipe out competition from local products, and very soon the towns of mainland Europe would become peopled with similar hordes of unemployed who would have nothing to lose and little to gain.

French, German, and Polish intellectuals began to catch up with developments in economic theory by studying thoroughly the basic principles of Adam Smith's science of the wealth of nations. Their main source was Jean-Baptiste Say who had systematized Smith's teaching and adapted it for popular reading.[31] All liberal-minded people saw political economy as a new revelation: here at last they had the first truly social science, which won them

over by its elegance and the logic of its deductive reasoning. It was compared
with Newton's physics. It began its career in the salons before becoming
accepted in the universities, and it was expected that very soon its popular
catechisms would find their way into the homes of the workers. From 1815
on, Say's lectures in Paris attracted crowds of people and the successive
editions of his *Treatise* were immediately sold out. The educated French of
the Restoration period became passionately interested in industry, preferring
it to the politics and philosophy which had brought them so much disappointment. This was the beginning of the epoch of industrial enthusiasm, the cult
of production and labor, of middle-class *arrivisme*.

Amid this enthusiasm, genuine though it was, a faint note of unease could
be discerned. There was a continuous shadow on the horizon of early capitalism. Say and Sismondi visited England again in 1819, a year which was
witness to workers' unrest and the Peterloo massacre in Manchester. Each of
them saw what he wanted to see. Say returned convinced more than ever
before in his faith in the future; Sismondi lost this faith, or at least began to
have doubts. The great schism in political economy and in the philosophy of
economic development had set in.

Naturally, there had been earlier pointers to this schism. The physiocrats,
in their polemics against the mercantilists, had warned rulers that it was not
possible to go against the "natural order of things" with impunity. This idea
drew its strength from rationalist metaphysics, with its supposition that the
physical and moral order of the world were organized by a law of nature.
Applied to history and economics, the idea of natural order envisaged,
generally speaking, a hypothetical course for human progress which would
have undoubtedly been followed, had not obsolete social institutions and
unreasonable government interventions prevented it.

In Poland, the idea of natural order in economics was eloquently popularized by a follower of physiocratism, Father Hieronim Stroynowski, in his
Nauka prawa przyrodzonego (*The Science of Natural Law*, 1785), which was
reprinted several times "for the public good." Stroynowski was by no means
an opponent of industrial development. Admittedly, he followed his French
masters, of whom Quesnay was the most important, in evaluating the benefits
of industry and commerce from the point of view of agriculture. However,
he did not question the existence of these benefits, a position which was not
contradicted by the theory that only agriculture and mining were "fertile"
branches of the national economy, because they produced pure income. His
argument was that industry should develop by its own efforts to meet the
growing surplus of workers, capital and produce in the field of agriculture. It
was absolutely wrong to wish, as the industrialists did, that the government

would accelerate this process: "The Supreme Authority should turn all its efforts to encouraging expenditure on land and agriculture, and leave all other fruitless expenditure to the natural order of things. Therefore, just as we should not tear people and capital away from agriculture where they are still needed and deliver them to workshops and factories, so, under the guise of strengthening national industry, it is not necessary, by example or by decree, to encourage citizens to increase their outlays on costly and elegant manufactured products to the detriment of expenditure which would benefit agriculture. In other words, all measures and decrees of the Supreme Authority which harm agriculture in any way and which diminish the amount of pure income derived from the land, cannot be truly and durably beneficial to the manufacturing industry and are undoubtedly harmful to the Nation as a whole."[32]

Polish authors had easy access to French, and to a lesser extent, German sources, but few of them knew English. Therefore prior to 1795 we find scarcely any evidence of their being acquainted with Adam Smith's treatise. But it was Adam Smith who adopted the French physiocrats' theory of natural order and gave it a broader and intellectually more fertile footing. According to him, the natural sequence in the development of the various branches of economy was simply a result of the hierarchy of natural human needs. "The cultivation and improvement of the country, therefore, which affords subsistence, must, necessarily, be prior to the increase of the town, which furnishes only the means of convenience and luxury."[33] In other words, towns and factories can, in theory, develop only insofar as agriculture in the surrounding area produces surpluses of produce and income which it no longer needs. "According to the natural course of things, therefore, the greater part of the capital of every growing society is, first, directed to agriculture, afterwards to manufactures, and last of all to foreign commerce." The problem was that the economic history of Europe failed to correspond to this logical plan; what is more, in modern times this plan had been turned almost completely upside down. "The foreign commerce of some of their cities has introduced all their finer manufactures, or such as were fit for distant sale; and manufactures and foreign commerce together, have given birth to the principal improvements of agriculture. The manners and customs which the nature of their original government introduced, and which remained after that government was greatly altered, necessarily forced them into this unnatural and retrograde order."[34]

Smith, of course, was talking here about feudalism. Feudal laws, serfdom, forced rent, primogeniture, difficulties in buying and selling land—all these institutions were "unnatural," as noted by the rationalistic social philosophy of the Enlightenment. But Smith meant something more: he was concerned with the causes of the great economic upheaval in Europe, with the genesis of capitalism (though this term was still unknown at the time). As he saw it, feudalism was not an obstacle to industrialization and the formation of a world market; on the contrary, feudalism actually provoked these developments, prematurely and in an unnatural way. For feudalism enfettered the country-side and agriculture by means of severe forms of coercion and exploitation, while the towns, thanks partly to the protection of the monarchs, liberated themselves much earlier, winning self-government and freedom of economic activity. Capital, enterprise and initiative therefore found a haven in the towns. From this base, commercial and industrial operations developed on a grand scale, while agricultural production lagged behind. Hence the inverted order. At the same time, however, another process was taking place: "At other times manufactures for distant sale grow up naturally, and as it were of their own accord, by the gradual refinement of those household and coarser manufactures which must at all times be carried on even in the poorest and rudest countries. Such manufactures are generally employed upon the materials which the country produces. . . . Such manufactures are the offspring of agriculture. In the modern history of Europe, their extension and improvement have generally been posterior to those which were the offspring of foreign commerce."[35]

According to Smith, this kind of extension (called "organic" in the nineteenth century) was to ensure faster, and above all more stable, economic development. "Compare the slow progress of those European countries of which the wealth depends very much upon their commerce and manufactures, with the rapid advances of our North American colonies, of which the wealth is founded altogether in agriculture."[36] America, at that time still in the pre-industrial era, provided the Scottish economist with the only incontro-vertible example of natural development; in Europe, it was obvious that development "contrary to the natural course of things" was prevalent. This tendency to digress from the natural order is also strengthened by all economic "systems," physiocratic as much as mercantilist, because each of them "endeavors, either, by extraordinary encouragements, to draw towards a particular species of industry a greater share of the capital of the society than what would naturally go to it; or, by extraordinary restraints, to force from a particular species of industry some share of the capital which would otherwise be employed in it."[37] Such measures always diminish the general value of the annual product of land and labor, and retard rather than accelerate societies in their progress towards welfare. "All systems either of preference or of restraint, therefore, being thus completely taken away, the obvious and simple system of natural liberty establishes itself of its own accord."[38]

An Inquiry into the Nature and Causes of the Wealth of Nations was first published in 1776. Had its author, who died in 1790, had the opportunity to see and comment on the course of the most stormy stage of the English Industrial Revolution in the late eighteenth and early nineteenth centuries, a revolution which was based on the world market, he would probably have seen it as a confirmation of his thesis about the distorted, unnatural course of development of the British economy. However, the second generation of the classical school, active in the period of the triumphs of large-scale industry, discarded this evaluative typology of the father of the school—a typology which was thoroughly historical. Admittedly, Ricardo occasionally used the phrase "the natural course of commerce," but merely as a category of theoretical analysis.[39] The natural course is the course which would have been followed at any moment had it not been for the distorting effect of grain tariffs, export premiums and other similar interferences on the international commercial and money market.

Meanwhile, it would appear that the axiology of natural development found most favor not in the fatherland of industry and political economy, but in countries which were just beginning to experience industrial development. Walerian Stroynowski, the younger brother of Hieronim, repeatedly refers to this axiology and these ideas. He was the author of a monumentally dull handbook of political economy, published in Wilno in 1816, in which he tried to reconcile Smith with Quesnay, whose theories were much closer to his heart. Stroynowski, once a deputy to the Four Years Seym, had been promoted to the rank of senator and private counselor to the emperor Alexander I. His book was mainly addressed to young people who were studying in Wilno to become civil servants, but the author took the opportunity to warn Russia against repeating the mistakes made by other countries with regard to the national economy. "Indeed," he wrote, "our civil servants, eager for fame, would like to gain this fame by ardently devoting themselves to their work, with a view to showing the incredible progress of this great nation in everything which rich countries have. But these commendable endeavors cannot bring about the intended benefits for the country: natural forces cannot be skipped over."[40] In his opinion, the main natural force restricting the possibilities of development was the workforce. It was only when agriculture became overcrowded that the crafts could, and should, develop. And they would develop of their own accord in keeping with the natural order of things, because in the event of a surplus of labor and capital both of them would seek new employment. For the time being, in Poland or rather in the Russian

Empire, investment in agriculture was most advantageous both for the owners of capital and for the entire nation. "Whoever tears people away from the land, from agricultural occupations, prematurely, and directs them to crafts and towns, inverts the order of things and diminishes the national income. It is true that in Europe almost all nations have followed this erroneous path and that others, on seeing their success, want to follow in their footsteps, taking no heed of the fact that the population is still insufficient for the country's agriculture. But the former nations have been present on the political scene for thousands of years and therefore they had enough time to make mistakes."[41]

The latecomer in Europe had no time to err: well-being would be attained slowly, but surely, with no experimentation—such is the message of Stroynowski's work. It is also significant that this enemy of any kind of government intervention in economic life makes only one exception to this rule: the government should help establish, and perhaps even set up itself, small, basic workshops, producing cloth, for example, in small towns. These enterprises would be based on cottage industries, and the treasury should not expect to derive profit from them, since their purpose would be to provide extra income for the local population: "such endeavors by the government constitute a beneficial and thrifty form of protection for the people, and in time they may bring returns and income."[42]

In this way, this conservative liberal trivialized the theory of natural development, providing it with an interpretation which would continue to be widely accepted until the enfranchisement of the peasants. The fear of a shortage of labor in agriculture and a growth in interest rates was a constant source of worry to the owners of estates employing serf labor. If this industry was really essential, the argument ran, then it should be local, so providing the peasants with some form of income in winter without allowing them to leave the village. The theory of natural development made possible the rationalization of these fears and for this reason appealed to the gentry.

However, in connection with Walerian Stroynowski, one other point should be mentioned—his warnings about Poland and Russia becoming infected with the spirit of European competition, the industrial race of states, which, he believed, was ruinous for their resources. The author of *Ekonomika powszechna (Universal Economics)* was convinced that industrial government experiments were forced through by capitalists who were only looking for ways of getting rich quickly, and, above all, by ministers of state who hoped to achieve fame in this way. This motif was soon to re-emerge—in Warsaw this time.

What is lacking from the work of Stroynowski and other economic treatises written before 1820 is an analysis of the dramatic course of contemporary capitalism. Yet, it was through observation of the sequence of events that the doctrine of natural development, apparently anachronistic if not downright backward, found unexpected support.

Having discussed the origins of this doctrine, we shall now return to the moment when Simonde de Sismondi of Geneva, following his visit to England in 1819, published his *Nouveaux principes d'économie politique*. Sismondi undermined the foundations of the classical theory: the conviction that the national economy, having once been put in progressive motion, will regulate itself automatically as long as the principle of free enterprise and the free market is observed. According to this theory, trade crises, unemployment and disturbances in the process of development may happen, but by their very nature are transitory phenomena, since all factors of production are automatically directed where they are most needed and, by the same token, where the rewards are greatest. Thus, supply and demand always strive towards mutual equilibrium, structural disproportions are leveled out, and the economic mechanism has built into it an instrument of homeostasis which is sensitive to every fluctuation. Transitory difficulties in growth may be cured only by further growth. If one factory that mechanizes its technological processes lays off part of its labor force, the latter will be absorbed by a new factory which will produce machines for the first one. Thus everything moves upwards in this best of civilizations the driving force of which is private interest, and the result is the maximalization of general benefits.

This rule of the homeostasis of growth was questioned by Sismondi, and from then on it would be challenged repeatedly. Not by everybody, of course. Sismondi and Say saw the same France, the same England, and the same crises, but turned what they saw into completely different models of the functioning of the system.

Political economy claimed to have discovered the natural laws of economic development. Sismondi's critique showed that the forced, uncoordinated English style of industrialization was far from being natural, and should be regarded rather as a state of artificially inflamed investment fever. "Dans la marche naturelle des choses, un accroissement de richesses donnera un accroissement de revenus; de celui-ci naîtra un accroissement de consommation, puis un accroissement de travail pour la reproduction, et avec lui de population; enfin ce nouveau travail pourra à son tour augmenter la richesse. Mais si, par des mesures intempestives, on presse l'une ou l'autre de ces opérations, sans rapport avec toutes les autres, on dérange tout le système, et l'on fait peser sur les pauvres autant de souffrance qu'on avait cru leur procurer de bien-être."[43]

Once again we find the "natural order" appearing as the norm from which reality has departed completely. For Sismondi, the departure was even more extreme than for the physiocrats and Smith, who were merely anxious lest the unnatural order of development, the premature growth of foreign trade and large-scale industry would upset the proper proportions between them and agricultural production. Sismondi seems to have gone further by showing us the latter stage of this process and its effects, which were more visible half a century later: the upsetting of the proportions and proper interrelations between production, income and consumption, that is, the permanent disturbance of the entire process of reproduction.

The social organization responsible for this state of affairs is "artificial," the economic system is "false." But Sismondi did not give a straightforward answer to the question of the genesis of capitalism. He was a historian and knew that no one had pre-planned this system, that it had emerged gradually in the course of the evolution of social relations. However, he draws particular attention to the role played at that time, especially in England, by legislation relating to commercial and agrarian activity and inheritance—legislation which had been influenced by the erroneous maxims of the economists of the mercantilist school, and later the liberal school. This indeterminist attitude contained a grain of optimism: if government interference could push economic development onto the wrong track, then rational interference, enlightened by critical economics, could bring it back onto the right course. Social forms, institutions and systems of ownership were the result of human activity: "l'ordre naturel du progrès social ne tendait point à séparer les hommes d'avec les choses, ou la richesse d'avec le travail; dans les champs, le propriétaire pouvait demeurer cultivateur; dans les villes, le capitaliste pouvait demeurer artisan; la séparation de la classe qui travaille et de celle qui se repose, n'était point essentielle ou à l'existence de la société, ou à celle de la production; nous l'avons introduite pour le plus grand avantage de tous; il nous appartient de la régler pour en recueillir en effet cet avantage."[44]

Contrary to various erroneous interpretations which he himself sharply rejected, Sismondi was not an opponent of industrialization, new technology and economic growth; he simply did not see them as autonomous values. For him, the supreme value was human life, specifically the protection and improvement of the lot of the proletariat. Criticizing industrial protectionism, he wrote: "On ne peut jamais compter avec assez de certitude sur les théories même les mieux établies, pour oser ordonner un mal immédiat, dans la confiance qu'il en résultera un bien à venir. On doit moins encore prendre une semblable décision lorsqu'on peut craindre qu'elle n'entraîne la misère et la mort de nombreuses familles qui se sont élevées ou qui ont embrassé leur industrie sous la garantie des lois existantes et de l'ordre établi; il faut d'abord songer à sauver les êtres qui souffrent, on s'occupera ensuite de l'avenir."[45]

He did not believe that interdependencies among economic factors are as "natural" and unchangeable as those in physics, and he urged that economics be treated once more as a moral science, that is, a science that would "weigh human feelings, needs and passions" and establish what aims and means of activity were desirable. He rejected the axiological indifferentism of Ricardo's school, and opposed the scientific and moral sanctioning of the kind of progress in production forces that multiplied, if only temporarily, the poverty and suffering of the working classes so apparent in the early stages of the Industrial Revolution. As an economist, he was constantly looking for ways to regulate the mechanisms of violent growth. In this search he anticipated many ideas which since then have become recurrent themes in economic thought and which have been verified by social and economic politics in the present century.

The growth of production was for Sismondi merely a means, while the aim was human welfare and dignity, and the most effective form of activity for science and government was (in the idiom of twentieth century economics) the stimulation of consumption and effective demand through a policy of full employment. As far as poor countries were concerned, Sismondi regarded cheap investments as the best policy, investments which would be labor-consuming and capital-saving, rather than the other way round.[46] His attitude to technological progress and to the introduction of scientific inventions (the issue with which his name was later to be associated most often) was purely pragmatic, free of any manifestation of conservative sentimentality: mechanization was desirable whenever there was a shortage of labor and whenever the supply of commodities lagged behind demand; when it was the other way round, it became harmful.

He was writing with France, Switzerland and Italy in mind, countries which were on the threshold of industrial revolution, and it was his opinion that economic development should take place at a restrained, even pace, not by large leaps and bounds, and with a planned counteraction to the concentration of production, wealth and income. Moreover, this version of the anticlassical program was free of the influence of economic nationalism, and of any attempt to stir up competition among states. England was dangerous not because its products were competitive, but because, as an example of an erroneous method of development, it could infect others: "je voulais montrer, dans la crise qu'elle éprouve, et la cause de nos souffrances actuelles, d'après la liaison qui existe entre les diverses industries de tout l'univers, et l'histoire de notre propre avenir, si nous continuons à agir d'après les principes qu'elle a suivis."[47] The last condition is an expression of Sismondi's belief that the generic features of continental capitalism had not been established once and for all, and that it was not too late to change course.

The state administration was to be at the helm of development. This, however, was not meant to protect the interests of the entrepreneurs who were able to take care of themselves, nor was it meant to artificially stimulate investment, but to rectify the division of social income, since "ceux qui encouragent une production indéfinie, sans se soucier de connaître ce revenu, poussent une nation à sa ruine, en croyant lui ouvrir le chemin des richesses."[48] Sismondi admitted that large-scale production which made use of constantly improving technological inventions would lead to the lowering of the price of goods, and consequently to a growth in demand. However, the key concept of his theory was that the growth of effective demand attained in this way would not compensate—as Say maintained—for the drop in demand caused by the simultaneous restriction of the use of labor and employment.

If this were the case, then governments had to support above all the growth of employment, wages and consumption: the production apparatus would then adapt to this by itself and, even if its cogs turned more slowly, it would avoid crises in selling its product. Up to then, unfortunately, governments had been doing things back to front: "they order stockings and hats in the hope that they will find legs and heads for them later."[49]

For Sismondi, the mass proletarianization of the workers and the extreme differentiation in standards of living constituted a grave social catastrophe. He was far from advocating radical egalitarianism, and regarded the socialist ideas of Owen and Saint-Simon as noble but naive. Nevertheless, he devised a whole set of compensating mechanisms—beginning with progressive taxes and labor legislation—which in time would become routine tenets of social policy. He wanted legislation to support agrarian reform and to allow the workers a share in the incomes of their factories. He opened the eyes of his contemporaries to some dehumanizing effects of the system of hired labor, and he justified the proletarian's right not only to work and ownership, but also to rest and participation in culture, viewing the degree of this participation as the only measure of the level of civilization. Defending himself against attack by the enthusiastic supporters of uncontrolled industrial growth he wrote: "Je prie qu'on y fasse attention: ce n'est point contre les machines, ce n'est point contre les découvertes, ce n'est point contre la civilisation que portent mes objections, c'est contre l'organisation moderne de la société, organisation qui, en dépouillant l'homme qui travaille de toute autre propriété que celle de ses bras, ne lui donne aucune garantie contre une concurrence, contre une folle enchère dirigée à son préjudice, et dont il doit nécessairement être victime. . . . Aujourd'hui, ce n'est pas la découverte qui est un mal; c'est le partage injuste que l'homme fait de ses fruits."[50]

The work of man was blamed, not the merciless nature of things. All sorts of labels were pinned on this humanist from Geneva who lived in the period of the beginnings of industrial capitalism: he was regarded as a reactionary and a radical, a petty-bourgeois socialist and a romanticist. But when we read his work a hundred and fifty years later, we discover in him a precursor of the democratized, corrective liberalism of the twentieth century and also, in spite of all the defects of his economic theory, a precursor of concepts for the development of overpopulated countries with a low national income. Sismondi's thought, unfettered by doctrine, has stood the test of time, something which cannot be said of many of his contemporaries.

Polish economists in the period of the Congress Kingdom closely observed what was happening in industry and commerce in England, watching the growth of its wealth and the impoverishment of its proletariat. They were aware of the fact that England was "the laboratory of economic development"[51] for the whole world, and they hoped to take advantage of the experiments carried out in this laboratory. They studied classic economics, and also the reservations voiced by Malthus and Sismondi. They found Sismondi's axiology particularly attractive, because their own reflections led them to similar conclusions quite independently of his influence. They saw all of Europe severing its links with feudalism and entering the epoch of a new civilization—a civilization characterized by the relentless growth of human needs and driven by free work and the spirit of enterprise. However, like Sismondi, they were not wholly convinced that the shape of this civilization had been predetermined and that it had to be everywhere the same as in, for example, Lancashire. To consider England as a laboratory and to consider England as the only possible model for one's own future were two different things.

The main dilemma for economic futurology was precisely the fact that British-style capitalism provoked admiration and distaste simultaneously: admiration for its dynamic development and distaste for its social effects.

It was distaste that Piotr Maleszewski, a Polish émigré, mainly felt. In a letter sent from Paris to Fryderyk Skarbek, he wrote: "When shall we be roused to feelings of righteous contempt for those horrible workshops, whose only purpose is to transform, by civil or military means, the laboring man into a physical man, and the physical man into a machine?"[52] Skarbek presented in dramatic terms the ethical paradox to which development through prole-tarianization gave rise: "Putting aside our admiration for the progress of various industries and the development of arts and crafts, the state of the richest and the most enlightened nations of Europe makes every friend of mankind painfully sorry for the lot of a large proportion of inhabitants for whom destitution has become an inherited calling, as it were. All the efforts of man seem to be directed only to one task: how to bring agriculture, industries, arts and crafts to the greatest degree of perfection, and what means should be used to produce the largest output at the smallest possible cost. Such aspirations were in keeping with the good of mankind as long as the nations strove to cultivate the first buds of civilization for the purposes of social improvement; they would still be in keeping with the good of mankind today, if human affairs proceeded along the tracks . . . laid down for them by nature."[53]

It should be noted that it was not the traditionalists, ill-disposed on principle to all civilizational novelty, or the political radicals, who dismissed all bread-and-butter issues as trivial, who made the first serious diagnoses of the generic vices of capitalism. It fell to the liberal economists to perform this task. It was their concern and responsibility since by virtue of their chosen profession they were morally obliged to believe that the future of weak nations would be resolved in the field of economic work, and they could not therefore cease to demand the energetic Europeanization of Polish life. However, when it came to pushing the peasantry from one kind of poverty to another, from feudal destitution to proletarian destitution, and when it meant using the slogan of historic "progress" to disguise this step, they balked. On this point their position was quite close to that of Sismondi. They wondered if the process could be brought about by less brutal methods, and, as became economists, introduced the rule of minimal costs into their own axiology. Consequently, they began to seek a variant of economic develop-ment which would not involve the shattering of all existing social structures and mass pauperization, with everything that it entailed.

Bentham's individualistic ethics provided Skarbek and Krysiński with the idea that the measure of the usefulness of a deed or product was the benefit that it could be expected to bring individual people who did not give up their personal rights to a better life in favor of the nation as a whole. In the light of this assumption, the growth of national wealth and the potential for production could not be regarded as a value and aim if it was not accompanied by a growth in the general welfare. This growth had to keep pace with the growth in wealth, or take place after only a short time-lag, and not in the remote future. In 1825, Skarbek wrote, with England in mind: "I shall never be able to reconcile myself with the idea that a nation can call itself rich while a major part of its population lives in poverty and destitution. . . . What use to the working people is this power which threatens the world with conquest? What use are all those wonderful industrial works and civilizational achievements extolled by the traveler? What use is the vain glory of holding the first place among the civilized nations? Finally, what use is this enormous wealth, which itself does not know its own magnitude, if the people does not have enough bread for its needs; if a major part of the people, like the first inhabitants of the steppes, must wander about the country like nomads in search of employment with rich capitalists; if an even larger number of capable workers become beggars of their own free will, and beg for alms in order not to die of hunger?"[54]

Earlier, in 1812, Krysiński, the most ardent advocate of the phasal theory of civilization, the theory of the "maturing" of nations, had combined this theory with a utilitarian assessment of their achievements: "The nations," he preached, "are aggregates of families, and the sum of individual welfares constitutes the welfare of a nation." He continued to advocate this opinion consistently, writing in 1829: "The objectives of today's science are purely practical; not metaphysical wealth, that is, wealth which is irrespective of time and place, but achieving the greatest possible happiness of the greatest number of individuals by means of wealth, increasing the prosperity of a country using the means that are most appropriate in the circumstances in which it finds itself, but without sacrificing the material being of the present generation—this is the objective, this is the aim of science."[55]

The problem of the lot of future generations tended to be neglected by large historiosophical syntheses, which saw things in terms of centuries and the hypostases of nations, classes and civilizations. But for the liberal utilitarianists it was to acquire a particular significance. Since the quality of individual existences is the final measure of the utility of both production and politics, then the question of sacrifices for the sake of the future becomes a tragic conflict of values, and not just a matter of working out the best strategy for achieving balanced growth. What level of sacrifice could be required of the present generation for the sake of the future, and more concretely, to ensure the financing of the industrialization of the country? Skarbek was aware of these issues. When Lubecki decided to finance investment in mining and metallurgy from the state treasury,[56] Skarbek suggested to the Society of the Friends of Learning that it organize a competition on the following subject: "Is it better for the government, in order to establish factories, which will be useful not only to the present, but also to future generations, to make large outlays surpassing the abilities of the present taxpayers, and to put the seal of perfection and durability on its achievements; or should it rather aim for less perfection and durability in its factories, and instead to spare the efforts of the present generation?"[57] The very wording of the question suggests what answer its author would prefer; but we may safely admit that Skarbek was concerned not only about the present generation as a whole, but also, perhaps above all, about the interests of the gentry proprietors who were likely to experience the burdens rather than the advantages of government-sponsored industrialization. Whatever the case may have been, the dilemma loses nothing of its pertinence, and indeed remains pertinent even today. This is not a scientific but an axiological dilemma, and it can only be solved arbitrarily, treating each case as a new challenge.

It is clear that the dislike of forced industrialization resulted both from fear of its actual economic costs and fear of the social effects it would bring in its wake. This critical reserve reflected the fundamental difference between Krysiński and Skarbek on the one hand, and Surowiecki and Staszic on the other, since the latter viewed Poland's industrial self-reliance as a precondition for its development and the regaining of its strength. For the economists who represented more cosmopolitan views this was by no means so obvious. Admittedly Skarbek, who always avoided extreme attitudes, perceived the harmfulness of the exclusively agrarian structure of the national economy—a structure which prevented the formation of a strong "internal circulation" and confined the country to exporting raw agricultural produce. A country which lacked developed processing industries and a "variety of employment opportunities" could not take an equal position in international exchange with industrial nations, and "freedom of trade without equality of trade is the most wretched of delusions and the most harmful of gifts."[58] This did not mean, however, that the small Congress Kingdom had necessarily to develop all branches of industry and strive towards making itself independent of other countries. Economists who, after all, had been educated in the classical school, regarded the campaign against things foreign in the name of supporting local products as a mental aberration. Failing to foresee the triumphs of economic nationalism all over Europe, they assumed that a free world market would prove lasting and that state borders would lose their significance. Under these conditions, the variety of economic structures and their mutual complementary nature would continue to be advantageous to all partners involved in exchange, each of them developing only those branches of production which, in view of the local conditions and resources, could operate and sell their products at the smallest cost.

There were, therefore, two clear strategies for development. According to the advocates of both of these strategies, feudalism, serfdom and the gentry were responsible for Poland's backwardness and poverty. But while Suro-wiecki thought that the only cure for poverty was to enter the industrial race of nations, Krysiński and Skarbek were of the opinion that Poland, weak and short of capital as it was, could hardly afford to compete in this race, and that participation could prove disastrous.

Once again, the familiar doctrine of natural development was used to justify this moderate strategy. This was the doctrine expounded at length by Skarbek in his *Théorie des richesses sociales* (1829) and, with some modifications, in the Polish version of this seminal work which appeared thirty years later.[59] It is worth repeating that this was a rationalist doctrine *par excellence*: a logically constructed measure for appraising departures from the regularity of actual processes rather than a historical generalization concerning these processes. The natural order of development implied the sequence which would have occurred, if it had not been for distortions caused by numerous local circumstances on the one hand, and by the artificiality and irrationality of laws, institutions and administrative decisions on the other.

For Skarbek, Western European industrialization constituted a drastic example of the "inverted order of things." The premature influx of capital to industry and commerce, before agriculture had a chance to attain a higher degree of perfection, was a developmental anomaly which sprang directly from agrarian feudalism. Investment in agriculture became unprofitable in a situation in which the direct producers were either deprived of the right to own land, or at any rate did not enjoy full rights of ownership and were legally disadvantaged in comparison with craftsmen and merchants. "The primary division of land proved an obstacle to ... the occurrence of the natural sequence of things in the development of national industry; because in the majority of European countries the land was owned by a small number of privileged hereditary squires, and for a long time it never even occurred to the laboring masses to aspire to exclusive ownership of land. It is to this circumstance that we should ascribe the general aspiration of the European peoples to giving priority to crafts and commerce before agriculture, because the two former occupations constituted the only path to affluence. . . . Such was the effect of the long-lasting feudal relations in European countries, and one may venture to say that it largely contributed to the fact that European nations pursued affluence and enlightenment in the inverse order."[60]

As can be seen, half a century after Adam Smith's treatise had appeared the Polish economist formulated even more forcefully the theory which claimed that accelerated industrialization was a result not of the decline of feudalism, but on the contrary, of its persistent durability. The theory pointed to the long-term consequences of this situation, which had been hinted at earlier by Sismondi: it was precisely the distortion of the natural sequence of changes that caused the upsetting of the fine balance between the branches of the economy and between global production and consumption. It was not capitalist industrialization as such, but its prematurity and the direction which it had been "forced" to follow, accompanied by the neglect of agriculture, that was to blame for poverty, unemployment and commercial crises.

So far, no attempt had been made to relate this thesis to Polish history: after all, the initial assumptions had not been fulfilled in a country where feudality hampered the development of towns even more than of agriculture. However, at the time when Skarbek was writing his treatise, these conditions had just changed. The towns, even those privately owned, were to all intents and purposes free, and commercial and industrial enterprise was no longer hampered, while in the countryside, in spite of the abolition of serfdom (in the Duchy of Warsaw in 1807) the rights of feudal ownership and *corvée* still survived. Under these circumstances, the flow of labor and capital from agriculture to commerce and industry became a real possibility, especially since the government of the Kingdom showed clearly that it wished to support new branches of the national economy. Thus, the theory of natural development gained in validity: not as a historic interpretation, but as a program and a warning with regard to future activity.

As early as 1807, Dominik Krysiński argued that "towns, factories, and manufacturing industries, though they have an influence on the nation's wealth, are of secondary importance for Poles." The state of the nation depended not on the superficial grandeur of large cities and factories, and the affluence of capitalists, but on "the condition of the nation's most numerous class," that is to say, on the property, housing conditions, clothing and diet of the peasantry. "*A well-ruled country is a country in which the government tries to increase the number of the owners of land, and in which the peasant has a chance to amass capital*; such a country, I insist, will become rich and more populous without manufacturing industries and without large cities. On the contrary, if income from agriculture is turned to establishing large manufacturing industries, if we endeavor by all possible means to increase the number of industrial workers, especially those of native stock, then we shall diminish the capital needed to improve agricultural production, and, what is more significant, we shall diminish the rural population, and by diminishing it, we shall unfailingly bring about the decline of agriculture."[61]

It is possible to detect here a significant conflict between economic predictions—a conflict which would continue in Poland for the major part of the century. Thus, the spokesmen of industrialization argued that the development of towns and industry would provide a lever for agricultural development, since it generated local commercial markets, raised the price of foodstuffs, and lowered the price of implements and other goods purchased by the peasants. The skeptics, on the contrary, reasoned in "either–or" terms: with the shortage of surplus capital and labor, industry would develop at the expense of agriculture, that is, in the final reckoning, at the expense of the peasants.

Which of the two sides was right? That depended on the timescale implicitly assumed. In the short term, society feels the burdens of original accumulation and investment more keenly than the results. Viewed from such a perspective, the skeptics were in the right. Krysiński, it should be noted, did not represent the interests of the gentry manorial farms, but supported the gradual appropriation of holdings by the peasants and the strengthening of their position. He regarded grain export as a social catastrophe, since it brought advantages to the large farms only ("And which are those countries that export the largest quantities? Those *where the people are slaves* and in which a huge number of individuals toil for a handful of people."[62]) However, as we have seen, unlike Nax or Surowiecki he did not view the development of local markets as an indispensable substitute for exports. Nor was this necessarily an inconsistency on his part. It is, after all, obvious that in a situation of near-starvation, a decrease in the burdens imposed on peasant farming will lead initially to a decrease in sales in favor of a growth in direct consumption. This may be regarded as good or bad, depending on whether one is interested in hungry mouths or historic progress.

Another factor which had a bearing on this issue was the frequently justified lack of confidence in the economic efficiency of despotic government, and the dislike of "administrative empiricism" which advocated the conducting of experiments on society without regard to theory. "The manufacturing industries and factories," wrote Krysiński in 1812, "are the favorites of government protection . . . and yet nowhere do we observe so much senselessness . . . so many effects opposite to what was expected, as in this part of the national administration. By neglecting to indicate which tasks are to be performed by individuals and which tasks are the duty of the government, very grave mistakes have been made . . . and manufacturing has been pushed in a direction that is unnatural and harmful to the nation."[63]

The opposition of the liberal economists increased in the period of the Congress Kingdom as a response to the growth of protectionism and *étatisme*. "Our present system of administration," noted Skarbek in 1820, "is based on the desire to draw everything into line with government rules and regulations. They have taken as their principle that they must try by all available means to increase domestic consumption, so that by virtue of the demand for home produce we become independent of foreigners; and they want to inculcate in us the industrial spirit, introducing all kinds of manufactures at once, with no consideration for the possibilities and needs of the country and heedless of whether these products will find markets. They make the prosperity of manufacturing and the stability of outlets dependent on open trade with Russia."[64] This was the beginning of the short-lived era of Lubecki, which caused the polemics between the two camps to rage even more furiously.

Minister Lubecki's point of departure was practically the same as his critics' and was, in fact, the same as that of almost all Polish writers on economics, beginning with the first partition of Poland: that is, an awareness that the well-being of the national economy could no longer rely on grain export. The English Corn Bill, passed shortly after the lifting of the continental blockade, proved conclusively how fragile a basis it was for any kind of calculation. The development of an internal market for agricultural produce was supposed to free the manorial farms of their dependence on exports, which were not always certain. There were also political considerations at stake. Lubecki never swerved from his loyalty to St. Petersburg, and his acceptance of the Tsar's sovereignty in Poland was above suspicion. Nevertheless, he wanted to counterbalance Russia's political domination with the economic and civilizational power of the Kingdom.

Like Staszic, Surowiecki, and many others, he was appalled by the inertia of rural gentry life, believing that it could only be overcome by industry, and that only the government was capable of initiating industrial development. "The position, alas, of the government in an underdeveloped country like ours is such that it has to take the initiative in everything and on every field, because the level of education, distrust and deeply ingrained habits discourage the citizens from embracing all innovations, which elsewhere can be left to the endeavors of private persons acting in their own interests. As far as we are concerned, we would fare badly in this respect if we applied the most elegant axioms of political economy, should they leave us at the mercy of this stagnation in which we have long been growing moldy. Our government is the commander-in-chief of inexperienced legions which have still to learn strict discipline, and must lead them onwards, instilling in them a sense of power and an awareness of the means at their disposal. With God's help, the government will be able to relinquish this role as soon as possible, and its powers of impulse, having put everything in motion, will commit themselves once more to the bounds of prudent rest."[65]

For the time being, therefore, everything was to be put in motion by the will of the minister of the treasury. Everything, that is, except one trifling matter: the relationship between the manorial farms and the peasants, which by tacit agreement was recognized as unchangeable. There was no provision in these long-term economic plans for creating conditions whereby the profitability of peasant farms could be raised and consumption for eight-tenths of the population could be increased. It is hard to see where this additional demand for industrial products was to come from in a situation where the peasant, forced to do so by financial burdens such as rent or taxes, participated in the market exclusively or mainly as a seller and not as a buyer. The "powers of impulse" stopped short at the village boundary. Contrary to what the classic economists believed, production did not open the way for markets.

The government program of industrialization was supposed to ensure economic independence for the Kingdom. "Our endeavors have already borne abundant fruit," boasted Lubecki at the very beginning of his mission. "We have forced out foreign woolen products, and linen products are the second on the list; our forges have every chance of developing rapidly."[66] This was indeed true, but at the same time it had already become obvious that the local market was insufficient even for the relatively modest production levels of the burgeoning manufacturing industry, especially when protective tariffs raised prices. Lubecki therefore decreased the reliance of the Polish economy on the uncertain corn markets of the West, but at the same time made it dependent on the equally uncertain, as it would soon transpire, textile markets of the East.

However, the main concern for his contemporaries was the costs involved in such an ambitious project of economic restructuring. The protectionist system meant the further intensification of what was already regarded as a thorough-going fiscal policy. The treasury drained agricultural surplus to the budget, channeling part of it into the construction of roads and waterways, and into credits and subsidies for craftsmen and manufacturers, and later allocating ever increasing amounts to government investment in mining. The liberal gentry opposition, both within the Seym and outside it, fiercely attacked Lubecki for the despotism of his unconstitutional measures, and also accused him of trying to squeeze capital for his industrial ventures out of the destitute. Admittedly, "destitution" was here a rather rhetorical figure of speech: the whole point of the dispute was the threat to the incomes and existence of large mortgaged land holdings. Lubecki did not deny that industrialization required sacrifices, but, he added, there was no other way of overcoming the hopeless stagnation of the nation. "No one takes in the fact that general prosperity will follow precisely from this destitution; no one wants to see that the national character is purifying itself in it, that this is the way to find the means which are best adapted to the situation of the nation and its skills, or that with the help of industry it will attain an independent and durable prosperity which nothing will wreck . . . Like a surgeon who must be oblivious to his patient's moanings in order not to endanger his life by his own excessive sentimentality, so must I too proceed unwaveringly on the road mapped out for me by duty, with the awareness that there is no difficulty in the world which cannot be overcome by this conviction."[67] In the face of such a noble mission, all the reservations of Lubecki's critics, who demanded a more precise calculation of the social costs and effects of the government program, must have seemed pusillanimous.

Many of them were, indeed, mean-spirited, and moreover often concealed the traditional short-sightedness of the country gentlemen for whom any investment—even their own investments, let alone national spending—counted as a loss if it brought in profits only after several years. A distillery was always the best investment, since it brought returns the following year. All kinds of interests and motives, including political ones, induced people to form anti-Lubecki alliances. Nevertheless, it is necessary to distinguish in this chorus of dissent the voices of economists, whose views were not necessarily narrower than those of the government minister.

If Skarbek and Krysiński needed a new example of the violation of the natural course of development, they were provided with one now. The Kingdom was repeating the Western mistake of premature industrialization, engaging in it, moreover, with an ostentation to which its economy, still half feudal, was not yet equal. The "preternatural urge," they argued, which the administration gave to one sector of the economy at the expense of another (that is, agriculture), dried up national resources and made it more difficult to effect a change in agrarian structure and improve the lot of the peasants. There was no advantage to be obtained by the nation "in engaging in all kinds of industry if it lacks sufficient production potential because of a shortage of labor and capital."[68] On the contrary, it was better to buy the necessary goods abroad than to produce them locally at a higher cost. The time would come when both the population and capital would grow to such a degree that they could not be absorbed by agriculture, and they would then flow to the towns, into crafts and commerce. "If the condition of the farmers improves to such an extent that a major part of them come to possess capital, if not land, and the earnings of the farm laborers are sufficient to ensure a dignified life for them, then a national industry will be created, and it will develop and aim at perfection, but the sequence of this progress will depend on how far the internal administration of the country allows things to run their natural course."[69]

Skarbek, admittedly, agreed to the channeling of public funds to some enterprises indispensable to the country, the running of which surpassed the capital capabilities of private individuals. For example, "the absolute need for natural resources which cannot be cheaply obtained by commerce, the justified hope of discovering rich mines, and occasionally the need to employ new labor, may be reasons enough for maintaining mining, which does not generate pure profit."[70] He saw this, however, as an exception to the general rule. He even thought that treasury accumulation was more apparent than real, since as a result of the harsh tax collecting system, state capital was often generated not from the collected income surplus but at the expense of active capital, diverted by the government from more profitable uses. Indeed, the costs of government production, burdened with an expanded bureaucracy of control and supervision, are always higher than private costs.[71]

In addition, the economists and journalists suspected, not without reason, that imposing government buildings and machines were, to some extent, merely intended to increase its prestige. Particular doubts were provoked by the government investments in mining and metallurgy which Lubecki forced through, and they were sharply attacked by the liberal opposition in the Seym in 1830. Shortly after, following the outbreak of the November Rising, Krysiński did not hesitate to deride "this costly *mining phantasmagoria* which consumes millions upon millions and which provokes sorrow and ridicule both at once."[72]

In his history of the rising which he wrote abroad, Mochnacki summed up Lubecki's industrial policy in the following way: "Given the present state of the science of national economics, no one can deny that the government should not exert an influence on the way national capital is used. Factories enrich the nation if they are created spontaneously. Factories which are established by the government and which without that government would never have been created, factories which are a fruit of the *prohibitive* system, prove a disaster for the customer, and harm natural local industry. This is a general rule." And, he went on: "It is said that houses are built from the foundation up and not from the roof down. In our case, agriculture takes precedence over manufacturing industries, and until the country recovers its independence, as long as all its produce is not absorbed by internal trade, all attempts at pushing it forward on the road to industrialization will be in vain. In Poland, only those hands which are superfluous in agriculture can be utilized in factories."[73]

These last statements by two fierce political opponents of Lubecki may be regarded as biased. Moreover, Mochnacki was still very much a Polish country gentleman, with all the ingrained dislike of commerce and industry that this entailed. However, this was not true of Jan Ludwik Żukowski, mentioned in the previous chapter, who was an ardent supporter of industrial progress. However, in a work written in 1830 even he displayed his fears that factory industries, for example the cotton industry, which had been transplanted to the Kingdom thanks to government protection, were not necessarily a stimulus to development. One has always to keep in mind, he argued, "that only those things are durable which have been introduced slowly and as a result, as it were, of the natural inclinations of the inhabitants." But in Poland things were being done in a different way: "No one seems to be concerned about the internal, autonomous generation of the forces of production. We only think of quick results, and when we see them, we no longer ask questions about the methods by which we have achieved them, how much they cost, whether their development has not harmed other ways of increasing prosperity, whether they have not hampered the progress of other effects of this kind, or whether they could not have been achieved by better and more advantageous means."[74]

The government's industrial program did in fact upset the balance between the various branches of the national economy: the relative overinvestment in metallurgy, coupled with the general stagnation in the twenty years after the uprising, produced a crisis which consumed a major part of the production potential which had been created. What is more, government industries, though larger and using more modern technology, produced goods which were more expensive and of poorer quality than those produced by the old-fashioned private furnaces and forges. In comparison with the whole of the economy, the new industries did not demonstrate the powers of impulse of which both Surowiecki and Lubecki had dreamt. This fact does not detract from their ideas, but, at least in some points, it confirmed the rightness of those who had been able to foresee the failure of the program, or who had become aware of what was happening early on and had drawn the appropriate conclusions.

In sum, the proponents of "natural" development had several objections to "artificial," forced industrialization. They were afraid: that this kind of industrialization was premature; that it was too rapid; that it began from the wrong end and that the sequence of investment was erroneous; that it was imposed by the state; that the enterprises it invested in were too large; and finally, that these projects were too costly, based as they were on expensive imported technologies. All these criteria were connected, and all of them were relative and depended on some arbitrarily adopted norm—it is, after all, difficult to establish what is "too rapid," "premature," or "too large." There would always be others who thought that the same process of industrialization was belated, too slow, and enjoyed too little support from the state. Nevertheless, it is not our intention to claim that the whole dispute was futile and sterile, or that it was simply a clash of various class interests.

In the writings of Polish academics, especially on the history of economic thought, the problem is often treated simply as a dispute about the role of the state in the process of industrialization (which we have distinguished above as one of several criteria). This aspect, however, does not have an autonomous significance, but is clearly part of the general civilizational trends. Let us recall that in England, and from the 1820s on also in France, the slogans of free trade and free enterprise were used as weapons by the supporters of rapid industrialization; for this reason, Sismondi aimed his criticism at the dogmas of economic liberalism, and demanded state interventionism—not protectionist interference to stimulate investment, but a correction in the division of social income in favor of the working masses. Sismondi's theories, and his warnings against the unrestrained development of capitalist interests, exerted an enormous influence on Polish, and also Russian economic thought, but on the whole no one considered it necessary (or politically feasible) to apply the kind of preventive measures suggested by the Geneva economist. In countries with fledgling industries, including Germany, the confirmed industrialists as a rule accepted the principles of protectionist policy, while both the landowning agrarians, generally opposed to industrialization, and the supporters of "natural" development, had confidence in the dogma of free trade, expecting that things would go as they wished as long as the government relinquished its active control of industry and tariffs. The attitude to the interventionist policy was thus clearly instrumental, and the crux of the dispute about the future was the concept of progress and welfare and the vision of what kind of social structure was desirable for the country.

"I do not want to abandon the middle road," wrote Skarbek in his contribution to the discussion on "luxury,"[75] and this dictum aptly characterizes the civilizational model he had chosen. He did not feel intoxicated by the wonders of technology and modernity; nor did he set up a cult of plain, rural simplicity in opposition to them. For him, neither the state of affairs that had long existed, nor that which was only beginning to take root were automatically right; both had to prove their utility before the tribunal of economics.

He did not dream of Polish Manchesters and Birminghams, together with the unavoidable concentration of wealth and the sharpening of contrasts in human welfare. But despite that, he was no enemy of industry, provided that it developed slowly in keeping with the spontaneous flow of surplus capital accumulated in agriculture. Agricultural work, like crafts and commerce, was also a kind of "industry," requiring investment and science, and it was superior to them in that it stabilized the labor market and protected the country against the specter of mass proletarianization. For this reason, Skarbek believed, the greater absorption of labor which agriculture involved and the fact that it was less disposed to mechanization was an advantage.

He did not see the productivity of the manufacturing apparatus as a measure of the level of civilization, but, like Sismondi, thought that this was reflected in the ability of society to use the goods produced. It was of secondary importance where these goods came from, whether they were produced locally or imported. "A country which, for example, is fertile and in which agriculture is in a developed state and has a broad range of easily accessible outlets for its produce, may dedicate itself almost exclusively to agriculture, bringing factory-produced goods from abroad and leaving foreign trade to foreigners." A logical consequence of such an attitude was the discarding of the theory of "tribute" which agricultural countries allegedly had to pay to industrialized countries. And even if it was true that commercial and industrial nations made more rapid progress on the road towards wealth and education, this was merely a transitory bonus resulting from the relative backwardness of agriculture. In the long run, they were bound to lose their advantage.[76]

In this doctrine, capitalist industrialization was not an indispensable pre-requisite of economic development; this was rather conditioned by the growth of people's needs and incomes. Wherever such growth took place, production followed in its wake. It was not, therefore, necessary to worry about produc-tion, or the interests of capitalists; the latter knew best how to take care of themselves. Legislation and administration, if they were concerned with the prosperity of all, had to ensure a more equal division of wealth and incomes so that in both agriculture and industry there would be a large number of small-scale, rather than a small number of large-scale, owners and producers. Labor had to be as rarely as possible kept separate from ownership and had to lead to ownership, since wealthy countries are those which have the most numerous "middle class of industrial people" who combine the labor of their own hands with the possession of small amounts of capital or land.[77] This was to be an independent class capable of defending its earnings, its moderate affluence. "The more people there are dependent on the will of others, the poorer the country becomes;" therefore, the government must help the workers so that they are not forced by their position to succumb to the capitalists.[78] This would become possible when rapid mechanization was restrained (for instance, by introducing a tax on machines in order to level out the costs of production) and when steps were taken to counteract the pauperization of the peasantry. These measures would prevent overpopula-tion and competition on the labor market, and the establishment of savings-banks would make it easier for the workers to accumulate small amounts of capital.

Was this, as Marxist historians claimed, a "petty-bourgeois utopia?" It should be noted, first, that any coherent plan for socioeconomic development, in fact any model for the future, is a utopia in that life is richer and more eclectic than all models: no model may be implemented without considerable distortions. The industrialists' vision of the civilizational role of large-scale industry and capital, which would overcome all the torpor and decay of the backward country, was, in the Kingdom and elsewhere, to prove equally "utopian," although it definitely was not "petty-bourgeois."

Many historians of economic development and economic thought seem to believe that while the systems of feudal social organization that we know from history are many and diverse, the capitalist system is, in principle, one and the same; the differences that have been noted are ascribed either to the different level of development or the different roads followed towards capitalism. At the root of this view lies the undeniable supranational similarity of the organization of production, the systems of dependence and the types of institution which evolved within the large-scale capitalist sector. The problem is, however, that the notion of "capitalism" is often applied not only to this sector, but also to the complex socioeconomic whole in which this sector functions. It is not difficult, however, to notice that in this broad sense "capitalist" structures are also diverse: the scope of capitalist relations *per se* is different and they coexist with other segments of the economy and society in various ways.

In a country in which agriculture accounted for the lion's share of the total produce, it was quite legitimate to believe that the distribution of land and the level of agriculture would determine the totality of the process of economic growth and modernization. By the same token, one could justifiably maintain that, considering its fundamentally different agrarian structure, industrialization in Poland would proceed along a different course, at a different tempo and with different effects, than in the Western part of Europe.

In the early stages of industrialization, the influence of industry on rural relations meant above all inducing the surplus population to leave the land and expanding the market for agricultural produce. From this point of view small-scale industry, which consumes little capital, which is evenly distributed and which processes local raw materials, is incomparably more effective than large-scale modern industry, which forms islands of capitalism in different parts of the country and constitutes a largely isolated system in a backward economy. Therefore, the theory of "natural" development had a profound social and humanitarian significance.

Was this, however, a realistic proposition? That is, was "natural" development really development or merely stagnation? Skarbek's model was notice-
ably flawed: it lacked a consistent program for the enfranchisement of the
peasants, it naively assumed that the workers and smallholders were capable
of accumulation, and it idealized the conditions of international exchange.
However, it is doubtful whether the completion or correction of his assumptions would totally undermine the foundations of his theory. The argument
that large-scale industry cannot be created without a "powerful push" misses
the point, since Skarbek's program was not about large-scale industry at all.
The convincing argument is, rather, historic and hinges on the Poznań region.
In this part of former Poland, in spite of the Prussian style of enfranchisement
which was somewhat unfavorable to the growth of peasant possession,
economic and social development took a course close to the "natural" version
and it would be difficult to claim that because of it Wielkopolska fared worse
than the other parts of the divided country. Here the "petty-bourgeois utopia"
became a reality.

The concept of another, more lenient capitalism, capitalism with a human
face, was to play a tremendous role in the history of Polish social thought in
the nineteenth century. This was hardly due to Skarbek's influence, since his
works never circulated very widely. The idea of natural development, of a
"middle road," had to germinate here and be revived again and again, because
it was itself a "natural," although not the only, solution to the dilemma of
Polish civilization. The need for scientific and technological progress and
a rational economy was, after all, recognized by all but the most stubborn
traditionalists. There was also a growing understanding that such progress
was possible only under conditions which allowed an unrestrained flow of
capital, goods, manpower, hired talent and knowledge. However, it was by
no means easy to arouse enthusiasm in the Polish gentry and intelligentsia
for this surrender to the chaos of speculation and the prospect of large towns
inhabited by the proletariat. Fears about disturbing the social order must have
had an influence here too. For this reason the thought had to take root that
Poland did not have to go through that experience, that indeed it could not do
so, since agriculture, in which the major part of human and capital resources
were tied down, would stabilize the development of the other fields of the
national economy. The prognosis of a slower evolution, taking place without
the brutal uprooting of the masses of country people and without the polarization of society along class lines, seemed an attractive proposition.

It was particularly attractive to those landowners who had tried to adapt
their views and their property early to the challenges of the new epoch.
No wonder, then, that the theory of "natural" development won popularity

among the more liberally-minded of the landed gentry. The *Roczniki Gospodarstwa Krajowego (The Annals of the Country's Economy)*[79] argued that in exchange for its grain, wood and wool the country could get all the foreign products it needed at a lower price than if they were to be produced locally. With such a profitable form of exchange, capital would multiply, the price of land would rise, and interest rates would fall. Only then would it be profitable to establish factories in the countryside for the processing of local produce and mineral raw materials, that is, factories such as breweries, oil mills, sugar mills, tanneries, factories producing lard and candles, brickyards, glassworks, saw mills, etc. "This is the only method of increasing the wealth of an agricultural country, a long and protracted method, but when there is no other, then we should follow the path it points to." An agricultural country should not aspire to building factories which would not withstand foreign competition without government protection.[80]

Just as important was the fact that this kind of natural growth was to protect Poland against the kind of crises that repeatedly shook the West. When, despite everything, the European crisis of 1857 affected "our agricultural, nonindustrial Poland, which did not even have a stock exchange," one influential Warsaw journalist saw the reason for this evil in the fact that landowners who had floating capital located it in shares or Paris banks, instead of promoting the local food-processing industries and improving the lot of the lower classes: "To this purpose let us turn our own Polish capital, and we can then afford to pay little heed to commercial storms raging somewhere in the West."[81]

Be that as it may, it was often difficult to differentiate between "artificial" and "natural" undertakings. Obviously, the prime example of "artificial" development was the cotton industry, built in the Polish Kingdom by German manufacturers using American raw material and selling its products mainly on the Russian market. Moreover, this industry was protected by import tariffs, supported by loans and tax reliefs granted by the treasury, and it brought the working masses in increasingly large numbers to the new urban centers. Another novelty were the sugar mills which were often quoted as an example of proper development because they were based in rural areas and brought large profits to sugar beet growers. And yet it was these sugar mills that provoked the sharpest economic polemic in the Warsaw press of the time.

The controversy arose in 1860, and concerned not the Kingdom, but Volhynia and Podolia. When Russia imposed a high import duty on sugar, a real sugar craze began there. Discussion in the *Gazeta Codzienna (The Daily Gazette)* was initiated by its correspondent in Żytomierz, Apollo Nałęcz Korzeniowski, a man of letters and an ardent democrat who, however, as often happened, had rather conservative gentry views on economic questions.[82] "We do not deny at all that our country is capable of material development," he wrote. "... However, we believe that manufacturing, industry and commerce should not absorb agriculture here, but serve it as the lowest of servants, as behoves baser activities. . . . Let us also add that as long as our agriculture and its every branch does not attain a level of complete development it is the duty of local landowners, as well as capitalist proprietors, to direct their work and capital above all towards this development."[83]

This time agricultural industry, which after all was in the hands of the landowners, was also seen as detrimental to the agricultural economy. The discussion on sugar mills in the Ukraine became a dispute on the general grounds for industrialization. The wounded "capitalist proprietors" counterattacked. The sharpest response came from Zygmunt Fudakowski, an industrialist and a prominent organizer of the sugar industry in the Ukraine. He ridiculed Korzeniowski for his attempts at combining "naturalness" with "duty." After all, Fudakowski argued, "without the help of industry agriculture can hardly be brought to full development on the road of natural progress. On the other hand, a road can be said to be natural when development becomes an absolute necessity, when it results from the very nature of things." He argued that it was useless to wait for the appearance of "surplus" capital and a "surplus" population since such surpluses would never arise; that the requirement to process local raw materials was fulfilled by the sugar industry, but that it was not really binding. Such conditions were contrary to the principles of good political economy, that is, the political economy that "all of us are reading." Even though the import duty increased the price of sugar, the local sugar industry would still bring income to the country, since the country would improve its trade balance, its agricultural sector would earn money from the growing of sugar beet, and the local factories producing machines and vats are encouraged to develop.[84]

The polemic was sharp on both sides and, on the whole, very symptomatic. On the one hand, the theory of "natural" development, which had arisen as a compromise, a middle road, between two extreme attitudes and had reigned supreme in the press and in public opinion for twenty years, became more conservative. Its gentry version reflected the ambivalent feelings of the country gentleman, who saw native industry both as offering the possibility of profitable sales of grain and as a rival which deprived him of labor and credit and caused his costs to rise. This evolution of views can be clearly seen in Skarbek, whose *Gospodarstwo narodowe stosowane (Applied national economics)*, published in 1860, showed a gentry-oriented, conservative bias in comparison with his earlier works, written in the 1820s.

On the other hand, the radically bourgeois ideology which claimed that industrial development should be fostered, an ideology which for a long time had been out of favor, became revitalized in the early 1860s. In the *Gazeta Codzienna*, which oscillated between its landowning and middle-class clientele, these two bodies of opinion (which in fact corresponded only roughly to the class divisions) sometimes clashed (as in the matter of the sugar mills), and sometimes they simply ignored one another, each of them arguing its own cause.

It is characteristic that in 1860 both sides used almost the same arguments as had been used in the *Dziennik Handlowy* in 1786. Meanwhile, Poland had changed, and so had the world, the economy and economic theory, but the essence of the dispute between the two strategies of development remained the same, and was still relevant, still unresolved.

One more attempt was made, shortly before the uprising of 1863, to bring these two attitudes closer together and reconcile them—this time by Józef Supiński.[85] Like his teacher Skarbek, Supiński, a loner from Lwów, was a man who followed the "middle road:" "In education," he wrote, "as well as in industry, in administration, and even in pure politics, I dislike violent means and distrust extremists."[86] Leaving aside the complexities of his exposition, his very moderation explains his ideological defeat and the complete lack of response to his program. He tried to influence Polish opinion at a moment when views were becoming polarized and political emotions excluded any interest in long-term social and economic programs. It was not until the era of the positivists that the significance of his teachings came to be appreciated.

Supiński's great desire to form a system, his wish to create a "philosophy of the universe" and construct a scientific foundation for the study of society left no mark on the history of European thought. But his *Szkoła polska gospodarstwa społecznego (The Polish School of Social Economics)*, especially the first volume which appeared in 1862, was the only Polish contribution to the subject of economic and social development since the publication of Surowiecki's *On the Decline of Industry and Towns*. In Skarbek's works, the problem of economic development appears only marginally: like his masters from the classical school who had departed from Adam Smith's historicism, he was interested above all in studying static dependencies between economic factors. Supiński, on the other hand, believed that theory was mainly needed to predict the future history of Polish society. In this context, the theory of "natural" development again recovered its preeminent position and became the *leitmotif* of *The Polish School*, but in a new version, expanded and freed of the influence of particular interests, whether the interests of the landowners or any other class of society.

Supiński's attitude to the West will be discussed later. Here, it is enough to say that he was a liberal and a genuinely enthusiastic supporter of contemporary capitalism, full of trust in its developmental capabilities. An admirer of the natural sciences, he believed that the effects of agricultural chemistry and industrial mechanization could only be beneficial, discarding Sismondi's reservations in this respect. His analysis of the causes of crises did not go beyond the views put forward by Say and Bastiat: overproduction and commercial crises are merely the consequences of protectionist laws which still hamper the freedom of labor, industry, commerce and transport. This freedom, when it finally triumphs, will cure all ills, since, after all: "General abundance means a general state of well-being."[87]

But these were merely principles. A poor theoretician, he demonstrated a sharpness of vision only when he tried to apply his generalized view to the local conditions in the Kingdom, or Eastern Galicia where he had settled on returning from exile. This was where the difficulties unknown to the Western liberals began; this was where the school of "the national economy" began, and in this school Supiński was to prove a prudent and independent teacher.

Supiński's intellectual formation obviously inclined him to recognize that commercial exchange between a country which produced agricultural products and raw materials and an industrially developed country had to be profitable to both sides. However, every economist from a non-industrial country faced the problem of the "tribute" or "eternal levy," as Surowiecki and numerous other writers had called it. The conflict between these two contradictory views, as we have attempted to show, went back as far as the eighteenth century, and it could not be solved by means of an economic calculus. Supiński noted that there was a clash between two different time scales: "This relation of international exchange, which may be profitable at one particular moment or for a number of years, cannot be eternally profitable for either of the two nations," he wrote. For in an industrial nation, it would lead to crises and class hatred, and in an agricultural nation it would bring stagnation and routine. The first part of his thesis, concerning the influence of exchange on the condition of an industrial nation, seems naive, but the second part was by no means ingenuous. Supiński did not restrict himself to economic evaluations of the conditions of international exchange; he took a lively interest in the influence of the structure of this exchange on the state of civilization in the Polish lands. Only in such an expanded perspective did the free trade dogma lose its power of conviction; since technical expertise, accumulated knowledge and labor contribute so little to the exports of agricultural countries—countries, moreover, where agriculture is on a low level—then the most obvious conclusion is that "to prepare . . . agricultural produce and raw materials in order to supply them to foreign markets and manufactures is the task of half savage peoples and slaves."[88]

Industrialization is, then, a necessity—not as an aim in itself, but as a catalyst for cultural development, and not for just one class, but for the country as a whole. While this sounds fine in theory, the question remains as to the kind of industrialization needed. Here, once again, we find the old idea of "naturalness," transformed into a program of selective development. It would be against the order of nature to grow tropical plants in the north; similarly, "the adoption of industries and the establishment of manufacturing enterprises which flower somewhere else but which are not suitable to the people and the country, turns into an effort . . . to push against the order of the human world."[89]

Supiński sternly warned his compatriots of the dangers of investment fever, and of hastily launching themselves into ventures the results of which could hamper, rather than accelerate, "natural development." He based his argument on the realistic assumption that capital and intellectual resources were very limited. "So, since great works can be produced only with great resources, to attempt great things when the capabilities of the nation are so limited is to risk wasting them; . . . or at least it means the omission of intermediate links without which there is no whole and no success. To import costly foreign industries before developing the kind of industry which is suitable to the local climate, to the education and needs of the local population, and to draw capital away from agriculture in a poor agricultural country in order to build railways while there are not enough surfaced roads or people to travel on them—this is to destroy rather than to build up the meager national resources; this is to empty one's own home in order to open its door to strangers."[90]

The matter of basic importance, according to Supiński, was therefore "the choice of the details towards which the common endeavor should be directed," that is, the defining of national priorities in production. On this point the author of *The Polish School* clearly departs from the theories of the gentry economists since he did not consider the hierarchy of needs from the point of view of agricultural producers, but accorded priority to the most elementary needs of the masses, that is, to the production of cheap linen and cloth, hides, iron, simple implements and soap. It was only later that the developing industrial sector was to serve more refined needs, finally stimulating needs that had not yet appeared.

A similar gradation is applied to the forms of industrial production: considering the meager resources available, these should tie down the smallest amount of capital possible, and at the same time should be spread throughout the country as a whole. For this reason, no one should scorn peasant cottage industries which may act as a powerful stimulus to prosperity. Great investments, on the contrary, do not awaken but "stifle the spirit of real industry, which in the natural state of things should develop in the numerous small manufacturing works which are a hundred times more useful to the country than railways."[91]

Supiński's attitude to the building of railways, based on his observations in Austrian Galicia, is significant. There is no trace here of the kind of opposition to the new form of transport which was typical of the traditionalists. Supiński has nothing against it, apart from the fact that it consumes enormous resources and thus drains the national market of capital. If foreign capital appeared for the building of railways, that was fine. In fact, the inflow of foreign capital and foreign specialists was a welcome thing because it would enliven local production and strengthen the nation. This was "knowledge and work accumulated not by us but for us," that is, "a service offered by powerful peoples to weak peoples, and which weaker peoples sometimes reject because of deeply rooted prejudices, misguided patriotism, and ignorance of the laws which govern society." Using foreign resources was, in fact, a temporary necessity, as manufacturing enterprises established by strangers would gradually pass into local hands since "the local capital and local technical skills will form a blend with them."[92]

This summary sketch of Supiński's argument leads inevitably to the question of how all the "shoulds" and "musts" were supposed to become a reality? The question represents an *experimentum crucis* for every liberal who wants to provide a program for the future. Indeed, Supiński's reply was hesitant. As a liberal, he distrusted governments, and as a Pole he was particularly suspicious of the governments of the partitioning powers. His liberal mind optimistically clutched at the thought that eventually, one way or another, free enterprise would steer the country's development onto the most desirable social course: "When national resources are not channeled into artificial courses by the government or by the people who influence public judgment without troubling to familiarize themselves with the axioms of social economy, these resources will move of their own momentum, will not deviate from the natural road, and will be found to answer the people's needs."[93]

This hope rested on the tacitly adopted assumption that the hierarchy of civilizational needs established by the economist would be mirrored in the structure of effective demand; the division of industry into branches and its geographical distribution would in turn adapt itself to this demand. If this were true, then what was "natural" in the sense of a socially desirable norm would also become "natural" in the sense of a real process. Supiński did not define this transition, nor did he formulate this assumption clearly, but his writings seem to indicate that he regarded it as obvious. What hc was not certain about was whether the small-scale industrialization he envisaged could take place in view of the pressure of foreign competition. Finally, like many economists before him, he admitted that a nation which wanted to "shed its torpor" had, for a short time at least, to relinquish the general principle of free international exchange and provide a "shield" and a "guarantee" for its fledgling manufacturing industries, as well as "internal protection" by facilitating transport, training young people, setting up banks and establishing government store-houses in case "the market becomes blocked."[94]

In spite of all this, state protectionism is of secondary significance in Supiński's program, and he is rather coy about the whole matter of intervention. He definitely attached more importance to the economic education of society, which he saw as creating the motivation for individual forms of activity in a way that was in agreement with general national aims—aims which were neither too great, nor too small. "Medium is beautiful," could have been his comment as he considered how to narrow the chasm between Polish poverty and the visions of the industrialists. His own wording is slightly different: "Indeed, by hedging the earth with chimney-stacks which reach to the heavens and harnessing the local people to machines . . . we turn the nation into one huge manufacturing works. . . but by restricting oneself to raw materials, living without industry in this century that is based upon industry, we deliberately dry up our vital forces and proceed towards annihilation. . . . Where does true and durable prosperity rest? In diversification and variegation."[95]

He then proceeds to paint a picture of his own utopia in which marshes and rocks turn into fertile fields as in the Netherlands or Switzerland, the earth becomes "one beautiful garden," everywhere houses are comfortable and full of light, clothes are clean; there is a school in every village as in Denmark, and books in every house; village women, in all their finery, go to dances in the town, as in Tuscany; the towns are populous, the fields are irrigated by canals as in England; there are railways and telegraphic services; every bricklayer knows the rudiments of the theory of building; every young person from the country finishes primary school; every young person from the towns finishes secondary technical school, and the children of the gentry are all university graduates.[96] This was a middle-distance vision, and it was to be implemented by a middle estate, which would be formed in the countryside by a confluence of the more affluent and better educated part of the peasantry and the middle and petty gentry, and in the towns by a harmonious association of capital and labor: that is, by allowing the workers to have a share in the profits, and later by allowing them to enter into partnerships with the factory owners.[97]

Life, however, went on its own way, ignoring both the prognoses and warnings of the moderate economists, and the bold dreams of the visionaries. Twenty years after the appearance of the first volume of *The Polish School*, Supiński's longing for a "prehistoric idyll" would be ridiculed by a young Marxist, Stanisław Krusiński who, armed with a new theory of development, knew that the individualistic economy "must of necessity go through the purgatory of capitalism before it enters the heaven of solidarity and fraternity."[98]

In defense of the Polish economists of the period before peasant enfranchisement one can only say that they were strangers to eschatological problems: they did not seek to get to heaven by shortcuts, and even less so by way of purgatory. On earth, and only on earth, did they seek ways and means of making the life of the destitute country and its inhabitants more dignified and prosperous. Compared to the appearance of factory towns in the Kingdom or the destitution of Galician villages, their modest visions were undoubtedly "idyllic." But were they really "prehistoric?" Denmark, the Netherlands and Switzerland were all in Europe and used the same calendar as everywhere else. Only their livestock, their houses and everyday life were different.

Notes to Chapter 2

1. Józef Wybicki, *Listy patriotyczne* (Wrocław, 1955), pp. 144–8, 199.

2. S. Staszic, *Pisma filozoficzne i społeczne*, vol. 1 (Warsaw, 1954), p. 112.

3. See K. Zienkowska, *Jacek Jezierski kasztelan łukowski* (Warsaw, 1963), pp. 222–4, 237–40.

4. *Pamiętnik Historyczno-Polityczny*, 1786, 1, p. 61.

5. *Volumina Legum*, vol. 9, p. 180.

6. Zienkowska, *Jacek Jezierski*, pp. 180–1.

7. *Pamiętnik Historyczno-Polityczny*, 1784, 12, p. 1155.

8. Staszic, *Pisma filozoficzne i społeczne*, vol. 1, p. 74.

9. J. Woleński, J. Michalski, E. Rostworowski (eds.), *Materiały do dziejów Sejmu Czteroletniego*, vol. 1 (Wrocław, 1955), p. 320.

10. *Dziennik Handlowy*, 1786, 4, p. 165; 7–8, pp. 378–80; 1787, 5, p. 273; 10–11, pp. 624–35.

11. J. F. Nax, *Wybór pism* (Warsaw, 1956), pp. 203–4.

12. *Dziennik Handlowy*, 1786, 1–3, p. 48.

13. J. F. Nax, *Wybór pism*, p. 73.

14. Ibid., pp. 153–4.

15. Wybicki, *Utwory dramatyczne* (Warsaw, 1963), especially pp. 378–83, 437–8.

16. W. Surowiecki, *Wybór pism* (Warsaw, 1957), pp. 39–40.

17. Ibid., pp. 54, 68, 245 et al.

18. The Commission for National Education, set up by the Seym in 1773, was put in control of the schools previously run by the Jesuit Order (dissolved by the pope), and during the twenty years of its activity reformed and modernized the whole system of education of the Polish–Lithuanian Commonwealth in the spirit of the Enlightenment.

19. Surowiecki, *Wybór pism*, pp. 62, 132–6.

20. Ibid., pp. 57–8, 127, 219.

21. Ibid., pp. 116–17.

22. Ibid., pp. 45, 75–6, 145.

23. Ibid., pp. 108, 111, 124–5, 146.

24. Ibid., pp. 103–4.

25. Ibid., pp. 74, 81, 83, 115, 138.

26. Ibid., pp. 98–9.

27. Ibid., p. 338.

28. Ibid., pp. 342–3.

29. Ibid., pp. 53, 140–41.

30. Ibid., pp. 37, 220.

31. J.-B. Say, *Traité d'économie politique* (Paris: Calmann–Lévy, 1972).

32. H. Stroynowski, *Nauka prawa przyrodzonego, politycznego, ekonomiki polityczney i prawa narodów* (3rd ed.: Wilno, 1805), pp. 193–4.

33. A. Smith, *An Inquiry into the Nature and Causes of the Wealth of Nations*, ed. R. H. Campbell and A. S. Skinner, vol. 1 (Oxford: Clarendon Press, 1979), p. 377.

34. Ibid., p. 380.

35. Ibid., pp. 408–10.

36. Ibid., pp. 422–3.

37. Ibid., vol. 2, p. 687.

38. Ibid., vol. 2, p. 687.

39. D. Ricardo, *On the Principles of Political Economy and Taxation* (2nd ed.: London, 1819), p. 157.

40. W. Stroynowski, *Ekonomika powszechna kraiowa narodów* (Warsaw, 1816), p. 8.

41. Ibid., pp. 75–6.

42. Ibid., p. 370.

43. J. C. L. Simonde de Sismondi, *Nouveau principes d'économie politique* (3ème ed.: Genève–Paris, 1951), vol. 2, p. 193.

44. Ibid., p. 232.

45. Ibid., vol. 1, pp. 332–3.

46. Ibid., vol. 1, p. 300; vol. 2, p. 219.

47. Ibid., vol. 1, p. 26.

48. Ibid., p. 87.

49. Ibid., p. 329.

50. Ibid., vol. 2, p. 289.

51. D. Krysiński, *Wybór pism* (Warsaw, 1956), p. 105.

52. See F. Skarbek, *Elementarne zasady gospodarstwa narodowego*, vol. 2 (Warsaw, 1931), appendix, pp. 215–16.

100   IMAGES OF THE FUTURE

53. F. Skarbek, *Pisma pomniejsze*, vol. 2 (Warsaw, 1937), p. 89.
54. Ibid., vol. 1 (Warsaw, 1936), p. 363.
55. Krysiński, *Wybór pism*, pp. 30–31, 106–7.
56. Franciszek Ksawery Drucki-Lubecki (1778–1846), minister of the treasury in the Polish Kingdom in 1822–30; in this capacity, he initiated a system of protection and government subsidies for private industrial companies and developed a large-scale program of direct state investment in mining and metallurgy.
57. Skarbek, *Pisma pomniejsze*, vol. 1, p. xviii.
58. Ibid., pp. 172–3 (the quotation comes from a German article entitled "On circulation of money and its causes," translated and edited by Skarbek).
59. F. Skarbek, *Ogólne zasady nauki gospodarstwa narodowego*, ed. W. Szubert, 2 vols. (Warsaw, 1955).
60. Ibid., vol. 2, p. 78.
61. Krysiński, *Wybór pism*, pp. 8–9.
62. Ibid., p. 7.
63. Ibid., p. 68.
64. Skarbek, *Pisma pomniejsze*, vol. 1, pp. 516–17.
65. *Korespondencja Lubeckiego z ministrami sekretarzami stanu*, ed. F. Smolka, vol. 4 (Kraków, 1909), letter no. 205 of 3 December 1824.
66. Quoted after F. Smolka, *Polityka Lubeckiego przed powstaniem listopadowym*, vol. 1 (Kraków, 1907), p. 193.
67. Ibid., pp. 203–4.
68. Skarbek, *Ogólne zasady*, vol. 2, pp. 78, 88–9.
69. Ibid., p. 83.
70. Skarbek, *Pisma pomniejsze*, vol. 1, p. 317.
71. Skarbek, *Ogólne zasady*, vol. 2, pp. 209–10.
72. Krysiński, *Wybór pism*, pp. 147–8.
73. M. Mochnacki, *Powstanie narodu polskiego w roku 1830 i 1831*, vol. 1 (Warsaw, 1984), pp. 179–81.
74. J. L. Żukowski, *O panszczyźnie* (Warsaw 1830), pp. 146–7.
75. Skarbek, *Pisma pomniejsze*, vol. 1, p. 148.
76. Skarbek, *Ogólne zasady*, vol. 2, pp. 89–90.
77. Skarbek, *Pisma pomniejsze*, vol. 2, p. 30.
78. Ibid., pp. 14–17.
79. *Roczniki Gospodarstwa Krajowego*, published in 1842–1864 by a company representing an influential group of the affluent gentry in the Kingdom, headed by Count Andrzej Zamoyski. The journal combined mildly conservative social views with economic liberalism, and promoted economic and technical knowledge and modern methods of husbandry.
80. *Roczniki Gospodarstwa Krajowego*, vol. 16 (1850), pp. 141, 143.
81. F. S. Dmochowski, *Obecne kwestye gospodarcze i przemysłowe* (Warsaw, 1858), p. 148.
82. Apollo Nałęcz Korzeniowski (1820–1869), a poet, playwright and, in 1861, a radical national conspirator, arrested and deported to Siberia; the father of Joseph Conrad.
83. *Gazeta Codzienna* 1860, no. 225.
84. Ibid., nos. 264–266.

85. Józef Supiński (1804–1893), regarded as the first Polish sociologist and forerunner of Polish positivism; after the defeat of the November Rising he emigrated to France, and in 1844 settled in Lwów, the capital of Galicia.

86. J. Supiński, *Pisma*, vol. 4 (Warsaw, 1883), p. 60.

87. Ibid., vol. 2, pp. 203, 239, 315–16, 321–3, 334, 339–41.

88. Ibid., pp. 342–3, 349.

89. Ibid., p. 214.

90. Ibid., pp. 140–41.

91. Ibid., pp. 168–9.

92. Ibid., pp. 169–72, 344.

93. Ibid., p. 141.

94. Ibid., p. 352.

95. Ibid., p. 343.

96. Ibid., pp. 316–17.

97. Ibid., pp. 288–9; also vol. 3, pp. 185, 223.

98. S. Krusiński, *Pisma zebrane* (Warsaw, 1958), pp. 28, 48.

CHAPTER 3

The Gospel and Economy

The new civilization was feared because it seemed to threaten the autonomy of the nation's culture and its feelings of self-respect, impaired as they were as a result of the partitions. Nor was this the worst of evils since, after all, the gifts of the West could be sifted and given a Polish form before adoption. As discussed in the previous chapters, much thought was devoted to such ideas.

The excessively fast pace of industrial development was feared because it seemed to threaten the equilibrium of the national economy, and above all, because the specter of the unemployed proletariat lurked behind such development. But this fear could also be dismissed, since there was still the hope that in an agricultural country the development process would take a safe direction and proceed at a moderate pace, and that, as a result, the side effects could be avoided. Again, as has been shown above, a considerable amount of thought was devoted to this subject.

And what if the new civilization was the work of pagan forces? If it did not involve building but destroying? If it did not lead to progress but into an abyss? If it was against Christ, against morality, against everything which was righteous and holy? If this was the case, then how could this new civilization possibly be adopted or even recognized? Would this not be to invite doom?

Anxieties of this sort had long been accumulating. They took root not in nations jealous of their more developed neighbors but, on the contrary, in the main centers of change; what is more, such ideas germinated in the minds of those who were the most *civilisés* of their contemporaries. Throughout the entire Enlightenment era, the optimistic philosophy of rationalism and progress was accompanied by a current of skeptical reflection. The author of *The Fable of the Bees* was well aware that moral perfection was a grand illusion of the human mind, since progress in the fields of science, industry and social organization was by no means compatible with the preservation of moral purity. Purity does not create anything. Universal well-being is born out of the evil instincts of human nature. Therefore, Mandeville and Hobbes, discarding all sentiment, acquiesced to a dynamic of progress which had no pretense to virtue,[1] although their doctrine failed to attract many followers. Unfortunately, not everyone is fond of moral paradoxes.

This issue had been echoing throughout Europe ever since the "citizen of Geneva," on his way to Vincennes, experienced a sudden illumination and realized that the exertions of the philosophical mind stifle the natural disposition of the human heart. In his famous discourses, Jean Jacques Rousseau portrayed culture as a source of suffering and perplexity. The formation of society was the original sin of humanity. Human beings gained possessions but lost freedom. They succumbed to laws and lost the inborn gift of compassion. In passing from the state of savagery to the civilized state, they acquired the knowledge of good and evil, and used this knowledge to harm one another. The source of all their calamities is their inborn, almost unrestricted faculty for self-improvement; "this faculty, which, successively producing in different ages man's discoveries and his errors, his vices and his virtues, makes him at length a tyrant both over himself and over nature."[2] This faculty turns into idle curiosity, pride and an urge to excel over others, and this urge is the strongest motivating force behind knowledge and power.

Rousseau's indictment of civilization was so passionate and total that the moral rhetoric of the following two centuries could hardly add anything new to it: in fact, Rousseauist ideas are still being developed and transformed by countercultural movements and amateurish existentialists. Above all, according to Rousseau, human beings lost their own authenticity: "social man lives constantly outside himself, and only knows how to live in the opinion of others, so that he seems to receive the consciousness of his own existence merely from the judgment of others concerning him." In the eyes of the thinker, society is merely "an assembly of artificial men."[3] Civilization is a great edifice of make-believe, hypocrisy, oppressive forms, rituals and distinctions. The life of French high society under the reign of Louis XV, with its "spirit of gallantry," so detestable to Rousseau, served as a model for his condemnation, but the conclusions he reached went further and deeper. The indictment extended to everything which in the times of Turgot and the Encyclopaedists was associated with the idea of progress, or which was a side effect of this progress: that is to say, it encompassed the sciences and the arts, the state and the law, technology and medicine, wealth and luxury, slavery and marriage, life's comforts and the pollution of the natural environment, and also wars, murders, abortion, epidemics, fires and earthquakes. "When we consider, on the one hand, the immense labors of mankind, the many sciences brought to perfection, the arts invented, the powers employed, the deeps filled up, the mountains leveled, the rocks shattered, the rivers made navigable, the tracts of land cleared, the lakes emptied, the marshes drained, the enormous structures erected on land, and the teeming vessels that cover the sea; and, on the other hand, estimate with ever so little thought, the real advantages that have accrued from all these works to mankind, we cannot help being amazed at the vast disproportion there is between these things, and deploring the infatuation of man, which, to gratify his silly pride and vain self-admiration, induces him eagerly to pursue all the miseries he is capable of feeling, though beneficent nature had kindly placed them out of his way."[4]

These two early discourses by Jean Jacques Rousseau constitute, as it were, a prototype for many subsequent rebellions by intellectuals against intellectualism, by sophisticated minds against the sophistication of a culture which is capable of producing great works but completely incapable of curbing the brutality of the human world—a culture, moreover, that serves tyranny and violence by supplying them with the tools of enslavement.

Such a harsh assessment of the entire course of history, and of the process of enlightenment and socialization, seemed blatantly unfair, even absurd, and inevitably provoked dissent. It has to be admitted, however, that the fanatically extremist mind of the philosopher, who did not hesitate to point out the far-reaching consequences of his assumptions, was an important contribution to the analysis of the apparently coherent whole which the idea of civilization claimed to be. In the mid-eighteenth century, this idea was only just taking form with as yet no name of its own, and Rousseau immediately revealed its inner contradiction: "our minds have been corrupted in proportion as the arts and sciences have improved."[5]

As to the antithesis to this schizoid state among civilized peoples, Rousseau's answer is fairly ambiguous. He suggests as many as three different sets of values, all of them located in a half-historical, half-mythical past, and all of them having only one feature in common, namely, that in the philosopher's reconstruction they are based on a pre-reflective, unintellectual understanding of the moral imperative. Apart from that, they seem virtually incompatible. The first model was, of course, the savage state, the state of the ancient Germans and Scythians: "a just mean between the indolence of the primitive state and the petulant activity of our egoism." This state, innocent and blissful as it was, was the real youth of the world and should never have ended: "all subsequent advances have been apparently so many steps towards the perfection of the individual, but in reality towards the decrepitude of the species."[6]

The second model was Rousseau's beloved Sparta, the most virtuous, hardy and robust nation, a people who banished all artists and those who meddled in the sciences, thus protecting itself from the sophistication and depravity of Athenian culture.

The third model, which is of particular interest to us, was the Gospel, a canon, one might say, very remote from the customs of both the Scythians and the Lacedaemonians.

The religion espoused by the learned Rousseau was the faith and love of the unschooled heart. The simplicity of the Gospels and the apostles' faith was juxtaposed, not for the first, nor for the last time, with the sophistry of theologians and philosophers. The beginning of all the evils of heresy, schisms, religious wars and persecution was scholasticism, the hubris of those ecclesiastics "who were the first to dare touch the ark so that they might prop up with their poor knowledge the edifice supported by God's hand . . . and who captured Christ's teachings in syllogisms." The result was that in the enlightened age the place of saints was taken by casuists: "knowledge is spreading but faith is disappearing; . . . we have all become theologians, but we have stopped being Christians." According to Rousseau, a peasant can understand and worship God better than a philosopher who flatters himself that he has fathomed God's mystery. The Gospel is the only book of faith that a Christian needs, and it should be preached *non aristotelico more, sed piscatorio*, in the way it was preached by its first defenders.[7]

The gardens of blissful simplicity and human ignorance may have varied, but the development of man's mental faculties was always depicted as a voluntary departure from the paradise of innocence and a descent into the inferno of civilization. From here there could be no return; once lost, innocence cannot be retrieved; the only means of escape was to withdraw from the world or else to create a new community of free, equal, honest people amidst the anguish of the false world, by changing the institutions of this world and making use of its tools. However, we are not interested here in Rousseau's paths to freedom. Just as we quoted the physiocrats and Smith, so now we invoke Rousseau only in order to trace the beginnings of one path which, from then on, would weave its way across countries and epochs, right up to the present day—and beyond.

Rousseau saw mankind's progress as a tragedy in which evil and good were inseparable: they arose from one and the same source and were the outward manifestations of the same process—"man, embroiled in the process of his own socialization, reveals both his greatness and his weakness at once, fulfilling his calling and experiencing his own downfall."[8] This dual vision of human history, in the course of which values become split, is only gradually exposed in the philosopher's successive works. Meanwhile, the contemporary readers of *A Discourse on the Arts and Sciences* and *A Discourse on the Origin of Inequality* interpreted them, justifiably, as a grandiloquent indictment of, and lament on, the progress of the Enlightenment. Such an interpretation was music to the ears of those people—and they are to be found in every epoch—who bemoaned the downfall of morals. Not to be outdone, the defenders of progress counterattacked, men such as the dethroned Polish king, Stanislaus Leszczyński, who sang the praises of "those happy ages when the sciences spread the spirit of order and justice all over the earth."[9] From then on, all over Europe, countless paeans would extol the century of Enlightenment—and just as many satires would denounce it. The gloomy shadow of doubt would never leave the side of the light of Reason, and the historic progress of the human spirit would produce its own Condorcets and Chateaubriands at the same time.

In Poland, Krasicki's[10] moral axiology was akin to Rousseau's vision of a depraved world. Unlike the representatives of the main stream of philosophical criticism during the Enlightenment, this excellent fable-writer targeted neither the tyranny of "superstition" nor feudal laws and institutions. He directed the brunt of his criticism against moral depravity in the "corrupt world" of hypocrisy, against those who, in their attempts to elevate themselves, revealed the most abominable sides of their own nature. The contemporary world was one big vanity fair. All its vices—both the detestable, such as duplicity and avarice, and the ludicrous, such as dandyism and slavish adherence to fashion—had in fact one root: egoistic individualism which released in people an insatiable taste for rivalry, a rivalry which was brutal and harsh, though camouflaged by the veneer of "politeness." There was rivalry surrounding social position, genealogy, wealth and bequests, luxury, favors at court, popularity in the salons, all that was artificial and vain—and also contest for learning. Knowledge, according to Krasicki, whenever it rises above the practical needs of everyday life and above the view of history which sees it as a collection of moral parables, is nothing more than "impudence of the mind," an expression of the same feverishness which distracts people from the practice of simple virtues in human society. Just like Rousseau, Krasicki thought that the main culprit was philosophy, or sophistry, including both scholasticism, which attempted to rationalize faith, and libertine rationalism which attempted to undermine this faith. According to Krasicki, the latter was more dangerous, since it was fashionable and triumphant: it was one more symptom of the moral crisis affecting that "allegedly enlightened" age.

Once again we see here a return to the Augustinian idea, always present in Christian culture, of a curtain screening the divine mysteries—mysteries which man should not attempt to probe since such attempts are always doomed to failure. The bane of the age were thus "pseudo-philosophers who discard revelation and base their alleged religion only on the rickety foundation of reason."[11] There was another reason why dogmas should not be probed: fear of divine justice and obedience to the teachings of the Church constituted the bond which held the human community together and linked the interests of religion with the universal well-being of mankind. The century which was to be called the philosophical age, would come to be regarded as the "most unhappy epoch of mankind," because of the skepticism of the unbelievers.[12]

The world was wicked, because people had become wicked. Thus the world could be put right in a simple way: it was enough for people to become better; for them to become better while living in a world which they made depraved and which made them depraved in turn. It was possible to weave all kinds of values into the banal fabric of moral teachings, whether religious or secular. The disenchanted moralists of the Enlightenment, who saw this age as an epoch of decline, conjured up, in thought and in their writings, all sorts of communities whose existence, they believed, was in accordance with the potentially unblemished nature of humanity. The most characteristic feature shared by all these communities, whether they were assigned to primeval forests or the antipodes of civilization, located on nonexistent isles or projected forward into the year 2440, was the lack of individual traits among their members who competed only in the practicing of virtue, and did not differ much from one another even in this respect. The inhabitants of Utopia had to be happy, and they would not be happy if they felt some unassuaged desire, especially such as could be satisfied only at the expense of others, or else by denying God. The ideal solution for the human comedy was the condition in which human desires never surpassed the available economic, technological and intellectual resources of a given community. The authors of these tales devoted their anxiety and imagination to the creation of a world free of anxiety and imagination, a world brought to a standstill by its own goodness, an isolated world which knew only the changeability of the seasons.

A morally perfect community could be based on joint ownership of goods and complete unfamiliarity with the idea of private possession, or on perfect equality of ownership, or on an ideal hierarchy of estates, on condition that everyone was satisfied with their place within the community. In the Utopian visions, a similar function was often performed by the ideal of patriarchal authority, an authority that was not tyrannical, but protective, not alienated, but personal, so that a community or nation was similar to a loving family which obediently followed its father's will. Idyllic simplicity, honest customs, "moderate wealth," and "blissful ignorance:" all these key words of the eighteenth-century sentimental utopia delineate the natural limits of freedom in an imaginary community which knew no rebellion or violence, and had no legal codes since every one of its members wanted to be what they were, to have what they had, and to know what they knew. In Krasicki's novel,[13] a young Polish nobleman makes an adventurous journey across Europe; then, while sailing round the world, he is shipwrecked and cast up on the shores of an unknown island, Nipu, where time has stopped. "Fear of novelty," the wise Xaoo explains to him, "for us outweighs any prospect of advantage, no matter how desirable. We hold the certainty of our unshakable situation higher than anything else."[14]

Mikołaj Doświadczyński has to admit that the old sage is right when he sees that the Nipuans are happy without science, technology, travel and a knowledge of foreign languages; that they are skillful, industrious and well nourished, although they have no knowledge of agronomy. This last point should be kept in mind, since, as we shall see later, agronomy recurs again and again in Polish conservative thought as a symbol of superfluous progress.

The ideal of the "unshakable situation" of peaceful societies could be modeled at will on remote isles or in the ahistoric times of "barbarity." However, this was not sufficient if one wanted to pass judgment on the situation in contemporary society, which was allegedly the result of growing moral (and often also physical) decadence over past generations. The conviction that people were more wretched than their fathers, not to mention their grandfathers and great grandfathers, is a common feature of moralistic views of the world. The metaphor of dwarves standing on the shoulders of giants appears in many ideological structures. Thus, in the moral writings of the Enlightenment period we find many variations on the ancient legend about the beautiful youth of mankind, the *aurea prima aetas,* whatever its place in history is. Various epochs were singled out as the "golden age," the time of good sowers, brave heroes, and of the true love of God and country. Krasicki's ideal periods were the age of King Casimir the Great (1333–70), or the later times of the victorious wars against Turkey. The period chosen is of little importance; the fact remains that at some point in the past the world began to deteriorate and the state no longer stood *moribus antiquis virisque.* This view does not fully reflect the actual degeneration of the political ethos of Poland: it was more an attempt to provide a setting for a myth than for real historical events. What mattered was that the model was placed in an irretrievably lost past. Such retrospection is always an instrument used to criticize the current condition of society, although, as is well known, it can serve a revolutionary cause just as well as a conservative one.

It is important to remember that Krasicki did not create an opposition between nationality and civilization, nor did he separate Poland from Europe. The protagonist of his novel is a true country gentleman, with a slight veneer of culture acquired in the salons of Warsaw and Paris; he even has some knowledge of Voltaire. But all these experiences have failed to fill the spiritual void within him. Sarmatism or Enlightenment, Poland or France, these were only different varieties of the gaudy brilliance of the world, the refinement which merely concealed arrogance and ignominy.

It is hard to return to the distant age of Virtue. It is just as difficult to improve the existing world overnight. But as early as the ancient thinkers, one comes across the notion that it is possible to hide away from this world by retiring to one's country estate. The poetically gifted bishop, the courtier of the kings of Poland and Prussia, was also aware of this truth *in abstracto*. He knew that the court was a vanity fair, that the town and the *beau monde* were breeding grounds of depravity, and that the country and home were the only place where real values were to be found.

The home represents an oasis of simplicity, of directness, and of transparency in interhuman relations. One may not be free of worries there, but one will definitely be free of envy, and of all striving for sham values. The home as a retreat from the world, and the country as a retreat from the madding crowd of rapacious civilization: this is one of the great archetypes of literature, one which has been used again and again to express the longings of people and cultures weary of their own over-refinement.

The return home symbolizes, however, something more than a promise of rest; it is also a return to the pure source of truth, virtue and happiness, to those sources which have not yet been poisoned. For this reason, home, the rural home of the country gentleman, constituted the last hope for rebirth, and a means of solving the paradox of the improvement of a depraved world by its depraved inhabitants.

The ancient stoical motif of purification by a return home, the withdrawal from the world, coincides with Rousseau's ideal of naturalness; and both have points in common with the cult of the native hearth, created by those who had yet to see the wide world and who, in fact, were not particularly eager to do so. This tradition, too, had long been present in literature and had become conventionalized. From the sixteenth century on, Polish literature abounded in accounts of the life of the honest man, and eulogies to the peaceful, joyous life of the countryside. As soon as Warsaw began to acquire a cosmopolitan air during the reign of Stanislaus Augustus, it came to represent the antithesis of this rural simplicity. It was seen in this light not only by country squires, but also in the work of comedy writers and moralists of various hues; from the magnate who treated writing as a pastime, to the man of letters who earned his living by the pen. All of them, each according to his means, were happy to take advantage of the intellectual refinement and social entertainments of the capital city, but proved equally willing to write satires and sermons paying tribute to the virtues of country life.

In the 1760s the *Monitor* published a number of eulogies on the town, as a place where young gentry swells could polish their manners, and acquire good taste and political knowledge; they were soon discontinued, however, without leaving any marked impression on the moral doctrines espoused by the gentry. For the more the gentry were attracted by the capital city, whether it was for diversion, to attend a Seym session, or to do business, the more they felt obliged to express their contempt for Warsaw society, and the more they yearned for their country retreats. In the end, the whole of the Enlightenment subscribed to this tradition, sanctifying it in verse and in prose. Contempt for the town, especially for the capital city, was a commonplace in European literature,[15] and Polish moral writings were no exception.

Jerzy Michalski has compiled a whole anthology of examples of this stereotype of Warsaw, where it is claimed that the capital is dominated by intrigues, political cabals, greed, shamelessness, debauchery, falsehood, hypocrisy, godlessness, vanity, luxury and foreignness: that is, everything which is opposed to nature. Country life, on the contrary, is in keeping with nature because it is simple, honest, free, decent, and modest; it is in the country that the faithfulness and sensitivity of the heart have been best preserved. "Rousseau's anti-urban statements, which facilitated this evolution, fell on fertile soil, because they pandered to time-honored beliefs."[16] At the same time, Michalski repeatedly states that it is difficult in these works to determine where originality ends and imitation begins, in other words, where the borderline lies between authentic conviction and the literary conventions represented by the parable and the pastoral genre. But does one not fall into the same trap as Rousseau by making such remarks? For one assumes then that such a borderline actually exists, and that it is possible to differentiate between that which is natural and that which is artificial; to separate the true needs of the human heart and natural wisdom from notions and feelings which are enfettered by cultural conventions.

Political radicals of that epoch, such as Jakub Jasiński[17] and Franciszek Salezy Jezierski,[18] also succumbed to the dictates of convention. This was an astonishing paradox: a militant spokesman for the emancipation of the towns joining the ranks of the anti-urban preachers. But the paradox is only an apparent one, since strident criticism was not aimed at the town of the burghers, craftsmen or merchants, but at libertine Warsaw, with its swaggering and dandified airs, and its abundance of temptations for the pockets of the newly arrived gentry. Similarly, the numerous laments and satires on impudent "philosophy" were not directed against real scholarship or educational reform, but against the salons where the illuminati flaunted their Voltairean ideas. In any case, in the moral writings of the Enlightenment the town is the abode of laziness, while the country represents work—with the divine blessing. The moralists extolled the gentleman squire (provided he lived in the village and looked after his estate) as a man content with his modest wealth and his knowledge gleaned from life rather than books, and who is ready to serve his country when the need arose, but is virtually uninterested in the "wide world" beyond the village.

After the partitions, however, what had been perhaps merely a literary conceit or a philosophical consolation for the loss of hope of a career in the wider world became a refuge for those threatened by the new order. The gentry demesne, safe until then, was put in a critical situation. Austrian and Prussian officials interfered in the patriarchal relationship between the lord and his peasants. After the Duchy of Warsaw was formed, the introduction of the Napoleonic Code and the legal emancipation of the peasants (1807) endangered the time-honored links of personal dependence and brought the threat of their replacement by money relations, relations based on calculation. The Warsaw papers began to write about the equality of the estates and about the principles of "rational husbandry."

The whitewashed manor house, engulfed on all sides by the waves of change, had a mission to endure and to safeguard what had not yet been changed: religion, peasant serf labor and tradition. Its task was to protect these ideals from the partitioning powers and from things foreign, from despotism, godlessness and liberal innovations, from confiscations, creditors, inspections and revolutions. If every change brought a threat to values, if the sequence of tradition was broken outside the squire's village, then the only consistent reaction was to isolate oneself and remain in isolation. It was easier to maintain this isolation in the lands formally incorporated into the Russian Empire or in Eastern Galicia than in the Congress Kingdom or the Poznań region. However, even in the latter regions the syndrome of defensive, passive traditionalism revealed immense powers of survival. Its ideological credo is to be found in novels, pastoral poems, accounts of daily life and diaries rather then in social discourse. It could not produce a coherent doctrine because by the nature of things it was anti-doctrinal, habitual and unrefined: it expressed the intellectual horizon of those people who, for spiritual nourishment, were content with almanacs, heraldries and Sunday sermons.

However, the gentry manor house created something which was much more important and durable than a doctrine: it created a collection of sacred values, a catalogue of native virtues on which Polish literature and ideological camps of various hues would draw throughout the period of foreign domination. The pivotal value of this system was the pastoral ideal: the profound conviction that the country air had the natural property of conserving physical and moral health, serenity and simplicity of customs, respect for one's parents, and love of God and fatherland. The idealization of country life gained a new function: the ownership of land no longer brought political privileges, but it was generally believed that this institution was the last retreat of nationality. The pastoral way of life, free of all cold calculation and reckoning, was an inborn characteristic of Poles and of Slavs in general. The landed estate was something more than a farm: it was the cradle of gentry values, the repository of all things Polish and of faith. Serf labor was not exploitation, but a natural relationship involving patriarchal sovereignty and protection, a bond of mutual need, love and confidence; if it sometimes left room for abuse, this was tempered by the inborn serenity of the Polish character.

This was a system of values which was absolutely immobile; there was no room in it for evolution. It was coherent and closed, and could only be threatened from outside. Thus, every departure from this pattern seemed to herald decline. This included agronomy:

"Since agriculture is man's general state
It cannot change its course through inventions
. . .
Everywhere one finds flails, forks, rakes, ploughs and harrows
All of them marked with the stigma of ancient times."[19]

As well as this unlearned traditionalism of the gentry, there was also the more self-conscious conservatism of philosophers, bishops, aristocrats and counselors of state. This conservatism did not deny its manor house provincial roots; on the contrary, it often emphasized them. Such was the case when the landowners from the Galician departments of the Duchy of Warsaw organized a protest against the Napoleonic Code and the centralized, French style of government administration in order to defend old Polish laws and traditions. Later on, too, it was not uncommon for highly philosophical and refined minds to take the same stance, idealizing rude simplicity, ignorance and serf labor. We can observe here one of the numerous paradoxes in which the conservative idea was to become caught up whenever it reached the level of thought or became a system of beliefs, rather than remaining a simple defensive reflex.

The perfect embodiment of the paradoxes of the intellectual logic of conservatism can be seen in Józef Kalasanty Szaniawski, the director of education and censorship in the Congress Kingdom. It would be difficult to find anyone more thoroughly educated, better read and more independent in his thinking, and at the same time more fanatical in his attempts to defend young people against the dangers of education, reading and independent thought. Who better than a man who had himself experienced in his youth the poison of Jacobinism could find the ideological antidote for it? Who could provide more powerful arguments against foreign influence than those found in French and German books?

However, Szaniawski was an exception to the rule in that his gradually growing dislike of all progress was not due to any enthusiasm for rural life. He was a philosopher and civil servant in the Congress Kingdom—a rare combination—and these two roles were closely intertwined in his mind. As a philosopher, he tried to provide a justification for a bureaucratic conservatism in which the government and the administration, and not the manor house and the demesne, became the foundation of the social order, nationality, and authority.

For authority was the key, indispensable principle of the conservative view of the world, the principle that united all varieties of this ideology. Reforms were regarded as admissible if they were an expression of the will of protective authority and if they did not destroy the established hierarchical order of the world. All the squire in his ancestral village had to do was to ensure that the authority of the father over his family and of the lord over his peasant remained intact. Above the squire, there was only God. The conservative politicians who entered the public arena and took upon themselves the responsibility for the fate of the nation had to provide the missing rungs of the hierarchy between the squire and God.

The ideal national society which the conservatives discovered in the past and which they wanted to rescue or restore was a union of estates and corporations: its elements were firmly joined together by the principle of mutual obligations, not divided by conflicting interests. "Every entity," Szaniawski wrote, "must be organic, and the perfect organism must rely on an appropriate gradation." If this was the case, there was an obligation to respect not only the separate spirit and institutions of every nation, but also, within every nation, "the individuality of social divisions and classes."[20]

The breaking away of both classes and individuals from their hereditary position in the social hierarchy had to be regarded as a disruptive and disorganizing factor. Following the short-lived liberal leanings of Alexander I, the Polish conservatives regained their former influence on the political level in around 1820. Their social doctrine consisted in the defense, and wherever possible the restitution, of the rights of the estates. In the constitutional period, the conservative–clerical faction effectively opposed all attempts at the division of church and state, and succeeded in revising some clauses of the Napoleonic Code, especially in the field of marital regulations. It also managed to prevent various middle-of-the-road draft reforms of the agrarian system, and blocked the granting of civil rights to the Jews. It found the broadest scope for its activities in the area of education. The conservative line on educational policy was formulated by Bishop Adam Prażmowski in the following words: "If the peacefulness of society, and its durable and propitious existence depend on the fact of its division into classes, and if each of the classes is satisfied with its situation and performs its obligations within this situation, one ought not to cause ferment by implementing an erroneous educational system, and any system which educates people beyond their position in life is erroneous."[21]

In other words, "the peacefulness of society" could still be ensured provided the onslaught of socially destructive forces was checked. There are striking differences between the diagnoses of Polish conservatives living in the age of the Holy Alliance and the bitter judgments passed by moralists of the era of Stanislaus Augustus. The latter felt themselves to be submerged in a world of falsehood in which almost nothing, save the virtues of home life, was worth preserving, and the only consolation was faith in the healing powers offered by a return to bygone innocence. The writers of the later epoch, who could draw on the whole experience of the revolutionary period, saw, when peace was regained, that not everything had been lost, nor had the maggots of despondency eaten away the healthy stem of national consciousness. The Catholic faith and its mainstay, the church, had survived and had even become stronger, the home had survived, even Poland still more or less existed, and in spite of the decrees and new codes the organic tissue of society was still intact. And the nation's elite had survived, and was still capable of assuming leadership in the work of defending the unchangeable values of the spirit and of life.

The situation was not hopeless: the menace had been exteriorized, and now revealed itself under the guise of three great upheavals on the philosophical, political and industrial level—upheavals which all sprang from the same poisoned well of "materialism."

However, the philosophical upheaval had already lost its infectious vigor. The age of conceited Reason had come to an end. The political and social upheavals which threatened the destruction of all thrones and privileges and the profanation of all that was held sacred, also seemed to have died down. Only one upheaval, the technological, industrial and commercial revolution, had continued to spread without let or hindrance, allowing new arrivistes and new classes to advance, and awakening new desires and new passions. The semantic field of the word "civilization" came to encompass this new change in society. Under the old order, and even under Napoleon, the essence of civilization was represented by the literary salons of Paris, refined taste, polished manners, elegant living and sparkling intellect, and a facility for passing judgments on all matters. Beginning with the Restoration period in France, other symbols and associations came very much to the fore: machines, stock markets, capital, new world powers and new dictators of fashion. The consequences of this shift in emphasis were by no means trifling: this "civilization," which Joseph de Maistre still regarded as the final phase of the centuries-long decline of mankind, suddenly entered a youthful, triumphant phase.

This, of course, did not mean that one had to like it. Wherever the expansion of the capitalist methods of production and urban lifestyle penetrated, it had, and still has, its enthusiasts and its enemies. As discussed, one of the sources of hostility in countries colonized by industry was the desire to defend the national identity, tradition and customs. But this was not the whole story. After all, even in the metropolises of the West there was no lack of people who, for various reasons, refused to accept the new rules of the economic game and the new (or was it really so new?) ethical code. Once this stance had been adopted, the key object of thought, first in Europe and then beyond, was no longer the criticism of urban culture, but of bourgeois culture. The liberals and the utilitarians were convinced that the new civilization, by breaking the fetters of feudal slavery and increasing the national wealth, had created more favorable circumstances than ever before for the uniting of individual and social aims. Now a dissenting voice was heard, namely, the view that this civilization, which had given its blessing to economic and political activity motivated by egoism, would lead to social anarchy, the triumph of violence, and the deterioration of Christian brotherhood among people and among nations. As if the previous centuries had not known avarice and profit, only universal love!

This over-generalized criticism of the bourgeois civilization of the West often erupted into emotional invective, expressing itself by means of a fairly limited repertoire of stereotyped epithets which was, in principle, the same the world over, from England to Russia. It was claimed that this civilization was "artificial," "degenerate," "contaminated," "false," "haggling," "rationalized," "materialistic," "egoistic," "anarchic," and "soulless." These are all commonplaces found during this epoch, including in Polish writing.

The dislike of civilization was now directed against economic theory. This may seem strange, as if one were to blame meteorologists for bad weather. But there was some sense in it. In the eighteenth century and frequently in later periods as well, philosophy, especially Voltairean philosophy, was generally held responsible for the deterioration of customs and mores. There was a fairly general conviction that books shape the ways in which people think and act, including those people who do not read them. This belief was even held by the traditionalists and the prophets of downfall, and it is perhaps this belief in the power of the word that more than anything else reveals the triumph of the Enlightenment. This triumph was rather ironical since it consisted of faith in the destructive power of the word, in the demoralizing influence of theory on life. Philosophers had their share of responsibility in this since their whole program was based on didacticism, aiming to change the world by persuasion; and although the age of mass culture and propaganda had not yet arrived, nevertheless, in enlightened spheres, they did indeed have the status of dictators of intellectual fashion.

The situation of political economy had been similar ever since it started competing with philosophy. Like the philosophers, the economists could not really make up their minds whether they wanted to explain relations as they were or create a moral-political axiology and, based on this, a normative science of reasonable conduct—a science which would be useful not only for rulers but also for individuals. A sizable part of the literature on economics was in fact made up of handbooks offering advice, while the remainder were for the most part theoretical models for the kind of capitalism that could exist if everybody behaved rationally. And since every general assumption of rationality introduced some arbitrary value judgments, it was not completely baseless to charge the economists with promoting new moral principles. Of course it does not follow from this that Adam Smith and his followers created capitalism with all its particular rules of play—a claim made by some critics of economics (economics in general, rather than any definite theoretical system) in the first half of the nineteenth century.

When Fryderyk Skarbek published his translation of Ganilh's *Economic Dictionary* in Warsaw in 1829, adding to it extensive appendices and an introduction, he was violently attacked by Feliks Bentkowski, the critic, bibliographer and editor of *Pamiętnik Warszawski*: "It seems to me that the principles proposed by the author . . . undermine the social union, debase people by turning them into simple calculating machines, and uproot the principles of morality and good manners which, after all, mean something in a social community and are said to be a prerequisite for the existence of nations." Moreover, he argued, by suggesting to people and nations that "wealth" or a "good life" were what they should aspire to, "today's political economy" encouraged selfishness, avarice, and dishonesty, destroying nobility and the disinterested practicing of the arts. Money, he said, should be a means, not an end.[22]

Skarbek's response to this attack was no less acrimonious: "[My opponent] regards wealth as an abundance of money, and refers to aspirations towards a good life as greed and self-interest; in order to make me an easier target, he omits all references to the word *civilization* in my reasoning. ... he never mentioned that I regard civilization as an inseparable accompaniment to wealth."[23] He goes on to explain that human beings are capable of having more than one aim. He reacted indignantly to the accusation that the kind of education which taught that work and thriftiness were ways of improving one's lot could undermine morality and the principles of social life. Turning this charge against the enemies of economics, he insinuated that they yearned for a return to the days when the people had lived in servitude, poverty and backwardness, breaking their backs to keep their masters in the luxury to which they were accustomed.

This dispute may be regarded as a blueprint for future discussions, for it was to recur again and again with only slight modifications. The enemies of economic theory saw it as a trivial and amoral apology for moneygrubbing, while its defenders urged respect for the material aims of labor, adding at the same time that they were only describing people and their behavior, in their role as producers, middlemen and consumers of goods, which after all did not exhaust the long list of human aspirations. They were told in turn that in this way they brought about the fragmentation of the person as a uniform moral entity.

However, the analytical fragmentation of human life was not the charge most frequently leveled against economics, which was also accused of something completely different, namely, of absolutism, of aspiring to become the new religion of the epoch of commerce. "The economic tendency," the young Aleksander Wielopolski noted, "wants to usurp for itself the dignity of the whole, and regards all other strivings, forces and moral constructs in the nation as tools and means of elevating industry; it seeks to discover the measure and hallmark of national dignity and power and to display them at fairs, refusing to recognize them in any other field."[24]

In its juxtaposing of moral and material strivings, religion and economics, agriculture and industry, conservative thought coincided with the current of literary sentimentalism which fostered the ideal of a simple life, modest and self-sufficient wealth, and peaceful, homely bliss. This ideal, whose Polish roots, as has already been mentioned, go back to the fifteenth century (the way in which this motif was employed and transformed in the eighteenth century has also been briefly described), was revived and conventionalized in the poetics of the pre-romantic idyll and the concordant social imagination.

Kazimierz Brodziński was the leading Polish exponent of the aesthetical and ethical ideals of a civilization friendly to the human race. In the Slavic country which he envisioned for the future, the climate and the people would be moderate, the Vistula would be regulated (by no means a modest proposal), towns would be properly planned and built, and the international exchange of goods and works of culture would be developed; however, all this would be achieved without stock markets and the pursuit of profit, without the smoke and hubbub of the pitiless world of capitalism. One might call Brodziński a pioneer ecologist since, without renouncing progress, he wanted to prevent in advance the pollution of the natural environment. In his dreams nature and culture attained a relatively harmonious unity: nature was not to be wild and primeval, but brought under control by the hand of a good husbandman. The central figure in this landscape was the farmer, the ploughman, a figure enlightened and industrious, but one whose needs were modest.

In political economy the growth of needs was the precondition of development, while in moral economy it threatened the natural state of humanity with extinction. When viewed from this perspective, bourgeois civilization seemed more than anything else to be a temptation to indulge in wanton consumption. "Industry, and with it luxury, attacked us simple men on our weak side. It started by pandering to our passions and bodily comforts. Like a silkworm, it spun its long thread of declamatory arguments, and forced its way into the modest manor-houses of our squires, contaminating their agrarian thought; it even donned the gown of the scholar to spread its influence from university pulpits!"[25]

It seems to be a feature of early capitalism that the more widespread industry was, with its products and the type of economic mentality associated with it, the more vehement was the verbal reaction to it. The relationship between the ideological attitudes articulated in literature and the practice of social behavior is by no means straightforward. Cultural patterns can sanctify and justify ordinary behavior, but sometimes they also happen to be designed to act against this behavior, to thwart it, and their intention seems to be rather didactic or compensatory. Heroic literature does not always grow out of the soil of the heroic ethos, and the condemnation of the cult of gold is often most widespread precisely when people are consumed by gold fever. Thus it was by no means certain that those who condemned towns were always staunch admirers of rural life.

Warsaw and Lwów attracted more and more noblemen in the 1820s and, as a result, the town was once again put on trial, appearing in the role of a gambling den where fashion, usury, laziness, debauchery and all the other cardinal and venial sins reigned. Antiurban sentiments were voiced in practically every work of Polish comedy; thus what was a thoroughly urban genre, written for townspeople, stubbornly continued to uphold the values of pastoral life. The rural gentry may have been portrayed as having many vices but its moral foundation was healthy, while the towns were ruled by profiteers and the *nouveaux riches*. With one stroke of the pen, everything in the town became false: romanticism was changed into a pose, religion turned into hypocrisy, and marital fidelity into deceit.

This bourgeois civilization, which channeled all human energies into purely carnal pursuits—making money, trading and consuming—seemed indecently trivial. And by the same token, the theory of such a civilization, that is, political economy, was trivial as well.

The ostentatious, blanket condemnation of the capitalist modernization of life and thought should not therefore be seen as an attribute of one ideology only. Various currents of the cultural heritage contributed to it. First, there was the spontaneous suspicion of all things new on the part of the farmer, accustomed as he was to the stable, cyclical routine of work and ritual, to the old implements and tools in the home and on the farm. Then there was the moralizing and economic views of the gentry which upheld this routine, including in its approval the doctrine regarding occupations that were worthy or unworthy of a gentleman. And, obviously, there was the teaching of the Catholic church which laid down for each and every individual the path to salvation in accordance with the obligations of his estate, that is, demanding humility from the poor, alms from the rich, and the moderation of desires from all. The Catholic church was much slower to adapt to the new rhythms of life than the Protestant congregations: it fought longer against charging interest and, above all, it denounced from the pulpit the accumulation of money and all kinds of social advancement. Additional influences came from the legitimate and illegitimate ideological heirs of Rousseau who propagated the cult of naturalness. Related to this was the sentimental utopia of a happy, secluded home and, finally, the poetical theme of the pastoral or farming idyll which canonized the model of artificial naturalness.

We are quite consciously mixing here the so-called different "levels of consciousness," or forms of articulation: common, everyday attitudes, and elitist doctrines, amateurish verses, sermons and philosophical disputes. All of these tend to merge and lodge in the human mind, or at least in unsophisticated minds, and it then becomes very difficult to decide what came from where in the popular view of the world. We will therefore continue with this same eclecticism.

As mentioned, the currents of older and more recent tradition were fed in the nineteenth century by new sources throbbing with contempt for bourgeois calculation and economic theory. We have already outlined postrevolutionary conservative thought which was so concerned about the upsetting of the former social order. But so far we have omitted to mention the insurrectionary democrats in the period after 1831, living in exile, dreaming of the day when they would return to their home country and topple the old feudal social hierarchy—but for the sake of freedom and equality, not for production and commerce. In terms of contempt for the bourgeoisie, no aristocrat, bishop or man of letters could equal these pilgrims and emissaries of Poland and its people. How scornful they were of the France of the House of Orleans, the France of bankers, lawyers and shopkeepers; how alien and repulsive did they find the cities of England and America! They were chilled by the calculating selfishness of the West, so indifferent to their lot and to their cause: confronted by this lack of interest they must surely have believed themselves to be emissaries from another, better world, a world which was subjugated and oppressed, but still capable of love and sacrifice.

Never was the gap between the sublime ideas and the everyday life of a nation so great. On the strength of their evangelical faith in the moral superiority of the oppressed and the persecuted, the Polish visionary poets entrusted the task of the redemption of mankind to a nation which was incapable of satisfying its basic material and intellectual needs, and which had ceased to play any role in European life. To an outsider, what difference could there be between Poland and a Serbia or an Ireland also heroic, subjugated, uneducated and hungry? For those whose eyes were blinded by the romantic philosophy of history, this was an irrelevance. The hierarchy of spirits and the stages of economic development were two contradictory or simply disparate systems of values.

Those who saw the soil and the vast expanses of unploughed land wanted to reconcile the two systems, but they could only do it in the same high-flown style. For if economic work was to become one of the national aims then it had to be made holy, just as poetry, the national struggle, and the making of sacrifices had been sanctified; it had to be proven that industry, contemptible though it was, was a path which the spirit could follow. Europe had already embarked on this road of self-perfection after long centuries of barbarity. "This is patently demonstrated by the general spread of culture, the high level of wealth and the visible superiority of the power of this part compared to the rest of the world. This can be seen above all in those sublime ideas, purified of the minutest earthly blemishes. In other words, nobility of mind equals material power, and the power of mechanical forces equals nobility of mind." Alas, there were still some European countries which could not boast of having attained this state. "Our motherland," argued Jan Ludwik Żukowski, "is one of these countries."[26]

In Poland this kind of sublimation of productive work was still a rare phenomenon. But Żukowski's language and ideals reveal a clear kinship, probably not accidental, with the French propaganda of industrialism which was spread during the Restoration period by the editors of *Le Censeur Européen*, *L'Organisateur* and *Le Producteur*. France had just begun to gather its strength and accumulate capital in order to start an industrial revolution, and the word "l'industrie" which, like the Polish word "prze-mysł," signified all economic activity, became the pivot of the new ideology and of the corresponding catalog of social virtues.[27]

The new ideology immediately came into conflict with all critiques of industrial civilization and political economy, accepting their challenge and the area of combat chosen by them. This meant that the ideological battle for the economic foundations of the new society *in statu nascendi* was to be fought not in the economic sphere but in the field of ethics. The supreme authority of the whole school, Jean-Baptiste Say, still refused to recognize this necessity. He accused his predecessors, above all the physiocrats, of constantly confusing "the law" and reality, that is, things as they should be and as they actually were. "L'économie politique n'est devenue une science qu'en devenant une science d'observation." If an economist argued for or against something, fought against some "prejudice" or defended some principle, he did so, claimed Say, in a purely technological spirit. Thanks to a knowledge of economics, statesmen and industrialists could foresee "les suites d'une opération, comme on consulte les lois de la dynamique et de l'hydraulique, lorsqu'on veut construire avec succès un pont ou une écluse."[28] The critics, however, were not concerned with how the bridge could be built, but with where it led and what was to be found on the other bank.

A whole pleiad of early-nineteenth-century conservative and romantic authors, especially in Germany and France, attacked the philosophical and moral foundations of economics which, they alleged, degraded human nature in that it saw material needs and the desire for profit as the only motive impelling people to action, and did not take the least notice of honor and sacrifice, duty and compassion. This kind of economics, they argued, was the mentor of a corrupt society, the symptom and herald of the moral decline of civilization, the philosophy of human subjugation to money and mechanics.[29]

They received their answer, or rather two slightly different answers since the industrialist camp held common views only up to a certain point.

The most eloquent defense of liberal industrialism is arguably a work bearing the significant title of *L'industrie et la morale considerées dans leur rapports avec la liberté*, written by Charles-Barthélémy Dunoyer.[30] Following in the footsteps of his master, Say, Dunoyer refuses to state what "should be." He ridicules the idea, contained in the Declaration of the Rights of Man and of the Citizen, that all people are born free. Freedom, he argues, is acquired, it is a gradable concept. People are not born free, but they can become free, to a greater or lesser degree. He dismisses the argument of Benjamin Constant and the other "dogmatists" that human beings have the right to be free. In order to identify the conditions which enable them to gain this right, he argues that one must take into account the entire history of mankind, beginning with a look at the savages, then the nomads, then the early settlers who forced slaves to work for them, then at those peoples which no longer had slaves but which were divided into estates, each estate enjoying its own rights and privileges. One must then examine those societies in which all privileges have already been abolished and in which everyone is driven by the ambition to advance in society, and finally, one must consider purely industrial nations in which the passion for power has been replaced by a passion for work—and , claims Dunoyer, there is only one such nation in the world, and that nation is the United States of America. According to him, an analysis of all these stages shows immediately and without any shadow of a doubt that at each successive stage of development enterprise and productive work have increased, and at the same time, contrary to the claims of Rousseau, Chateaubriand, Bonald, and all sentimental skeptics and preachers, the level of social morality has grown. "Let them harangue as much as they want to against those people who allegedly want to restrict human activity to physical matters: I say that industry is always advantageous to intellectual and moral life; I say that a system in which our existence becomes more pleasant ("la plus douce") is also one in which this existence gains in quality and dignity."[31]

Thus, material progress facilitates moral progress, and together they contribute to the growth of human freedom. If this is the case, human history is nothing but the history of freedom which can be measured with the same impartiality and exactitude as light or electricity. "So our freedom increases the more power, activeness, industry and knowledge we have, the more capable we are of satisfying all our needs, the less we are dependent on things: every kind of progress expands our ability to act, and every new skill is a new freedom."[32] All the truly good things of this world—life comforts, finesse, knowledge, art, freedom, peace, security, property, equality—exist in harmony; they increase together and one never has to sacrifice one of them in order to secure another. Dunoyer dismisses those accusations leveled at civilization which allege that it destroys customs, debases men's characters and causes societies to decay. "This impeachment of civilization is not new. The idea that our species degenerates as it progresses is as old as the world." A whole volume could be compiled of such judgments: they are, he says, not just the views of a few eccentrics, but represent a general superstition concerning progress.[33]

For Dunoyer, civilization entails the general ennoblement of society, and antisocial civilization is a logical contradiction. The development of science and productive capabilities, and the increase in material goods will extinguish the centuries-old desire for conquest and plunder, domination and exploitation; the struggle for colonies will prove to be an excessively costly adventure, and state frontiers will lose their significance, for free people will attach more importance to small local communities in which they will live together of their own free will.

Politics—the true source of depravity—will come to an end. No form of government, no Montesquieuesque division of power can assure the peaceful coexistence of different classes with opposing interests. Only political alchemists can cherish such illusions. Of decisive importance is the economic system. In those places where slavery, privileges, monopolies and the spirit of domination disappear, social peace will prevail irrespectively of the political organization. Rivalry between producers is not war, but innocent competition ("des rivalités innocentes") which is an incentive to better work. In the field of productive activity, the success of one person does not deny another the chance of success: "Everybody can prosper here together, all peoples of the world can prosper together."[34]

Everything is thus geared towards the perfection of humankind, and if there are any blemishes on the crystal perfection of the future, they are there because such is the "nature of things." In Chapter Ten of *L'industrie et la morale,* the herald of the kingdom of freedom turns momentarily into a worried Malthusian, although he quickly comes to the conclusion that there is no form of evil that will not ultimately contribute towards progress. This vision of things was taken further by Frédéric Bastiat, who argued that free competition, acting as a counterbalance to personal interest, results in the ethics of brotherhood; from here it was just one step to the conclusion that all social reforms could only spoil the economic harmony of capitalism.[35] In this way the brilliant view of the future imperceptibly shaded into an apology for the not-so-brilliant present, as so often happens in history.

At the same time, Charles Dunoyer's history of mankind is thoroughly secular. There are no divine plans in his book, only "la nature des choses." Moral principles are not commandments; they are merely the result of social development. "It is often said that Christianity civilized us: it seems more reasonable to say that civilization ennobled ("a épuré") our Christianity. The letter of the Gospel has certainly not changed, but our understanding of the Gospel has evolved; our religious sentiments and principles have kept in step with all our sentiments and with all our principles; they have become purer and more reasonable in accordance as we have become more refined."[36]

Claude Henri de Saint-Simon, who in the same period and in the same city was working on an alternative model of the moral defense of progress and civilization, followed a different course in his reasoning. His model was incomparably more grandiloquent, visionary and comprehensive. At first glance, it seems to have grown out of the same ideological background, from the same enthusiasm for productive work, science and enterprise, from the same idea, shared by all industrialists, that society is divided into bees and drones, and from the same faith in the convergence of interests of all classes and occupational groups who actively contribute to the expansion of industry. These are common features, but in spite of the numerous similarities Saint-Simon's sociological imagination, kept in check initially by the convention of scientific determinism, took, from the very beginning, a different route: it was no longer a historical report, with sorties into the future, on the evolutionary progress of industry, freedom and virtue, but a plan for the total and immediate redemption of the world, and for the creation, by human forces, of God's kingdom on earth.

Such a plan necessarily had the Gospel as its starting point. But the Gospel was only a fragmentary revelation; it only proclaimed the negative principle of coexistence: thou shalt do no evil to thy neighbor. The second part of the moral code, concerning the obligation to do useful work, had not yet been revealed by God, which, in Saint-Simon's view, had enabled the church and the theologians to distort the very essence of Christianity. They had separated heaven and earth and had taught contempt for material goods and the order of this world. This was to no avail, because religion is a system, and a system can have only one principle. This one principle was established by God, and the rest had been invented by the clergy. "God has said 'Men should treat each other as brothers.' This sublime principle comprises all that is divine in the Christian religion. . . . Now, according to this principle given to men by God as a guide for their conduct, they should organize their community in the way which will be most advantageous to the greatest number; they should make it their aim in all their undertakings and actions, to promote as quickly and completely as possible the moral and physical welfare of the most numerous class."[37]

Saint-Simon's God was a utilitarianist familiar with the work of Bentham. He was also an economist, though at first it was not quite clear which school he represented. It is obvious that he sanctified all industrial work, but that was not enough. Did he give his blessing to contemporary France, or to the Europe of the Restoration period? On this point Saint-Simon had some doubts. This epoch of bourgeois *arrivisme*, of "looking for a place for oneself," which for Dunoyer seemed to be the final vestibule before entering the blessed age of industry, came to be regarded by Saint-Simon more and more as a critical period of chaos. And his disciples knew for certain that it was the very opposite of the order which they were waiting for.

If the brotherhood of people was the supreme moral value, then history should not be seen as the successive development of freedom, but as a progress of association—a completely different thing. The opposite of the principle of association was the principle of antagonism, a weaker principle but capable, nevertheless, of hampering progress. The contemporary social condition, coming after a revolution that destroyed but did not build, was a continuation of the state of war: of war between individuals, between classes, and between states. Competition was not the harmonious coexistence of aspirations, but a form of chaos, because "by keeping every industrial enterprise separate from others and forcing them to struggle with one another, it depraves both individual and social morality."[38]

The God of the Saint-Simonists finally parted company with liberalism. For Saint-Simon's followers, social morality was not born out of the wisdom and conscience of the individual. It was senseless to claim that the individual by himself was best able to estimate the relationship between his deeds and the interests of society, interests which were to be watched over by the two "sad deities" of individualists: conscience and public opinion. These deities were supposed to reward and to punish. Unfortunately, faith in these fallible organs could only lead "to opposition against any attempt at organizing a *central administration* for the moral interests of mankind, to a hatred of all *authority*."[39]

This is obviously written in the style of the conservatives, and utilizes their categories and their accusations. Indeed, Saint-Simon's disciples began to quote Condorcet less and less frequently, turning instead to De Maistre—with the difference that in their doctrine man was now alone in a crowd, and there was no way back to the maternal, protective warmth of the vanished communities of earlier times. He could only escape forward, into the future, into a more general form of association. Is this not, they asked, just what industry demanded?

People of France, make one last effort: power to the producers!—this appeal recurs with obsessive frequency in Saint-Simon's oeuvre. Down with politicians, generals, barristers and clergymen. The work of the nation should be directed by competent people: by scholars, artists and industrialists. Someone who knows how to organize his own work will also be able to administer the huge workshop which the nation is becoming. Such a person will be able to control public education, which will have as its foundation pure evangelical morality and whose objective will be the mastering of the positive sciences. The general supervision of all this will be in the hands of the Academy of Reasoning and the Academy of Feelings. "*As soon as artists place the earthly paradise in the future, as soon as they show that the establishment of the new system will lead to this paradise, this system will, beyond any doubt, come to prevail.*"[40]

This would happen first in France, and then throughout the world, a world united by the New Christianity that was called upon to weed out selfishness and ensure peace, brotherhood and welfare for mankind. "It is called upon to link together the scientists, artists, and industrialists, and to make them the managing directors of the human race, as well as of the particular interests of each individual people. It is called upon to put the arts, experimental sciences and industry in the front rank of sacred studies, whereas the Catholics have put them among the profane branches of study."[41]

In the New Order, the opposition of science and religion, corporal and spiritual needs, self-interest and morality would lose all meaning. The industrial system would be both moral and rational, because it would abolish the chaos of the market: instead of competition between individual capitalists, the Supreme Hierarchy, taking in the whole of the great industrial workshop at a glance, would assign various tasks of production in accordance with the register of general and individual needs. Universal agreement would replace universal struggle, and as a result all crises and bankruptcies, every form of adversity and poverty would vanish. "To put it briefly, industry is *organized*, everything is mutually united, everything has been foreseen. . . ."[42]

The workers would confidently entrust their fate to the best and the wisest. No one was doomed to relying on himself alone, everyone could find a place for himself within this system. However, freedom would not be destroyed since the ruling over people would be transformed into the administering of affairs, into organizing the process of work and education. "The fear that despotism based on knowledge can ever exist would be as ridiculous a chimera as it would be absurd, and such fear can germinate only in minds which are absolutely foreign to all positive ideas."[43]

Only from that point on, from the moment the monarch or the parliament peacefully introduced such organizational changes, would harmonious progress begin, free of all the destructive cataclysms of history. This progress would be threefold: physical, intellectual and moral, that is, it would involve the development of industry, intelligence and love. By working towards the improvement of his own lot and the lot of other people, man could be said to perform religious work.[44] This, according to Saint-Simon, was the Gospel of the Lord.

The thinking classes of the epoch looked forward to the future with great longing ("soif d'avenir"), convinced that the future had already begun to bud, that the present carried it in its womb. Saint-Simon was absolutely convinced that he was not creating a utopia; he believed that he, better than anyone else, could divine and reveal to the world the destination to which the road trodden by civilization for centuries would inevitably lead. Even his moral preaching was presented as scientific, based on human experience. In his view, one had to know how to interpret this experience, how to read the Gospel of the Lord, the signs of history—and one also needed a flash of inspiration, or illumination. Then suddenly the entire mystery of the world would be revealed as a deductive system stemming from one key principle. There were, however, a number of such illuminations, each of which revealed to the chosen one a different principle and, in consequence, a different future. Such forecasts can be arranged in some typological order and each of them assessed on a scale stretching from the kingdom of maximum freedom to the kingdom of perfect organization. Still, all these prophets, the sober ones and the inspired ones, those who believed in divine providence and those who believed in positivism, were certain that the child yet to be born would be more beautiful and brighter than anything ever seen on earth so far. It was true that the present had only given birth to premature, hybrid monsters, but even these miscarriages had proved necessary for the earthly realization of theodicy. Whoever conceived the purpose of history, had no doubt that humankind, by subduing the earth, was moving closer and closer to the land of justice.

In Poland, August Cieszkowski[45] aspired to be the herald of this land of justice. From the words of the Lord's Prayer, interpreted as a prophecy, he wove an Adventist vision of the return of Christ bringing peace, the descent of the Kingdom of God to earth, and the ascension of the earth to heaven. However, there is nothing apocalyptic about this vision: no excessive depravity among humans, no horrible cataclysms, no Judgment. Mankind was to enter this promised heaven on earth serenely and almost imperceptibly through civilizational work, learning and the improvement of technology, and through an increasingly widespread and fair social organization. And this heaven on earth would not be a celestial choir, but simply a higher level of social life existing and working in peace and well-being. In this Kingdom of God there would be factories and railways, and the people would earn and spend money; and it would not be the Holy Spirit but the caring terrestrial government that would see to it that, as in Fourier's phalanstery, everyone received the social minimum. "This minimum will comprise not only those objects which today we regard as indispensable; there are also others things, today regarded as luxuries, which will soon be seen as indispensable, and the *sphere of needs* will expand at the expense of the *sphere of luxury*."[46] Thus, in the future, "our daily bread" would comprise not only foodstuffs, clothing and fuel, but also free elementary and vocational education ("the intellectual minimum"), hygiene, social insurance, physical training and, finally, cultural entertainment. In Holy Writ, where all this had been promised, the heavenly manna sent by God to the Israelites in the wilderness was a portent of the social minimum. In the future, the means for all these benefits of the "social system" would be supplied not by God, but by industry and its surpluses, and also by the saving in expenditure when superfluous armies were abolished.

This Kingdom was really intended for the people, for all people, since in the epoch of the Paraclete there would be no barbarian peoples, and all would have a chance to enjoy the benefits of civilization.

"The Messianism of a sober economist," or "everyday Messianism," is how Andrzej Walicki described this prophesy.[47] Indeed, Cieszkowski's eschatological, religious imagination is not very sublime; his God does not approach in wrath and with thunderbolts, nor does he provoke fear or mystical admiration. The point of this prophesy is the combination of the sacred and the secular which it entails. The great systematic presentation of a religious and dialectic philosophy of history becomes the setting for the lucid forecasts of the author's sociological imagination, which is bold and matter-of-fact, and yet free of Fourier's precision which seems so ridiculous in its attention to detail. This vision anticipated much of what was to happen a century later in several kingdoms which were far from godly, but its greatest defect was the fact that it offered too facile a solution for the dramatic conflicts of modern life.

Such conflicts were familiar to the author of *Ojcze Nasz (Our Father),* who was a perspicacious and knowledgeable observer of Western societies. Like all contemporary critics of liberal civilization, he saw its main weakness in the wasting disease of individualism which affected in particular the middle classes; its symptoms were the isolation which existed among individuals and among local and occupational communities, their egoistic exclusivity, and their lack of common links or a shared objective. Political economy consolidated this fragmentation of interests: "It has been concerned only with means, and not with aims; with abstract notions of values, and not with the aim of these values; with dead wealth, and not with the use of this wealth; that is, it has been concerned with things rather than people."[48]

Cieszkowski described how, in a society without a sense of community in which private or local interests take precedence over the common good, the system of political democracy is nothing more than the "power of number," and the promise of equality never progresses beyond the level of pure abstraction. Clashes of interest within states are at least regulated by the law, while such conflicts among states are resolved by force since international law is not supported by any sanction, any guarantee. "Indeed, civilization is a bitter irony . . . as long as there exists among the societies of the world . . . this state of nature contrary to man's destiny."[49]

Such diagnoses of the diseases of the West were fairly common (in both the West and the East) in the 1840s and were easily accommodated within the structure of conservative thought. The difference was that in Ciesz-kowski's case this diagnosis did not spring from the conviction that the world in general was getting worse. On the contrary, he maintains that whatever state it might be in at present, it is still better than it was. In the Middle Ages there was more "individualism" that served to separate people, and less "association," than in contemporary capitalist countries.

From the "general human" standpoint which Cieszkowski took, the dream of rescuing or restoring small, closed and, on the whole, oppressive neigh-borhoods or corporations was, just as in the case of the Saint-Simonists, a clearly illusory solution to the dilemma of human loneliness. The road could only lead forward—towards larger and more general forms of association, towards mankind. Modern civilization was rich in technological inventive-ness and legal idealism: by its own efforts, and with God's assistance, it could produce the means of overcoming its own limitations and defects.

God's Kingdom on earth would not be given to the people; it would be won by them, by their thought and their toil, and by the constant perfection of social life. "Organic" progress, free of "convulsions" and of "the contra-dictory feelings of revenge and hatred," would not be achieved through class struggle, and even less so through conflicts between nations; it would be achieved as the objectives of these classes and nations gradually draw closer to each other.[50] The principle of equality, until then abstract, would be complemented by the principle of hierarchy and organization, and this marriage would conquer the world and tame individualism. Under democracy the new, open aristocracy of reason and merit—a kind of "popular patrici-ate"—would secure the uniting of progress with the preservation of the values of live tradition. The government, by "organizing institutions" without any attempts at acquiring monopolies, would, however, restrict the anarchy of free competition by applying a planned "protective" redistribution of budget resources, thus harmonizing private interests with the public good.[51]

If people could form nations without losing anything of their individuality, then nations would be able to unite, first under one legal system, and then under one government; they could first form a "European union," and finally a united mankind.

Europe had already taken the path towards an ever broader integration and an ever more universal synthesis, and the other continents would soon follow. The creative human genius was already working towards this. This genius was revealed in the sciences, arts and industry which, in Cieszkowski's idiom, constituted the various "roads of the spirit," a free spirit which was able to create a new reality, both material and spiritual. "Intellectuals" and "industrialists" alike acted as its demiurges. Every new discovery or invention had at the same time an instrumental and symbolic significance, and the two meanings could not be separated: for example, the telegraph, a technical means of communication, was at the same time a symbol of the process by which the nations were coming closer together.

"Almost every phenomenon of the day has an important social objective. We find this even there where we would least expect it. For example, the discovery this year of three methods of producing *artificial fertilizer* is a very significant portent. For we are coming closer to a radical reform of the world, a reform which will be the rebirth of nature and in which original sin and its effects will be obliterated both morally and physically. Thus the earth will be freed of the burden of curse and from then on it will give birth not just to thorns and thistles. For this purpose it needs fertilization, which will be possible thanks to these fertilizers. Hence, our deep interest in this problem is proof of our awareness of its further consequences. The same may be said of railways and sugar-processing plants. The former will bring peoples closer together, as well as prolonging man's lifespan (because he will no longer lose so much time in vain), the latter will, literally, sweeten his life."[52]

This peculiar, apparently trivial association of myth with agronomy, and of fertilizer with the Redemption is not, of course, an attempt to desanctify myth, but rather to sanctify agronomy. In the Bible, simple pastoral or agricultural chores are repeatedly used to convey mythical messages, and a figurative sense is superimposed on the literal, economic sense. If such a double function can be performed by the ritual of sowing and reaping, by the olive tree and the vineyard, then why not fertilization and sugar beet, or railways and credit? When man changes his crops and customs, God learns a new language, and that is all.

The Gospels were used for their teachings about the vanity of temporal goods, and the pointlessness of excessive concern about tomorrow. In a world which considered earthly treasures ever more precious, Sunday sermons were becoming completely divorced from daily matters. Cieszkowski's faith ignored this hypocritical split by adverting to St. Matthew's parable of the multiplication of talents and by making holy weekdays devoted to profit-bearing work. Blessed are the industrialists, inventors and workers, for they shall inherit the earth: "Because in the future the industrial class will be the true army of mankind, which under the banner of the spirit will win ever new trophies from nature, trophies which will never be associated with defeat, which will never cause tears, but will assure happiness for the future generations while providing numerous advantages to the present one."[53]

No fear of the social costs of progress is expressed here, provided this progress did not destroy the social order—something which the socialist demagogues encouraged. With evolutionary development, all threat of moral or economic crisis would vanish, the very problem of crisis would cease to exist. There was no split of values since all goods were placed on one scale. Indeed, the messianist Cieszkowski's confidence in the humanism of technological civilization surpassed that of the most trusting and grandiloquent futurologists of the Enlightenment.

The finalist view of the future of the world contained in *Our Father* was a radical attempt at assuaging the dramatic anxiety which pervaded the epoch of steam engines and romanticism: anxiety lest modern civilization developed in a direction which would be contrary to that morality which was supposed to form its axiological foundation. Cieszkowski, following Saint-Simon, nullified this conflict by recognizing the functional, if not generic, unity of the needs of the soul and the body, of moral and material values, and by sanctifying them jointly in his prophetic vision of the epoch of the Holy Spirit in which secular history would once again merge with sacred history. Economics, he believed, was not contrary to the Gospels when it oversaw work in the Lord's vineyard and showed how Christ's promise could be fulfilled.

On the other hand, Cieszkowski's millenarianism stood in obvious contradiction to Church orthodoxy, which is probably the main reason why most of his work, which he himself regarded as epoch-making, remained in manuscript form until his death. Nevertheless, unlike Saint-Simon who treated the canons of Christianity very pragmatically, Cieszkowski was a deeply religious thinker. He read the words of the Lord's Prayer like a palimpsest which had revealed its hidden sense to him in a moment of youthful illumination.

Henryk Kamieński[54] was faced with the same dilemma in his attempt to create a philosophy of economics, though he did not receive any divine inspiration. He was also one of those Europeans who resisted the pervasive feeling that the world, corrupt and plunged into the chaos of contradictory passions, had lost its moral compass and had gone adrift.

Thinkers, who are concerned with a vast range of social phenomena, almost never reconcile themselves with the experience of chaos and of the unpredictability of the course of human affairs. In the epoch of early capitalism it was clear that the old links between the estates were rapidly declining and that the ritual rules of life were being destroyed. It is no wonder then that European thought reacted by producing a multitude of ingenious systems of the philosophy of history, which rationalized the overwhelming need to find a global direction and meaning. Later on we shall discuss the catastrophists, who constructed history against themselves. For the moment, let us consider positive systems, that is, systems in which the course of human civilization is revealed as the gradual, uninterrupted implementation of a chosen ideal. Each of these systems is, fundamentally, the result of wishful thinking, with the difference that rationalization masks the emotional *fiat* and turns dreams into predictions or acts of prescience. Rationalization consists here in the conviction that one can derive a whole line of history from some supreme axiomatic principle—that is, one can discover the future.

Kamieński, no less than Cieszkowski, was convinced that the future could be fathomed, although he did not invoke biblical prophecies. He cited a number of axioms of social philosophy which were as simple, as general, and, it seemed, as intuitively obvious as in geometry. What prompts people to action, he claims, are their own interests. Human beings wish to free themselves from their enslavement to matter, that is, from conditions in which all physical and spiritual forces have to be utilized for the satisfaction of existential needs. Destitution and all forms of primitive existence are the signs of this state of enslavement which cannot be reconciled with human spiritual nature. Therefore, the struggle with matter in order to be free of its overwhelming power means the liberation of the human spirit and human creativity. Thus, striving for an increase in public welfare and labor productivity is not merely a prerequisite of progress; it is itself progress, a general and indispensable progress, because all that is human is realized in this striving. Savagery is not the natural human state: the state of nature "is before us, not behind us."[55]

Kamieński was still engaged in the Enlightenment dispute about the mutual relationship between "nature" and "civilization," and in this dispute he took an opposite stand to the tradition of Rousseau. For Kamieński these two notions, these two states of mankind, were not mutually contradictory; in fact, they were one and the same. The growth of human needs and skills and the development of social institutions did not mean the annihilation of "natural-ness," but rather its implementation since the human species' most natural feature was its ability to create consciously, through its activity, a "human world," that is, a society which "succumbs to the absolute law of indispensa-ble progress, and therefore keeps changing its present shape for more perfect and finer ones." The measure, or the scale, of this creative activity was, he claimed, the growing unity among people, their closer contacts on earth, the breaking down of barriers, and the incessant progressive movement, the changeability of the forms of life. Indeed, "who can doubt the spiritual superiority of an American of the United States over a Greenlander or Lap?"[56]

Thus, clothed in a new dress and couched in different language, we find in Kamieński's work the grand promise of those philosophers who, fascinated with inventive human genius, made human beings the sovereign rulers of their destiny. Alienation disappeared like ghosts at dawn. Romantic objections to the coldness of the world, the brutality of history and the triviality of the market vanished. The longing for outmoded forms ceased, as did the feverish waiting, in hope or dread, for the future judgments of God, History or the Proletariat.

Chaos disappeared. "Indeed, chaos disappeared when the idea of creation became light." The day was bright once more, and humanity was marching along the signposted route towards Synthesis. In order for it not to stray and lose its objective, it was directed by the social sciences, that is, moral, material and political economy. The task of moral economy was to illustrate the genesis of ideas and sciences, those "acts which *precede* the general reality of progress." Material economy concerned itself with the understanding of the creativity of the human spirit in its struggle with matter. Finally, political economy was the theory of "social arrangements" (or sociology).[57] Together, they revealed and described the aim of history.

"*The necessity of the progress of mankind!*" For Kamieński this aim is so closely associated with human nature that it was sensed by the heart and the imagination even before the mind revealed it. "This was an idea which inflamed the mind, and it *will become the light* which will illuminate everything."[58] Literally everything. Kamieński's rationalist enthusiasm left no secrets undisclosed, it allowed for no ambivalence or hesitation. The grand synthesis of the sciences would illuminate the grand synthesis of history: the future would become comprehensible, crystal-clear, and mankind would never err or stray, because it would know.

At this point we return to the dispute about economics, that is, about the moral element in industrial civilization. The status of "material" economy was debased both by its adherents and by its enemies; this was so because economics "was not viewed in connection with the grand objectives of mankind, and was not explained according to the unmistakable laws of the general synthesis of the sciences." Placed in that teleological perspective, can it still be charged with vulgarity? Kamieński's generally monotonous discourse shifts into expressive oratory as he furiously replies to the conservative and romantic moralists: "Enough contemptuous cries aimed against material economy! . . . As if it were concerned with the vegetation of society! As if its aim were to sanctify matter by decreeing that the progress of civilization means that man produces more and consumes more! As if it were a base, pedestrian science which compares civilizational progress in man with bestial utility . . . Our science, which allegedly breathes crude materialism, is abused by those who see the sanctification of *the material development of society* as a tribute to and subordination of oneself to matter . . . I ask them, then: is it man's spirit which pays tribute to matter or matter which pays tribute to the spirit when man does not have to concern himself laboriously and exclusively with the satisfaction of his physical needs? When the globe takes on new shapes every day according to his needs? When navigational technology and steam power transfer him like lightning to distant parts? When the barriers of time and space disappear in order to facilitate the dissemination of thoughts, thanks to the pliability of matter which preserves these thoughts and transfers them under the guise of statues, paintings or books?"[59]

Elsewhere, the target of his remarks is even more obvious: "In the various nations, human thought flowers in scientific endeavor only when agriculture and the crafts assure them prosperity. . . . As the crust of poverty that oppresses them crumbles, they can see everything more clearly and then their spirit is liberated. . . . Thus, in a way we come to stand in defense of the material aspirations of the present age, aspirations which are often opposed by the so-called *romantic* view of those people who, together with their precious feelings and thoughts, claim to be misunderstood by the present age. Poor misunderstood ones! The fact is that it is they who misunderstand the present times. They fail to find in what they claim to be purely material the strong development of the human spirit, one of the most sublime spectacles that the world of thoughts can present."[60]

For Kamieński, it was obvious that civilization was proceeding unwaveringly towards the implementation of brotherhood among people. The epoch of brotherhood would be the supreme moment in universal history when mankind would be ennobled to the extent that it would work out of a sense of vocation and divide the fruit of its labor according to the needs of all. For the time being, however, until this moral revolution should come about, "unity among people is like a commercial company and from this element one is not able to produce a more sublime idea of brotherhood."

This was the favorite metaphor of the conservatives. How often were the liberals accused of attempting to turn society into a commercial company! But in the context provided by Kamieński the metaphor is only intended to underline the fact that this society had not so far been a community of the highest order; only disinterested activity, activity motivated by a calling, "can raise a simple company based on financial reckoning ... to the power of holiness."[61]

Until then, self-interest had determined people's actions. It had always done so, and Kamieński saw nothing wrong in that. For him self-interest was a force which never ceased to work for the benefit of society, since nothing could be gained without reciprocity. The point was that this reciprocity had to become gradually more balanced. So far this had not been the case. In history, every social system had made it possible for one class to monopolize ownership, and had created various forms of physical and economic coercion to guard these exclusive rights: for this reason, the reciprocity of services was not balanced, labor did not receive what was due to it, and the division of wealth was unjust.

This was also the situation in capitalism. Kamieński does not actually use this name, although he examines this system. In his treatise on poverty (1843), he develops an idea which is familiar to us from the work of Sismondi and Skarbek. The progress of capitalism has two sides: a bright side and a gloomy one. "It seems that we are dealing with two contradictory bodies of opinion which cannot reach an agreement on this significant question of progress and the widespread use of machines: on the one hand, we have the interests of humanity, outraged by the fact that the workforce is sunk in an abyss of destitution; on the other hand, we have the universal interests of industry and man's domination of the earth which he owes to his ever increasing ability to mold matter. Why, alas, does this progress not work for the good of all mankind? Why does every step it takes forward result in the horrible oppression and the destitution of the lowest classes of society in those foreign countries which, on the surface, are resplendent in industrial glory and seem to represent the utmost in beauty and goodness—but under this deceptive cloak hide shameful wounds?"[62]

Kamieński, however, rejects Sismondi's palliative for this evil. It does not do to check improvements in technology, because such improvements are always absolutely beneficial for humanity, freeing it from the yoke of terrible toil and increasing human productivity. Unemployment and poverty are not caused by the development of industry, nor by technology, but by an unsound social system, that is, by the monopolistic control of capital which deprives the people who most need it of the right to work. This exclusivity must be restricted; when everyone has the choice to work for themselves or for someone else, then it will be easier to guarantee the universal right to work and to improve the division of wealth, especially when this wealth increases as a result of progress in industry and new inventions.

Kamieński does not go into details of how this is to be achieved. After all he was not an economist, but a philosopher of economics. Nevertheless, the course of his reasoning almost coincides with the ideas of Skarbek, and also of Sismondi, though he did not read the latter very carefully. His work represents a humanitarian critique of the capitalist economy as viewed from the position of unorthodox, democratized liberalism. The fundamental evil of this economy was the fact that it had produced an economic oligarchy; free competition on the labor market was evil by virtue of the fact that as a result of the concentration of ownership, competition on the labor market was not free enough. Kamieński wanted to popularize and democratize capital while still maintaining the progress of mechanization; unlike the professional economists, he was unaware of the fact that it was technological progress that necessitated the concentration of capital. For this reason, the conflict that he perceived so sharply and dramatically seemed to him easy to resolve. All that was needed was a principle which would allow for a fairer division of the fruits of labor, a principle closer to the ideal of the balanced reciprocity of services. Sismondi's fair division was to be supported or implemented by the state. Kamieński does not mention the state; he writes about "universal will" which always discovers a more just and egalitarian principle whenever an old principle proves to be outmoded and hampers further progress. For the law of necessary progress means the "*inevitable progressive development of the idea of justice*, in the course of which we can discern various stages, but never any denial."[63] Therefore, even if in some moment in history, as a result of the existence of exclusivity and coercion, private interests prove antisocial, this is only a temporary disturbance; soon harmony will be restored, and selfishness will again be the doer of good.

Both the conservatives and the socialists accused the civilization of capitalism and democracy of unleashing individualism, which allegedly brought about the disappearance of the community links without which social ethics could not exist. Liberal philosophy had to find an answer to this basic charge, and was subsequently obliged to revise this answer a number of times. The axiom of Kamieński's theory was the conviction that, owing to the rule of reciprocity, individual interests constituted the main factor of socialization. This axiom distinguished him from the socialists. The time would come, he believed, when individual advantage as the driving force of human activity would give way to the higher motives of brotherly love, but this could not be enforced by any external agent: "therefore all attempts to undermine the existence of the well-conceived interest, with the help of means which cannot replace it in its social activity, are doomed to failure. If they were to have any chance of success, this *would mean the destruction rather than the progress of human society.*"[64]

Cieszkowski and Kamieński were two Polish counsels for the defense in the ongoing trial of industrial civilization and economics. Both, however, were far from being apologists for real Western capitalism; both treated it merely as a transitory phase of social evolution. In accordance with the historico-philosophical tastes of the epoch, the defense of civilization demanded the laying aside of current interests and every kind of particularism: the beneficiary of the Great Promise was mankind *in toto*, even if confined to the sphere of European culture in the imagination of the proponents of this gospel.

It was of no importance when the Promised Land would actually be reached. What mattered was confidence in the course of universal history, in its direction and its final sense as revealed by philosophical apriority. What mattered was faith that this civilization, which was the fruit of human greed, inventiveness and labor, contained, so to speak, a moral instinct which would bring it back onto the right track each time it deviated from its course.

Paradoxically, these two voices were hardly known to their contemporaries, and were heard only by a meager audience in Polish intellectual circles of the mid-nineteenth century. Nevertheless, *Our Father*, though it remained for the most part in manuscript form, and *The Philosophy of Material Economy* offered the most comprehensive strategy for the defense of civilizational work by placing its axiology and aims against the broad background of a universalist philosophy of history.

Only fragments of this dramatic defense, at times mercilessly mutilated, entered general circulation. Journals in Poznań and Warsaw published similar ideas and slogans, products of Polish sentiments and French books, all of them testifying to one thing: that faced with the formidable prosecution comprising traditionalists, reactionaries, romanticists, revolutionary democrats, socialists, Slavophiles, preachers and comedy writers, economic theory and practice needed something more than pragmatic arguments with which to defend themselves. It was not enough to demonstrate that beet could be used to produce sugar, or that money generated money. Industry and economics were obliged, as it were, annually to display for public inspection their certificates of morality.

Such certificates were not convincing enough, considering that the course of contemporary events did not inspire confidence in the progressive, conflict-free development of civilization. In the 1840s, the Polish Kingdom entered a long period of economic and intellectual stagnation; Paskevitch's[65] policy of isolation proved effective—perhaps too effective. Private capital was unable to become independent of protectionism and government loans and orders; the border area between private and state interests became a twilight zone that offered many opportunities for illicit transactions. A number of notorious cases of corruption did not help to build a sense of trust in the morality of merchants. The brilliant career of the financier Piotr Steinkeller,[66] the model pioneer of capitalist enterprise, provoked admiration and envy, but his star began to wane at the end of the 1840s, demonstrating that under Polish conditions talent and vigor were not enough to ensure success. More cautious and determined steps were taken in the Poznań area. There one could discern the first buds of organic work and its ideology,[67] but they were still too young and too weak to have much impact on the community as a whole.

The lofty visions of the prophets of industry were strangely out of keeping with the stagnant life around them, in which the spirit showed no particular urge to subdue matter. Attempts were made, however, to drive the spirit to other kinds of action. The uprising of 1846, had it been even momentarily successful, could have led to the enfranchisement of the peasantry by a Polish resolve, and lifted the country out of its state of stagnation, imposing on it the idea of democracy. However, things took a different course. The gentry held the revolutionary party almost as responsible for the slaughter in Galicia as the Austrian government.[68] The conservative party regained its former position, taking advantage of the psychological shock caused by the peasant rebellion.

In the sphere of ideas, the Springtide of Nations had consequences of a more complex and global nature. Europe, which for thirty years had enjoyed peace and relative stability, received a powerful shock in the years 1848–49, and there were more such shocks in store for it. Both the liberals and the conservatives were equally terrified by the workers' uprising in Paris and by the first manifestation of the ability of socialism to influence the masses. They were no longer sure whether the values and institutions they cherished constituted a barrier strong enough to withstand the advancing wave of social and moral "anarchy." The European left wing, crushed by the ultimate triumph of reactionary forces from Paris to Pest, tried to cure itself of its liberal illusions by looking for new, more radical forms of eschatology. "When there is but a sense of the approach of menacing events which will shake the foundations of the old order, does man's tendency to treat his own epoch as an exceptional epoch—and also perhaps man's need for impressively constructed myths—produce conditions conducive to viewing history as a drama the epilogue of which is nigh. This epilogue may be the end of the world, the *dies irae*, but it may also be the advent of the ultimate epoch of happiness and justice."[69]

The Springtide of Nations also revealed a new direction for the course of European history to Polish and Russian émigrés. What was most significant in their case, however, was their profound disillusionment with the Western nations which had refused to or were unable to support the cause of freedom in the East, and which had lost the fight for freedom in their own countries because of their decrepitude. Faith in the West, in liberalism and in the brotherhood of all peoples seemed crushed. Lack of confidence in the immanent values of European progress pushed some people to the cult of tradition and others to revolution; some it pushed to dreams of a Slavic community, others to ultramontanism—but it always led them towards an imagined world where the faith and community of people were still alive, a world as far away as possible from the hollow idol of "materialism." Bourgeois liberalism, both political and economic, made various claims about its ability to implement the ideals of freedom and justice, but whatever its claims were, they were resolutely opposed on both sides. The forces of reaction maintained that liberalism had given birth to anarchy and social revolution. The democrats felt that it had allied itself with the forces of reaction, thus betraying the cause of the people and of freedom. Europe seemed to have split into two mutually hostile camps: into the international force of order and the international force of revolution; into two intransigent and irreconcilable positions which—as in *The Un-divine Comedy*[70]—would soon have to engage in a mortal battle which would settle everything. The spokesmen of both parties were fond of quoting Christ and were equally passionate in their condemnation of individualistic egotism, middle-class morality, stock exchanges, the Rothschilds, and parliaments.

In Poland, there was no room for democrats in any of the partition zones. For a whole decade only the conservatives were allowed to be heard. It was their era. Had not their warnings come true? Godless, materialistic Europe, corrupted by philosophers and economists, had spurned the spiritual leadership of the Church and the natural social hierarchy and was now on the brink of an abyss. In the period following the Springtide of Nations, a voice was heard in Poland for the first time, which constantly recurs in Europe's intellectual culture, philosophy and art, that is, the prophecy of an imminent catastrophe, the voice which echoed in the writings of the French counter-revolutionaries half a century earlier, and in the works of Joseph de Maistre. It was no longer a question of the lot of Poland: the issue was the decline of the West, the premonition of some great eclipse, the end of the old world. Previously, perhaps Krasiński had been the only Pole to sound the depths of this yawning chasm. Now, after 1848, every provincial moralist used it as a threat.

There is a wide range of texts which prove this point. Henryk Rzewuski,[71] never slow in voicing unpopular views, had for some time been engaged in an intellectual exploration of the pessimistic philosophy of history. His starting point was the thesis, fairly widespread during the romantic period, regarding the autonomous growth of national cultures and the lack of points of comparison between them. Added to this was the conviction that each nation realizes its own particular destiny given to it by God. Rzewuski expanded this thesis to include all civilizational phenomena. "Civilization," he argues, "is not unitary, and each great human epoch has had its own separate civilization. Civilization . . . means the development of a certain idea in time, an idea sown in the womb of some particular nation. There are different ideas, hence there are different civilizations; they are identical only insofar as they are subject to the same organic laws, which means that a nation in its collective state reveals this idea through the various stages of its growth, zenith, decline, and, finally, demise."[72]

The fact that civilizations are mortal and the history of mankind is a cycle involving both rise and fall was not a new discovery. It had been current in ancient times, and had been revived during the Enlightenment, a period of rivalry between the theory of historic cycles and the theory of linear progress. Eighteenth-century philosophers and historians were fascinated by the ruins of Roman civilization, and sought in them some indication of the future fate of Europe. Rzewuski also tried to discover a lesson for the future in history, but in his own peculiar way. It is interesting that this proponent of variety among nations treated Western Europe as one nation; in principle as a French–German nation since he was willing to make an exception in the case of England which respected her aristocratic tradition, while the rest of Europe was of no importance for him. It only remained to give the organic cycle—from birth till death—a theocratic content, and one could divide the whole of history into periods, and assess them.

Thus, according to him, the sun of European civilization reached its zenith in the Middle Ages when the positive and organic spirit of Christianity was triumphant, science was subordinated to religious dogmas, and wisdom could be discovered not in books but in myths, in the live oral tradition. This was the beginning of all the great ideas of mankind, all great institutions, all new indispensable inventions, such as powder, the art of navigation and the now long-forgotten secrets of craftsmanship. Up to the present time, "everything that is durable among people is a legacy of the Middle Ages."[73] Beginning with the sixteenth century, with Luther, the Reformation and humanism, came a negative and critical epoch, an epoch of decline, of slow demise. The human mind, confident in its own faculties, wanted to free itself of the power of faith and authority but was only capable of negation: philosophical negation, or rationalism, under whose influence everything became trivial and paltry; social negation, or revolution; and materialist negation, or the triumphs of industry and commerce. All of these were branches of the same poisoned tree of pride.

For Rzewuski, industrialism represents "the convulsions of societies that are on the brink of decline." Happy Middle Ages did not know today's machines, steam engines in particular. "As to those machines, I know that here also many farms use threshing machines, machines for reaping, for harvesting, for haymaking, etc., so that soon agriculture will no longer need people. Congratulations, but still I have more faith in abundant crops when I see my fellow man make the holy sign of our redemption before throwing the seeds on the ground, than when these seeds are scattered by a mechanical sower whose cogs and wheels are supposed to supplant the rules of agriculture given to our first father by God himself. Such innovations may enrich some, but the masses will certainly not benefit by them, since they will be short of bread. Our Savior said: man doth not live by bread alone, but also by the word. Today's prophets, apostles and advocates of industrialism tell the befuddled people: you have no bread, but in order to sustain your existence we shall feed you with our philosophical, political and economic theories."[74]

As for economics: "We keep hearing our fellow countrymen extolling the agricultural policies of foreign countries and urging us to imitate them. However, it is easy to prove that our time-honored farming practices, which the majority of our landlords still uphold, are not inferior to any of the foreign methods. . . . There, it is unthinkable that a landowner should be able to manage without having the initial capital which will stimulate production; here, though the kindly gentry landowner may lack capital assets, and is often burdened with debts, he does not throw up his hands in despair. Magnanimous as regards his peasants, he is their father, not their oppressor, as is the case abroad; he works on his land without resigning from public life; he supports his family on a decent level, brings up his children well, cherishes old Polish hospitality, happily offers his best Hungarian wines to his neighbors, buys books that have just been published in the language of his forbears, takes journals, pays his taxes and the interest due to credit societies, and his honest work provides him with the means of paying for all of this."[75]

This patriarchal idyll conforms perfectly to the moral and literary convention of gentry traditionalism. But in the author's absolutist world view, each social image becomes an element of the universalist plan of history. This idyll represents an area that has not yet been spoilt by the corrupting civilization of reason which is "so brilliant in its phenomena, and so base in its spirit." Indeed, the lay culture of the West, its science, philosophy and economics, its alleged progress—these are all products of the Antichrist, and those Catholics who would like to reconcile them with the spirit of the Christian faith delude themselves. Their efforts are all in vain: "We need to fight against civilization, and we must do so without any respite. Because this civilization is basically evil and godless, and though it may die, it will never allow itself to be cured."[76]

It may die, and it will die, because it no longer has any ideas, only speculation and machines: "The Europe of reason and philosophy has preserved tattered bits of canvas hanging on flagstaffs, but its banners are gone." Poland has no banners either, because it belongs to the West, and together with the West has come to the end of its days. *Vae victis!*

Rzewuski was, indeed, consistent in his extreme presentation of anti-occidental ideology. In his reasoning, the iron logic of doctrine went hand in hand with a passionate rancor. He analyzed the same symptoms which the liberals interpreted as proof of the youthfulness and powerful dynamism of Western civilization, of its ability to realize human dreams of power, but he saw in them evidence of decrepit old age. The axiomatic system was inverted and, as a consequence, the evaluation of historic facts changed. The final demise of the West after 1848 was simply a matter of time, and, in his view, the sooner it happened the better. A new Christian civilization founded on authority and faith, a new cycle of history would then be started by the one country which had resisted the deadly poison of decay, that is, the young, unlearned, unphilosophical Russia. "[Russia] is the only country whose sons would not fail to rally to her banners."[77]

This conclusion, which Rzewuski confirmed by devoting his life to servile collaboration with tsardom, was loathsome not only to the Warsaw intelligentsia, but also to the majority of the Polish traditionalists. First, it offended their sense of national dignity. Second, in the mid-nineteenth century the general consensus was that one ought to be at least somewhat "progressive," even if this was very superficial. Even the Church, the rock of patriarchal conservatism, began seeking some kind of *modus vivendi* with secular science, capitalism and moderate measures of social reform.

Nevertheless, the conviction that "so-called progress" was simply the death knell of a civilization which had denied its own Christian roots was fairly widespread in Polish conservative thought, and it intensified after the critical year 1848. At the same time, there was a sharp difference between the conservatives in the Prussian and Austrian partitions and those in the Russian zone. The regions of Poznań, Galicia and Kraków had already introduced agrarian reform, and whether this reform was good or bad, it had been carried through. With their experience of revolution and their links with the metropolises of Vienna and Berlin, the local squires and journalists had a feeling of belonging to the West, to the Western current of events. The criticism of contemporary European civilization in the Kraków journal *Czas* or in the *Przegląd Poznański* was, in a way, criticism from inside, supported by arguments drawn from Western conservative literature. Things were different in the Kingdom, Lithuania or Volhynia, isolated as they were from the European revolution and counterrevolution by the tsarist *cordon sanitaire*. In the 1850s, ideological debate among the gentry was dominated by the problematic question of peasant tenure which still awaited a solution. Because of the backwardness and isolation of the Russian zone, the problems of the capitalist world still seemed remote, and there was the feeling that they could be avoided. This context favored the revival of the Slavic idea, not as political speculation, but as a product of an epigonistic, post-romantic belief in the civilizational division of Europe. This belief was also shared by the revolutionary democrats in exile.

However, this difference among the partition zones was a difference of points of view and stylistics, not of axiology. The main points in the moral condemnation of civilization differed little between Paris and Moscow, and even less so between Kraków and Volhynia. The European political and social crisis of the late 1840s, generally understood as the demise of liberalism, gave birth to numerous prophets of disaster. In Poland, apart from Rzewuski, the most eloquent of these prophets was Józef Gołuchowski, who was a philosophy professor in Wilno in his youth, and later became a landowner in the Kielce region. He wrote two books on the agrarian question which were published anonymously abroad; the first was written in 1847, and the second in 1849–50. These contain the essential points of the catastrophic school of thought of the mid-nineteenth century.

Every bit as long-winded as Rzewuski, but less doctrinaire, Gołuchowski did not attack science, education and technology. He complained about the laziness of both the upper and lower classes in Poland, the general contempt for work, the squandering of income, and the general decline of estates and farms, and he quoted the industrious puritan Netherlands as an example to be followed. But it so happened that France, with its permanent social upheavals, and not the Netherlands, had become the symbol of the West. Gołuchowski speculated about the force that put contemporary civilization in motion, and found this force in the awakening of human desires. On this point, in fact, more than one liberal economist would have agreed with him, though these "desires," or the growth of needs, would have been treated as a very welcome development.

The conservative Gołuchowski knew better. Arguments about the triumph of the human spirit over matter did not convince him. He saw the exuberant desire to possess and to use as a demon which had been inadvertently freed and which was intent on destroying the entire social structure. "I believe there are two reasons for this. First, civilization, by pandering to excessively sensuous tastes and becoming increasingly emancipated from the rule of religion and morality, corrupts the wealthy, and, following their example, the masses, by awakening in them a multitude of previously unknown sensuous desires which cannot be satisfied because once unharnessed, desire gallops ahead of all means of gratification. . . . Second, competition is nothing less than the race of human labor, whose own self-interest is the jockey who urges it on with the sharpest of spurs; this competition has something antisocial in its nature. . . . In the final reckoning, this is, properly speaking, a war of all against everyone."[78]

For Gołuchowski, civilization, which had become the apotheosis of materialism, carried in its womb the seeds of annihilation and produced its own grave-diggers. For how could those who consumed defend themselves against those who wanted to consume? Socialism and communism proceeded from the same principle of sensuousness, with, in their case, the admixture of the diabolical envy of the dispossessed. The fierce struggle of individuals, classes and parties made the very existence of a nation increasingly improbable: a nation which "no longer strives to be great but, having disintegrated into the individual gluttony because of the pursuit of egoistic aims, madly tears itself apart." Social revolution in the West was unavoidable, but it would build nothing, and destroy much: "God has chosen Satan as the instrument of his work." The infernal trumpets could already be heard, the framework of the edifice was shaking, and it was possible that the catastrophe would come in the lifetime of the existing generation. Europe deserved such a catastrophe since it had not heeded the voice crying in the wilderness. "Universal disasters, universal plagues, are pitiless in their destruction of individuals, the innocent perish side by side with the guilty, because in the face of the greatness of supreme justice individual innocence is of no consequence in this world. The triumph of evil, which seems to be at hand, will respect it even less."[79]

Slavdom could still save itself from the universal revolutionary deluge, provided it learnt something from the experience of the West, that is, provided it turned back from the wrong path, and did not try to imitate the West. "There is still time; let us think long and hard because at this moment our whole future is at stake."[80] Soon, it would be too late.

There was still time because, fortunately, the peasants in Poland and Russia still had limited desires and modest needs, and were easily satisfied. They had yet to learn envy, they had yet to covet the ordeal of civilization, in relation to which they were still in a state of pathetic childlikeness. There was still time for the landlords to win them with love, goodness, religion and education, and to elevate them to a position in which they could enjoy ownership and wealth and participate in society. Here we can perceive the wisdom of the native, Slavic policy, a policy which united rather than separated, which built rather than destroyed.

It was not yet too late, but time was short because the demagogues on the one hand and the absolutist government on the other were trying to abolish property rights, divide estates, and awaken and exploit latent desires. This was the Western way, an imitation of the methods applied by the Austrian and Prussian governments. But forced enfranchisement, which takes from one to give to another, could not solve or complete anything. Once awakened, desires would know no limits. The Polish and Russian peasant had less respect for private property than the Western proletarian, and the government was no less solicitous in its efforts to cajole him than the forces of destruction which tried to use the burning issue of agrarian reform for their own political aims. Among the Slavic nations, which had no industry or proletariat and which were far behind the rest of Europe, it was enough to violate the right of ownership, the foundation of social order, and the flood-gates would open. "Then you will have a social revolution, but several centuries prematurely and without all those wonders of civilization which preceded revolution in the West; because if you discard the modest degree of development which has been achieved in the Slavic lands, barbarianism will come into its own again."[81]

This was not the end of Józef Gołuchowski's undivine comedy: for there was no guarantee that the process would be confined to the Slavic territories.

There was an additional factor in operation: the stifled aspirations of the Polish people to independent existence. Since all previous attempts at recovering independence had proved futile, it was inevitable that people should come to the false conclusion that Poland's road to salvation lay in social revolution. This misconception had infected the desperate, talented youth of the country. Young people, who felt no attachment to the contemporary social system since it prevented them from breathing freely, found themselves the victims of illusory hopes. "When this happens, the social revolution will become organized, and acquire the invaluable assistance of intellectual strength without which no work can endure; in such a case it may be successful and will not be immediately destroyed by the anarchy of the mob. Later, it will become obvious how false these hopes were, but by then the harm will have been done. The Polish and Russian landowner will be the first victim: Poland will collapse, Russia will collapse, and a volcano will open in their place, engulfing in its destructive lava Austria, Germany and the rest of Europe. . . . Like the march of the northern peoples in ancient times, this new vandalism will crush more prosperous countries and extinguish, perhaps for several centuries, the fine light of civilization."[82]

The Polish conservative prognoses of the mid-nineteenth century wavered between hopes of Slavic salvation and premonitions of total apocalypse. Polish defense against Western capitalism and socialism was not strong enough and the enemy was busy creating diversions behind its lines. For the defenders of the hierarchical order, this was a time of anguish; they believed that God was on the side of the landowners, but contemporary history was no longer the work of God. Several years had to pass before they became accustomed to the permanent movement of bourgeois civilization and saw that they could still defend permanence, property and tradition on the ground of this civilization. For the time being, however, they felt besieged and hopeless. Only those who consciously engaged in negotiations with liberalism could suggest a realistic social and economic program. The staunch conservatives were able to perceive the existential evil of capitalist competition, but in its place they could offer only moralistic preaching and a naive faith that the landowners' paternal love of the people would be a sufficient antidote to class conflict.

The conservatives were tireless in their exhortations to the landowners to love their serfs. After 1848, evangelical love among the estates became the main theme of conservative writing. Only such a love could save the world from barbarity. It was to serve as the foundation of a new social structure and a new economy, which would be neither aristocratic nor capitalist, but simply Christian.

It is important to note that this theme appears not only in conservative writings. The dream of Christ's Poland and a world ordered in accordance with evangelical teachings is found in at least three different variations at the time: the communist version (in the agrarian utopias of left-wing émigrés); the messianic version (in Mickiewicz and Cieszkowski); and the conservative version. There were also mixed conceptions, such as Leon Rzewuski's Christian socialism, understood as "the aim of applying evangelical teachings to the relations of production."[83] These variations differed profoundly as regards their attitude to the institution of ownership and the interpretation of the egalitarian idea. They did, however, have a common starting point, namely, their condemnation of economic individualism and their feelings of repulsion towards a world which was an arena for the ruthless rivalry of greed and force. All these doctrines, whether right-wing or left-wing, rejected the capitalist road of development and placed their hopes in the moral transformation of humanity rather than in modern industry or new models for the political organization of society.

The 1850s witnessed a strong sense of a crisis of values in Europe. It is not surprising, therefore, that in Poland, too, various amateurish philosophers and economists produced a large number of schemes for ethical utopias.

In his two volumes of learned elucubrations, generously embellished with hundreds of quotations from the Old and New Testaments, Antoni Morzycki traced the winding path of social progress from the day of the creation, condemning everything in the history of mankind which he saw as a manifestation of the "speculation of pure reason," "pagan rust," the "contradicting thought" of materialism, and the selfishness of the rich and of the state. New names were added on every page to the list of the enemies of brotherhood and progress: we encounter Homer as the extoller of armed conquest, followed by Roman law, which recognized only the "reciprocity of interest," and more or less the entire civilization of the ancient world; then comes Machiavelli, the Reformation, Absolutism, Voltaireanism, Rationalism, the French Revolution (the bestiality of the people being a consequence of the bestiality of the government), Napoleon, Metternich, English colonialism, and of course Hegel, Feuerbach and the other "dreamers of the post-Hegelian school"; on the Eastern side, we have Ivan the Terrible who debased Russia, Peter the Great who Germanized it, and Catherine II, that "embodiment of the spirit of eighteenth-century philosophy and all its cynicism, a philosophy which was submerged in the abyss of a materialism bathed in the glaring light of reason." The Church is not spared either. Since the times of Constantine this Church has become more and more secularized, "it has increased its numbers to the detriment of its spirit"; since Trent, it has replaced its councils with the authority of papal congregations supported by the Jesuit order; finally, the popes, Pius IX included, in their excessive concern about their state and monarchic rights, "have forgotten their mission on the slippery throne of earthly government."[84]

Such a general, radical and pessimistic indictment of almost the whole history of civilization, harsher than that of Henryk Rzewuski, was unprecedented in Polish literature. The basis of this judgment, and at the same time the measure of genuine progress, was "social love combined with reason," a love which was interpreted literally and regarded as a possible foundation for social structure. Morzycki dreamt of a world that would really apply evangelical principles in everyday life, a holy and prudent world; he found models for this world in the Essene or first Christian communities, in some medieval orders and—of course—in Slavdom. Apart from these, history only showed what violence and hatred could achieve, and what reason without love and without God could attain. The last product of this "pure reason" was political economy. It was the economists that invented the rules that enabled individuals to get rich, it was the economists that saw the poor as instruments, as beasts of burden. The individualism of economic theory was contrary to Christ's order of social love. God inflicts poverty as a punishment on those peoples which, befuddled by "these pagan know-alls," greedily rushed forward to implement the principles of political economy. No new idea could be expected from this quarter. France, Germany, England and Spain had rejected the living thought of progress: this "civilization of egoism and violence . . . is the bane of human kind, and the main task of the present epoch is to retreat from the cold, stifling caves of this civilization, even if they are brightened with flowers."[85]

Morzycki strongly believed that this epoch of "baptized paganism" would soon come to an end. A new historical epoch was approaching, the synthetic, cohesive, creative epoch of the "harmonization of elements," a truly Christian epoch. In this new epoch, human beings would free themselves from their enslavement by the state, just as they had already freed themselves from enslavement by their masters; and "*all superiority, authority and power will cease.*"[86] But the progress of unification in love would not stop at the level of national egoism. The future would bring the reconciliation of peoples in brotherhood and peace. This was already being achieved by the development of overland and water transport, industrial exhibitions, and trade, since in this way peoples were getting to know each other and were coming closer to one another. "Evangelical truth is spreading across the world. . . . And when the time comes, peoples that did not know one another before this will sit down to a common feast." The "signs which distinguish separate states" would disappear, and the churches which had been separated for centuries would unite, mankind would become one family and one Church of Christ, and this Church would become a universal state and its gospel would be recognized as the common law.[87]

Morzycki raised the question of who would bring this about and how. According to him, in the epoch of the independence of the individual, the German intellect had been the leader, but its mission was now over. The epoch of the association of people and nations would be led by the Slavs since the social idea of the Slavs always had been and still was social love. Among the Slavs, the Poles were the true people of the gospel. But the Polish spirit could achieve the work of love only through Russia, the only power which had not been shaken by the convulsions of 1848–49, and which now awaited the fulfillment of its destiny. Only Russia could meet the challenge of the proud, corrupt, renegade England which exploited Ireland and overseas countries. The Revelation of St. John applied to Russia and England in its prophecy of the triumph of the East over the whore of Babylon, the mistress of the seas. Providence had chosen Russia to gather together the whole of Slavdom under one tribal banner, to lead it in the fight against Germanism, and to inspire it with the spirit of love and brotherhood of peoples. Admittedly, Russia had not as yet fully embraced this spirit, but under Polish influence, concluded Morzycki, its government was becoming more lenient and more Christian, in a word, more humane, than the Western states.[88]

This is an extraordinary mixture of ideas, taken from all kinds of sources and eclectically linked in the author's mind. Morzycki borrowed from the reactionaries and the democrats, the socialists and the messianists, the Slavophiles and the pan-Slavists. Attempting to establish the sources of these ideas is of less importance than identifying what it was that kept all the heterogeneous ingredients together and turned them into one historiosophical system. The unifying factor was the author's unbending hatred of "Germanism," the term applied by Morzycki (and several others) to the whole of Western civilization, the state of the Franks included. That a country squire from the Polish Kingdom should publish, towards the end of the reign of Nicholas I, a long treatise in the Prussian partition zone, in which he proclaimed England to be the main enemy of mankind and saw in the tsar the instrument which would bring about the Christian brotherhood of peoples—all this might seem an intellectual aberration. It might, if it were not for the fact that loathing for the West, capitalism and liberal economics intensified slowly after the November Rising and became the dominant note in the poorly harmonized Polish orchestra in the period following the Springtide of Nations. Without this loathing, which was no less evident in socially radical literature than in conservative thought, the career of the Slavic idea in Polish minds would be incomprehensible since, after all, it was the least suitable time for such an idea.

It is true that Polish Slavophilism was not homogeneous; it was split by an acrimonious dispute between its main current, which saw "Latin" Poland, with its deep attachment to freedom, as the trustee of the idea of the ancient Slavic commune (in a democratic or patriarchal society), and a smaller group which consisted of the proponents of Russo-Slavism, who were always suspected of national apostasy.[89] The first current was programmatically antitsarist, therefore it was not affected by any new evidence of the policing role played by Russia in Europe, such as its intervention in Hungary. However, the idea of Slavic civilization without Russia always appeared lacking as a philosophy of culture or history. The opposing of the Slavic evangelical character to both the "pagan" West and the "Asian" East, that is, Moscow, was an excellent way of relieving the Polish complex, involving as it did the doctrine of the ethical superiority of the oppressed. However, the prognosis drawn from that fact, namely, that a nation that was politically nonexistent could first morally redeem its fellow Slavs and then the mercantile West, could not survive without a messianic prop rationalizing a faith in the power of the helpless. Besides, the simple traditional opposition between Poland and Europe or Poland and the West brought to light the disturbing inequality of potentials. The reducing of the West to "Germanism" and the simultaneous elevation of Poland to "Slavdom" performed the function of a magic rite: the use of the respective names established an equilibrium between the parties in this spiritual antagonism. (It is worth noting that the West did not even deign to notice this antagonism.)

The Russophile current had no need to resort to magic. Adam Gurowski[90] (following his "conversion"), Wacław Maciejowski[91] and their followers witnessed the synthesis of Slavdom and the antithesis of the West in the state of Nicholas I, and immediately gained a realistic picture of the balance of the forces involved. This piece of geopolitical realism, however, was compensated for by the disarming naiveté they displayed in entrusting the mission of the liberation of the peoples and the unification of Europe to tsarist Russia and the Slavic nations united under her command.

All the variants of Polish Slavophilism, each in its own way, thus proved to be paralogisms. The intricate historiosophical scaffolding was constructed around the simple naive belief that agricultural nations, slow to develop and still untired by the journey of civilization, were, by their nature, honest. Romantic philosophers, beginning with Herder, deduced from this that the future belonged to them; they would provide models for the more economically advanced. That economic progress was the reverse of moral progress had always been the conviction of thinkers, poets, émigrés and farmers who could not adapt to the hustle and bustle of urban life. Urban-industrial civilization, they felt, killed altruism, and thus, contrary to all appearances, was anti-Christian. This civilization had to be opposed with the simple truths of the gospel, and, finally, these truths would conquer Babylon.

Those who were certain of this victory predicted the annihilation of the West, an apocalyptic catastrophe which would be followed by the moral rebirth of the world. Such were the origins of the successive paradoxical versions of catastrophic conservatism produced by the imaginations of radical visionaries. Those who did not share their faith and powers of imagination, but who felt an equally strong loathing for the corruption of bourgeois civilization, could only indulge in nostalgia for the world of pastoral simplicity and homely virtues, a longing for that which had passed, was passing, or would pass in the near future.

Such a world was already becoming extinct; it survived only in literature where its moral position was weak, even if still attractive. In Aleksander Fredro's[92] late comedies we witness the town invading the country. New men, energetic, crude and rapacious, appear in the manor houses of the gentry bringing with them corruption, exploitation, lack of ceremony and "agricultural typhus." They turn the whole world upside down. However, this world, which has resisted change until the present, is equated with inertia, quietism and decrepitude. It offers a weak, unconvincing alternative: impotent tradition, elegiac tones. This is a commonplace found in the literature of many countries: *morituri*, old merry England, the cherry orchard where the axe has already been applied to the roots.

Traditionalism, unless it was mature enough to revalue its legacy, sought refuge in ever remoter corners far from the main routes of the civilizational invasion—but even there it failed to find any invigorating signs of moral robustness. In his Volhynian novels, Józef Ignacy Kraszewski[93] presented a picture of country life which was far from idyllic, and he did not hesitate to castigate the squires for their exploitation of the peasants and brutality towards them. In other passages, he offended his readers with passionate diatribes against the idleness and parochialism of the class of noble landowners for whom "genuine life means vegetation on their patches of ground between the pigsty and the barn." In a cycle of articles published in the *Tygodnik Petersburski* (1837–41), he attacked the laziness of the Polish gentry, their aversion to reading and their "mental stagnation," referring to them as *The Moral Diseases of the Nineteenth Century*.[94]

At the same time, however, he spent the next twenty years complaining without respite about everything that came from the West, especially France: philosophy, literature, technology, laws and manners. One of his novels, similarly entitled *Diseases of the Age* (1857), is the lament, moving in its naive openness, of a gentry thinker horrified at the fact that even Volhynia had been invaded by that dry, cold, terrible civilization, a civilization based on calculation which had no consideration for "people, their customs, their past, habits, memories, and predilections," a civilization which caused even the birds to stop singing. "The world will be transformed into a huge economic–industrial–commercial enterprise, people will become commercial agents, books will be replaced by registers, and life will be replaced by double-entry accounting . . . and perhaps . . . some will like this, but we, who are older and slower of mind, miss our simple gentry past! . . . Let us have more heart and less agronomy, for God's sake; the theories of Bastiat and List cannot take the place of the gospels. . . . Improvements may be brought about slowly and gradually, and they should arise only when necessary, without our imitating things foreign which will Germanize us, denationalize us, Anglicize us, obliterate our native Slavic features. . . . How can we possibly rejoice at that progress which tears our life away from us and turns us into apes of the West?"[95]

These two moral polemics are not identical. The first censures human vices, even if they are the vices of a whole class, as well as cultural failings, but not the foundations of the social system. The second, however, expresses a fundamental skepticism as to the possibility of humanizing bourgeois "progress"; it does not deny its economic achievements, but it warns against the "materialism with which the West is infecting us, which we apply ourselves as a redeeming medicine for our old diseases, unmindful of the fact that this medicine is the cause of much more harmful diseases."[96] This text, and hundreds of other criticisms of capitalism written from a conservative or romantic position, expresses the conviction that feudalism, with all its faults, is a "warm" and humane system, based on personal ties, while capitalism, with all its virtues, is a "cold" system, based on rational and objectified ties. "There is something cold, something that does not appeal to the heart and the imagination" in the spirit and character of the contemporary epoch, is how a writer in the Kraków journal *Czas* put it. This feeling was fairly general in the twilight years of romanticism.

The Polish laments, however, were unique only in their stylistics and in the fact that they still had a defensive character. But the main features of the moral critique of civilization were, to all intents and purposes, the same in London, Kraków and Wilno.

The same *Czas* journalist we mentioned above reviewed, in 1857, several English books on the ethics of the capitalist institutions of Britain—the Bank of England, railway societies, and the stock exchange. This reading furnished him with evidence of the moral corruption of modern society, in which "the spirit of speculation pervades all relationships" and the arrogant, insatiable thirst for knowledge "wants to embrace the whole of creation" but does not seek God. "Only political economists do not lose faith in the principles of their science, only they continue to sing the same tune of progress and civilization. Stock brokers take on the role of reformers and proclaim a new order of things. . . . The people surge into the palaces showing the triumphs and masterpieces of industry. . . . Everywhere . . . [we see] the cult of matter, and it seems that in our times the steam engine, the telegraph and bank drafts have replaced ideas and become the agents of progress."[97]

The spirit of speculation is a force of destruction: "this untiring revolutionary places treacherous mines under the deepest foundations of the social order." He also destroys art and literature by harnessing them to the utilitarian service of the "needs of the time" and by stripping them of imagination and beauty. And since "the whole society has begun to take part in the game," as in England, the stock exchange has become its culture, foisting "legends, customs, laws, and language"[98] on it. Political life and parliament have also succumbed to these laws.

Thus far, this represents a fairly banal and, at that time, widely accepted catalog of capitalist sins. But the author goes further: he shows how a civilization based on capitalism betrays its own principles, and how liberalism destroys its own most sacred values: the result of the development of credit and of monopolies is that individual ownership and independence become a mere fiction. "No civilization had such great and radical contradictions as ours. . . . On the one hand, individualism is growing stronger, while on the other hand, social centralization threatens to submerge every individual being."[99]

The author also describes how freedom and individuality have to contend with the growing centralization of the administration: "Only a strong mechanism is capable of rallying and uniting atomic individuals who wander around without any moral or national force to bind them together. Bureaucracy is an artificial mechanism of this sort, a mechanism which threatens the independence of modern societies."[100]

Thus, speculation and industrialism constitute the greatest breakthrough in the history of mankind: they are the beginning of a new epoch. But this, he claims, is an inhuman epoch, symbolized by the construction of railways which leads to large-scale nomadic movement: hordes of barbarians without

religion, morality or family ties being conveyed by English railway-contrac-
tors from various parts of the country. Anyone who has seen this and who has
pondered the social contradictions that are revealed in the process must ask
himself: "do we really improve ourselves or gain anything from this much
talked about civilization?"[101]

The conservatives' fear of materialist progress was not completely unfounded. It expressed above all the anxiety of the middle gentry who lacked
the knowledge, capabilities and capital necessary for embracing "reasoned
husbandry"; hence their distrust of experiments and their tendency to idealize
the values of the passing world in the hope of prolonging its god-fearing
existence.

Conservative opinion was also, as in the case of Kraszewski, interested in
defending more universal values which were under threat: people's sense of
rootedness, community and tradition. The world of constant change and
expansion, the world of competition and rivalry was perceived as a demonic
enemy which uprooted and destroyed the cultural and local identity of the
individual. In this diagnosis, the old-world traditionalism of the Polish squires
found confirmation in the strand of conservative thought that had matured in
the metropolises of capitalism and that drew its sustenance from long years
of observing the daily successes of this epoch. By the mid-nineteenth century,
conservative thinking had already worked out its own rudimentary theory of
the society of the masses in which human beings, deprived of their history
and alienated from the community, were formally free, but had in actual fact
been enslaved by the increasing concentration of power in the hands of the
economic and administrative authorities.

The conservatives of the mid-nineteenth century voiced almost all the fears
and warnings connected with unhampered economic growth which are still
to be heard today and will continue to be heard for a long time. They were
aware of the phenomena of anomie and alienation, the lonely crowd and
environmental pollution, the ideology of consumption, exploitation, étatisme,
rivalry between powers, and imperialist wars for new markets. However,
while the left, whose diagnoses were generally similar, worked hard to seek
and devise alternative solutions—even if naive or maximalist—to the problems of social and economic organization, the conservatives could offer little
but exorcisms. With the exception of England, of course, where they greatly
contributed to the development of factory laws and a modern parliamentary
culture which would later serve as an instrument of social reform.

Christian social thought in Poland enjoyed much support, although ideologically it was divided. It tended to be the domain of laymen, without
participation on the part of the institutionalized church. It is striking that

Christian social thinkers lacked any understanding of the fact that capitalism was not an invention or a draft project, but resulted from the association of the desire to possess with scientific and technological inventiveness. Capitalist models for the organization of production spread since, in an epoch of unhampered population growth, they assured the even faster growth of productivity, and also because they offered a range of goods and wages which could attract the pariahs of feudal society.

The Christian moralists responded to all of this with their noble homilies, and their idea that human nature must be changed. They knew, better than anyone else, that man does not live by bread alone, and believed that if man tried to live by the Word, then God would not deny him bread either. After the disastrous famines of the 1840s, from Galicia to Ireland, this appeared a rather forlorn hope. The struggle against the demon of economics could not replace, unfortunately, the battle against potato blight and cholera. It was not the industrial proletariat whose bellies were bloated by famine on the Vistula, and it was not the fault of agronomy that gentry agriculture was declining.

For this reason, the conservative camp and the supporters of an ostentatiously Christian approach had to develop a different line of argument, a more practical and optimistic combination which would reconcile the gospel with economics and technology, and the Polish gentry with Western capitalism. This orientation, which we have already presented, albeit in a different context, was also moralistic, since moralizing pervaded all Polish social and economic thought at that time. Propaganda in favor of credit societies or new methods of fertilization always had to be justified by showing that they served more sublime values.

The ideological texts of Andrzej Zamoyski and his associates[102] abound in such Christian moral justifications. But their moralizing was of a different kind than that of the prophets of doom. The reason for the emergence of a school of liberalized conservatism was the conviction on the part of some gentry-based intellectuals that antioccidental, anticapitalist jeremiads were historically sterile. They understood that economic and social changes were the result of spontaneous, unplanned activity. They could not be stopped or given a different course by sermons, and there was no point in trying to do this. To be sure, the task of "true conservatism" was to see to it that the process of change remained natural and organic, which meant that "social demagogy" could not be allowed to force this process in an artificial, revolutionary way. It is, however, worth quoting the ideologue of this camp, Ludwik Górski, writing in the wake of the Springtide of Nations: "to trust the power of tradition to such an extent as to discard everything which represents progress or change in the ideas and needs of the age, to censure all attempts at keeping our society at the same level of civilization with the rest of Europe, is to substitute prejudice for truth, and backwardness for tradition; it is to expect reward without doing anything to earn it; it is to put oneself in the position of an attacked man who has lost his weapons and who, rather than seeking a new weapon, brandishes his bare arm in the conviction that he can defend himself; in short, it is both erroneous and ridiculous."[103]

Tomasz Potocki stated overtly that it was necessary to break away from "reaction" and by prudent reforms anticipate the threat of a revolutionary solution to the peasant question. "Genuine conservatism . . . does not involve stifling the spirit of the time, but steering it."[104] Thus, the attitude to tradition was to be critical and selective: it was no longer a matter of preserving the *status quo*, the landowning gentry had to guide the transformation of society firmly. An ideal model was the Tory party in England, a country admired by the liberal conservatives, where, as Andrzej Zamoyski put it, "practical enlightenment, and slow but sure advances prevent progress by leaps and bounds."[105]

They knew well what kind of progress they wanted. These feudal land-owners, still using forced peasant labor and only slowly replacing it with money rent, were enthusiastic supporters of free competition. The better educated among them studied the works of liberal economists, Say and Chevalier included, regarded political economy as the queen of all sciences, and admired agronomy more than philosophy and poetry. Admittedly, not everything coming from the West was commendable. Poland needed to develop an immunity to the toxins of philosophical materialism, religious skepticism and, most of all, socialism, this "plague of modern ideas," but it had to be open to new technology and the principles of the capitalist economy. In the system of education which they advocated, just as in the case of the puritans, individual interest paved the way for the welfare of all, and sober calculation was combined with moralizing pathos. "Let us remember that accountancy represents God's thought in the form of figures," cried one writer at the time, a representative of the party which tried to overcome old prejudices in order to turn the gentry into modern farmers and agricultural industrialists.[106] Indeed, their Christ was a good bookkeeper.

Andrzej Zamoyski agreed with Chevalier that the progress of liberal capitalism meant at the same time a growth of morality in public life. For the new civilization was based on three fundamental principles: individual freedom, equality in law and reciprocity among the nations. Freedom meant the abolition of serfdom, free choice of occupation, and respect for property. Thanks to freedom, man confirmed his sense of responsibility and was led to follow the commands of his conscience without excessive legal coercion.

Equality in law meant "complete reciprocity between the producer and the consumer, between the seller and the buyer, between the employer and his man-power," which would bring all the social classes closer together. Finally, freedom and reciprocity in commerce would bring the various nations closer together and unite them. By this token, the Western countries of Europe were world leaders not only in the industrial and intellectual fields, but also in the area of morality.[107]

This did not mean that the landowning Occidentalists, who on the whole accepted technological progress and the capitalist rules of play, were blind to the social dangers inherent in the Western model of industrialization. They were concerned about periodical "industrial–commercial tremors" and the effects of mass proletarianization. However, they did not see them as sufficient reason for taking fright, turning back and sticking to natural economy. As one of them wrote, "even if some of the extreme consequences of the present western movement cast a shadow on the whole, we are too close to the beginning to worry about the end. The ocean waters hide menacing rocks in some places, but no one who has to travel gives up sea voyages, in particular since others have already discovered those rocks and marked them with suitable warning signs."[108]

The modern landowners already knew what kind of civilization the Poles needed. They also knew what kind of morality they needed. Fryderyk Skarbek wrote in 1848 that the common people should not be required to observe a strict morality which would not allow for anything between virtue and perfidy. "Morality," he went on, "is good in as far as it is practical and in as far as it can be practiced by everybody;" such morality, he said, must involve personal advantage, and not sacrifice.[109] The maxim was also applied to the landowning class. The founders of the Agrarian Society were not sentimental; they asked for reason, not charity, and advocated a love of the people that would bring returns. Piety, industry, and thrift were for them the three main virtues, a combination that revealed their affinity to the bourgeois ethical code. Their favorite moralist was Benjamin Franklin, but tailored in such a way as not to raise excessively the expectations of the thrifty and industrious peasants.[110]

This was the basic inner inconsistency of the marriage of conservatism and liberalism. Skarbek, becoming increasingly conservative with age, still argued that the aim of civilizational progress was "not only to provide [all men] with the means of subsistence, but also to expand their sphere of desires and joys, and above all to bring about an improvement in their way of life." In this view, it was futile to dream about the moral improvement of the people as long as the masses lived in a bestial state of "torpor and inertia" and their aspirations reached no higher than their basic needs. But he also expressed the fear that the aspiration to a better life on the part of the working classes might grow faster than the means amassed through godly work and thrift, since such a situation threatened to upset the social order. "In such a state of affairs, the aspiration to a good life takes on the form of an unassuaged desire . . . [Such a desire] produces passions, leads men astray, and even causes crime; it ceases to foster morality."[111]

Skarbek's argument was that the people should acquire civilization in a manner befitting their station, and that they should not imitate the life of the upper classes since this would breed envy, while envy in turn would breed rebellion and revolution. This meant that equality in law was a good thing, provided everyone knew their place and their aspirations were not too high.

This is also how the problem was understood by the landowners from Zamoyski's circle. They were unable to decide whether society was a free market or an organic union of hierarchically ranked classes. The eclectic character of their doctrine reveals itself in their programs for reform and in their practice in everyday life. They wanted to free the peasant from the obligation of corvée and later enable him to buy out his holding, but at the same time they wanted to make sure that the gentry continued to control the village community. They disseminated Franklin's ideal of the self-made man in didactic tales for peasants, and pointed out, in the same tales, that happiness could be attained only by remaining in the social estate into which one had been born. They extolled enterprise while ridiculing the *nouveaux riches*, and proclaimed that "money legitimizes man's value in society" while underlining the significance of the gentry as an "archconservative" body for the nation. A propensity for half measures characterizes almost all the writings of the landowning liberals. Their irresolution resulted from the mutual permeating of two hierarchies of values which could not be integrated into one coherent system. Each of the hierarchies imposed a different interpretation of economic change, a different attitude to urbanization, to social mobility, to the spread of education, even a different reading of catechism.

Of this body of people, Tomasz Potocki took the most Western stance. He accepted with almost no reservations the liberal axiology of capitalism, and argued that unrestricted economic freedom, the abolition of privileges, equality in law and inequality in ownership embodied the social principles of Christianity.[112] The opposite extreme was represented by Jan Mittelstaedt, who in the late 1850s resolved to create his own system of Christian political economy for the benefit of the Polish gentry.

Mittelstaedt belonged to the extreme right wing of the Agrarian Society. While everybody else in the Kingdom was speaking of enfranchisement,

Mittelstaedt proposed that the gentry expropriate the peasants and turn them into manorial laborers. (He had one estate in the Kingdom, and another in the Poznań region, where he purchased a number of peasant farms after the introduction of agrarian reforms.) His book is the work of a God-fearing agronomist: on one page he writes of manure, and on the next about eternal redemption.[113] Admittedly, we can find a similar juxtaposition of the sacred and the secular in Cieszkowski, but there is a difference: Cieszkowski blessed fertilizers (artificial fertilizers, in fact), while Mittelstaedt hired Almighty God as the manager of his estate.

In his "Outlines of political economy in accordance with the Christian religion," we find again and again the kind of reasoning typical of romantic Slavophiles. Material progress had failed to bring man happiness; society fell into atoms; the Germanic peoples (that is, the English and the Germans) had only superficially adopted the Christian faith, and the French, though more noble, were also pagans since they had "proclaimed the stock exchange their new temple and worship at the shrine of the golden calf." Adam Smith had sacrificed spirit for matter; the socialist reformers meant well but had failed to invent anything worthwhile; the rich were dying of dyspepsia and the proletariat were dying of hunger; everywhere technological and intellectual progress proved to be harmful and only served to bring closer "the sorry end of Western civilization."[114] The Slavs would not embark on this hopeless road of theoretical speculation and practical reason. The people of God would introduce sound economic principles without any theorizing: "we find it easier to govern our lives by simple reason enlightened by the teachings of the Savior than by the sophistry of Western Europe." It was easier for the Slavs because they were a meek and agrarian people, a people whose spirit had been tempered by poverty and suffering. It was they who would begin the epoch of social love which would rescue the world from spiritual death at the last moment.[115]

In commerce, the argument went, social love could be embodied beautifully provided the interest rate was low, since otherwise only the usurer would get rich. There were to be no customs duties on grain exports, "because *the more we give other nations, the richer we become.*" Competition was a good thing, only it was not to be run on pagan lines; mutual rivalry was to manifest itself in love and sacrifice. After all, God divided the nations according to their capacity for material and spiritual production, the way workers are divided in a factory. "Let the Polish Kingdom produce the best wheat and practice the Christian virtues; let the Italians supply us with oranges, lemons and the fine arts; let the Russian Empire provide us with precious furs, hides, raw materials, etc. Through commerce the nations come to need one another, . . . and come to know and love each other better."[116]

Christian virtues had finally been linked with the price of wheat and Slavic eschatology with the low interest rate. There was nothing easier than to apply these principles to the rural economy since it was all a question of figures, and the figures were irresistible: "in the future, the men and squires will speak eloquently in the language of figures or the Gospel, and all vain talk will cease." Till then, the author explains "how prudent and beneficial it is to love one's neighbor."[117]

So, the squire was to love his neighbor out of self-interest. As regards the people, Mittelstaedt says, those economists commit a grave error who wish to encourage them to be more industrious by pointing out the material advantages to be gained, "or, worse still, who attempt to generate artificial needs in the producing class, cultivating industry and diligence in the worker so that he will have the means of satisfying these needs: only Germans, for whom philosophy has taken the place of religion, can work like that; but woe to us and to our workers when live faith is extinguished in our hearts, because then the world will become a battlefield of wild beasts where the stronger and the craftier are victorious and trample on and devour the weaker." Mass consumption, he argued, should be checked rather than encouraged; a peasant who "learns to smoke Havana cigars, drink champagne, wear fine costly clothes, and eat Strasbourg pâté" would not be civilized. People should rather be encouraged to work "not by need but by the feeling of love." It was necessary "to convince our people that each of us works in the service of God." However, the author adds sadly, "our people have not yet acquired the moral disposition to work from a sense of love, spontaneously, of their own accord; therefore, we still have to force them to work." According to him, the simplest way of achieving this, after the abolition of serfdom would be "a year's service." This would be beneficial for the demesne, since a farmhand did not even have to earn enough to support his family: the "rest of the food they need may be purchased with the earnings of his wife and adolescent children or with the money raised by breeding poultry and pigs."[118]

This, he argued, would also be most advantageous for civilization. Mittelstaedt was no Henryk Rzewuski, who idolized the simple sower and loathed the cogs and wheels of noisy machines. On the contrary, the new Slav welcomed modern life enthusiastically, along with rational, western-style farming which needed a lot of land and a handful of people to cultivate it and breed animals. He already sensed the significance which electrical power, then practically unknown in Poland, would acquire in the near future. This Christian who criticized pagan England was in fact a British landlord, a modern farmer, a grain merchant and a pastor all in one: "let wind, water, steam and electricity do the work for people . . ., let rickety carts harnessed to peasant horses disappear, and let everything operate according to the laws of mechanics."[119]

Or, rather, according to the laws of mechanics, the gospel and economics. It is easy to sneer at this author who reached the ultimate in utilitarian hypocrisy, turning every idea into business and every piece of business into an idea. The method was fairly common, but we are not concerned here with unmasking his class hypocrisy. Our aim is to demonstrate how persistent was the problem of moral assessment of cultural and economic systems.

In the mid-nineteenth century, liberal economic thought found itself in an impasse: attacked from the right and the left, it devoted more time to justifying capitalism than to studying its mechanisms. The Polish followers of modern trends, for whom the West of the present was the Poland of the future, had no trouble in finding suitable arguments in Bastiat's *Economic Harmonies*, Chevalier's *Letters on the Organisation of Labour*, or Baudrillart's lectures. In 1858, Henri Baudrillart won the first prize in the competition of the Academy of Moral Sciences in Paris for his essay *Des rapports de la morale et de l'économie politique*; subsequently he taught this subject at the Collège de France and published his lectures in 1860. The following year a fairly free adaptation of his book appeared in Warsaw. This was an unsophisticated apology composed of maxims which had been current for the past fifty years about the moral advantages of capital, ownership, free labor, public education, industry and railways. The cultural universalism of this attitude is significant: industrial civilization is good for all peoples, not only for Europeans. Human races do not differ as regards their skills, they only differ as far as the level of education is concerned. Once the East was the leader of universal progress, now this role has been taken over by Europe. In industrial work, physical strength counts less and less, while intellectual and moral strength have become more significant; therefore "the most moral peoples nowadays are those who have the largest capital." If this is the case, then it is ridiculous to yearn for primeval, barbarian simplicity.[120]

Baudrillart personalized economic forces and categories in a Christian spirit: land, labor and capital are merely "auxiliary elements of production"; the economic subject is man who is gifted with a soul and a body. This sounds fine, but the true nature of liberal moralism always revealed itself when it came to discussing the soul and the body of the worker. As so many before him, the professor of the Collège de France rejoiced at the fact that the steam engine had such a positive influence on the family life of workers and that it "called women and children to work." He found it marvelous that large-scale production was replacing the small, scattered workshops of previous times and saw in it the fulfillment of the principle of the economy of effort. "In the face of the beneficial effects of manufacturing, the grievances of Owen, Sismondi's declamations and the sentimental complaints of small producers die down." According to Baudrillart, the worker in the factory fares better than the craftsman; his life is better regulated, his labor is less toilsome but his working hours are longer, which means that he has less chance of being corrupted by idleness. Moreover, the manufacturing worker works with others: "*the sweetness of company* makes his work easier and has a beneficial effect on his life." Here, the Polish translator, or rather adapter, of the work adds that while for the German worker it is enough that he is paid fairly, the Polish worker, who has a Slavic soul, also needs to feel attached to his master, and requires "kindly encouragement." In this respect, the clergy can help because "with Christian humility the hardest task becomes the *sweet labor* which the Heavenly Father expects from us."[121]

Zygmunt Dangel, the author of an introduction to political economy which in fact contains whole pages copied from the Polish edition of Baudrillart, was also full of sweetness. "Only those truths which are taken from Christ's teachings are economic truths," he wrote, from which it can easily be deducted that economics is simply synonymous with morality. However, Dangel argues that the socialists have no right to invoke Christ, because Christ preached charity and not communism. "Thus, socialism and political economy represent a contradiction, or two oppositions engaged in permanent battle, in which the latter tries to consolidate and implement man's freedom of spirit and of matter, while the former violates divine laws by restricting self-reliance." Therefore, the uprooting of socialism is the duty of economics, a science which "leads mankind through supreme wisdom, supreme philosophy, and supreme morality, according to the path laid down for us by Jesus Christ."[122]

As further reading of this text makes obvious, Jesus Christ was a declared supporter of free trade, and an enemy of the "protectionist system" which was the worst superstition of backwardness. "Free trade is a banner under which all *libre échangistes*, all true economists of the present age, fight against the legions of medieval superstition and prejudice. Free trade is the morning star which illuminates the nation's education . . . Finally, it is the foundation and he who builds on it finds increasing confirmation in his life of the words of the Holy Scriptures, namely, that he was created in the image and likeness of God as the Lord of All things, the power of whose Spirit dominates the whole world."[123] Such is the language of textbooks of this period.

Józef Supiński,[124] writing at the same time, did not take the name of the
Lord his God in vain. He also belonged to the generation which sought a
synthesis between Christian moral philosophy and economics. But he aimed
higher: he discovered divine thought not in manorial accounts, but in the
general plan of the universe and in the progress of human societies. No one
since Kamieński had censured so harshly the anti-economic moralists from
the ranks of gentry traditionalists or romanticists. Every inch a liberal,
Supiński claimed that "only the material power of the nation, of this aggregate
of individual beings, can bring it freedom, education and independence. For
this reason, the science of social economics, which you call crude materialism, does not sap the principles of morality and education, because it itself is
based on education and morality. By mapping out the roads leading to
property, power and order, it removes the sources of ignorance, humiliation
and corruption. . . . Its truths can harm, and in the future they definitely shall
harm, only those who try to hamper universal progress for their own aims."[125]

He then erupts into a glorious tirade against those who pronounce curses
upon industry, the accumulation of resources, and enterprise, against the poets
and admirers of the dead past who impudently impose their own phobias on
their own people and try to turn them away from their means of rescue. "Do
not try to make us hate England and France, because England and France rule
the world and we are heedful of the whole world; do not call their life a 'fetid
water-hole', because this water-hole produces people whose works cause
your own light to be dimmed; do not try to tarnish their thriftiness by calling
it egoism, because this egoism makes such sacrifices for the commonwealth
of which we cannot even dream."[126]

While the author sneers at the mystical initiations of theology and romantic
poetry, he can perhaps be seen as a mystic himself, a mystic of learning and
progress: "Everything passes," he wrote, "save the eternal truths which lie
far away, hidden from us and separated from this world by aeons of time.
Impatient man fills with his own being the void which he cannot endure."
The exact sciences reveal the mystery of God and this Polish *homo impatiens*,
just as Condorcet before him, also predicts that man will enjoy a "permanence
close to immortality." He is dazzled by electric sparks which "carry words
across the world at a speed for which a thunderbolt is no match, with a magic
force which causes time to vanish." He goes on to delight in the kind of
futuristic visions that we find in Auguste Blanqui: "There is one law for
everybody. . . in the face of this law a private wrong becomes a public
offense. . . . The expansive towns shine with a life and brilliance never known
before. . . roads and water routes criss-cross fields covered with lush crops. . .
the lands and the seas are free of outlaws. . . schools for the people. . . ever

more universal political rights. . . banks, shares, savings societies, financial openness, population censuses, steam, railways." This is no utopia. This is the human spirit changing the face of the world. "Who can fathom the further course of this progress? And who can predict the future of the whole of mankind?" Centuries are mere days and hours. A new, brave world is close by. "Yes, it is a new world, a burning world in which the two worlds of Christ merge into one, because the equality descends from the clouds to take root in the earth. ... Nations grow together into one uniform body which will one day live by *work and knowledge*, untroubled by fear, protection, fame, poetry and slavery. The farther back we go, the more mysticism, art and phantasms we find; the farther forward we go, the more truth and unembroidered facts we see."[127]

Supiński is not describing an utopia, but a whirlwind of social life. Man rids himself of anxiety about his soul and about his possessions; he rids himself of the demons of the past and becomes the master of his own lot. This is infinite progress, in which there is a "prevalence of natural truths and divine laws grasped by human knowledge." Rather than creating illusory worlds: "Let us live peacefully in the world where the Creator placed us; this world will not give birth to a Columbus who will discover More's island or the happy state of Father John."[128]

He could also have added that this world would not give birth to a Doctor Faustus since, after all, God readily reveals the secrets of nature to daring scholars, and thus impatient mankind would not have to pay with the loss of its soul for the power and multiple skills it received. It was only the romanticists and some conservatives who sensed some demoniac element in machinery and the liberated masses. The imagination of the progressives had not yet reached the stage where it could consider the possibility of a division of values. They had not yet sensed the tragedy of the undivine comedy. They still had trust in human reason and in the wisdom of history. They saw the future as a land of plenty, where eternal peace would prevail among the different classes and nations, and so they had no fears about the fate of the world. In the poor landscape of their own country they obstinately continued to stitch together the *sacrum* and the *profanum*: the great promise and the small affairs of everyday life. But the thread was to come unraveled again and again.

Notes to Chapter 3

1. Cf. J. B. Bury, *The Idea of Progress: An Inquiry into Its Origin and Growth* (New York, 1955), p. 178.

2. J.-J. Rousseau, "A Discourse on the Origin of Inequality," in *The Social Contract and Discourses*, transl. by G. D. Cole (London, 1938), p. 185.

3. Ibid., pp. 236–7.

4. Ibid., p. 239.

5. "A Discourse on the Arts and Sciences," ibid., p. 133.

6. "A Discourse on the Origin of Inequality," ibid., p. 214.

7. Rousseau, "Odpowiedź królowi polskiemu," in his *Trzy rozprawy z filozofii społecznej*, ed. H. Elzenberg (Warsaw, 1956), pp. 84–5, 91–2.

8. B. Baczko, *Rousseau: samotność i wspólnota* (Warsaw, 1964), p. 170.

9. S. Leszczyński, "Odpowiedź króla polskiego," in Rousseau, *Trzy rozprawy*, p. 63.

10. Ignacy Krasicki (1735–1801), a Catholic bishop, poet and novelist, regarded as the greatest representative of eighteenth-century classicism in Polish literature; best known as the author of fables and satires in verse.

11. Quoted after R. Wołoszyński, *Ignacy Krasicki: utopia i rzeczywistość* (Wrocław, 1970), p. 348.

12. I. Krasicki, *Pisma wybrane*, vol. 3 (Warsaw, 1954), p. 257.

13. *Mikołaja Doświadczyńskiego przypadki* (1776), a novel of adventure in which the hero learns about the world by experience, hence his name Doświadczyński, meaning "Experience-seeker."

14. Krasicki, *Pisma wybrane*, vol. 3, p. 179.

15. See J.-P. Hulin, *La ville et les écrivains anglais 1770–1820* (Lille, 1978); R. Williams, *Culture and Society 1780–1950* (Harmondsworth, 1979), and *The Country and the City* (London, 1973); et al.

16. J. Michalski, "Warszawa' czyli o antystołecznych nastrojach w czasach Stanisława Augusta," in *Studia Warszawskie*, vol. 12 (Warsaw, 1972), p. 77.

17. Jakub Jasiński (1761–1794), a poet, soldier, Polish "Jacobin," the leader of the insurrection of 1794 in Wilno; died in battle in the defense of Warsaw against Suvorov's army.

18. Franciszek Salezy Jezierski (1740–1791), a priest, educator and a radical political writer in the days of the Four Years Seym, an advocate of burghers' civil rights.

19. D. Bończa-Tomaszewski, *Rolnictwo: poema oryginalne* (Kraków, 1802), quoted after A. Witkowska, *Sławianie, my lubim sielanki. . .* (Warsaw, 1972), p. 103.

20. J. K. Szaniawski, "O naturze i przeznaczeniu urzędowań w społeczności" (1808), in H. Hinz and A. Sikora (eds.), *Polska myśl filozoficzna Oświecenie—Romantyzm* (Warsaw, 1964), p. 256.

21. Quoted after M. Manteufflowa, *J. K. Szaniawski: ideologia i działalność 1815–1830* (Warsaw, 1936), p. 86.

22. Quoted from the foreword by K. Krzeczkowski to F. Skarbek, *Pisma pomniejsze,* vol. 1 (Warsaw, 1936), pp. xxii–xxiv.

23. Ibid., p. 506.

24. A. M. Skałkowski, *Aleksander Wielopolski w świetle archiwów rodzinnych*, vol. 1 (Poznań, 1947), p. 198.

25. Brodziński's tirade, as remembered by K. W. Wójcicki, quoted after A. Witkowska, *Kazimierz Brodziński* (Warsaw, 1968), pp. 218–19.

26. J. L. Żukowski, *O pansczyźnie* (Warsaw, 1830), pp. 142–3.

27. See N. Assorodobraj, "Elementy świadomości klasowej mieszczaństwa (Francja 1815–1830)," *Przegląd Socjologiczny*, vol. 10 (1948), pp. 139 90.

28. J.-B. Say, *Traité d'économie politique* (Paris, 1972), pp. 25, 42.

29. L. Epsztein, *L'économie et la morale aux débuts de capitalisme industriel en France et en Grande-Bretagne* (Paris, 1966), pp. 105–13.

30. Ch.-B. Dunoyer, *L'industrie et la morale* . . . (Paris, 1825).

31. Ibid., p. vii.

32. Ibid., pp. 37–8.

33. Ibid., pp. 91–7.

34. Ibid., pp. 342 50.

35. Epsztein, *L'économie et la morale*, pp. 66–9, 82–4.

36. Dunoyer, *L'industrie et la morale*, p. 242.

37. H. Comte de Saint-Simon, "New Christianity" (1825) in his *Selected Writings*, ed. and transl. by F. M. H. Markham (Oxford, 1952), p. 83.

38. *Doctrine de Saint-Simon: Exposition.* Première année: 1829. Ed. C. Bouglé et E. Halévy (Paris, 1924), p. 267.

39. Ibid., pp. 326–8, 377–8.

40. Saint-Simon, "Organizator" (1820), in *Pisma wybrane*, ed. J. Trybusiewicz, vol. 2 (Warsaw, 1968), p. 324.

41. Saint-Simon, "New Christianity," in *Selected Writings*, p. 105.

42. *Doctrine de Saint-Simon*, p. 261.

43. Saint-Simon, "Organizator," *Pisma wybrane*, vol. 2, p. 318.

44. *Doctrine de Saint-Simon*, pp. 221–2, 486.

45. August Cieszkowski (1814–1894), an unorthodox Christian philosopher and economist who also wrote in German and French. He developed a system of national Messianism, only part of which was published during his lifetime. Some of his works are available in English in *Selected Writings of August Cieszkowski*, ed. and transl. by Andre Liebich (Cambridge, 1979).

46. A. Cieszkowski, *Ojcze Nasz*, vol. 3 (Poznań, 1923), p. 215.

47. A. Walicki, *Filozofia a mesjanizm* (Warsaw, 1970), pp. 76, 88; see also his *Philosophy and Romantic Nationalism: The Case of Poland* (Oxford, 1982), pp. 295–307.

48. Cieszkowski's notes, published in A. Walicki et al. (eds.), *700 lat myśli polskiej. Filozofia i myśl społeczna w latach 1831–1864* (Warsaw, 1977), p. 338.

49. Cieszkowski, *Ojcze Nasz*, vol. 3, p. 63.

50. Ibid., vol. 1 (Poznań, 1922), p. 168.

51. Cieszkowski, *De la pairie et de l'aristocratie moderne* (Paris, 1844), and *Du crédit et de la circulation* (Paris, 1839), quoted after *Filozofia i myśl społeczna w latach 1831–1864*, pp. 328–36.

52. Cieszkowski's notes, ibid., pp. 336–7.

53. Cieszkowski, *Ojcze Nasz*, vol. 3, p. 214.

54. Henryk Kamieński (1813–1865), a democratic political writer and conspirator, philosopher and economist; persecuted by the tsarist police and administration, emigrated to Switzerland in 1851.

55. H. Kamieński, *Filozofia ekonomii materialnej ludzkiego społeczeństwa z dodaniem mniejszych pism filozoficznych*, ed. by B. Baczko (Warsaw, 1959), p. 54.

56. Ibid., pp. 36, 38.

57. Ibid., pp. 39–41, 50, 117.

58. Ibid., p. 50.

59. Ibid., pp. 53–5.

60. Ibid., p. 346–7.

61. Ibid., pp. 315, 318.

62. Ibid., 364–5.

63. Ibid., p. 100.

64. Ibid., pp. 325–6.

65. Ivan F. Paskevitch (1782–1856), Russian Field Marshal. For his role in the crushing of the Polish uprising of 1830–1831, he received the title of the Duke of Warsaw and was appointed Tsar Nicholas I's Viceroy in the Polish Kingdom, an office he held until his death.

66. Piotr Steinkeller (1799–1854), the best known Polish industrialist and businessman in the 1830s; though full of energy and ideas, he eventually went bankrupt.

67. "Organic work," the name usually given to economic, educational and cultural efforts aimed at raising the civilizational standards of Polish society and at strengthening the nation's resources and self-organization in the face of adverse policies conducted by the partitioning powers.

68. In February 1846, an anti-Austrian rising was about to break out in Galicia, which was to grant the peasants the ownership of their plots. However, incited by Austrian officials, the peasants turned against the gentry, murdered many landlords and plundered manor houses in some parts of Western Galicia. This "fratricidal slaughter" prevented the outbreak of the rising.

69. S. Ossowski, *Dzieła*, vol. 3 (Warsaw, 1967), p. 166.

70. *Nie-Boska Komedia (The Un-divine Comedy)*, a visionary drama written by Zygmunt Krasiński, a young romantic poet; published anonymously in Paris in 1835. In the final act, the revolutionary forces under the command of a fanatical leader defeat the last defenders of religion and tradition but are then held back by a miraculous vision of Christ.

71. Henryk Rzewuski (1791–1866), a talented, arch-conservative novelist and publicist, a Russophile and Paskevitch's courtier.

72. H. Rzewuski, *Pisma*, vol. 1 (St. Petersburg, 1851), pp. 42–3.

73. Ibid., vol. 1, p. 60; vol. 2, p. 41.

74. Ibid., vol. 1, p. 59.

75. Rzewuski in *Dziennik Warszawski*, 1852, quoted after A. Zajączkowski, *Z dziejów inteligencji polskiej* (Wrocław, 1962), p. 104.

76. Rzewuski, "Cywilizacja i religia," *Dziennik Warszawski*, 1851, nos. 21, 22.

77. Rzewuski, *Pisma*, vol. 1, p. 49.

78. J. Gołuchowski, *Rozbiór kwestyi włościańskiej w Polsce i w Rossyi w r. 1850* (Poznań, 1851), pp. 194–5.

79. Ibid., pp. 18, 199–200, 533, 689.

80. Gołuchowski, *Kwestya włościańska w Polsce* (Leipzig, 1849), p. 109.

81. Gołuchowski, *Rozbiór kwestyi włościańskiej*, p. 199.

82. Gołuchowski, *Kwestya włościańska w Polsce*, p. 295.

83. L. Rzewuski, "O dążnościach reorganizacyjnych w społeczeństwie," in A. Walicki et al. (eds.), *Filozofia i myśl społeczna w latach 1831–1864*, p. 969.

84. A. M. Mora [A. Morzycki], *Fundamenta budowy spółecznej zastosowane do Narodu Polskiego*, 2 vols. (Poznań, 1852–53), passim.

85. Ibid., vol. 1, p. 224; vol. 2, pp. 127–30.

86. Ibid., vol. 2, pp. 156–9.

87. Ibid., vol. 1, pp. 112–13, 133, 182–4.

88. Ibid., vol. 2, pp. 293–322.

89. See Z. Klarnerówna, *Słowianofilstwo w literaturze polskiej lat 1800 do 1848* (Warsaw, 1926).

90. Adam Gurowski (1805–1866), a conspirator before, and a radical journalist during the November Rising; in 1832, one of the founders of the Polish Democratic Society in exile and spokesman for its left wing. In 1834, under amnesty granted by the tsar, he returned to Warsaw, where he supported Russian pan-Slavism with no less zeal; condemned as a renegade by Polish opinion, he again left for the West and eventually settled in the USA, where he made himself known as a political writer.

91. Wacław A. Maciejowski (1790–1883), a historian of the laws and customs of the ancient Slavs, a Polish propagator of the Russian orthodox variety of Slavophilism.

92. See note 55 to chapter 1.

93. Józef Ignacy Kraszewski (1812–1887), a novelist, publicist and historian, the most prolific and the most popular Polish writer in that period; lived in Wilno, Volhynia, Warsaw, and, from 1863, in Dresden as an exile.

94. J. I. Kraszewski, *Wybór pism*, vol. 9, ed. P. Chmielowski (Warsaw, 1893), pp. 50–74.

95. Kraszewski, *Choroby wieku: studyum patologiczne* (Wilno, 1857), vol. 1, pp. 6, 9, 153; vol. 2, pp. 5, 25.

96. Ibid., vol. 2, p. 144.

97. M. Słomczewski, "Charakter i niebezpieczeństwa cywilizacji przemysłowej," *Czas—Dodatek miesięczny* 1857, vol. 7, pp. 583–6.

98. Ibid., pp. 631–42.

99. Ibid., p. 587.

100. Ibid., p. 663.

101. Ibid., p. 647.

102. See note 79 to chapter 2.

103. L. Górski, *Wybór pism* (Warsaw, 1908), p. 180.

104. Krzyżtopór [T. Potocki], *Poranki karlsbadzkie* (Poznań, 1858), p. 29.

105. S. Kieniewicz, *Między ugodą a rewolucją: Andrzej Zamoyski w latach 1861–1862* (Warsaw, 1962), p. 38.

106. *Roczniki Gospodarstwa Krajowego* 1858, quoted after R. Czepulis, *Myśl społeczna twórców Towarzystwa Rolniczego (1842–1861)* (Wrocław, 1964), p. 122.

107. A. Zamoyski, "O postępie," *Roczniki Gospodarstwa Krajowego*, vol. 22 (1853), pp. 42–75.

108. Z. Fudakowski, "Dziennikarstwo i przemysł," *Gazeta Codzienna* 1860, no. 262.

109. F. Skarbek, *Pisma pomniejsze*, vol. 2, pp. 349–51.

110. Czepulis, *Myśl społeczna*, pp. 151–2.

111. Skarbek, *Pisma pomniejsze*, vol. 2, pp. 344, 347, 360–62.

112. Krzyżtopór [T. Potocki], *O urządzeniu stosunków rolniczych w Polsce* (2nd ed.: Poznań, 1859), p. 13.

113. J. Mittelstaedt, *Zarysy ekonomii politycznej zgodne z religią chrześcijańską zastosowane do gospodarstwa wiejskiego* (Warsaw, 1859), pp. 106–8.

114. Ibid., pp. 5–8, 12–15, 22–25.

115. Ibid., pp. 10, 17, 29–34.

116. Ibid., pp. 53–4.

117. Ibid., pp. 58–9.

118. Ibid., pp. 109–12, 116, 133.

119. Ibid., p. 99.

120. J. Niemirowski, *O związku moralności z ekonomią polityczną. Podług wykładu H. Baudrillart, profesora w Collège de France* (Warsaw, 1861), pp. 97, 110, 123.

121. Ibid., pp. 71, 83, 204–11.

122. Z. Dangel, *Ogólne zasady ekonomii politycznej*, vol. 1 (Warsaw, 1862), pp. 16–29, 109–10.

123. Ibid., pp. 310, 318–20.

124. See note 85 to chapter 2.

125. J. Supiński, *Pisma*, vol. 2 (Warsaw, 1883), p. 30.

126. Ibid., p. 158.

127. Ibid., vol. 1 (Warsaw, 1883), pp. 258–62.

128. Ibid., p. 263.

PART TWO

Ambiguities of Progress
from 1864 through the 1880s

CHAPTER 4

Vicious Circles

Paradoxical as it may seem, in the course of the last three centuries many developing countries have found themselves with too many educated people. The development of secondary, and in particular higher, education, supplemented by courses of study abroad, tends to run ahead of the general growth of civilization in any given country and of that country's ability to utilize the qualifications of its people.

This phenomenon has always caused strong social tensions. It added a new element to the list of inequalities in the areas of civil rights, wealth, income and power: a drastic inequality in the division of knowledge and skills, and in access to cultural goods. The enormous distance that separates the illiteracy and civilizational primitivism of the masses from the sophisticated intellectual culture of the educated elites is typical of all countries in the early phases of the modernization process. Moreover, the acquiring of an education, especially by young people from the lower and middle classes, always awakens expectations for social gratification. Those who have spent years studying tend to feel they deserve to occupy a higher rung on the ladder of income, prestige and political influence. If society, the government and producers are unable to fulfill these hopes, then educated people turn against the prevailing system.

It is generally accepted today that the expansion of higher education at a faster rate than the growth of possibilities for the employment of graduates contributed in large measure to the political ferment in West European countries in the first half of the nineteenth century by creating a reserve of alienated intellectuals who entered public life as champions of radical social change.[1]

Such intellectuals, whose expectations of advancement had been frustrated, appear again and again in the guise of ideologues and leaders in almost all radical left- and right-wing movements up to the present day. In the Russia of the second half of the nineteenth century it was these intellectuals, and not the civil servants and professionals, who were referred to as the "intelligentsia." This provides an extremely interesting subject for comparative studies.[2]

It is not always the case, of course, that the frustrated expectations of a section of the young, educated populace, and various hindrances to the process of its social integration push it towards revolutionary ideals and actions. People give vent to their sense of being unwanted by competing (e.g., with other ethnic groups), by emigrating, by forming subcultures on the social margins, by joining bohemian artistic movements, etc. Alternatively, the feeling of being superfluous may simply lead to resignation and bitterness, to reconciling oneself, for example, to the boring existence of a provincial teacher, or to remaining an unrecognized genius.

In Poland, a group of such restless, rootless intellectuals first emerged in the times of the Four Years Seym (1788–92), when they played a significant role. In the years following the partition of Poland, a sizable group of "redundant elements" graduated from Wilno University, earlier than from any other college in the Russian empire.[3] The romantic movement and the conspiracies which preceded the November Rising were in large measure the work of students and young graduates. They rebelled partly as a result of their ardent patriotism and enthusiasm for the new developments in European politics and literature, but were also influenced by their lack of prospects and the feeling that they would be unable to make any constructive use of their education and aspirations.

In the period following 1831, despite the loss of the intellectual elite due to emigration and the lack of Polish institutions of higher education (with the exception of Kraków), we find many references to the difficulties encountered by teachers, doctors, lawyers, and even engineers in their search for work and patrons.[4] For the legions of young people of gentry or burgher origins who had a secondary (or uncompleted secondary) education, the most tempting career was still the civil service; it is true that it was boring and sterile, and served the interests of the partitioning powers, but it did not demand any special qualifications and, once one had managed to get through the period of apprenticeship, it provided some kind of stability. Although it is customary to ascribe the predilection for office work and the scrambling for government positions to the influence of the gentry tradition, this is by no means peculiar to Poland; the same was true, for example, of France at that time, something which outraged the "industrialists" with their contempt for bureaucracy.

The notions of "overproduction" of talent and education *(Geistige Überproduktion)* and "intellectual proletariat" seem to have been coined in Germany in the period following the Springtide of Nations, and the choice of terminology was obviously influenced by socialist literature.[5] The problem of the "overproduction of intelligentsia" was openly discussed in the Galician press, where the blame was put on the traditional school and university curricula which were not adapted to the country's economic needs. In 1864, a contributor to a Lwów weekly wrote that the contemporary educational system "creates yearly a multitudinous intellectual proletariat, which is not only useless, but indeed injurious to the nation.[6]

In the Russian partition zone, the problem became more acute in the years preceding the outbreak of the January Rising in 1863. Here in particular, the strong dependence of the intelligentsia on their government-employer which scrupulously monitored the loyalty of its functionaries gave rise to an attitude of servility and careerism in some, and a feeling of frustration, temporarily stifled, in others. The authors of the conservative camp and the more perspicacious representatives of the governing spheres were the first to realize the danger of such attitudes. Thus, for example, Józef Miniszewski, a eulogist of the gentry tradition, suddenly started complaining in his moralizing tales that the Poles were inferior to the Germans as regards management, and that young people were attracted by government positions rather than by commerce and industry since their fathers wanted them to learn "a bit of everything"[7] instead of encouraging them to master one useful skill. The same author, after he had become the spokesman of Margrave Wielopolski,[8] was still lamenting the "overcrowding of offices" and the growth of the legal "proletariat."[9] Wielopolski himself mentioned the emergence of the "bureaucratic proletariat."[10] It is worth noting that when the Main School in Warsaw opened in 1862, out of six hundred students as many as four hundred enrolled at the legal-administrative department, which remained the most numerous department until the closing down of the school.[11]

Wielopolski's reform of the school system failed to change the traditional nature of the instruction provided: it was geared to supplying new, better qualified people to the educational system, judiciary and administration rather than catering for the needs of the national economy. Admittedly, the development of the educational system and the re-Polonization of the civil service in the Kingdom would have, in time, provided these young officials with better career opportunities. This, however, happened too late. It is difficult to judge to what extent obstacles to promotion contributed to the radicalization of the intelligentsia in the early 1860s. But it is certain that the Warsaw conspiracies, the organization of "Reds,"[12] and later the civil and military organization of the insurrection of 1863, were, generally speaking, the work of young educated men, among them functionaries of the various government departments and Polish officers from Russian military colleges and army staffs.

In the period following the collapse of the uprising all these factors continued to operate, determining the professional structure and the material conditions of the intelligentsia. It has been estimated that in the late 1860s over 70 percent of Warsaw's "intellectual workers" (a broad category comprising all non-manual jobs) were employed by the state. Transport, industry, commerce and private banks provided employment for a mere 15 percent of the Warsaw intelligentsia, and a still smaller percentage were employed in the professions (those whose income came directly from their clientele). Forty percent of Warsaw doctors were in government employment (which did not exclude private practices), and the number of architects working exclusively to private orders was smaller than the number permanently employed by the administration, the municipal authorities and the railways.[13] Just as before the uprising, it was hard to get a job or private practice, and while there were still no signs of durable unemployment, this was probably due to the loss of life during the uprising, the deportations to Siberia, and a new wave of political emigration.

The balance between the supply of "intellectual workers" and job vacancies in the Kingdom, which had long been precarious, was upset in the late 1870s and the early 1880s. The last, relatively numerous groups of graduates of the Main School were entering the labor market,[14] not to mention graduates of Russian and Western universities which had become more accessible to Poles since the late 1850s. As a result of the persecution of all things Polish in the Lithuanian and Ukrainian gubernyas of the Empire, and the policy of intensive Russification in these lands—which preceded all attempts at Russification in the "Vistula-Land," as the Congress Kingdom came to be officially called—part of the young intelligentsia moved to the Kingdom from the East.

In this period, more and more young members of the gentry were drawn to the towns by the prospect of finding work. So too were many former leaseholders and overseers of landed estates who had become redundant as a result of the crisis in the gentry economy which set in following the agrarian reforms of 1864 or as a result of the repressive confiscation of property by the tsarist authorities. In addition, some Siberian exiles and a small number of emigrés returned home following the 1867 amnesty. As a rule they lacked any means of subsistence, and their presence therefore increased even more the pressure on the labor market.

This pressure was considerably greater than the growth of the number of jobs. Moreover, the abolition of separate government institutions in the Kingdom and their replacement by agencies of the central government entailed a considerable reduction of personnel, even before the increased influx of Russian functionaries. This process lasted some twenty years. After 1876, the judiciary was affected by cuts in the number of Polish employees; at the same time, wherever it proved feasible, Polish secondary school teachers and Warsaw university professors were replaced with Russians, and, as a rule, Poles were not appointed to vacant positions. They were also eliminated from higher posts in administration of state demesne and forests. The final victim of this process was the Bank of Poland, which was turned into a branch of the Imperial State Bank in 1886.[15]

The Russification of the Kingdom was the next disaster to hit the country following the collapse of the uprising. For the Polish intelligentsia and for students it also meant a threat to the material foundations of their existence. The kind of education they had acquired had not prepared the intelligentsia for economic self-sufficiency. The impoverished rural gentry were even less capable of supporting themselves, and many of them moved to the towns in search of work, usually in some kind of office.

In the face of restricted access to the civil service, teaching and the judiciary, the young intelligentsia inclined more and more towards the professions open to them or towards private employment in railways, banks or industry. However, it soon transpired that the national economy, and its undeveloped capitalist sector in particular, could not absorb those thousands who had lost their positions in the nonproductive sphere which, until then, had provided them with some means of subsistence.

The "young press"[16] began to sound the alarm as early as the beginning of the 1870s. Since it could only hint at the political causes of the crisis, it had all the more scope to enlarge on the economic and educational causes and effects. Aleksander Świętochowski had just published, at the age of twenty-three, such provocative articles as "We and You," "Public Opinion," and "Tradition and History vis-à-vis Progress." These were militant ideological manifestos of the young generation. "We and You" in particular was reminiscent of the romantic attacks on the classics half a century earlier. The "olds"[17] perceived in these articles, and not without good reason, not only an ideological rebellion, but also a demand for a place for young people. Soon after, Świętochowski openly spoke out in defense of the interests of his generation: "A number of young people who leave university are to be found dispersed throughout society, waiting for the opportunity of a job; a small number have received positions where they can exert some influence; and a fairly numerous group is to be found representing the spiritual interests of society. The largest group is waiting.... For new legions of individuals skilled in some kind of work, often very necessary work, arrive by the day, while the job market keeps shrinking. Hosts of brave forces wander through the byways of life, unexploited, waiting on the wings! A very singular situation. Society suffers from thousands of unsatisfied needs, and the people capable of satisfying these needs are forced to remain inactive, and are assigned to the category of redundant forces."[18]

Three months later, Świętochowski again asked what should be done. "How can we employ the squadrons of inactive, healthy, brave forces which ask for work in vain? This is the key issue of our social existence, the thread that binds together all the main questions of the moment." He questioned whether it was really worthwhile studying and acquiring qualifications when "Lawyers become private tutors, philologists take up employment in commercial banks, mathematicians teach Latin at private schools for girls, and naturalists work in notaries' offices as scriveners. A hotch-potch of talents, dispositions, predilections, a true tower of Babel built of human brains. And everywhere there is poverty and despondency. . . . One can observe a whole multitude of such minds, almost seven-tenths of the general mass of spiritual forces, being wasted in inactivity or stifled in disagreeable conditions." This, he says, is how the intellectual proletariat is born. This word, "this tattered rag . . . round which the scum of society gather, is for us a banner which rallies the noblest and bravest of legions. Through lack of work, thousands of healthy, talented, useful and needed individuals have come to form a proletariat, and thus, by a strange quirk of fate, have become akin to the most putrid layers of society."[19]

The high tone of these words and the rhetorical exuberance of the epithets expressed the experience of the first post-insurrectionary generation of educated young people: the experience of feeling superfluous, of encountering obstacles to their aspirations as they entered adult life. Świętochowski probably did not have first-hand experience of this feeling, for he found an outlet for his talent unexpectedly quickly. Many others followed the same path: student poverty and difficulties in starting a professional career have often been used to explain the attractiveness of journalism for these young people. It was a field of activity which yielded a small income but did not demand too much exertion, and in addition it brought popularity and enabled one to exert an influence on public opinion.

However, the problem of the superfluous intelligentsia and the lack of work soon ceased to be a feature of one generation only. Lack of perspectives and the waste of talent became the fate of the whole of the Polish intelligentsia, irrespective of age. Only the young, who had not yet given up, felt the paradox of their position particularly keenly: they believed that their country desperately needed them and the knowledge they had acquired, while at the same time they felt completely superfluous. The ideologues of "work at the roots"[20] would seek ways of breaking out of these vicious circles.

The First Circle:
The Semi-intelligentsia with no Professional Training

Mainly because of censorship, but also because they were in favor of a policy of adapting to conditions which could not be changed, the positivists did not engage in any criticism of the government or the tsarist system. However, they were passionately dedicated to the cause of educating society. In the face of the reduction of the Polish administrative staff, most of whom were not qualified to work anywhere else except in the civil service, the "young press" could not but stress how pernicious was the high respect for state employment which prevailed in society, an attitude which allegedly stemmed, as did contempt for physical work, from the gentry tradition. By reversing this hierarchy of values, it was hoped to alter the unsound occupational structure of the enlightened strata.

An anonymous contributor to the journal *Niwa (The Field)* reminded readers that "intellectual work", just like physical work, was a commodity subject to the law of "offering and demanding." Since under the changed conditions clerks were needed much less than before, one should turn to those "branches of social labor" whose products were in demand. This lecture on economics was followed by a moral sermon. The author ridiculed the stupidity and laziness of the clerical "social parasites" whose "heads are as empty as their stomachs." He asked: "why should we feel ashamed of working with a dirty laborer, if this noble work gives us a decent income, higher even than what clerks of the middle grades earn?" When he talked of working "with a dirty laborer," the author obviously had in mind the position of a factory overseer, since he claimed that young people be provided with a secondary technical training before taking up new occupations: "Either we should open private technical schools, or else we should raise funds to send young people to foreign institutions. In fact, we should do both."[21]

A year later, Eliza Orzeszkowa[22] put forward the same argument when writing about the foolish ambitions of the sons of impoverished country squires and their search for a position, nothing more than a position, which she regarded as a "snail-like retreat into the shell of ideas which have been established once and for all." She described how the seeker of a position who had spent a couple of years at secondary school could not, at that time, hope to climb higher than a "clerk's stool," and how even "that is difficult to come by and calls for protracted endeavors and much bowing and scraping." The native proletariat sprang from these "office hands," a pitiable proletariat, but "no less dangerous for the durability and prosperity of our social existence than the proletariat whose gloomy multitudes have dimmed the brilliant horizon of France."[23]

She argued that there was just one answer to all the laments about the shortage of positions: "the labor of one's hands, gentlemen!" The country needed trained, cultured craftsmen who could form the much-needed "middle social stratum," a reservoir of labor and energy. Of course, there was nothing wrong with them receiving a secondary education. Indeed, Orzeszkowa's ideal was general secondary education for all (although she probably meant only the scions of the gentry and the townsmen). The problem was, however, that "to turn a young man who, descrvcdly or undeservedly, has a school-leaving certificate, into a modest laborer working with his own hands seems to our society a bizarre thing, a horrible thing, almost a crime crying out for vengeance to the ancestral peerages and maternal dreams of sons who will be geniuses." For this reason, "one of the most urgent social needs" was for craft schools. Such schools, she argued, should be financially supported by capitalists who would simply be acting in their own interests; their curricula should be drawn up by the intelligentsia; and the gentry should send their sons there, rather than to general education secondary schools.[24]

The name is significant: these were to be "craft schools," and not vocational schools, a term that was rarely used. This was the first problem tackled by the journal *Przegląd Techniczny (The Technological Review)* established in 1875. In its first issue, its editor claimed that factory industry "seems to want to completely eliminate crafts," exploiting for this purpose the superior capital resources which were made available by shareholders' companies, and also the genius of its inventors. But factory production, it was claimed, was inferior to craftsmanship as regards artistry, and probably only talented master craftsmen would survive in the future. For such master craftsmen, old-fashioned training as apprentices would not be enough: they would need schools where they would be able to acquire a general, theoretical, technical, economic and aesthetic education. Such overall knowledge would enable the craftsmen to defend their independence against industrial competition, and also to preserve their sense of personal dignity. This was the aim to which the "contributions and legacies of well-intentioned people"[25] should be devoted.

Bolesław Prus[26] returned again and again to this subject in his writings. From 1875 on, he was in constant touch with the Employment Office in Warsaw, a small private labor exchange for the intelligentsia and specialists. The problem was, Prus reported, that half of the customers of the office were "people for all trades," that is, with no training at all. "The employers . . . are looking for metallurgists, gardeners, bookkeepers, mechanics, etc., while the applicants, who are ready to take any job (the majority of them dismissed clerks), can, admittedly, read, write and do sums well, and know some legal and administrative regulations, but are incapable of working as gardeners or mechanics." It is true that the demand for jobs was considerably higher than their supply in almost all occupations; for example, in the "technical" section there were four candidates for each vacancy. However, as Prus reminds his readers, although "jobs are in short supply, a specialist will find one seven times more easily than a non-expert." Meanwhile, "there are thousands of people without any occupation, and there are even more children who study Latin and Greek in order to swell the ranks of the half-educated proletariat." Thus each time the question was raised, it ended with an appeal to factory owners, to country squires, and to craftsmen to collect funds for vocational schools. "Without such schools, the present generation is lost for productive work, and the next generation will also be lost."[27]

The government was not interested in changing the secondary school curriculum, which was rather a reflection of its conservatism than of any deliberate political decision. Indeed, if political considerations had prevailed the educational authorities would have been more inclined to support the vocational training of Polish youth at the expense of general education with its emphasis on philological subjects. Sponsors were also slow in coming forward.

Fifteen years passed before the government gave its consent to the establishment of private vocational schools, but even then hardly anybody took the opportunity to found schools of this sort. Świętochowski blamed "the social attitudes of the majority" which continued to give greater value to office work or the position of station master, or even the job of conductor on the horse-drawn trams in Warsaw: "This is a pretty sight indeed! On the one hand, we have great crowds of people without work, and on the other, vast areas of activity suffering from a shortage of hands. It is no longer just sweet reason, but the rod of experience that tells us that we must prepare ourselves for productive occupations. Alas! In spite of this rod, fathers and sons continue to dream of offices and 'positions' in general . . . Some prefer to copy court writs or be clerks for twenty roubles a month, rather than work as a gardener and have enough bread, and a nice job which will also be useful for the country. . . . It's ridiculous and sad. And as long as we do not rid ourselves of this ridiculousness and this sadness, all our palaver about social revival will be fruitless."[28]

Fruitless it was, but for a different reason. The positivists saw themselves as determinists and realists: the point of departure for their general program and the concrete projects they supported was the existing state of affairs, and their aims were very much tailored to their means. However, the conclusions they reached were always moralistic. Indeed, how could they be otherwise, when they had no influence on the authorities and no capital, and when their weapons consisted merely of two or three severely censored journals?

Tradition, gentry prejudices, snobbery, dreams of the trappings of office—all these undoubtedly played some part. But when all is said and done, this figure of evil who was so severely castigated by journalists and writers, namely, the secondary school pupil, continued to do as he had always done. He went where he could, learnt what the government told him to learn, and then, having neither the means nor the inclination to continue his studies, took up such job as he was able to perform. That is, instead of becoming an educated worker, he became a half-educated member of the intelligentsia. In the final reckoning, he probably still fared better than those who, having barely learnt to read and write, became apprenticed to master craftsmen or went to work as unskilled laborers in factories or on building sites.

Finally, the wretched secondary school pupil was blamed because, as Prus and dozens of others after him wrote, "this moderately educated part of the nation, which calls itself the 'intelligentsia', seems to be cut off from the masses and has little if any influence on their life."[29]

The Second Circle: The "Academic" Intelligentsia

Things were more complicated with the so-called academic intelligentsia, that is, with university graduates. The local university[30] produced mainly doctors and lawyers, two professions which could hardly be described as useless. Doctors in particular occupied an important place in the program of organic work. In many parts of the country the doctor was the only educated man. He had access to places where education did not reach, and thus was expected to disseminate hygiene, combat superstition, and popularize learning. In a word, he was supposed to act as an outpost of progress.

The university also educated secondary school teachers and academics. Not much was written about teachers, or if it was, it did not find its way into print. This was a taboo subject and, for the advocates of activity within the law, slightly awkward. Polish teachers were removed from state schools, or else removed themselves; those who could sought employment in the small number of private schools, mostly for girls, while those who managed to keep their positions became, willingly or otherwise, instruments of Russification. With scholars, the matter was different. The lack of academic institutions in the Kingdom meant that the work of the scholar was not a profession, but a vocation, and moreover a vocation which in the epoch of positivism was regarded as the most noble, even by the conservatives.

Logic demanded that the movement whose motto was "Knowledge is Power" should support young people's thirst for knowledge and higher education and their eagerness to learn a profession. However, the situation on the labor market produced tremendous confusion in this field and attitudes tended to fluctuate. There were clearly too many people with a secondary education and no skills. No one questioned the necessity of reducing their numbers. But what about those with university education and special quali-fications? Were there too many or too few people in this category? This question continued to trouble Warsaw journalists until the late nineteenth century.

At first, the lot of scholars was seen as one which demanded stoicism. This was in keeping with the tradition, in Poland and elsewhere, of surrounding scholarly research with an aura of heroism. According to Ryszarda Czepulis, most of the appreciations of scholars which were published in Warsaw journals after their deaths portray them as martyrs to their work, men whose achievements, no matter how modest or second-rate, involved great sacrifices on their part.[31] In the West, Samuel Smiles portrayed them in a similarly conventionalized way in his *Self-help*, the Polish translations of which were very popular, and Eliza Orzeszkowa followed suit in her "Letters on Litera-ture."[32] Such an image was not wholly unjustified. Many a scholar earned his living by giving private lessons or by writing for various journals, and there were many who could only dedicate themselves to their studies after a long day at the office. This phenomenon is unavoidable whenever the academic interests and aspirations of individuals from outside the propertied elite cannot find support in academic institutions. Some thought this situation advantageous. Adolf Dygasiński asked rhetorically in 1884, "doesn't this ascent of the Golgotha of learning give man tremendous strength and endur-ance?"[33]

With time, however, the realities of life caused some positivists to question this ideology of martyrdom in the cause of learning, especially since in theory they were advocates of harmonizing the interests of the individual with those of society. "We can see no just reason for forcing superior minds to wear a crown of thorns," wrote a contributor to *Niwa*, in opposition to Smiles' theses. Such a doctrine, relieving society of all responsibility, would lead to the tragic impotence of the intelligentsia: "The impotence of those impoverished tal-ented youths who have to interrupt their studies for lack of funds . . . the impotence of those enlightened minds toiling under the yoke of tedious drudgery, who are prevented by poverty from making the most of their knowledge and abilities—these are all manifestations of this impotence of the intelligentsia." "Self-help" is not enough if talents are to be exploited and utilized creatively, argues the author; what is needed are "schools, universities, learned associations, societies, clubs, and editorial offices." Editorial offices were, in fact, very critical of themselves in this respect. The travails of journalism were said to check the intellectual development of young people, and turn them into dilettantes with regard to every field of knowledge: "Instead of gifted psychologists, historians, natural scientists, lawyers, or astronomers, literature is left with smart columnists." All of these vicious circles could only be broken with the organized assistance of society.

But who was supposed to organize this assistance and who was going to support it financially? The author of the quoted article from *Niwa* reasoned that it was highly profitable for all countries to invest in learning and academics. But the year was 1874, and the tsarist system was wreaking havoc on Polish culture, education, literature and the press. The only way left was to appeal to public generosity in order to create societies for the encouragement of academic studies, as had been done in the Poznań region. Some counted on the help of small contributors, but most pinned their hopes on the philanthropic spirit of the rich; the soulless indifference of those who "know only the glitter of names or the brilliance of gold"[34] was harshly criticized.

This period saw the beginning of a second wave of emigration. In fact it was not a wave at all, because, unlike 1831 when poets, soldiers and politicians fled the country *en masse*, there was now merely a small, almost imperceptible, but steady flow of the best brains, and those with the best chances, abroad. The positivists were against emigration on principle, but they understood the motives and could only helplessly watch this tragic export of talent, well aware of the fact that by the nature of things scholars lose touch with their country and its needs more quickly than poets: "And so our intelligentsia is densely scattered all over Europe, while in Poland such people were few and far between; the German *Zeitschrifts* are full of contributions by Polish scholars, while Warsaw is incapable of publishing a single large academic journal. There is no doubt whatsoever as to the extent that [Polish] literature and the whole country lose by this."[35]

These alarm signals and appeals eventually resulted in the foundation of the Mianowski Fund for Academic Assistance. By itself, however, this fund could do little to improve the material conditions for conducting research. Academic emigration continued, and even a number of the most prominent representatives of the positivist camp defected; some of them went to Galicia, others farther afield.

The emigration of young people—those who went to foreign universities never to come back—seemed to pass unnoticed. No one paid any attention to the departure of Władysław Natanson[36] or Maria Skłodowska[37] who devoted all her resources to ascending the "Golgotha of science" in Paris, and finally succeeded, while in Warsaw she could at best have become the headmistress of a private school for girls.

Doctors and lawyers had fewer reasons to emigrate and fewer chances of finding a job abroad. The majority of them, including those who graduated from Russian or Western universities, settled permanently in Poland. Their fortunes differed, depending on the skills, ingenuity, connections and initial capital of each individual. The professions quickly became stratified. The picture painted by the press of the time is undoubtedly oversimplified. It is, however, not hard to understand why the polemicists who took part in discussions on the overproduction of the intelligentsia were more interested in the "marginal utility" of higher education than in average achievements. No one denied that there were some celebrated doctors, lawyers, and notaries who charged exorbitant fees, kept their own coaches and servants, and belonged to high society. But this was not the real issue.

Numerous diaries and press reports leave no doubt as to the existence of "overcrowding" in the professions. It was not easy for young medical and law graduates of limited means to establish themselves. And since the demand was, on the whole, much smaller in the provinces, the larger towns, principally Warsaw, became particularly "overcrowded."

This phenomenon was not restricted to the Kingdom: it also caused anxiety among enlightened public opinion in Russia. According to figures from the *Otechestvenneye Zapiski* quoted by Bronisław Białobłocki, the ratio of doctors to the whole population of the Russian Empire was ten times lower than in the United States, five times lower than in Britain, and two times lower than in Germany. "And despite all that, we can observe in reality a dreadful hyperproduction of doctors. For example, a vacancy in the most remote place, where a doctor in a *zemstvo* can earn 1200 to 1300 roubles annually, will attract from 20 to 90 candidates. In the newspapers, we frequently come across reports about the extreme destitution of young, job-seeking medics, about doctors dying of starvation, or about doctors taking up jobs as tutors, copyists, etc."[38]

As to the legal profession, the situation had been aggravated by reforms to the judiciary which took place in the 1870s. This resulted in a major reorganization of the members of the profession not only in the Kingdom, but also in Russia itself, and meant that graduates of the privileged St. Petersburg

School of Law were given priority before university graduates when it came to appointments and promotions.

The following is a rather telling report from a provincial town, one of many similar pieces, published in the Warsaw paper *Głos (The Voice)* in 1891: "We attended secondary school in Suwałki and Maryjampol. On leaving school we dispersed and moved to various places: to Warsaw, to the Empire, depending on the means at our disposal and our plans for the future, but all of us without exception went to university.... [Having graduated] almost all of us returned to our native parts ... none of us wanted a brilliant career, we only sought a piece of bread.... You know that almost all of us, with few exceptions, graduated in medicine or law and in both these branches we encountered overcrowding.... There is an excess of lawyers and doctors in the *gubernya* capital, and we found all positions occupied.... Some doctors found employment in small hamlets where they have to struggle with poverty, quacks, and a lack of books, journals and implements; working among the common people, they gradually win their trust and finally acquire a medical practice; some stayed on in Suwałki, but they did not fare much better; the rest dispersed all over the world.

"The situation of the lawyers is worse: over a dozen of them returned and each year a couple of new ones appear. None of them can make a living in the town, since there is extreme overcrowding in this field, and the scope for work is smaller. A lawyer has two choices of career: to become a magistrate or obtain a legal practice. Considering that a law graduate has far less practical knowledge than a medical graduate, we can understand why the idea of young lawyers settling in small towns is virtually impracticable, or at least very risky."[39]

The majority of the rural population and part of the urban population still did not make use of medical services; in cases of emergency they sought the assistance of quacks, village midwives, folk-healers, herbalists, and apothecaries who concocted mixtures of their own recipe. Lawyers encountered similar competition from the so-called "pettifoggers." The low demand for their services and the small clientele was more the result of the country's low level of development and low educational standards than of material poverty.

In discussions in the press, the ambiguity of such terms as "need" and "scope for work" caused much controversy: they meant one thing from the point of view of civilizational ideology and educational progress, and something different in the idiom of economic practice. This antinomy left its mark on positivist thought from the very beginning.

All the positivists sooner or later drew the same conclusions from observing developments on the labor market: they advised young people against higher education. "The number of clerks, lawyers, teachers, and doctors," wrote Świętochowski as early as 1872, "cannot be quickly multiplied, and moreover an excessive increase in their numbers is in fact harmful for society. Meanwhile, the number of producers can be allowed to grow almost infinitely, because each producer is at the same time a consumer, and thus maintains a balance in trade. . . . The whole point is that the father, rather than dreaming of a professorial or judicial career for his son . . . should prepare him for a career as a merchant, a craftsman, a farmer, or an industrialist."[40]

Bolesław Prus, a sober-minded observer of life, always believed that progress should begin with planting potatoes and not roses. Although he valued learning and saw a multitude of uses for it, he gave priority to practical commonsense: "Today," he wrote, "the future of a university graduate is neither brilliant nor even secure. . . . Shouldn't then the badly-off parents of adolescent sons contemplate some occupation for them which would be more secure than an academic career? . . . It is a fine thing for society to give out a hundred university diplomas and classical school certificates each year. But it is a bad thing when the capital spent on education does not accrue interest."[41] This was indeed a bitter dilemma for the advocates of organic work: what timescale was to be applied when calculating the interest on the capital spent on education? And was this interest to be calculated from the point of view of family spending or national development?

As far as national development was concerned, not all publicists were convinced that the main issue was the proper utilization of professional qualifications. In any case, the intelligentsia was not always seen purely in professional terms. An anonymous contributor to the *Przegląd Tygodniowy (The Weekly Review)* argued in 1880 that education by itself did not make one a member of the intelligentsia; what was needed was an understanding of social obligations. The hallmark of the intelligentsia was a "vibrant creative power . . . an incentive which leads the nation onward, mapping out and clearing the path like a vanguard." And if this was the case, then people needed to believe in their own potential, in their own mission rather than lamenting and complaining about the "hyperproduction" of intelligentsia.[42]

However, at the threshold of the 1880s the problem was given a new political context. Following the assassination of Tsar Alexander II by a Pole, Ignacy Hryniewiecki, the nationalist section of the Russian press, led by Mikhail Katkov's *Moskovskiye Vyedomosti*, accused Polish students of being the leaders of the terrorist group of the Narodnaya Volya. While the more lenient censorship rules of Mikhail Loris-Melnikov's administration were still in force, Polish public opinion took advantage of the opportunity to reply. It almost unanimously rejected these accusations by proving that the Russian universities were the main hotbeds of "nihilism."[43] Katkov's party, which had gained some influence over the government in the early part of Alexander III's rule, still maintained that Poles should have restricted access to universities because the number of students exceeded the needs of society and because the consequent growth of an unemployed educated proletariat in the towns constituted a threat to the state. These arguments did not go unheeded. Universities in the Russian Empire started introducing the *numerus clausus* for Poles and Jews, although applying the same measures in Warsaw university proved more difficult.

This was a complex problem for the positivists, since for the last ten years they had been writing about the excessive interest in higher education. *Prawda (The Truth)* admitted that "the question of the proletariat and the forced unemployment of the graduates of our university calls for serious consideration." At the same time, however, it pointed out as explicitly as it could, given the strict censorship, that this was a result of the fact that these graduates had been barred from teaching and the judicature, and from some other careers: "It would seem that we have an excess of intellectual powers, but we only do not have the possibility of utilizing them properly. Considering the seriousness of these issues, it is surprising that there are journals in Russia which have nothing better to do but throw dust in the eyes of the people and stop the mouths of their opponents with mud."[44]

Several months later Świętochowski returned to the subject, but this time he took the conventional line, claiming that "the number of people with university diplomas not only surpasses the present reduced needs of the country, but would even be excessive if the needs were normal." The source of this state of affairs, he argued, was "our innate . . . aristocratic disposition and the insufficient democratization of our society." It was this disposition that made young people see secondary school only as a "stopover" on the way to medical or legal studies, since they found trades degrading. "How many of these people could become well-off bakers, shoemakers, tanners or carpenters!" And he concluded by saying: "The intelligentsia of our society today forms a register in which the medium and lower notes are lacking and only the highest notes are produced. Meanwhile, our voice should be able to range over the whole scale."[45]

This was not consistent reasoning. The argument about the lack of the lower and medium strata of the intelligentsia (with reference to education, of course) had no support in facts, nor was it consistent with earlier and later statements by the same author, who more than once produced evidence that there was a surplus at these levels. It had been suggested earlier that a baker with a secondary school diploma should take the place of a clerk or a teacher among the ranks of the intelligentsia. This time, however, it was not a question of consistency or originality. The problem was how to prevent the growth of a class of educated plebeians at the university and around it, who, seeing no professional or material prospects for themselves, would become easy prey to socialist agitation. The positivists were genuinely afraid of revolutionary ferment: not so much because they saw in it some direct threat to the bourgeois social system and private property, but rather because the slightest incident in Warsaw could serve as a pretext for a further tightening of the police regime in schools, the press, and, indeed, in every other field.

"Towards the end of the winter of 1883," Ludwik Krzywicki recalled years later, "the whole complex of inner symptoms at the university began to herald an approaching storm." Student circles were being reborn, the "socialists" were engaged in fierce polemics with the "patriots." Following years of apathy, the desire was being born again among students to manifest their position in some way, and Apukhtin's[46] policies only poured oil on the flames. In April, the famous university "rebellion" took place, with very grave consequences.[47] The newly founded underground social-revolutionary party "Proletariat" began to make its presence felt more and more among workers, students and secondary school pupils. The police became more watchful. The charismatic party leader Ludwik Waryński was arrested on 28 September. With the help of informers, almost all organizers of the workers' party cells were arrested a month later. In mid-November appeals from the Workers' Committee appeared on walls, factory gates, on pavements, and in churches; they ended with the following declaration: "we are sharpening our knives for traitors and oppressors!"[48] The warnings were no empty threats: they were soon followed by attacks on *agents provocateurs*. The newspapers were silent on the subject of the "Proletariat," but the city was seething with rumors. It was known that its leaders were young, educated, intelligent. On 15 December, the Warsaw conservative journal *Niwa* published an editorial entitled "The Academic Proletariat."

The article, which was ascribed to Teodor Jeske-Choiński, contained almost nothing which would not have been argued for earlier by the progressive supporters of organic work. It repeated the same warning to young people who, guided by misconceived ambition and at the cost of considerable sacrifice on the part of the whole family, pushed their way through to higher education in the hope of earning lucrative fees as doctors or barristers in the future; the truth was that, in the majority of cases, these incomes "do not equal the interest on the capital invested in the protracted, arduous educational process." On the positive side, it reminded readers that "there is a shortage of experts everywhere you turn," that the country needed "skilled technicians, craftsmen, merchants, industrialists and farmers." This was almost the same message that was preached by Prus, Orzeszkowa and Świętochowski. Only the tone of this article is different: it is irritatingly patronizing, even downright contemptuous for the *common people*. Choiński does not grudge higher education to those who have the means and who study for pleasure and not for a career. Meanwhile, "everybody craves learning! learning! The caretaker, the janitor, the craftsman, the farm supervisor, they all want education!"

While the title of this article was nothing new, in December 1883 it had a different ring than previously. It sounded like a denunciation—especially since the author casually remarked that the misguided, under-educated secondary school leavers and university students tended to join the ranks of malcontents of all persuasions.[49]

If this article provoked violent opposition it was probably because it appeared in a journal which, by this time, had become the paper of the renascent conservative landowning faction, advocating reconciliation with tsardom, and also because it appeared at that particular moment. Białobłocki, writing in the *Przegląd Tygodniowy*, managed to smuggle in an unveiled allusion to the similarity between the warnings given in *Niwa* and the *Moskovskiye Vyedomosti*, but all the polemicists of the day seemed to be more or less aware of these political undercurrents.

In his correspondence from Dresden for the *Biesiada Literacka (The Literary Feast)*, Kraszewski[50] described Choiński's article, with some exaggeration, as the "propaganda of obscurantism" and as Malthusianism applied to education. There can never be too much education, he argued. The proletariat is not produced by an excess of education, but by exaggerated expectations on the part of graduates: after all, even a university graduate, when he cannot find any other job, can become a craftsman. The "hyperproduction of intelligentsia" and "false radicalism and impatient attacks on the established order" can be prevented by Christian altruism and "the colonization of the wilderness, by bringing the light where it is lacking."[51]

Adolf Dygasiński[52] wrote in a similar vein in the *Przegląd Tygodniowy*. This was a surprising about-face in his case. The leading author of the positivist camp relegates the existence of the "educated proletariat" to the realm of myths: "Where can you see this surplus population of educated people? Are the universities swarming with unpaid *Privatdozenten*, who suffer the torments of hunger and hatch dangerous plots while waiting to get a position? Do we find in archives and libraries legions of scholars who have written weighty tomes which cannot be printed because of lack of interest. . .? . . . There are no educated proletarians here, because there is a lot of work and a lot of bread for them. Doctors are greatly overpaid, and yet there is still room for quacks and faith-healers. Barristers and solicitors are not dying of hunger, and yet there is no shortage of work for pettifoggers and other shysters. . . . And the aristocratic *Niwa* is annoyed because the plebs want to be educated and become full citizens, while the gentry go bankrupt both materially and morally. This will not do! Such paltry articles will not stifle the spirit of the time."[53]

The editors of *Niwa* seemed taken aback by the vehemence of the response to their editorial and by the peculiar realignment of forces that this entailed. In his response to the polemicists, Choiński admitted that the headline "academic proletariat" was not really apt and that a better term would be "academic careerists." He rejected the class interpretation of his article: he did not mean that the plebs should be barred from education, he simply wanted to say that only those who had the talent and predisposition should proceed to higher education. He found it amusing that the iconoclastic *Przegląd Tygodniowy* wanted to teach *Niwa* respect for higher ideals and had accused it of materialism. But he insisted on reminding his readers of the harsh economic realities, as opposed to "progressive declamations."[54]

Jeske-Choiński's attempt to soothe the controversy was undermined by his colleague from *Niwa*, Władysław Olendzki, who reaffirmed the overtly conservative interpretation of the journal's position. He argued that higher education should attract "above all such candidates as were truly independent as regards their means, and from among the rest, only exceptionally talented people who have a vocation." He called it a sad state of affairs when poor career-seekers graduate after years of poverty, availing of the generosity of the public to do so (mentioning charity-balls to support students as an example), and then dare to ask for positions, work and bread. "What can society say to the poor wretch who has been led by his own folly to push his way into the higher realms of learning? It will answer with silence because society does not have at its disposal university chairs or even minor positions which it can dole out on demand, because for each academic post, no matter how modest, there are hundreds of philosophers, jurists, masters and doctors of various kinds." Poor youths, he argued, should be taught some useful trade immediately, because otherwise they will become "a burden to themselves and to society" and will lend an eager ear to evil promptings.[55]

A month later, the same author again defended the thesis of the existence of an academic proletariat: "We understand this collective term as signifying the entire surplus, which cannot be denied, of graduates and undergraduates of all departments of higher educational establishments: doctors without a practice, barristers without clients, philosophers, mathematicians and politicians [sic!] without chairs, positions or bread, without a point of departure and without an ultimate destination; people who are wasted, embittered, and deranged, in other words, beaten and shattered, people suitable for all jobs and for no job!"

The socialists joined the debate belatedly since some who were party members were behind bars awaiting trial, and others, the "legal" ones, had been expelled from the university and were now scattered all over the world. The only socialist author in Warsaw who was still free was Białobłocki.[56] His calm, reasonable article sounded the final accord in the dispute. Białobłocki did not take issue with *Niwa* over the facts concerning the situation of the intelligentsia; rather, he reinforced *Niwa*'s diagnosis with his own observations. However, he expressed his astonishment at the idea of redirecting the redundant surplus of the intelligentsia to technical trades and to production, since in this field "there is the same overcrowding as everywhere else."

The reason for the overproduction of intelligentsia was, Białobłocki maintained, the poverty and the low cultural level of the common people. There was nothing original in this statement, since Prus and other "organicists" had said the same. However, Białobłocki had little faith in craft schools and other panacea of this kind, believing as he did that the prevalence of supply over demand on the labor market was an inseparable feature of the development, and even more so of the underdevelopment, of capitalism. He seemed more or less to ignore the political realities of the Kingdom: he saw the phenomenon on a European scale, as "an evil which cannot be removed under the present circumstances, and which must be reckoned with."

This was, however, a relative evil, an evil for the interested party only, and not for society as a whole since, he argued, the dispensable were in fact indispensable. Due to their independence, the bread-seeking "specialists of the intelligentsia" with no career prospects constituted the only chance for the development of social thought: "the educated proletariat . . . which does not represent the interests of any social stratum, can impartially explain to society the course of inter-class clashes."[57]

This marked a turning point in the long and heated discussion of the situation on the labor market for the intelligentsia. Until then, the whole issue had been viewed above all in utilitarian and economic terms, though admittedly with a political undertone. The ever-present and growing reservoir of people whose qualifications could not be utilized had been treated with contempt by some, and with compassion by others; whether or not it was feared, from a social point of view it had always been regarded as pure loss. In the mid-1880s, the idea was born that this marginal group had some value of its own. Soon afterwards, it would be said that only the "proletarian" part of the intelligentsia had any value at all.

This turn around called for a fundamental change of views on the professional and social functions of the intelligentsia. Until then, the main concern was whether doctors had patients to treat, whether barristers had clients to defend, whether teachers had pupils to teach, or whether academics could conduct research and publish their findings. It is true that the program of organic work charged the intelligentsia with the duty of voluntary social work, but even in this it did not, on the whole, lose sight of specialist qualifications. In this new perspective, qualifications became a secondary, unimportant matter. The main task of the intelligentsia as such, or of the "educated proletariat," irrespective of the kind of education it had received, was to shape social thought and ideas, and national and class consciousness. "Specialist" became a term of ridicule. Competition on the job market would be overshadowed by competition on the market of ideas.

The Third Circle:
The Technical and Industrial Intelligentsia

Still, almost all the complaints, of progressives and conservatives alike, regarding the surplus of intelligentsia could, in the end, be summarized in the same message: a call to undertake productive work; to seek employment in factories and handicrafts, in farming and gardening, no matter where, provided this work built, produced, enlarged the national wealth, and laid a solid foundation for civilization. And also, although this was not said openly, provided it laid the foundations for the independence of the Polish nation in some undefined future. That industry was waiting for a young, vigorous, skilled workforce was an axiom which, on the whole, hardly anyone, apart from the socialists, dared to doubt, although everybody was aware of the worrying reports emerging from this civilizational battlefield.

The most noble of the technical occupations, the one that called for most expertise, was engineering, above all civil engineering, that is, the construction of roads, bridges and railways. This profession fired the imagination of young people, and was attractive to them because of its pioneering character, the romanticism of traveling and the colorful life that went with it, and also because of the high earnings. The engineer was the favorite hero of the positivist novel and of journalism; as an exalted demiurge he pushed the world onto new (railway) tracks and declaimed grandiloquent tirades about progress. He combines practical knowledge with broad intellectual horizons, thus embodying the ideals of the progressive camp.

Following the January Rising, plans were drawn up to build new railways. The engineering profession became popular among young people of gentry and burgher backgrounds, although there were no colleges in the Kingdom to teach it. There was a great rush to enroll in Western technical colleges and in institutes in St. Petersburg. Mathematicians and physicists, who saw no future for themselves at universities and schools, began to study engineering.

The myth burst like a bubble. As early as the 1870s, it was observed that the number of engineers could not be absorbed by the country's economic life.[58] An increasing number of reports appeared on the alarming shortage of jobs for engineers. The enthusiastic supporters of progress were put in a difficult situation. "In our recent romances," wrote Bolesław Prus, "engineers were idealized as heroes: they made fortunes, they were loved, they alone could boast fine black beards and undaunted noble characters. No wonder then that many a young school leaver hoped to find employment under the banner of blissful civil engineering where the movement to build railways was gaining momentum."[59] Alas, too many people had flocked to this banner. Świętochowski's self-criticism came slightly later, in 1882: "Some years ago, when hard experience was rousing us to endeavor, when public opinion was proclaiming that we should follow a practical path, we took this to mean that we should push our young people into the fields of natural science and mathematics. That was the beginning of the epoch of engineers and technicians, an epoch which is still with us. Unfortunately, there have not been enough roads and factories for them."[60]

In spite of that, each autumn young Poles crowded to various renowned technical institutes in St. Petersburg: to the colleges of communication, technology, mining and forestry. It was difficult to gain admission—there were ten, sometimes fifteen candidates for each place. But the fortunate ones, those who passed the competitive entrance exams, had little trouble obtaining government grants, and their conditions of study were reasonably good. Until 1884, when religious and territorial quotas were introduced, Poles (coming from both the Kingdom and the Empire) constituted almost half of the student body at some institutes.[61] However, on returning to their country after graduation, many of them could not find employment.[62] This also happened to graduates of Western technical colleges and engineers who had already acquired considerable experience working abroad.

By its nature, engineering was a cosmopolitan profession. Many disappointed engineers therefore sought work in different parts of the world; some went to the West, some even as far as the antipodes while others found jobs in Russia. The Polish engineers of that period traveled the world—they could be found everywhere, from the Andes to Sakhalin!

But the question still remained: why? It is true that in the period following the severance of the Russian alliance with Germany, checks were placed on the granting of concessions for railway building in the Kingdom, but industry was developing. It seemed, however, that this industry did not want Polish technicians.

One could fill volumes with the complaints and threats addressed to German industrialists who refused to employ local engineers, masters and clerks. The constant alarmist reports about the invasion of German capital were in fact concerned less about the capital itself, or competition and profits, than about the fact that foreign industry brought in its wake foreign specialists and supervisors while, at the same time, there was no employment for Poles. This provoked understandable bitterness, which increased when Polish industrialists likewise started bringing in foreign specialists. "It is indeed a horrible irony and a cause of both pain and shame," wrote Świętochowski after 1874, "that foreigners entrust to our compatriots the digging of the world's largest tunnels and the building of the most magnificent bridges, and we have no confidence in our own ability to build or manage a small local factory."[63]

This was, however, the reality: technical colleges and institutes taught how to build tunnels and bridges, but not how to manage "a small local factory." Prus understood this perfectly well. Before he himself became a fierce enemy of foreign capital and German economic expansion, he had tried to explain that industry had to be governed by economic calculation and not by sentiment. "Our chauvinists," he wrote, "do not take into consideration the facts of the present and the past, and they loudly complain that a large number of factories are in the hands of people of German origin, and that these people entrust all better positions to foreigners." According to Prus, the reason was that Poles had applied themselves to studying crafts and technology too late, and that they approached the matter from the wrong angle. While the Polish "craftsman" (that is, skilled factory worker) was inferior to his German counterpart as regarded theoretical knowledge, the Polish engineer lacked sufficient practical experience. Specialization was chosen with no concern for real needs; therefore there was an excess of civil engineers and a shortage of mechanics. The obligatory summer training for students was, according to Prus, "nothing more than going round a factory in the shortest time possible." "Industrialists claim that a young graduate is very 'raw' material indeed; he is incapable of supervising workers by himself and consequently cannot hold a managing position," while he regarded anything below that as beneath his dignity.[64]

Such remarks were very apt. Taking into account the level of organization and concentration of industry and construction work in the Kingdom at the time, and the fact that they used mainly imported machines and technology, what was needed above all was mid-level technical personnel. Industry needed "masters capable of working at their benches and teaching workers;" it also needed people to supervise small workshops and factories. Meanwhile, young Poles were trying to learn how to be "top managers of industry," professionals whose knowledge the industrialists could neither utilize nor appropriately remunerate.[65]

This assessment of the situation is confirmed by other sources. In any case, there was certainly nothing new about this state of affairs; indeed, it had lasted uninterrupted for over a hundred years, since the establishment of the first manufactories. However, in the time that had elapsed since then, Polish society had produced its own technical experts, some of whom were outstanding specialists, but had failed to keep pace with the new, quickly changing technology.

Of course, some role was played here by the foreign capitalists who had more confidence in people who spoke their language and understood their culture, although this was probably true more of administrative personnel than technical staff. It is known, for example, that in the period between 1858 and 1869 the German board of the Warsaw–Vienna Railway Society had a policy of barring Poles from higher positions. It is also true that when this railway was taken over by Leopold Kronenberg and put under Polish management its services did not deteriorate in any way.[66] Nevertheless, too much was made of this national factor. It has been established that when the textile and metal industries introduced new technology in the middle of the nineteenth century, they simply could not do without foreign engineers, masters and qualified workers. The technological revolution imposed its own requirements, and technical education could not keep abreast of them. Local traditions of occupational structure also played a role; in Łódź, which had the most Germanized industry in the Kingdom, factory owners did not on the whole bring in masters from abroad; instead, they educated and promoted the best and most knowledgeable local weavers, although the results were not so different as regards the ratio of Polish to non-Polish employees.[67] "Anyone who has visited local factories," someone wrote, "cannot have failed to notice that they only rarely employ engineers who have studied in St. Petersburg; all the positions are occupied either by people without any theoretical background who have learnt their craft by direct practice, often in the same factory which they now manage, or else by graduates of foreign colleges. St. Petersburg technicians do not seem to come up to the requirements of local

industrialists." Young school leavers were therefore advised to start as workers or apprentices in a factory, steel-mill or coal-mine, and only then, after
several years of practical training, "go for a year or so to a technical college
in order to . . . learn things about the latest developments in their chosen
field."[68]

Organic work, by definition, had to manage without state support. Moreover, it had to put a check on the state's destructive activity in relation to
culture. Planned associations of intelligentsia and capitalists were to provide
a material basis for this work and its activists. They were intended to promote
a dynamic, modern civilization as a counterbalance to the routine of bureaucracy with its petrified conservatism. The fact that industry, in spite of its
development, failed to live up to the expectations of the "organicists" in this
regard was perhaps the severest blow their program received.

As for the crafts, small workshops were close to the heart of the advocates
of organic work from the very beginning. There were several reasons for
considering them superior to factories. First, until the end of the century,
large-scale industry was concentrated in a few regions, while vast areas, on
both sides of the Bug and the Neman rivers, remained virtually unaffected by
its influence. Second, industry was largely in foreign hands, while the crafts
were entirely domestic. In industry, the poor man could at best dream of
reaching some minor position, while in the crafts he could expect gradually
to save enough to enable him to set up on his own. Finally, the workshop
made the traumatic process of adaptation to urban life easier for those of a
rural-gentry background.

The author of an article about schools for apprentices published in 1878
had certainly not read Marx's analyses of the phenomenon of alienation, but
that did not prevent him from realizing that: "Personal work, but independent
and autonomous, which produces goods bearing the imprint of the worker's
individuality, work in the environment of one's family, which allows for
private ownership and human freedom, this is the new objective which faces
the industrial class."[69]

Was it a new objective, or an objective that went back as far as the Middle
Ages? If it was new, then it was certainly not for the "industrial" class, but
for those who had been deprived of a career elsewhere by the agrarian crisis,
the Russification of schools and offices, and the uneven development of
capitalist industry.

The petty-bourgeois nature of Polish positivism has been frequently underlined. As the sociologist Stanisław Rychliński aptly observed, the heroes
of didactic novels used grandiose words to sing the praises of the great
inventions of the age, while the ideal for both men of letters and journalist

moralists was not the builder of transcontinental railways, but the honest, thrifty, efficient craftsman.[70] Should this be seen as yet another example of "the lowering of the ideal?" Or does it rather represent the chasm between the ideal and the rude reality, a chasm which characterizes many ideologies, including the romantic ideology of independence?

The ideology of organic work fanned the aspirations of the gentry, the townspeople, and, first and foremost, the intelligentsia; it encouraged them to educate themselves, to bring their country into Europe and to gain a better, more affluent life for themselves. At the same time, for purely practical reasons, this ideology had to keep a check on the aspirations it had awakened. The positivists' motto was "Knowledge is Power." There were, then, dreams of power and of industrial and civilizational victories, but also dreams of positions, of any bread-winning job.

Naturally, the "redundant" impoverished intelligentsia we are talking about here constituted only a minority of the growing legion of "intellectual workers." Indeed, all sorts of people could be found in its ranks: undereducated "men of all trades and no skills" and perennial students, but also highly qualified specialists who lacked the drive to make a career, and some intellectually outstanding individuals. The minority was growing bigger. In our analysis of the marginalized strata of the three most numerous social and occupational parts of the intelligentsia as discussed in this chapter, we have encountered, in each case, the same vicious circle which neither the spontaneously developing economy nor ideology was capable of breaking. Sometimes it seemed as if the country had come to a standstill.

But it had not. The scale was changing. Towns were expanding, houses and hospitals were being built, industry was developing and becoming modernized. This was accompanied by increased employment for the professional intelligentsia, although the increase never matched the number of people seeking jobs and careers.

This is a disproportion which is typical of the early stages of capitalism. It seems that in all developing countries the aspirations of more or less educated people are always far ahead of the rate of economic development and the standard of living of the masses. In poor countries, especially those with access to foreign universities, it is quicker, easier and cheaper to produce an intelligentsia and an intellectual elite than to raise the level of general needs and the means to satisfy those needs.

The abyss separating the level of elitist culture from the living conditions and average cultural level of the masses, which is characteristic of many backward countries, may sometimes pander to the vanity and snobbery of educated and "well-bred" people, but it works against their vital interests inasmuch as they have skills to sell. The professional interests of the intelligentsia require that the demand for their services should increase, that is, they require a general advance in human needs in the fields of education, hygiene, medicine, housing, travel, literature, entertainment, administration of justice, etc. These same interests also require that the means of satisfying new civilizational needs be accessible to the widest possible social spectrum.

However, the needs and means of the main mass of the nation grew at a slow pace in the Polish lands in the nineteenth century, much slower than the pace of industrialization—a situation which is only normal. The plough of belated capitalism ploughed only some fields, and did so superficially, leaving large areas of civilizational wasteland untilled. For this wasteland to be utilized it was necessary to carry out a planned redistribution of the social product, but this redistribution could only be assured by the granting of state or territorial autonomy. The tsarist regime did not have any social policy to speak of. Municipal self-government was introduced by Wielopolski in the Kingdom in 1861, but it was abolished as a punishment for the uprising. As a result, to quote once again Rychliński, "while in the West the rapidly expanding self-government system represented the collective needs of society, softening the negative effects of capitalism which was not concerned about the common interests; that is, it raised the level of hygiene in the towns, expanded the network of roads, extended its assistance to the growing town poor, built schools, and established cultural institutions, the Polish Kingdom was, in the same period, almost completely deprived of such organs of collective activity."[71]

The aim of the program of organic work was to enable the intelligentsia to take the place of these nonexistent local-government bodies by engaging in voluntary work, although it had neither funds nor universities, and did not even have the right to form associations. The only instrument these authors and apostles of the visionary program had was a censored press. With the help of words, they tried to animate their country which was stagnating in poverty and torpor. Their faith and energy enabled them to continue the struggle for a decade. As late as 1880 the *Przegląd Tygodniowy* wrote: "We cannot conceive of reasonable liberalism, of moderate democracy in any other way than as the elevation of the common people, in towns and countryside alike, so that they will be able to make use of all the achievements of our century. ... To leave alone any section of the nation with its limited production and consumption means the voluntary condemnation of society to stagnation or even death."[72]

Soon afterwards, however, the epoch of General Hurko[73] began, and the press of the Kingdom contains increasingly frequent reports about the apathy and torpor of the provincial intelligentsia, which was "incapable of caring" about anything more serious than a game of whist.[74] A keen observer of the times, in a gossipy account of the situation in Warsaw written in 1886 for the Galician paper *Czas*, mentions the "general despondency" caused by the total lack of hope: "Those born and educated in an era when the country enjoyed slightly happier conditions are dying out; the young are inactive and hopeless, and contemplate a future without sunshine or prospects, with a bitterness which each day only serves to enhance."[75]

This bitterness, inactivity and despair bred all sorts of rebellion: against the bourgeois industrial and commercial civilization which was allegedly destroying the true values of Polish folk culture; against capitalist exploitation; against the Jews and the Germans who, it was claimed, barred the progress of true-born Poles at every step and turn; against the hypocrisy, conventions and tastes of the philistines; and, finally, against the partitioning powers.

And, on the top of it all, there was the rebellion of the intellectuals against their own impotence.

Notes to Chapter 4

1. L. O'Boyle, "The Problem of an Excess of Educated Men in Western Europe 1800–1850," *The Journal of Modern History*, 1970, 4, pp. 471–95.

2. See O. W. Müller, *Intelligencija: Untersuchungen zur Geschichte eines politischen Schlagwortes* (Frankfurt, 1971).

3. D. Beauvois, *Lumières et société en Europe de l'Est: l'Université de Vilna et les écoles polonaises de l'Empire russe 1803–1832*, 2 vols. (Paris, 1977).

4. R. Czepulis-Rastenis, *"Klassa umysłowa": Inteligencja Królestwa Polskiego 1832–1862* (Warsaw, 1973), pp. 87–8, 232–4.

5. See L.G. [Ludwik Gumplowicz], "Korespondencja z Wiednia," *Dziennik Literacki*, 1866, pp. 331–3.

6. L. Powidaj, "Polacy i Indianie," *Dziennik Literacki*, 1864, p. 788.

7. [J. A. Miniszewski], *Listy cześnikiewicza do marszałka* (Warsaw, 1858), pp. 144–5.

8. See note 48 to chapter 1.

9. J. A. Miniszewski, "O służbie publicznej," *Dziennik Powszechny*, 1862, no. 157.

10. A. M. Skałkowski, *Aleksander Wielopolski w świetle archiwów rodzinnych*, vol. 3 (Poznań, 1947), p. 123.

11. When Margrave Wielopolski was appointed Minister of Education in the Kingdom (1861), he gained Alexander II's permission to reopen Warsaw University under the name of Szkoła Główna (the Main School). As such, the School survived only seven years: in 1869 it was transformed into a Russian university. For the student enrollment figures see S. Kieniewicz (ed.), *Dzieje Uniwersytetu Warszawskiego 1807–1915* (Warsaw, 1981), p. 348.

12. The "Reds," the popular name of a clandestine organization which was born in the wake of large-scale patriotic manifestations in Warsaw in 1861 and which subsequently started preparations for an armed rising and the enfranchisement of the peasants.

13. J. Leskiewiczowa, *Warszawa i jej inteligencja po powstaniu styczniowym 1864–1870* (Warsaw, 1961), pp. 101, 112, 137.

14. S. Borowski, *Szkoła Główna Warszawska 1862–1869: Wydział Prawa i Administracji* (Warsaw, 1937), pp. 245, 286 et al.; S. Dobrzycki, *Wydział Matematyczno-Fizyczny Szkoły Głównej Warszawskiej* (Wrocław, 1971), pp. 117, 122–5.

15. [S. Krzemiński], *Dwadzieścia pięć lat Rosji w Polsce (1863–1888)*, (Lwów, 1892), p. 167.

16. The "young press," the name given to some Warsaw periodicals edited by young protagonists of liberal positivism in the early 1870s. Aleksander Świętochowski (1849–1938), an influential editor, publicist and writer, was the intellectual leader of this "progressive" movement.

17. The "olds" (or the "old press"), the name given to the conservative defenders of the integral national and Catholic tradition.

18. [A. Świętochowski], "Młodzi," *Przegląd Tygodniowy*, 1872, p. 178.

19. [A. Świętochowski], "Co robić?," *Przegląd Tygodniowy*, 1872, pp. 289–90.

20. "Work at the roots," the basic part of the program of "organic work," consisted mainly in fighting illiteracy and improving the civilizational standards of the rural population, the tasks which the intelligentsia and the gentry were called upon to perform.

21. *Niwa*, I, 1872, pp. 204–5.

22. Eliza Orzeszkowa (1841–1910), a prominent Polish novelist of the period of positivism; lived in Grodno outside the borders of the Kingdom; in her numerous articles on social questions and literary criticism contributed to the Warsaw "progressive" papers, she gave voice to liberal and humanitarian views.

23. E. Orzeszkowa, "O jednej z najpilniejszych potrzeb społeczeństwa naszego," *Niwa*, III, 1873, pp. 102–3.

24. Ibid., pp. 124–5, 154.

25. *Przegląd Techniczny*, 1875, pp. 1–8, 81–7.

26. Bolesław Prus (the pen name of Aleksander Głowacki, 1847–1912), the leading Polish novelist of the positivist period whose works include *The Doll* and *The Pharaoh*; he was also a publicist and for many years contributed weekly columns to Warsaw papers; these "chronicles," as they were titled, still constitute a rich source of information on the daily life and the social problems of the Poles in the late nineteenth century.

27. B. Prus, *Kroniki*, ed. Z. Szweykowski, vol. 1(2), (Warsaw, 1956), pp. 241–2, 446; vol. 2 (Warsaw, 1953), pp. 176–7, 224, 285, 513–14, 522–3.

28. A. Świętochowski, *Liberum Veto*, ed. S. Sandler and M. Brykalska, vol. 2 (Warsaw, 1976), pp. 105–7.

29. B. Prus, *Kroniki*, vol. 5 (Warsaw, 1955), p. 109.

30. The Russian university was opened in Warsaw in 1869 as a successor to the Szkoła Główna (see note 11 above); its faculty consisted mainly of Russian professors, while the student body was mixed. Polish was banned as the language of instruction.

31. R. Czepulis-Rastenis, *Ludzie nauki i talentu: Studia o świadomości społecznej inteligencji polskiej w zaborze rosyjskim* (Warsaw, 1988), pp. 317–19.

32. Orzeszkowa, *List I: Wiek XIX i tegocześni poeci, Niwa*, IV, 1873, p. 258.

33. A. D. [Dygasiński], "Z prasy: Proletaryat naukowy," *Przegląd Tygodniowy*, 1884, p. 23.

34. "Niemoc inteligencyi," *Niwa*, IV, 1873, pp. 1–5, 24–7, 105–8.

35. [Świętochowski], "Wywóz naszej inteligencyi," *Przegląd Tygodniowy*, 1874, p. 282.

36. Władysław Natanson (1864–1937), a physicist theoretician; after studies in Cambridge and Dorpat failed to obtain an academic position in Warsaw; in 1891 moved to Kraków where he was soon appointed professor of the Jagiellonian University.

37. Maria Skłodowska-Curie (1867–1934), one of the founders of the science of radioactivity; Nobel Prize winner in physics (1903, together with Pierre Curie) and chemistry (1911); she left Warsaw in 1891 to study at the Sorbonne and settled for life in Paris.

38. B. Białobłocki, "Nadprodukcja inteligencyi," *Przegląd Tygodniowy*, 1884, pp. 249–51.

39. "Odpowiedź na list przyjaciela z Warszawy," *Głos*, 1891, p. 431.

40. [Świętochowski], "Co robić?," *Przegląd Tygodniowy*, 1872, p. 290.

41. B. Prus, *Kroniki*, vol. 2, p. 294; vol. 5, pp. 393–4.

42. "Zadania inteligencyi naszej," *Przegląd Tygodniowy*, 1880, pp. 605–7.

43. *Prawda*, 1881, nos. 13, 14.

44. [Świętochowski], "Niezużytkowane siły," *Prawda*, 1882, p. 193.

45. [Świętochowski], "Wyższe tony," *Prawda*, 1882, p. 362.

46. Aleksandr Apukhtin (1822–1904), the superintendent of the Warsaw school district in 1879–97; a zealous executor of the policy of forced Russification, he introduced a police regime in schools of all levels.

47. L. Krzywicki, *Wspomnienia*, vol. 1 (Warsaw, 1957), pp. 238–52. Ludwik Krzywicki (1859–1941) was a prominent sociologist and social anthropologist, in the 1880s and 1890s a Marxist, closely connected with the Polish socialist movement.

48. L. Baumgarten, *Dzieje Wielkiego Proletariatu* (Warsaw, 1966), pp. 285, 301–2.

49. [T. Jeske-Choiński], "Proletaryat naukowy," *Niwa*, XXIV, 1883, pp. 881–8.

50. See note 93 to chapter 3.

51. J. I. Kraszewski, "Listy z zakątka," *Biesiada Literacka*, 1884, pp. 21–2.

52. Adolf Dygasiński (1839–1902), a popular novelist with a bias towards naturalism, also a publisher, journalist, teacher and author of pedagogical writings.

53. *Przegląd Tygodniowy*, 1884, p. 23.

54. T. Jeske-Choiński, "Ziarna i plewy: polemika," *Niwa*, XXV, 1884, pp. 203–10.

55. J. Soplica [W. Olendzki], "Sprawy bieżące," ibid., pp. 230–32.

56. Bronisław Białobłocki (1861–1888), a literary critic influenced by the socialist ideology. Died young in poverty.

57. Białobłocki, "Nadprodukcja inteligencyi," repr. in his *Szkice społeczne i literackie*, ed. S. Sandler (Warsaw, 1954), pp. 81–90.

58. Leskiewiczowa, *Warszawa i jej inteligencja*, p. 115.

59. Prus, *Kroniki*, vol. 2, p. 52.

60. Świętochowski, "Wyższe tony," *Prawda*, 1882, p. 362.

61. N.S.B., "Głos z Petersburga," *Przegląd Tygodniowy*, 1884, pp. 377–8.

62. Prus, *Kroniki*, vol. 8, p. 214.

63. Świętochowski, "Wywóz naszej inteligencyi," *Przegląd Tygodniowy*, 1874, p. 282.

64. Prus, *Kroniki*, vol. 2, pp. 283, 524; vol. 8, p. 215.

65. Ibid., vol. 7, p. 9; vol. 8, pp. 135–7. See also *Niwa*, XVIII, 1880, p. 476.

66. K. Strasburger, "Działalność Leopolda Kronenberga w dziedzinie kolejnictwa," in *Leopold Kronenberg—monografia zbiorowa* (Warsaw, 1922), p. 120. Leopold Kronenberg

(1812–1876) was an influential Warsaw banker who invested large amounts of capital in industry and railways; he founded the first School of Commerce in Warsaw.

67. *Głos*, 1888, pp. 619–20.

68. *Przegląd Tygodniowy*, 1884, p. 345.

69. *Przegląd Tygodniowy*, 1878, quoted after S. Rychliński, *Praca organiczna w Królestwie Polskim po powstaniu styczniowym*, doct. dissert. (1931), ms. in the Library of SGH in Warsaw, p. 134.

70. Ibid., pp. 60–63.

71. Ibid., pp. 594–5.

72. "Zadania inteligencyi naszej," *Przegląd Tygodniowy*, 1880, p. 618.

73. Gen. Iosif Hurko (1828–1901), Warsaw governor-general in 1883–94, a ruthless executor of Tsar Alexander III's policy of Russification of the Polish Kingdom, which was officially renamed as "Privislinskiy Kray" (Vistula Land).

74. *Głos*, 1891, p. 380.

75. A. Zaleski, *Towarzystwo warszawskie: Listy do przyjaciółki przez Baronową XYZ*, ed. R. Kołodziejczyk (Warsaw, 1971), p. 437.

CHAPTER 5

Affirmation and Negation

The Warsaw positivists were aware of the disparity between their grand visions and their meager resources almost from the very outset. They wrote in the press with grandiloquence and with a profound faith in the justness of their cause, but without any certainty of its ultimate victory. Unlike their predecessors from the *Gazeta Polska*[1] *(Polish Newspaper),* they had doubts concerning the automatism of progress, the self-motivating creative power of work and capital. But the situation had changed and it had become incomparably more difficult to set the whole process in motion. Earlier, in around 1860, there had been the possibility of an alliance between the progressive intelligentsia and the nascent middle class. Economic and political development were proceeding at the same pace, in spite of some periodic crises. The reconstruction of the Polish educational system had just started, and it seemed feasible for the moderate democrats to take control of urban local government institutions. And finally, it was believed that Wielopolski's conciliatory "civil government" could not manage without some kind of cooperation from the intelligentsia and the middle class, and that this cooperation would force it to take a more liberal line.

In 1871, the structures which could have provided the foundations for progressive work were in ruin. The middle class had survived, but it was indifferent to the fate of the national community. Kronenberg[2] had given himself over exclusively to business and renounced all ambitions to shape public opinion or take part in political life. In fact, other than in Galicia, it was no longer possible for anyone to take part in political life any more. The Government Committee[3] was bringing its work to a close. Poland had reached rock-bottom.

The tutors of the Polish enlightened classes, people in their twenties, who were unfurling their banners at that time, had an easier task than their predecessors in one respect only. For this was the first time that the camp of organic work had no opponents or rivals on the left wing. For the next decade they were the "Reds," but reds who refused to form conspiracies and to take up arms.

Until then all "organic" undertakings and programs, in Poznań, Warsaw or Lwów, had been the work of men in their forties, usually former insurgents, exiles or political prisoners. Younger people had not been interested—this moderate idea had not fired their imagination. The successive revolts of young people, never more than a handful, were rebellions inspired by the poetry of immediate action against the dreary prose of social and intellectual work; they were rebellions which preferred maximalism to compromise. It was only when the country reached a nadir of defeat and hopelessness that the poetry was finally extinguished and the new young men could express their revolt in the language of prose. Nevertheless, they were absolutely convinced that they could offer "society" such words of truth as no one before them had ever revealed.

This conviction was shared by their readers, even the most unreceptive of them. For ideas were quickly forgotten and each had a line of predecessors in this country where the continuity of political life and social thought was interrupted every ten years or so.

This new vanguard was unknowingly voicing opinions that for the most part had been expressed a long time before, but it was wording them more forcefully and at a time when order prevailed in Warsaw,[4] which meant that an article in the *Przegląd Tygodniowy* could easily become the most important event of the week. They took advantage of this respite and could not complain of not being heard. Whether they were actually understood is another matter. For they used, as Eliza Orzeszkowa put it later, "a prison idiom," and the game they played with the censors was, at the same time, a game with the readers. It was not merely a question of substituting euphemisms for certain forbidden words. Some of Świętochowski's articles are completely made up of hints, parables and allusions, and to decipher them required a special kind of hermeneutics. "Indeed," Świętochowski wrote years later, "we developed to perfection the art of invisible writing which the readers' intelligence could decode, just as a chemical is used to reveal invisible ink."[5] They brought their art to such a state of perfection that even today they still mislead some commentators and researchers who ascribe to them widely divergent views: the rejection of independence and appeals for an agreement with the tsar on the one hand, and nationalism on the other; bread-and-butter ideals and bombastic trivialities; an endorsement of acquisitiveness and an attempt to justify bourgeois exploitation. Their contemporaries too, especially those writing from the safety of Galicia, leveled a whole range of accusations at them.

The year 1871 was a quiet one: Polish political thought had been paralyzed following Sedan, and social thought had come to a standstill with the fall of the Paris Commune. In the Russian partition zone, the tsarist administration had drawn more political gain from the emancipation of the peasants than anybody else.[6] Relations between manor and peasants had reached an all-time low. The establishment of a peasant commune under the protection of the Russian government put an end to various patronizing illusions about the gentry gradually helping the peasants to become part of the nation. The gentry, in any case, was almost completely engrossed by the problem of trying to make ends meet in the critical situation after the agrarian reforms. In these circumstances, the whole *raison d'être* of the liberal-conservative ideology disappeared, based as it was on the leading role of the gentry in the process of restructuring agrarian relations.

There was, therefore, no programmatic sociopolitical thought either on the left or the right in the early 1870s. There was no thought of revolution, for there was no one to implement it, and the memory of disaster was too fresh. But nor was there any thought of reconciliation, since the tsarist administration neither desired nor needed it.

The sublime moment in 1861 which had seen the "fraternization of estates"[7] was a thing of the past. Ten years later, the nation was divided into alien classes which were unconnected by any moral ties, and which were all incapable of producing their own ideology or social movement. The only uniting force to be discerned among the debris was the church, a church that suffered persecution but which drew strength from its spiritual resistance and therefore provided the only rallying point for the passive idea of survival.

As often happens in the wake of tremendous defeats, social consciousness underwent a regression. Now that people's hopes for change had been so brutally frustrated and every leap of the national imagination into the future had proved a bloody, senseless risk; now that people had to live in a truncated reality, a refuge and a purpose could be found in the world of values which had been tried and tested and had proved durable. The repository of these values was the Polish Catholic tradition of the rural gentry described briefly in chapter 3. However, this cultural canon had not remained unchanged either. For several decades it had been submerged in a sentimental romanticism devoid of rebellious nonconformism. It had also become enveloped in the somber legends of past skirmishes and uprisings. As Bohdan Cywiński so aptly remarks, in every uprising "the idea of revolt and revolution came from restless, socially radical elements, often seriously at odds with religion or at least with the Church, and in each case the leaders and ideologues were joined by the sons of gentry families, thorough traditionalists, every generation of whom paid an extremely high price for a revolution whose very idea was alien to them."[8] The idea may have been alien, but the history was theirs, and the relics of the successive upheavals, whatever their ideological provenance, were worshiped in the spiritual museum of the national memory.

The old gentry traditionalism, laced with the painful recollections of the recent past, was the soil out of which the concept of Polish-Catholic intellectual formation grew, a concept which is sometimes regarded as the essence of things Polish. This was not an "ideology:" it did not try to rally people to its cause, it had no program and did not organize collective activities. It was merely meant to serve as a stronghold of nationality and faith, joined in a single, sacred bond. Anything foreign was inevitably seen as a diversion and an attempt to breach the walls of the fortress. For this reason, the foundations of Polish traditionalism in the periods following the partitions, the November Rising and the January Rising, did not change. It rested on the unbending conviction that all scientific, philosophical and social novelties coming from foreign countries weakened Polish defenses and led straight to apostasy and the loss of national identity. The main threat to Polishness and the church were seen as coming not from Russification or even Germanization, but from "Frenchifying" and "materializing" influences. The mainstay of Polish-Catholic identity was meant to be faithful loyalty to native customs, and a disregard for what was going on in the wide world or in the nearby town.

However, not all was well with these native customs. At the beginning of the century, the traditional values of the manor house and the parish really did reflect the customary style of life in large areas of the country. After the January Rising, remnants of the old life seem to have survived in some Lithuanian *gubernyas*. In the Kingdom and the Ukraine, the manorial farm became commercialized, the gentry was changing into a merchant class of speculators, and the patrimonial lordship of the manor house and its protection of the tenants, which in any case had always been idealized, was abolished once and for all. Untapped resources of native culture still remained in peasant villages, but these resources, although discovered and exploited by the romanticists, would become an ideological value only towards the end of the century at the same time as the birth of the peasant movement and populist leanings on the part of some members of the intelligentsia.

Meanwhile, traditionalism marked the final stage of a culture which was still gentry-based. This culture was becoming increasingly less authentic, having less and less to do with the gentry's everyday lifestyle, their motivation and behavior, and their utilitarian mentality and morality. Of course, there is a gap between the sacred and the real in every culture, and it was particularly glaring in the gentry culture all over Europe. Chivalrous myths were often invoked by merchants and usurers, the ideals of brotherly equality were exploited by magnates, and the idyll of the serene life of simple villagers was cultivated by courtiers and townsmen. Nevertheless, for a long time this sacred and symbolic sphere stood as a strong canopy over the crumbling edifice of the noble estate. The moment this estate ceased to exist, both *de facto* and *de iure,*[9] the problem for the younger gentry was how to find their place in the structure and culture of a society which was becoming increasingly middle class. This untouchable deposit of tradition and myth revealed its impracticality and fundamentally compensatory nature. The result was a growing breach between the sphere of practical activity which was concerned with individual adaptation to a new economic and social situation, and the sacred sphere of shared cultural symbols in which the various deposits of passive nostalgic patriotism, piety and fear of change found sustenance.

The idealized Old Polish customs and costumes, especially those associated with chivalry, continued to charm people on the stage, in the national operas of Stanisław Moniuszko,[10] and in the historical tales which were still popular. This provided people with values which were lacking in a banal existence, and the need for this compensation became greater as this existence and the chores of everyday life became ever more mundane and colorless.

More important for Polish culture than this traditional strand was the return wave of romanticism. Polish poetry of the 1830s and 1840s was written mainly outside Poland, in Saxony, Switzerland and above all in Paris, where it was also published. Volumes of poetry were secretly smuggled into Poland, or at least to the Russian partition zone and were often confiscated by customs men and gendarmes. During investigations against political activists, the fact that somebody owned or even read certain works could be used as evidence against him. When a legal edition of some of Adam Mickiewicz's poems appeared in Warsaw for the first time in over thirty years in 1858, it was drastically censored and all patriotic "germs" removed. Under these conditions, romantic poetry had a strong impact on the minds and hearts of young rebels. There was some justification in the accusation that it drove these young men to hopeless struggles for freedom and led to their destruction.

Nevertheless, this poetry survived the heroic sacrifices of 1863 and the ensuing reprisals. It became even more widely read: new editions appeared in Lwów and Poznań,[11] commentaries were written, men of letters engaged in heated discussions about it. Works appeared which had never before been published, including Juliusz Słowacki's[12] mystical writings which were previously unknown. Paradoxically, the editors, critics and ideologues of the generation which came to be known as the positivists, by fostering this poetry, established and consolidated in the Polish cultural consciousness the basic canon of romantic literature which has remained virtually unchanged until today. The place of honor was now given to *Pan Tadeusz*, which until then had occupied a lower position. It was only now, after the death of the authors and the demise of any hope of an insurrection, that romanticism truly became the nucleus of Polishness, the "homegrown food" of literate Poles.

Contrary to what later historians and schoolteachers preached, the rationalists of the 1870s, people like Świętochowski, Orzeszkowa, Chmielowski and Spasowicz,[13] somehow managed to combine the cult of "positivist" knowledge and the motto of useful work with a painstaking cultivation of the legacy of the national bards. They did so not because they separated artistry from ideology—such aestheticizing attitudes were completely alien to them. "Romantic literature," Ewa Warzenica writes, "was seen by 'the young' as forming a proper basis for the national education of young people."[14]

This attitude was an acknowledgment that the entire poetic oeuvre of Mickiewicz established the highest measure of national culture since it was his work more than anyone else's which was the focus of attention. It also reflected the conviction that the fiery words of Polish exiles could create unifying spiritual bonds in the period of the most ruthless persecution of this culture and the deepest fragmentation of the national community. Since then, romantic poetry has been recognized as a common heritage, unquestioned even by those ideological groups to whom the romantic attitude towards the world was completely alien.

It became increasingly difficult to take issue with the philosophical, moral and aesthetic axiology of romanticism, in view of the charisma of the authors and works in which this axiology found its most profound expression. The sanctification of romanticism in the national consciousness not only as the main literary and linguistic model, but also as the conventionalized pattern of the experience of common fate, gave this poetry an extraordinary unifying power, though at the same time it hampered the crystallization of intellectual currents. In Poland, one was hardly allowed to define oneself and one's own values against Mickiewicz; one could only annex him and ascribe him ideologically to oneself. It was, therefore, necessary to create a Mickiewicz who was a positivist, as well as one who was Catholic, socialist, conservative, nationalistic, mystical. . .

The young "positivists" of the 1870s were the first to fall into this axiological trap. It was they who cultivated and disseminated the romantic legacy in Poland. When Father Franciszek Krupiński's pamphlet criticizing this legacy was published, the *Przegląd Tygodniowy* described his attack as unfortunate, though admittedly it defended the author's right to oppose "established opinions." The anonymous journalist defended romantic poetry against what is still the most sensitive charge leveled at it, namely, that it is responsible for the effects of "utopian politics:" even if the impact of poetry were as powerful as that, he wrote, "which still needs to be proven more forcefully, then its harmfulness would be due not only to the very nature of poetry, but also to the conditions of the development of society which was unable to perfect other organs of spiritual activity in an equal measure."[15] The Warsaw advocates of organic work were fairly consistent on this matter: it was not they but the Kraków "Stańczyk" group[16] who attacked the *liberum conspiro*, utopian politics and historical synthesis of Lelewel.[17] Even if the positivists had wanted to make such a reassessment and had been capable of doing so by themselves, they would probably not have been allowed to do it because of censorship. As Świętochowski admitted years later, "this language of Aesop can, albeit with difficulty, be used to write about anything except history."[18] However, it is doubtful whether they would have wanted to make such a reassessment: after all, for them, unlike the "Stańczyks," the romantic model of patriotism belonged to the sacred sphere of shared symbols and attachments.

Nevertheless, they based their own teaching on completely different principles derived mainly from Western liberal thought. Mill and Mickiewicz, Spencer and Słowacki—could there be any more different intellectual models? The canon of national culture and literature proposed by the "young camp" seemed to be composed of two incompatible parts, but this was exactly the kind of reading list that was adopted. In the secret libraries of self-education, compiled by the societies of students and secondary school pupils, the works of Mickiewicz, Słowacki and Krasiński,[19] and the novels of Kraszewski and Jeż,[20] rubbed shoulders with volumes by Draper, Buckle, Mill and Spencer, and later with the works of Marx, Lassalle and Lafargue.

This peculiar syncretism of positivist education is, however—considering the epoch—a completely understandable phenomenon. The peaceful coexistence, and even mutual complementarity of such different, often contradictory visions of the world and history expressed the two different functions which literature, in the broadest sense, was expected to perform: the preservation of existing values, and the propagation of new ones.

In view of the complete lack of any institution which could unite the divided nation, the memory of the past and the idea of the motherland seemed to be a precondition for the preservation of national identity, the only defense against the intensifying processes of Russification and Germanization. The generation of the period following the January Rising had, however, three different canons of national tradition from which to choose, all of them aspiring to perform this function. The first of these, which might be described as the classic one, was the canon of petrified gentry tradition described above.

The second had been created by the "Stańczyk" group, who were concerned with re-evaluating the historical heritage according to their own criteria of political thinking. The third was romantic. There were no others.

Faced with such a choice, the young progressive representatives of the intelligentsia did not hesitate long. The gentry-clerical tradition they found obnoxious because of its provincialism, its intellectual torpor and its aggressive intolerance of modern European intellectual currents. They obviously felt closer to the critical re-evaluation of tradition by the "Stańczyks," especially the secular, occidental version represented by Michał Bobrzyński.[21] Nevertheless, the conservative doctrine of the "historical stratum," which implied the consolidation of the nobility's elitism, was not in keeping with the democratic inclinations of the young intelligentsia; moreover, the case the Kraków writers made for a strong state and government, together with their uncompromising condemnation of rebellions, conspiracies and uprisings, could not expect to get a welcome reception in the Russian partition zone.

The high patriotic tone of great romantic poetry was more in harmony with the idealism of the young supporters of organic work. They opted for romanticism, though not as a view of the world and history. They took from it its fervor, its faith in the mission of youth, its Promethean individualism, and, finally, its opposition to the stagnation and spiritual mediocrity of a defeated people. The positivists' romanticism was fragmented and selective.

This generation did not, in principle, have any reason to fear a new uprising, and hence were not wary of the romantic passions. The main enemy of the program for organic work was social inertia. Admittedly, they could perceive a cause and effect relation between the "volcanic eruptions" and the long periods of psychological torpor which followed them, and this was one of the main reasons for their dislike of such eruptions. Nevertheless, they had to contend not so much with the danger of a new eruption, as with the effects of the previous one. They demonstrated extraordinary inventiveness in their search for the right words to describe this condition: they used such expressions as passivity, inertia, apathy, despondence, indifference, fainting, paralysis, fear, impotence... Ever since Mickiewicz's *Ode to Youth* had been published in 1827, the struggle against inertia in Poland had, in fact, always employed the stylistics of romanticism, irrespective of whether the authors were concerned with "deeds" or "work."

While accepting the lofty calls to action contained in the poetry written in exile, and the courage of its imagination and of its blasphemy, the "young camp" rejected those components of the romantic heritage which it saw as opposed to this active attitude. It discarded messianism, the idea of a chosen people with a great mission—in short, it dispensed with the whole romantic philosophy of history. Finally, in its first manifestos dating from 1871–72, it ostentatiously and passionately rejected the notion of poetry as a "lament," and the apotheosis of national martyrdom.[22] Radicals among the intelligentsia felt that these components of the romantic legacy which they rejected only paralyzed the nation by setting up its ideals in the past, instead of mobilizing its energy to work for its rebirth in the future. These ideals, together with the myths of the gentry and the conservatism of the church, belonged to the tradition of inertia, and not to the tradition of life.

On a first reading, Świętochowski's famous articles against "tradition," and the controversy they caused, appear no more than empty words. Such a view, however, would be premature. The author, writing in the columns of the carefully censored *Przegląd Tygodniowy*, had to mask his real message, couching it in an excessively grandiloquent style. But the problem he was discussing was a major one: the restructuring of the intellectual formation and the psychology of the Polish enlightened strata. In other words, he was trying to change the model of national culture.

Since the time of Napoleon, this culture had lived on memories, enveloped in a cocoon of nostalgia. Both gentry traditionalism and rebellious romanticism consolidated this bias. It survived for a long time, becoming a characteristic constituent feature of Polish spiritual life. The intellectual, pictorial and mythological wealth of Polish historical literature in all its genres is astounding when we compare it with the poverty and schematism of futuristic thinking and visions. Disputes about the future never reached such a high emotional temperature as disputes about the past, because Poles felt themselves to be the lords and masters only of their past.

The whole of the positivist intellectual upheaval can be encapsulated as a fierce attempt, though eventually not very successful, to change this trend. The management of one's own future in highly unfavorable conditions became the main axiom of the new model of culture and the main task of the intelligentsia.

"The tradition of all the dead generations weighs like a nightmare on the brain of the living." This is what Marx wrote[23]—human society cannot be modeled at will, according to rationalistic designs, because even a revolutionary has to operate in certain given conditions that have been passed down to him. Świętochowski was no revolutionary, and borrowed this juxtaposition of tradition and progress from Spencer rather than Marx, adapting it to Polish conditions. Although his article of 1872 contains sentences almost identical with that quoted above, their meaning is different. "Tradition" as meant by Marx, that is, a set of circumstances which restrict the freedom to project social change, is not a curse for Świętochowski, but the basis of action: "Could we discard everything that has been done so far in the past and start everything anew? Never. History is a trail which has been traveled by thousands of generations; each newly arrived generation should learn the whole course of this route, stop for a while on the place where its predecessor stopped and then further trace the path of science and life."[24]

The curse was "tradition as an absolute principle of life," a tradition which, by sanctifying truths, extinguished intellectual inquisitiveness. Perhaps this should rather have been called orthodoxy—the kind of national-conservative orthodoxy which makes us believe that the very course of history confirms our values—although in a country which was subjugated and humiliated such faith was paradoxical and could not survive without the support of complex philosophies of history. But Świętochowski was obliged to use the word "tradition," taking pains to differentiate this meaning from others, since the word "tradition," like "nationality" or "nativeness," acted as a talisman against more daring thoughts of reform. The reckless assault of the young journalist on the "deification of the past" was a protest against the stagnation of ideological life. The belief that the national past was the only repository and guarantee of collective ideals led to the claim that no idea which was absent from tradition had any right to exist in contemporary times. Świętochowski's aim was to nullify the misleading argument *ex historia*. He, perhaps more than any of his contemporaries, was aware that no system of values could be logically extracted from historical experience; on the contrary, such systems are employed in the interpretation of this experience. "So, the past gives us no ideals, models or principles." Or else, he added more pertinently, it gives each of us different ideals, models and principles, depending on our individual needs and predilections.[25]

The word "tradition" in the post-romantic epoch had become sacrosanct. For this reason, many saw Świętochowski's article merely as a profanation and a provocation, without making any effort to recognize the precise meanings that the word had as used by the author. The questioning of the significance of tradition was seen by its orthodox adherents as a bold attempt to undermine the very principle of the continuity of national life. The outrage caused by this article contributed to the schism within the "young camp." The moderate and polite Julian Ochorowicz[26] wrote in another journal that "the soil of tradition nourishes the flower of progress:" one cannot exist without the other, and "so we pay tribute to both of them." He made the remarkable discovery that to walk "is to put one foot in front of the other, while the other foot remains behind." He reminded Świętochowski that the impatient Jacobins had wished to change everything at once, and pointed out the evil consequences of that fancy. The moral of all this was that "the future of a society depends on the moderation of the progressive party." Finally, he drew up an indictment of the above mentioned article by his radical colleague: "The past is an open book; from our history should we draw principles to guide us in life, in our history should we look for pointers to progress."[27] Unfortunately, the author failed to tell his readers how this search was to be carried out.

All parties to this dispute indulged in clichés. However, while behind Świętochowski's sublime phraseology there were some significant theoretical and practical ideas, Ochorowicz's banalities were intended only to keep the conservative camp happy. As we have seen, the tragedy of this camp in the Russian partition zone stemmed from the severance of all links between the sphere of cult and the sphere of practical activity. Remarks about the need to respect the past, tradition and the faith were accompanied with a discussion on the price of wheat. The tsarist government was consciously determined to destroy the past—tradition, faith, nationality, and language—and the paralyzed gentry community was incapable of any act of resistance. The conservative camp preserved nothing save religious and social orthodoxy.

The more detached the canon of ideals and dogmas became from the problems of daily life, the more fearful and aggressive was the response of orthodox opinion to any real or imaginary threat. In their view evil forces lurked everywhere, trying to shatter the rock of tradition and faith, for which purpose they assumed ever new names: atheism and materialism, ("so-called") progress and ("false") learning, capitalism and socialism. But there was one enemy, whose stifling presence was seen and sensed by everyone, but who could not be named or pointed out. This state of affairs led to some strange crusades. Court martials were still operating in the Kingdom and in Lithuania, and the scaffolds at Warsaw's Citadel had not been yet dismantled, when the *Przegląd Katolicki* began publishing a long series of articles entitled "Catholicism and Dissidence." According to those articles, the source of all contemporary evil was protestantism, which, long before Max Weber's thesis, had been recognized as the demiurge of capitalist civilization. For protestantism "has inculcated coarse materialism with all its consequences in the hearts of the peoples that it has won over." According to the author, it had frozen all feelings of compassion, even among priests, and had stifled human pity for those suffering poverty and disease, a proof of which was, for example, the lack of hospitals and orphanages in England and Germany. Protestantism had destroyed the moral power of modern societies and subordinated their entire industry and energy to the desire for profit, wealth and a good life. Hence the vanity and vain superficiality of American civilization, while England, "tormented and perplexed by materialism, atheism, moral degradation, heresy and godlessness, must eventually fall into the bloody hands of socialism; and when its vengeful, destructive sword has pierced her, she will have to grant the remnants and ruins of its palaces to the generation which today vainly begs for a bit of food from the servants of the wealthy."[28]

In the course of the following years, the *Przegląd Katolicki* identified the main threat to faith as "positivist knowledge," by which it meant the progress of the natural sciences. Its editor, Father Michał Nowodworski, an erudite theologian, was far from regarding revelation and science as two different cognitive orders unable to compete with one another. He followed the contemporary line of the church, which itself assumed a quasi-scientific attitude in its struggle with science. In 1868, for example, Nowodworski reported on the latest discoveries and theses in the field of geology, palaeontology, anthropology, Darwinism, and historical demography, in order to prove that they contradicted the Bible, and demanded that "false science" bow to the truths revealed in the Book of Genesis. Holy Scripture, he argued, was the only source of infallible truth, while the claims of reason led to the land of eternal skepticism. "Uncertainty, the doubting of everything, the great summit of reason, all this is a horrible torment for man. Complete unawareness is much better." For him, a science not based on religion could only disseminate "idleness, avarice and license . . . which devastate communities." The principles of Christian faith could not be reconciled with the "intellectual current of the present moment:" "positivist" knowledge had to be challenged by revived scholasticism, since only scholasticism could satisfy the general hunger for "universal and encyclopaedic" science, and also solve the major social and economic problems of the day.[29]

Secular conservative orthodoxy focused its attention on slightly different problems, but it also regarded itself as a rock resisting hostile waves which buffeted it from all sides. In the early 1870s the Kraków daily, *Czas,* prophesied the annihilation of European civilization. The paper was not an enemy of civilization: on the contrary, it claimed that Poland had always been a part of Europe, together with Europe forming a bulwark against Asiatic despotism, just as now it was making a stand against pan-Slavism. "We are a nation permeated through and through by western civilization; all manifestations of civilization in our state have always been genuinely Polish."[30] For civilization meant, after all, the inner power of peoples and states which had grown over the centuries, their laws and government, their Christian spirit and tolerance. According to *Czas,* the nineteenth-century scientific, industrial and social revolution was the antithesis of this civilization; it was the beginning of catastrophe. It saw contemporary European monarchies as being like ancient Asian states "which likewise rested exclusively on material power and overthrew each other successively, and left no historical legacy behind. . . . The brutal apotheosis of the state, material power as the exclusive basis of the state edifice, the destruction for the sake of the state of social foundations and institutions, this ruthless trend, this political materialism had always threatened Europe from the East, because it was characteristic only of Asiatic civilization." Now, only now, was this brutality nestling in the very entrails of Europe, and even more so in materialistic North America.[31]

The anonymous author of this diagnosis traveled by rail across Europe in 1872. All around him he saw a world heading towards annihilation: "In no country and at no time before has the habitual and widespread worship of the golden calf engulfed the whole of society to this extent, from the very top to the lowest level; never before has it so systematically purged itself of all other feelings and aspirations as now in Vienna. . . When six years ago we reported in your daily on the Paris exhibition, a similar ominous thought came to our mind . . . at the sight of this tower of Babel erected amidst a confusion of all tongues, which, however, did not rise up to the sky like its biblical counterpart . . . but sank deeper and deeper into the ground in order to oppose its earthly power to that of heaven. . . . We asked then where material progress would eventually lead us, and we came to the conclusion that the hour of the forces of destruction was near."[32]

Now he claimed the prophecy was being fulfilled. The world was divided into just two camps: the camps of affirmation and negation. Negation took various forms; it could be religious, social or national negation, including the negation of political freedom by bureaucratic (meaning Vienna) centralization. Negation was approaching the gates of Kraków, because Kraków, too, could soon become similar to the Western molochs which "are social agglomerations, random collections of people who have nothing in common and who exploit another."[33] These views on inventions, civilization and negation appear to have been copied from Rzewuski.[34] However, the same idealization of pre-capitalistic society, when people did not exploit one another, the same catastrophic vision of history, the same clichés and phraseology appear spontaneously again and again throughout the entire epoch of bourgeois civilization. They are, moreover, universal and have nothing specifically Polish in them. Nevertheless, this rejection of modernity had a particularly paralyzing force in Poland, a country which had just shed serfdom but had not yet overcome poverty and illiteracy, a country which had no government or educational system of its own, and which lacked raw materials and financial resources.

As usual, the vanishing values were to be saved by country life and the common people. A Swiss-style village, for example, or Kraków peasants. "The Swiss village represents an ideal of beauty of its kind, and although civilized . . . it presents a picture not only of welfare, but also, one might say, of peasant comfort, while remaining, however, ideally pastoral." The Galician village did not, admittedly, present a picture of peasant comfort, but then the Kraków countryfolk were a rock of tradition and nationality. "National sentiment is a conserving element; it cannot exist without monuments of the past and without a people who, by its very passivity and inactivity, preserves unchanged through whole centuries national elements such as faith, language, customs, and even costume. Tradition is becoming increasingly obliterated in the more intelligent members of our society, as we exchange it for any cheap foreign trinket; all of us, from the aristocracy to the peasantry, are succumbing to the currents of decay so fast that we are no longer capable of preserving anything."[35]

As early as the romanticists, the peasants were beginning to replace the gentry as the preservers of national tradition. Nevertheless, the fact that such self-criticism appeared in a conservative newspaper addressed to the land-owning class was in a way the sign of a new epoch and a loss of self-belief on the part of the gentry. This, however, did not mean that it had renounced its historic role. Even in the Russian partition zone, the would-be shapers of gentry opinions were waking from their torpor. Their weekly, *Niwa*, once again tried to adapt the program of organic work to the needs of the squires, that is, it attempted to turn it into a program for the preservation of gentry estates and tradition, which were regarded as the nation's "spiritual territory." Both land and tradition were to act as a bastion against the influence of cosmopolitism, the Germans, the Jews, and, presumably, the Russians. In 1880, a *Niwa* editor would issue an appeal to "The absentees,"[36] demanding that the old families return to their social posts.

Earlier, readers from the higher aristocratic spheres had been outraged by two much discussed novels by Józef Ignacy Kraszewski, *Morituri* and *Resurrecturi*.[37] One of the responses to these novels, namely *Głos szlachcica polskiego (The Voice of a Polish Gentleman),* published anonymously in Lwów in 1880, is particularly noteworthy since this pamphlet contains the entire canon of orthodox gentry thinking. The author passionately defends the princes of the house of Brański, a noble but completely impractical branch, whom Kraszewski, then an emigré living in Dresden, doomed to historical extinction. But he is even more outraged by the suggestion that the ruined gentry could retrieve their position by turning to market gardening. This shows the author of *Resurrecturi* to be not only the grave-digger of his own class, but a renegade. The anonymous writer argued that it was right and fitting that the gentry were ashamed to work at some occupations and that they lived according to the customs of their forebears, and not the customs of shopkeepers. Its emblems were the cross and nobility, and not some "resurrection" which would be achieved through the worship of the golden calf and utilitarianism.

The gentry were "so far the exclusive heirs to the entire historic national past." Not long ago, the gentry "voluntarily and spontaneously gave up half of their land for the benefit of their younger brothers, the peasants," but they still had control of the other half of the land and the defense of that land was their patriotic and religious mission. The gentry were alive and did not need to be resurrected. He regarded as disgraceful Kraszewski's advice to the gentry "to enter triumphally riding a carrot and holding a bunch of asparagus under their arm and to occupy the position from which they have been pushed aside by public, personal and also general conditions."

The gentry had their holy order: Religion, Motherland, Family and Tradition. These were to be defended. "Let us imagine the nation as a stronghold. If we carelessly let a stranger as regards blood and customs into this stronghold, then beware! The stranger will espy the weak points of the stronghold and point them out to the external enemy, and then deliver the stronghold and its garrison into the hands of the destroyer." The stranger was positivism, materialism, atheism, the so-called rights of man, Hegelian philosophy, Darwin, democracy, and shopkeepers. Within the stronghold, people were to stick to God and the national spirit, and "preserve the old order."

The ancestral Polish gentry, exposed as it was to scorn from all sides, did not, he argued, have the right to change anything in their order. They had to defend tradition, to pray and to endure until "the miracle of unification is born of our faith." And then:

"The Polish gentry with God and the people

Will free the country from slavery by miracle. . ."

The whole practical program could be summarized in two admonitions of "national service:" first, let us not collude with Moscow or the forces of revolution; and second, "Let us guard, defend and keep our fathers' inheritance" because "one does not trade in land as if it were pepper or haberdashery . . . Let us remember that by defending our fathers' inheritance we defend the Fatherland!"[38]

This is an untypical text, extravagant in every respect, which shows the limits to which a certain kind of mentality can be pushed. And though it would be hard to find an equally fanatical statement elsewhere, the conservative press of the day was full of examples of this orthodoxy based on tradition and rank, an orthodoxy which had more influence on the social consciousness than Michał Bobrzyński's modern toryism.

Without an awareness of this background, one cannot understand "positivist negation." The main feature of the young avant-garde was what can be called an engineering attitude: they wanted above all to know what was to be done and how it could be done. This explains the intended reduction in the content of the national cult: for the problem was how to eliminate this splitting of the consciousness between a deep level in which sacred beliefs and hopes were stored, and a completely separate layer, capable of adaptation, which motivated everyday attitudes. The positivists wanted to connect that which ought to be worshiped with that which had to be done. The process had to be two-sided: the program of practical activity had to be subordinated to the overtly articulated ideal values, and, at the same time, it was necessary to exclude from pragmatic thinking political axioms which, under the existing conditions, did not lend themselves to proper instrumentalization. Świętochowski would later remark that he did not wish to get rid of dreams but of illusions.[39]

The non-illusory dreams would be translated into the idiom of social practice by the intelligentsia, which the positivists usually defined as a nonsociological category. True, the ideologues of progress, as we have seen, were concerned about the well-being of those educated individuals who offered their skills for sale, and identified themselves with such individuals very closely. However, in his declarations of program and in newspaper columns, the Envoy of Truth[40] on the whole avoided stressing socioeconomic distinctions: he defined the intelligentsia not according to its condition but its mission. And the mission was twofold: it involved the transformation of social consciousness and social ethics, and the transformation of the conditions of life. Thus, towards the end of the century and later, the intelligentsia was often seen as the intellectual avant-garde, standing "at the head of the spiritual interests of the whole community," as a creative force which led the nation and took responsibility for the common fate; it was, or was meant be, "the lever of progressive development." The intelligentsia was a "thinking and feeling class," and by definition it embraced those who "reflected on themselves" and who had "self-knowledge."[41] Thus understood, the intelligentsia could include a country squire and a village teacher, a doctor and a poet, a wealthy merchant and a starving student. And each of them could choose not to belong to this class. But since the squire and the merchant could only just squeeze through the eye of the needle of the doctrine of social duty, in the final reckoning the "thinking and feeling" intelligentsia was composed mainly of professionals.

This confusion of meanings grew out of the programs of organic work, but even today causes a lot of misunderstanding. We have grown accustomed to superimposing one concept of the "intelligentsia" on the other, and in this way we confuse duty with reality, and the idea with the social condition. The growth of a body of intellectual workers—professionals, public and private functionaries, scholars, men of letters, and artists—was not something peculiar to Eastern Europe, and in spite of all efforts it is difficult to prove that education combined with professionalism made for a stronger supraprofessional unity in this region than anywhere else. What was perhaps specific for this part of Europe was the notion that the intelligentsia had a pioneering and missionary role to play, since in that part of Europe which enjoyed political freedoms and which had citizens and not imperial subjects, the formulation of programs had already become the preserve of parties, civic associations and social movements, and their implementation was in the hands of parliaments, governments and local-government institutions.

A small group of daring young men who called themselves the "progressive party" put a heavy burden of responsibility on the shoulders of the intelligentsia, demanding from its members not just one sacrifice, but the "reawakening of the vital powers of society" and persistent "efforts to bring about a revival."[42]

The first, still fairly general, indicators as to what that work actually should be were based on Western books. Świętochowski and Mikulski's important series of articles, entitled "Work at the Roots" and published in 1873, shows, however, that the main merit of this avant-garde was not so much that it discovered the theory of civilizational development, as that it revealed the destitution prevalent in their own country. True, there were other authors who had done this before them. But this was the first time that Polish destitution became the initial premise of a social program. The revolutionary democrats before 1863 expected the educated class to love the people, to sacrifice their lives and privileges, and to liberate Poland by setting free the popular forces which were under the yoke of agrarian feudalism. These were lofty ideals, but the generation of thinking intelligentsia that emerged after the last uprising could not be blamed for treating them with a certain measure of skepticism. The blood sacrifice had been made, and enfranchisement, whether it resulted from a decree of the National Government or a *ukase* of the Tsar, was an act of historical justice. But none of that resulted in an increased rye harvest, nor did it add a single citizen to the stateless nation. The peasant ceased to be the subject of the squire and became the subject of the Russian or Austrian emperor, and the superintendent of the commune or tax collector continued to bleed him dry, just as the manor had done before. The abolition of corvée and rents proved to be merely an indispensable condition for another kind of enfranchisement: allowing the rural population a share in the most elementary products of civilization and culture. This sort of enfranchisement, however, could not be introduced by revolutionary or government decrees.

When compared to the program of work "at the roots" or Prus's *Chronicles*,[43] the unconscious spiritual aristocratism of the romanticists and revolutionary democrats of the past epoch is obvious. They were obsessed with Poland, and some of them, the most noble and sacrificially-minded, were obsessed with dreams of a free people's Poland. But the idea of Poland was still a cause held by only a small percentage of the country's population—and no democratic catechism could do anything about that. The time of conspiracies and uprisings had passed, and still the peasant, just as in the era of Staszic, did not care, and could not care, "whether Poland is a Polish nation in the world." The peasant's lot, his most vital truth, was endemic hunger, a high infant mortality, one of the lowest soil yields in Europe, illiteracy, a lack of knowledge of laws and regulations, usury, vodka and tuberculosis.

After Sedan, it was useless to expect the miracle of a resurrection, and it was equally futile to expect that an independent Poland would miraculously cause loaves to multiply or spread universal education. The ideals had to be adjusted, brought down to the "roots." This "lowering of ideals" would later provoke criticism of the liberal positivists from both the left and right. The source of this "lowering of ideals" was the otherwise banal discovery that Poland lacked not only independence but also soap, school primers, places of work and study, water supplies and sewage systems, and, above all, the cultural unity without which a "nation" remains only an abstract concept. It was also realized that perhaps it was not necessary to wait for better times before beginning the construction of this civilizational infrastructure, since the interdependence of cause and effect might prove to be quite the opposite from what had been assumed. For this reason Świętochowski suggested that the society should "work where the field is open," and furiously attacked the "political troubadours."[44]

In order to restructure the hierarchy of objectives, it was necessary to look at one's own country as if from outside and without sentiment, the way Montesquieu and Voltaire had viewed Bourbon France. However, in a country that is colonized and humiliated, such bluntly critical assessment is psychologically much more difficult, being seen by many almost as a form of national apostasy. Romanticism imparted to the Polish intelligentsia—just as the Slavophiles imparted to the Russian intelligentsia—the conviction that an understanding of the motherland demanded a kind of mystical initiation, and therefore could be gained only from the inside, through participation in the national historical mystery play. Perhaps this is the reason why the masterpieces of Polish romantic poetry remain incomprehensible to most foreigners. The exteriorization of the vantage point led to the destruction of the myth about the unique character of Polish history. Michał Bobrzyński went furthest in this direction when he demanded that Polish history should be seen as part of the course of general, or more strictly West European, history. For Bobrzyński, Poland was a nation just like any other, with its own periods of greatness and defeat. What was unique was the fact that its history had been written in such a way after the partitions as to exclude it from the operation of general laws, and make it exist in some unreal spiritual sphere. In the final pages of his *History of Poland* (1879), he ridiculed the portrait of the model gentleman whom Polish men of letters claimed to have existed in the preceding two centuries, adding the sarcastic remark that "it is not said, however, whether this ideal Pole paid his taxes regularly."[45] This was more than merely a revised view on the reasons for the downfall of the state; this was a criticism of a cultural system in which the question of tax belonged to the low, unessential sphere of reality.

Świętochowski subjected to the same harsh criticism the general conviction that the peculiar moral and political attributes of the Polish national character made it immune to infection by foreign ideas. "The faith in some peculiar properties of our soil has not died out . . . In our lifetime Europe has been swept by a number of currents . . . which have been kept at bay with the assurance that 'they will not find proper soil here'." This was the response to Darwin's theory and positivism, and later to socialism and antisemitism. And this was not going to change "until we take the crown of the chosen people off our heads and start seeing ourselves as ordinary mortals." There were, he admitted, differences among the nations, but "precisely this conviction that we are not a dead or severed branch of the European tree, that the tree's juices run in our veins, this conviction should sustain the thought that here, on 'our soil' the same symptoms may develop as anywhere else."[46]

The stubborn insistence on making Poland ordinary, on observing it through the eye of an outsider who had broken away from the vicious circle of cultural initiation, became the methodological point of departure of the "negation" which the positivists were accused of. In this respect, they were true heirs to the Enlightenment, but at the same time they began the long line of "scoffers" who contended with the burden of the Polish tribal myth. In the eyes of the West, the idea of Poland having a universalist mission, or of her being the bulwark of civilization, was a ridiculous claim, based, moreover, on obsolete geopolitics. Unlike the Galician neo-conservatives who still believed that the eastern reach of Polish gentry settlement was the border of

European civilization, the liberals from the Russian partition zone noted the progressive Europeanization of Russia, and were not at all sure whether Warsaw was closer to Paris than St. Petersburg. At the same time, the menacing power of Bismarck's Germany was growing in strength in the West, and its shadow would loom large over all Polish political thought in the last thirty years of the nineteenth century.

In such a context, the idea of Poland's universalist mission lost its point for the positivists. "Then, what was the purpose of all our efforts to make Europe safe, when this Europe does not need us? ... Let us forsake the illusory thought that we are an indispensable condition for European equilibrium, an indispensable dam checking the waves of Asian barbarity, the bulwark of the world ... We should try to justify the Poles' right to existence not by claiming that Europe cannot sleep peacefully without them, that they are the most faithful guardians of Europe's barns and granaries, but by the fact that they exist, for themselves and by themselves, that they form a separate, quite numerous nation, that they have their own, reasonably developed civilization which adds to mankind's progress and enriches it with significant original elements. Those whose right to life stems from these sources, will be understood and finally respected by the whole world."[47] So far, they claimed, Poland did not command respect, since it had not adopted a modern scale of values and remained "perhaps the least democratic nation in Europe;" it still cultivated, "in its notions if not in its relations," the caste system which allowed for the separation of "aristocracies of birth, of money, of rank, and of learning." Poles were disliked in Europe for their arrogant airs, lack of respect for work, and "stubbornness bogged in tradition." The Polish reputation as a "gentry" nation was based to some extent on exaggeration and misunderstanding, but after all "it is not without reason that the whole society has gained an oft-repeated nickname, covering itself with ridicule, and presenting itself to the world as a long obsolete anachronism."[48]

The above examples demonstrate the dual nature of the European idea as interpreted by the Polish liberals. They were aware of the untrammeled growth of state nationalisms in Europe, and rejected the lofty utopia of political universalism and the romanticists' faith in the unification and brotherhood of free and subjugated peoples. They saw that it was useless to rely on European political alignments, and that traditional faith in the friendship and assistance of France, which had been defeated and was as selfish as any other state, lacked any foundation. Those peoples which were beset by pan-Slavism with its annexionist tendencies on one side and pan-Germanism on the other, had to develop their own resistant brand of nationalism if they wanted to survive.[49] Only a small number of Polish positivists regarded social

Darwinism as a fitting theory of society; Świętochowski did not approve of it as far as individual or class interests were concerned, but he used the concept of the "struggle for survival" when working on his strategy of national resistance. In this restricted sense, he may be called the precursor of Polish nationalism.

However, this is just one side of the liberal doctrine of "adapting" programs to current conditions. For them Europe had ceased to exist as a political idea, but it continued to live as a vital civilizational idea. Subjugated and backward peoples had to join this civilizational entity or perish. Tradition was not an effective shield. Former political and territorial rights, the blood spilt in the defense of the freedom of one's own and other nations, or, finally, the exotic otherness of gentry culture could not be used to make a case for national rights in the contemporary world. The argument that "I was, therefore I am" was vain and useless. It seemed that almost all positivists quoted the Czechs as models to be followed by the Poles: once the Czechs did not exist, and then they did. They had become a nation to be reckoned with thanks to their persevering efforts to develop their own internal autonomy and democratic culture. In order to strengthen internal forces, the wall erected by parochialism between Poland and Europe had to be demolished—"the wall in which here and there significant breaches have already appeared, but which still separates us from even passive participation in universal development." They saw the acquisition of modern technical and social knowledge as a powerful instrument in the "struggle for survival," and gibes at the triumphs of the Western genius as simply self-defeating. "There is no choice here; we have only one road left to us: to join in the stream of general civilization, to adapt ourselves to it, to subject our life to the same impulses, the same rhythms which govern the development of other nations. Otherwise, they will never recognize our rights and our needs, and will continue to regard us as if we were some ancient relic which can be made comprehensible only with the help of an archaeological dictionary."[50]

This may have been merely replacing one myth with another. The "tribunal of civilization," before which nations were supposed to prove their rights,[51] may have been as misleading a hypostasis as the conservative interpretation of tradition or messianic soteriology with its faith in the morality of the historical process. There would be more than one occasion on which men would have doubts about the tribunal of civilization, and indeed all other tribunals of history except the judgments and sentences delivered by cannon fire. Nevertheless, the theory of civilizational competition among nations was the greatest universalist and future-oriented myth of the nineteenth century; its only serious rival would be the doctrine of universal social revolution. The myth of civilizational contest carried a powerful energy load, and directives for pragmatic activity could easily be derived from its axiology.

But what did the "progressive party" really mean by that protean word "civilization" without which no nineteenth-century social doctrine could have managed, regardless of whether it was used as a negative or positive reference? If we were to believe right- and left-wing critics, the ideology of civilization was to be merely a kind of new mercantilism, a handbook of capitalist greediness written for individuals and for nations. Civilizational growth was seen as the philosophy of shopkeepers, who recognized only that which could be measured, weighed and calculated in money. "Doctors, mechanics, engineers, natural scientists and merchants," a critic of positivist novels lamented, "have overrun literature *en masse*, chasing away knights, poets, artists, journalists, orators and preachers." And none of these practically-minded characters "has done anything which would go beyond the limits of the daily needs of society. . . . They are indifferent to the supreme mysteries of the cosmos and the misfortunes of great nations."[52] There are hundreds, if not thousands, of similar statements, worded in a more or less romantic style. However, while the critics only unmasked the poverty of positivist ideology, the catastrophists were absolutely disgusted with the spiritual impoverishment of the civilized world in which, as one poet wrote,

"Thoughts are being dwarfed, the volcanoes of the heart are extinguished;
History no longer resounds with the archangelical chorus of faith,
The age of reason, like a horde of licentious soldiers,
Stuffs itself with the flesh of conquered matter."[53]

Condemnations of this sort were nothing new. It seems that in all literatures a revulsion for bourgeois morality and rationalized middle class civilization is a natural reaction to the progress of this civilization. As far as Poland and Russia are concerned, the reaction was peculiar only insofar as this repugnance had a clearly preventive quality. A proud contempt for material goods and modern production technologies is one thing in a wealthy country—as, for example, in the case of the American transcendentalists—and something completely different in those parts of the world where four-fifths of the population is chronically undernourished and lives in the most primitive conditions, far from civilization. It was very strange indeed, as Eliza Orzeszkowa aptly noted, that industry was condemned "in a country where this industry is only at the infant stage of development."[54] In any case, it was the opponents of the civilizational program who consistently reduced its contents and meaning to trivial economic factors. Their charges prove groundless when one actually looks at the positivist programs. The economic views of the Polish liberals will be discussed in the next chapter. Here it is enough to say that they regarded the satisfaction of a certain minimum of elementary existential needs as a necessary step in the liberation of the creative potential of individuals, and regarded the country's economic development as a prerequisite for the growth of its internal power and of its culture. The idea of reducing "civilization" to "capitalism," and of confining values to the economic sphere, was not only alien to them, but contrary to their basic world view.

The defense of the nineteenth century undertaken by Eliza Orzeszkowa in 1873, constitutes the most articulate and complete exposé of the ideals which positivism associated with the notion of civilization in its early, optimistic phase. Orzeszkowa's literary dialogue was a diatribe against the sentimental criticism of industrialism—a criticism that drew its arguments from the aesthetics and ethos of pastoralism. The author's imaginary traveling companion is, like Brodziński, Kraszewski and many others, a defender of the natural environment, of primeval nature, the rural landscape, the peace and quiet of forests and lakes. He is also a defender of a person's right to disinterested contemplation, to the cultivation of non-utilitarian values. In any such debate, the steam engine was an indispensable element. From the mid-nineteenth century on, railways had been the symbol of modernity, with its blessings and scourges, all over the world. Some saw them as symbolizing the power that human thought and inventiveness exerted over matter, space and time; others, on the contrary, regarded them as a symbol of the power matter exerted over humanity.[55] Thus, Orzeszkowa's interlocutor is aware not only of the engine's smoke which pollutes the clean air, and the noise that destroys the peace of nature, but he also perceives in the railway a sign of the mechanization of human life. In the age of the steam engine, "everybody hurries, rushes, bustles, knowing neither why nor where." Human beings lose their subjectivity; they can no longer steer their own course because they themselves are controlled by Mechanism: "You are not people making a journey, but goods being transported."[56]

A hundred years have passed since then, and these arguments are still in circulation and are becoming, in fact, more popular. The only difference is that the railway has been replaced by supersonic aircraft. A particularly endearing feature of Orzeszkowa's writing as a journalist is that the ideas that she contested are always presented in their most noble version. Today, it is her replies rather than the refuted charges that may seem naive. She knows why and where mankind was rushing. She appears in the guise of a precursor of futurism, an admirer of terrific speed and momentum, of the beauty of machines and factory smoke which she describes drifting across the sky the way Adam Mickiewicz depicted the clouds in *Pan Tadeusz*. However, she is more interested in ethical arguments than aesthetic effect. A destitute wretch cannot admire nature. Agriculture without support from industry, learning and commerce will not provide enough food for the hungry. In humanity's attempts to subdue the forces of nature, the moral law is on the side of civilization and the pertinent question is "whether this religious concern about protecting the primeval beauty of nature against all harm, with no regard given to human needs, suffering and security, whether this is not simply a deification of the 'flesh of matter', a fetishism which idolatrously worships blues and greens, steppes and waters, oaks and weeds?" In any case, she argues, industry will one day appear on the banks of the Vistula and the Neman, and if we fail to develop it, others will do so in the future. "Then . . . we, who take pride in calling ourselves an arch-poetical people, will be allowed to make an appropriate number of pipes of white birch bark, and to tend and pasture the flocks of our lords, on rivers which flow with honey and gold, but not for us."[57]

This was only the starting-point—it was not machines that were the main defendant in the trial of civilization. The catastrophists were obsessed with the dwindling of the spiritual dimension of humanity. Their lament was that the era of heroes, of faith, love and sacrifice, had come to an end; the steamroller of commonplace flattened everything, reducing to the same level people and nations who were totally dedicated to the pursuit of profit. And this is where the speech for the defense begins, made on behalf of the nineteenth century, the "great accused":

"I have written statutes in which I have made all people, irrespective of their birth and the color of their skin, equal as regards the right to learning, honors, profits and happiness …; I have discovered how fatal physical poverty and intellectual backwardness are for the physical and spiritual health of man, and I have started the work of alleviating or, if it is at all possible on this earth, completely eliminating these disasters, by liberating social relations from the clutches of superstition and wrong; this I have done by improving the social economy, and by making institutions of public education open to all; I have stretched my protective wings over deserted children, decrepit old age, and helpless debility. . ."

These ideas, Orzeszkowa admitted, were not strange to previous centuries, but it was only recently that they had been given the support of critical reason. There was the same difference between the charity of the past centuries and that of the present age as between alms and a modern hospital. She advised those who asked whether there was progress or decline in history to have a closer look at the changes in criminal justice: "No other work of the human mind contains more justice, wisdom and, above all, love than the improvement of the penal proceedings, the use of psychology and forensic medicine in the courts, the abolition of capital punishment, and prison reform . . . The magnificence and poetry of this work by far surpasses the bloody and boisterous expeditions extolled by Homer and Tasso."

The hallmark of modern civilization, she claimed, was free, bold thought and social reforms that took full advantage of scientific achievements. The fruit of this thought was "today's religious and political liberalism" which was building "the great edifice of civil equality and public freedoms."[58] Seven years later, Orzeszkowa was to add that the nineteenth century, which had been so often condemned, was the age of the development of compassion.[59]

Was this just one more civilizational utopia? Orzeszkowa did not write about the future; she used the past and present tenses. Was she describing an ideal, or the Western world as she saw it? She was, in fact, describing both the ideal and the reality, and she immediately perceived the growing gap between them. This ideological formation had reached Poland belatedly, leaving no time for any naive faith in civilization, which by then had revealed many of its inhuman features. The age of Condorcet and Bentham, the age of enthusiasm on the part of philosophers and economists for the progress of the human spirit through history, the age of faith in social harmony, succumbed to the fever of speculation in the epoch of the French Second Empire and could only expect a shameful death. Modern civilization was supposed to be a tightly-knit system of values; scientific and technological development was to bring about a general improvement in the level of education and wealth, accompanied by a gradual but continuous growth of equality and freedom, peace, and political democracy, and the ultimate result was supposed to be a society based on the principle of altruism. Instead, this system of values proved to be not solid, but cracked. The development of science, learning, technology and production was undeniable, but it resulted in both a hitherto unknown degree of comfort and a different kind of poverty from that known previously, in a growth of equality and of inequality, of freedom and of enslavement. The new chances for the development of a sense of community among mankind, and the new loneliness of the uprooted dwellers of the large crowded cities, were products of the same historical process.

Once the inner contradictions of industrial civilization had become manifest, it was vain and futile to further indulge in either outright praise or condemnation of the whole development. By the same token, the disputes between the traditionalists and progressives lost their meaning. The industrial epoch had to be recognized as a fact, an irreversible process caused by the spontaneous burgeoning of human inventiveness and enterprise. The recognition of this fact meant that the conservatives had thoroughly to revise their doctrine, while liberals saw that there was a chance their humanistic ideals would be implemented. In the name of this chance, they demanded that society place some trust, albeit limited and conditional, in modern civilization. Only one thing was certain, namely, that scientific progress multiplies the creative forces of mankind, by the same token increasing the ability of its intellectual elites to bring about a rational transformation of the natural and social environment. The question remained as to the principles of human community these instruments would serve. The liberals did not subscribe to the conviction that methods of production and of the exchange of goods determined every aspect of social and political culture.

One of the main points in the programs of organic work was voluntary association, a practical school of cooperation. It was a peculiarity of the Polish intelligentsia's liberalism that it did not go through the phase of individualistic philosophy which was so characteristic of more middle-class societies. Early liberalism opposed the growth of the state's sphere of competence everywhere in Europe, but in England or France it took advantage of state institutions of social integration, whether monarchical or republican. It was not difficult to call for an open market, or for free competition of individual talent and enterprise in those countries where basic human rights were already secured—the right to one's own native language and education, access to the law, the right to practice one's own religion, and to protection against the arbitrary use of power by government officials and the police. But ideas travel faster than political systems. The axiology of democratic liberalism, no longer confined to the gentry, was spreading in partitioned Poland as well, although here it found no support from official institutions; in fact all of them were entirely hostile to it. The first region to go through this process was the Poznań area (in the 1840s), and the fruit of this was the Society for Educational Assistance, and later the Polish League.[60]

The Warsaw "progressive party" questioned the authority of "tradition" and the constraining power of the system of petrified collective ideas. This was why it called for a free "exchange of opinions," but it never wanted to leave the liberated individual alone and helpless in the face of tsarist school supervisors, commissars and gendarmes. While the positivists disclaimed any aim of organizing society politically they dreamt of, and cherished illusions about, covering the country with a network of economic, educational, professional and other associations. This network was to form the backbone of a social structure; it was to be a substitute for a parliament and local self-government, capital and university. Prus in his *Chronicles* and Święto-chowski in his columns were merciless in their criticism of the Polish intelligentsia which was incapable of social action even in the more favorable conditions of Galicia or the German partition zone: "'the educated classes', their mouths full of noble slogans, are aware of vast tasks and general needs, and proudly talk about our 'thousand year old civilization', but they do not know what to do, and if they do know, they have no idea how to unite and organize themselves."[61] And, since they had no idea how to achieve their aims, the organic program lacked solid foundations.

There was also another, no less important reason for the positivist ideologues' dislike of individualism. When they announced their program, the doctrine of the free play of social and economic forces had already been morally compromised in the West, where it was perceived as the ideology of the strong and the ruthless. John Stuart Mill, the most authoritative and popular of the liberal philosophers, had already begun to back away from the classic interpretation of freedom as the lack of intervention, and had tried instead to reach a compromise with the reforming ideology of the socialists. His Polish disciples never wholly subscribed to the doctrine of free competition. They acknowledged—though not without reservations, of which more later—that the middle class had a useful role to play in the industrialization of the country, but this was not a sign of any true sympathy. Świętochowski would take special pride in the fact that *Prawda* did not print advertisements placed by large companies, and his remarks about "sharks" became more acrimonious as time passed by. "Capitalism is rotting," he wrote, "and it will continue to rot . . . because it draws its juices from man's evil instincts."[62]

Evil instincts, it was argued, were released by fierce competition for markets and profits, by class struggles and national conflicts. "Conflict," wrote Prus, "is usually an indication of either a faulty structure or faulty social relations. Where there is conflict, reforms are needed, preferably reforms reached through negotiation and mutual compromise. . . . In any case, conflict is disastrous, if not criminal, because it dramatically saps the nation's power. Constant references to it are a symptom of savagery."[63] Not everybody was as consistent as Prus in his advocacy of social and national pacifism, but on the whole the positivists did not subscribe to the social Darwinist vision of humanity divided into herds of wild beasts fighting one another. If they did accept this view, they did so with great abhorrence. As the years went by, they were provided with more and more occasions on which to demonstrate their abhorrence. And more and more frequently this feeling was caused by the discrediting of those ideas which they had adopted, at least in name.

The German liberals who supported Bismarck had simply used the principles of freedom as a screen for the ideology of force. According to them, Świętochowski wrote, "commerce . . . must be absolutely free, the interests of the capitalist must not be subjected to any restrictions and the state with its numerous army must not be hindered in its policy of conquest and denationalization. . . ." The Poznań politicians had to dissociate themselves from these national-liberals and seek an alliance rather with the German conservative circles which were more sympathetic towards Poland. The situation was similar in Austria, where an alignment of the Polish Circle in Parliament with the Right was necessitated and justified by the fact that "[Austrian] liberalism has brought the Slavic peoples violence and oppression, [while] conservatism has given them relative freedom and equal rights." These were bitter re-evaluations, and undertaken in self-defense, since through "naive deductions based on a common name" the odium of those "liberal" policies also fell upon the Warsaw liberals. However, Świętochowski said, the disturbing necessity of an alliance with reactionary forces did not weaken the value of progressive ideals: "This is only a condemnation of the stunted tribe of German liberalism which subjugated a great idea to selfish aims which could only be achieved by social and international oppression. Even if Bacon had been a thief, and Voltaire a sycophant, no one would reject the principles of induction and tolerance."[64]

The positivists did not reject civilization either, but its course was bringing them more and more disappointment. They gradually rid themselves of the youthful bravado and naiveté of their first manifestos. The claim made by some writers that positivism collapsed in the early 1880s is unfounded. On the contrary, it matured and gained in wisdom, having realized how divided all arguments are, how complex and unschematic the conflicts of the present, and how obscure the future. The literature and journalism of this second stage reflects a mature skepticism rather than ideological capitulation.

This skepticism concerned the health of social organisms and the diseases which beset them. Until the late 1870s this seemed a relatively simple matter: one could recognize the doctor by the diagnosis he offered. As we have discussed, for conservatives the source of health was adherence to the old faith, customs and native soil. "The illnesses of the age" were the illnesses of civilization, of modern life, of the big city. The process of modernization, by taking people away from their land, their village and their parish, broke down their resistance to both the theory and practice of materialism. Deprived of the protection of religion and tradition, civilization carried within itself the seeds of its own destruction: it provided nourishment for the most serious "illness of the age," namely, socialism, the spirit of nihilistic revolution.[65]

For the last few decades, the supporters of progress had been making a diagnosis which was the complete reverse of that offered by the conservatives. They maintained that what most needed to be cured were backward and ailing societies that lacked the will and vigor indispensable for a bold leap into the future. As one writer put it in the *Przegląd Tygodniowy*, "Rotten seeds will never bring forth healthy crops. When, however, we observe the societies of the West, where these principles, which are considered pernicious by many, have come into effect, we see them developing soundly and leading the march of civilization. We see that the path of reason, instead of pushing people back into barbarity, leads them to make new discoveries and improvements. We see that the strivings of our young people, those fanatical 'atheists and materialists,' are no less noble than their devotion to professed principles. When we see all of this, the conclusion we draw is that the breath of the spirit of the age is carrying humanity, and us to some extent, along the path of self-improvement and progress."[66]

This confidence did not last long. The social remedies of the liberals became more and more defensive. *Niwa* (before it swung to the right) conceded that technical progress does not automatically imply progress "in the sphere of thought, feelings and act." But it dismissed the objections of the moralists as being due to impatience. It saw "progress" as only a very general pointer, a summons to action, not "a magical spell which will work miracles." The future was not certain, but had to be conquered: "History only provides us with some pointers, it does not make of them irrevocable laws." The norm for progress was not, it argued, "a feverish state," but a lengthy "struggle of convictions and principles," the only struggle which the *avant-garde* of the intelligentsia unconditionally sanctioned and for which it demanded "absolute freedom" (this under the regime of Berg and Apukhtin!).[67]

Thus far, the liberals did not lose their faith in a better future. They knew that modern civilization also had its ailments; it was affected by severe economic and moral crises, it bred a proletariat, crime, wars, the cult of brute force, but this civilization, and this only, thanks to the ceaseless transmutation of matter, freedom of thought, and social inventiveness, was capable of curing itself. "It is necessary to open more windows to Europe and let its currents air our stuffy dwelling. It is not true that it is healthy inside, and that outside the plague is raging."[68]

However, this confidence weakened. The closer it came to the end of the century, the more difficult it became to distinguish conservative, democratic-liberal and socialist diagnoses of the illnesses of civilization, although the remedies were still radically different. The notion of civilization began to merge with the notion of capitalism, although initially it had been something very different, much more comprehensive and carrying with it entirely different connotations. It was not so much that civilization had shrunk, as that capitalism was expanding and implanting its own rules of play in all spheres of political and cultural activity. The main centers of this plague were the great metropolises of Europe: London, Paris, Berlin. It looked as though the whole world was simply a prey for the great predators. The age-old theme of a civilization which annihilated Indians returned once again, only this time, as well as the Red Indians, reports of whom were still circulating following the recent fighting in Dakota, Africans and Asians were affected. From this time onwards, much of the space in Świętochowski's *Prawda* was taken up with diatribes against imperialism, colonialism, and the arms race. For him, the mission of civilization and European "cultural expansion" had become a hypocritical screen for cynical pillaging and violence. "Unfortunately, present-day civilization either does not know or does not wish to use any other methods of proselytization, so while shuddering at its cruel methods, we must accept that this is necessary. The torch of progress must scorch before it illuminates."[69]

Understandably, one could not relinquish all remnants of belief in the moral law of progress, even if it was seen, for the time being, as "a progress of annihilation." Towards the end of the 1880s, there appears for the first time in Świętochowski's writings the millenarian thought which formerly had been alien to him and the whole intellectual structure of liberalism. This was the conjecture that the path to the millennium of peace and justice might lead not through a gradual accumulation of values, but through the bloody convulsions of nations. If this were true, then compassion for the living and the dying was at odds with the prospects for those who were yet to be born, just as the apostles of social revolution assumed. "Indeed, if culture cannot progress otherwise, by using other methods which are more honest and noble, then it were better that it finished its work: let it destroy what has to be destroyed as quickly as possible, and let it cease to deprave our feelings and principles by its bloody and abhorrent acts." Let it destroy. *Pereat mundus antiquus*. "When we consider today the three million people in a state of readiness for battle, and the millions spent annually on these forces, the dream of the apostles of eternal peace seems to be suspended like a rainbow somewhere in unattainable space. But, it has to be admitted, a beautiful rainbow. Contemporary society may laugh at these delusions, but it cannot take away from them their colors and brilliance. And although we may have to wait long, the peoples who today are burdened by wars will never cease to believe that an epoch will dawn when the time of turmoil and bloody ordeals will finally end. Civilization, whose coat until then will be red, will don a white cloak and only then can it truly be called human."[70] Positivist negation finishes with this utopia.

But how did this relate to what was happening, or not happening, in provincial towns like Mława or Kielce? Superficially, barely at all. The inhabitants of Mława or Kielce were not usually aware of what was going on in the outside world, and their concerns were of a more parochial nature. But even on this level there was the same nagging uncertainty as to whether the various values which made up one complex ideal were really mutually supportive. For it was initially taken for granted that knowledge, social prosperity, egalitarianism, freedom of economic enterprise, care for the weak and the dispossessed, freedom of expression, self-government of communes and associations, upbringing in the spirit of tolerance, the assimilation of the Jews, the emancipation of women, the defense of national culture, the improvement of health care, the decline of delinquency, and altruistic ethics of human solidarity—that all these aims were interdependent and could not clash. No wonder that when Prus, who was skeptical of every doctrine but had a childlike belief in statistics, dared to question whether the development of education was definitely accompanied by a fall in crime and an increase in morality, Świętochowski and the others denounced him as a virtual obscurantist who wanted to retard the progress of the people.[71] And yet, considering this catalogue of aims, it was inevitable that there should be conflicts, arising either from the very nature of these values, or from historical circumstances.

All decent European liberals and democrats felt obliged to demand compulsory elementary education for all. But how was that possible in Poland where schools were instruments for ruthless policies of Russification or Germanization? They felt obliged to inculcate society with respect for the law. But how difficult that was in a state in which the law was a screen for political lawlessness! A logical consequence of the Polish variety of protective liberalism was demanding state intervention in the working conditions in factories and mines. But this assumed a certain degree of trust in the state bureaucracy, which took every pain to stifle human rights and the right of the nation to develop freely.

A well-known way of settling conflicts of values is to take one of them as primary and absolute, and to subordinate all other values to this. Such a primary role could be claimed by the ideal of freedom of the individual, the national cause, the abolition of private property, economic growth, or God and faith. On closer inspection, neither "progress" nor "civilization" were suitable for that function, because an absolute cannot be a conglomerate.

The majority of the Polish intelligentsia were finally seduced by the simplicity of axiologically ordered ideologies. The moment they succumbed to this temptation, they parted ways with the program of organic work, a basic premise of which was a lack of absolutes and a policy of reconciling values which were seen as belonging together, although they sometimes clashed. The nation, by organizing itself into voluntary associations, would create a forum for negotiating such a reconciliation of values, since one could not rely on state institutions. Public opinion would be the arbiter of the disputes. The organ of this opinion was the scrupulously censored press.

The situation was difficult. The "progressive party," its leader claimed, had made every effort to energize society to act. This was true, although the means that it had for influencing society were far more modest than those which conservative opinion had at its disposal, and its influence was much narrower in scope. Observers from both camps were agreed on this. But it was also true that the "struggle for existence," the pursuit of profit, in short, middle class economic competition, released much more energy. Critics of the program of organic work were quick to point out that its whole policy boiled down to this. Thus, before Świętochowski assessed the inroads made by civilization on a global scale, he had to do the same for the Polish Kingdom.

The progress of recent years, he wrote in 1885, "has improved our social relations in many areas . . . it has led to an increase in production and more widespread education, but has diminished the general level of happiness and turned people's aspirations predominantly in the direction of practical endeavors. . . . It must be admitted that such a turn has its positive sides, insofar as for a long time we had been guilty of economic negligence and insofar as every kind of prosperity is invigorating. Despite all the deviations that the social organism has undergone, despite the abuses, misdemeanors, wrongs and violations, which are so densely interwoven into the fabric of economic progress in our day, we would not wish for it to stop, we would not wish to return to the old days of traditional ossification." But, he continued, one could not close one's eyes to the fact that the fierce scramble for roubles had caused a general fall in ethical standards and a loss of interest in science and art. No program could be blamed for that. Life itself tended to push human activity in a certain direction more firmly than mere words. However, the press (again the press, the highest and only national institution!) had the duty of urging people to make sure that economic growth was balanced by moral and intellectual development, so that we "do not become a society of well-to-do egoists and morons. We need material resources, but let us not consume all our energy in attaining them, let us not sacrifice all other aims to this goal."[72]

His assessment for the Kingdom was then similar to the assessment for European civilization in general. But soon it became necessary to add a commentary to the former: the economic crisis and the new tariff policy of the tsarist administration, which was meant to hinder industry in the Kingdom, made people doubt the durability of even the one tangible success which the Western model had achieved in Poland. Świętochowski, who was still the editor of the legal journal *Prawda*, but also one of the founders of the secret

Literary Society, wrote a pamphlet which was published anonymously in Lwów and was intended to be smuggled into the Russian partition zone. In it, he admitted that legal activity had failed: "oppression grew in accordance as our resistance diminished." Admittedly, organic work had led to economic progress, but recently even this had been hampered. The tsarist tax machine "draws its income from the poor." He described the Germans as a privileged group in industry; they were allowed to form local government organizations and societies. Polish economic impotence was mainly "due to our inability to communicate and work together, because of the lack of freedom of association, which is such a powerful instrument in civilized nations." Unemployment among the intelligentsia, the persecution of religion and the Polish language, the breaking of the character of young people in school, the Russification of the courts, the impossibility of providing education for the people, who "feel abhorrence for the Russian school and do not have the Polish one," and above all the "spiritual guillotine" of censorship—this was the Polish Kingdom in 1889. Although fifteen to twenty years earlier legal rights in Poland were only "a pale shadow of civilized conditions of life," people had decided to place themselves under the protection of those rights, in order to do everything possible within the limits of legal activity. "Alas, we soon cured ourselves of the illusion that Russia was a state based on the rule of law, and that one could live and act there in accordance with the law."[73]

Thus ended yet another chapter in the history of Polish "sober enthusiasts" who were accused of wanting to negate and destroy everything, and of being afraid of negating or destroying anything at all. They were accused of wanting too little and of not being able to achieve even the little they wanted. In addition, they were accused of cosmopolitanism and of "stifling the spirit."

Notes to Chapter 5

1. *Gazeta Polska* (until 1861 *Gazeta Codzienna*), a Warsaw daily bought in 1859 by the banker Leopold Kronenberg, propagated Western scientific and liberal ideas, and tried to stimulate economic progress in agriculture and industry.

2. See note 66 to chapter 4.

3. *Uchreditelnyi Komitet* (1864–1871), a committee of Russian officials sent to Warsaw by Alexander II in order to implement the enfranchisement of the peasants, introduce the principle of "self-rule" in the village communes, and remove all traces of a separate administration and finance in the Kingdom.

4. "*L'ordre régne à Varsovie*" was a memorable announcement made by minister Sebastiani in the French *Chambre des Députés* in October 1831, when he learnt that the Russian army had crushed the Polish rising.

5. A. Świętochowski, *Wspomnienia*, ed. S. Sandler (Wrocław, 1966), p. 101.

6. The Polish underground "National Government" on the first day of the Rising, 22 January 1863, issued a decree to the effect that all peasant services and rents should cease at once and the tenants should be granted property rights to their lots. The authorities of the Rising proved unable to implement this decree, and the reform was finally carried out by the tsarist government in 1864.

7. The patriotic manifestations in the Kingdom in 1861 were a solidarity movement of the townspeople, the intelligentsia and some groups of the gentry.

8. B. Cywiński, *Rodowody niepokornych* (Warsaw, 1971), p. 298.

9. The Constitution of the Duchy of Warsaw in 1807 formally marked the end of the division of society into estates. Later the tsarist administration tried to verify the diplomas of Polish nobility, but offered only symbolic privileges to those who passed the bureaucratic test. However, the gentry's sense of hereditary belonging to the noble estate continued much longer than their legal status.

10. Stanisław Moniuszko (1819–1872), the most popular Polish composer in the second half of the century, known mainly for his operas which are still often performed by Polish theaters.

11. There was more freedom of the press in the German Reich after 1870, and even more in autonomous Galicia, than under Russian rule.

12. See note 54 to chapter 1.

13. Piotr Chmielowski (1848–1904), a historian of Polish literature, literary critic and editor, one of the leading representatives of Warsaw positivism. Włodzimierz Spasowicz (1829–1906), a lawyer, political writer, critic and historian of literature, an advocate of Polish–Russian conciliation, lived in St. Petersburg and contributed to both Russian and Polish culture. See also notes 16 and 22 to chapter 4.

14. E. Warzenica, *Pozytywistyczny 'obóz młodych' wobec tradycji wielkiej polskiej poezji romantycznej (1866–1881)* (Warsaw, 1968), p. 135.

15. *Przegląd Tygodniowy*, 1876, p. 321.

16. *Stańczycy*, a group of conservative intellectuals in Kraków who became known in 1869 after the publication of a series of satirical pamphlets signed with the name *Stańczyk*, a legendary sagacious royal court jester in the sixteenth century. The "Stańczyks" derided patriotic bombast, condemned conspiracies, and advocated faithful loyalty of Poles in Galicia to the Austrian Emperor.

17. See note 69 to chapter 1.

18. [Świętochowski], "Stan ogólny Królestwa Polskiego," in an anonymously published brochure *Z domu niewoli*, 1 (Lwów, 1889), p. 33.

19. Zygmunt Krasiński (1812–1859), a romantic poet and playwright, representing conservative social views. See also note 70 to chapter 3.

20. Teodor Tomasz Jeż (the pen name of Zygmunt Miłkowski, 1824–1915), author of many historical novels, an emissary of the Polish Democratic Society in exile (active in particular in the Balkan countries), one of the spiritual leaders of the Polish *irredenta*. On Kraszewski, see note 93 to chapter 3.

21. Michał Bobrzyński (1849–1935), an outstanding historian, professor of the Jagiellonian University, dominant in the Kraków historical school, very critical of the Polish republican tradition; also a conservative pro-Austrian politician, governor of Galicia in 1908–1913.

22. Świętochowski, "Opinia publiczna," *Przegląd Tygodniowy*, 1872, p. 2.

23. K. Marx, *The Eighteenth Brumaire of Louis Bonaparte* (Moscow, 1967), p. 10.

24. Świętochowski, "Tradycja i historia wobec postępu," *Przegląd Tygodniowy*, 1872, p. 147.

25. Ibid.

26. Julian Ochorowicz (1850–1917), a positivist philosopher and psychologist.

27. Ochorowicz, "Tradycya," *Opiekun Domowy*, 1872, p. 138.

28. *Przegląd Katolicki*, 1864, pp. 599, 633.

29. *Przegląd Katolicki*, 1868, pp. 625, 673; 1876, pp. 407, 437.

30. *Czas*, 1872, no. 14.

31. *Czas*, 1872, no. 80.

32. *Czas*, 1872, no. 160.

33. *Czas*, 1872, nos. 84, 113.

34. See note 71 to chapter 3.

35. *Czas*, 1872, nos. 107, 207.

36. M. Godlewski, "Nieobecni," *Niwa*, XVII, 1880, pp. 79–91.

37. The novels tell the story of an old aristocratic family, brought to ruin by a crafty, ruthless parvenu; in spite of that, the son of the family does not lose heart and, abandoning the old prejudices of his caste, starts working with his own hands and cultivating a vegetable garden.

38. *Głos szlachcica polskiego (J. I. Kraszewski a zakon szlachecki)*, (Lwów, 1880), passim.

39. [Świętochowski], "'Precz z marzeniami'," *Prawda*, 1881, no. 25.

40. *Poseł Prawdy* (The Envoy of Truth) was how Świętochowski signed his column in the weekly *Prawda* (The Truth) that he founded in 1880 and directed for the next twenty years.

41. *Przegląd Tygodniowy*, 1872, pp. 178, 217; 1880, p. 605; *Niwa*, III, 1873, p. 97. Cf. A. Świętochowski, *Liberum veto*, vol. 2 (Warsaw, 1976), p. 263.

42. [Świętochowski], "Dlaczego?," *Przegląd Tygodniowy*, 1872, p. 169; also his "Partykularyzm," ibid., 1876, p. 364.

43. See notes 20 and 26 to chapter 4.

44. Świętochowski, "Wskazania polityczne," in *Ognisko: Książka zbiorowa wydana dla uczczenia 25-letniej pracy T. T. Jeża* (Warsaw, 1882), p. 50.

45. M. Bobrzyński, *Dzieje Polski w zarysie*, ed. M. H. Serejski and A. F. Grabski (Warsaw, 1974), pp. 403–4.

46. [Świętochowski], "Nasz grunt," *Prawda*, 1882, p. 25.

47. [Świętochowski], "Polityka przedmurza," *Prawda*, 1881, p. 38.

48. [Świętochowski], "Walka o byt," *Prawda*, 1883, p. 13; also his *Liberum veto*, vol. 1, pp. 440–41.

49. [Świętochowski], "Pangermanizm i pansłowianizm," *Przegląd Tygodniowy*, 1876, pp. 361–3; also his *Wspomnienia*, p. 61.

50. [Świętochowski], "Walka o byt," p. 86.

51. [Świętochowski], "Myślę—więc jestem," *Prawda*, 1881, p. 3.

52. T. Jeske-Choiński, *Typy i ideały pozytywnej beletrystyki polskiej* (Warsaw, 1888), pp. 213–14.

53. L. Sowiński, "Dział pieśni," as quoted by E. Orzeszkowa, "Listy o literaturze," *Niwa*, IV, 1873.

54. Ibid., p. 233.

55. See L. Marx, *The Machine in the Garden* (New York, 1964).

56. Orzeszkowa, "Listy o literaturze," *Niwa*, IV, 1873, p. 157.

57. Ibid., p. 233.

58. Ibid., pp. 260, 283.

59. Orzeszkowa, *Patriotyzm i kosmopolityzm* (Wilno, 1880), pp. 183–5.

60. The *Towarzystwo Naukowej Pomocy* (Society for Educational Assistance) was founded in 1841 by Dr. Karol Marcinkowski with the aim of helping gifted but indigent young people to complete their secondary school or university studies. The *Liga Polska* was founded in 1848 by the Polish liberal gentry and intelligentsia to defend Polish cultural and economic interests in the provinces of Poznań and Pomerania; it was dissolved by the Prussian government in 1850.

61. Świętochowski, *Liberum veto*, vol. 1, p. 664.

62. Quoted after M. Brykalska, *Aleksander Świętochowski redaktor "Prawdy"* (Wrocław, 1974), p. 87.

63. A. Głowacki [B. Prus], *Szkic programu w warunkach obecnego rozwoju społeczeństwa* (Warsaw, 1883), p. 119.

64. [Świętochowski], "Liberalne bankructwa," *Prawda*, 1883, p. 94.

65. P. Popiel, *Choroba wieku* (Kraków, 1880).

66. *Przegląd Tygodniowy*, 1872, pp. 371–2.

67. *Niwa*, III, 1873, pp. 25–7. Gen. Fyodor Berg (1790–1874) commanded the Russian forces which crushed the rising of 1863; he then became Alexander II's *namestnik* (viceroy) in the Kingdom, an office which he held until his death. On Apukhtin see note 46 to chapter 4.

68. Świętochowski, "Wskazania polityczne," in *Ognisko*, p. 53.

69. Quoted after Brykalska, *Aleksander Świętochowski*, pp. 120–22.

70. Ibid.

71. B. Prus, "Oświata," *Nowiny*, nos. 301–2; Świętochowski, *Liberum veto*, vol. 1, pp. 321–2; also his "Stosunek wiedzy do moralności," *Prawda*, 1882, nos. 47–48.

72. [Świętochowski], "Obecna doba," *Prawda*, 1885, p. 2.

73. [Świętochowski], *Z domu niewoli*, 1, pp. 11, 16, 37.

CHAPTER 6

Growth and Distribution

The liberal program of organic work and Polish socialism had a common point of departure: a direct knowledge of the extent of the poverty existing among peasants, farm laborers and workers. The sight of this poverty and the refusal to accept it produced a reflex of compassion for the starving and the degraded, which gave birth to the same moral imperative in the case of Prus and Waryński.[1] At this point, however, their paths parted.

The supporters of organic work saw the same, age-old Polish destitution. At one time, it had been confined to the cottages of peasants, who, it is true, had had to work for the squire, but who, as compensation, could count on his assistance in early spring or when their last cow had died. Now the destitute could count on no one but themselves; they roamed the country and the world in search of bread, and crept into the towns to display their tattered rags to the literati. Enfranchisement did not put an end to hunger, because not much farmland was acquired as a result,[2] and even less grain or roubles. The land did not produce more because farming methods had not changed. What had once been taken by the squire now fell into the government's hands; the priest took his share as before, and the moneylender charged more. As Malthus had predicted, the number of mouths which needed to be fed grew more quickly than did the yields of potato harvests; children had to be given a piece of land or compensation in cash, farms diminished in size. Many a villager had to seek employment elsewhere and be glad of any job that came up. What had all this to do with capitalism?

Capitalism gave some kind of chance to the destitute; this chance was meager, often illusory and always involved long wanderings and loneliness, but still it was better than the hopelessness awaiting them at home. If it had not offered some chance, people would not have left their native villages to work in factories, on building sites or railways, or in Germany[3] and America, in an alien, inhospitable world. If they had stayed at home, the same pot of white borscht and cabbage would have had to feed an even larger number of mouths.

This, at least, is how things were seen by naive advocates of organic work, who, as Karl Marx's young disciples explained to them, knew nothing about theory since they continued to believe, following Supiński and Spencer, that society was an organism. The left-wing students were correct: Polish society of the 1880s hardly resembled a healthy organism. The point, however, is that the other things in which the organicists believed did not depend on whether they used the model of the "organism," as Prus did, or whether, like Świętochowski, they managed without it. They believed that even if society were to rid itself of all the Dietrichs and Scheiblers[4] whom they heartily disliked, no one would be any better off—while some would perhaps be worse off. It was not necessary to assume a conflict-free harmony of class interests in order to sustain this hypothesis. It was enough to admit that mass poverty could not be eliminated without economic growth, and that this growth was impossible without capital. These indeed were the convictions of all the intelligentsia who supported organic work.

As early as 1872, Adolf Suligowski admitted that the abolition of serfdom and corvée had failed to eliminate poverty. But the thesis that poverty was caused by industry was for him tantamount to painting an idyllic picture of the past and generally putting the cart before the horse. With the existing population growth, he claimed that there was no other solution apart from building up a technological infrastructure for labor, which was powerless without the support of capital. Suligowski regarded knowledge, without which any progress of rational economy was impossible, as a form of capital. Since large-scale production reduced the prices of goods, it also increased demand: in this way, "luxury" goods slowly became everyday items. Above all, every new form of capital expanded the possibilities of earning money, which meant that "capital growth is in the interest of the working classes." The author, warming to his topic, argued that all resources should be turned into capital and invested in equipment and in the improvement of factories and roads, so that more was produced than consumed. This was the only way of improving the situation, and therefore, he wrote, "the laments of the ideologues are useless."[5]

This line of argument remained basically unchanged for the next twenty years, although the liberals began to perceive more clearly the factors that hampered economic development. They also realized that in conditions of free competition excessively optimistic expectations of a rapid improvement in the lot of the working masses could only prove vain. Development did not ameliorate social antagonisms; on the contrary, it exacerbated them. These observations prompted the ideologues of economic progress to listen carefully to the arguments of the socialists and to give them much thought, but ultimately to reject their basic assumptions. For although the organicists did not deny the existence of capitalist exploitation of labor, and were even ready to recognize the theory of surplus value, they still insisted that mass poverty was not caused by exploitation and the capitalist "expropriation of small owners," but by the country's general destitution and backwardness: that is, the low productivity of land and labor, rural overpopulation, a slow rate of development, illiteracy, and lack of skills.

Władysław Wścieklica's article, which enraged the Polish revolutionary socialists more than any before, included the following passage: "Therefore, we do not need a social revolution today to improve the well-being of society as a whole and of the various shades and hues of the working class in particular, but we need a *development in industry*. But," he added, "talking about industrial development to our socialists is a complete waste of time, because they . . . regard industry as the curse of mankind." We shall assess the aptness and honesty of this last sentence further on in this chapter. At this stage we only wish to stress that Wścieklica's conclusion was based on two points of comparison: first, that in relation to the general destitution of the country the skilled factory workers "are doing fairly well," and "simple" laborers were not dying of starvation either; and second, that "as our industry has developed, the lives of both the former and the latter have improved, and they are quite pleased with their lot."[6] The socialists found this second thesis particularly abhorrent. Indeed, the statement that the Polish worker of 1882 was pleased with his lot seemed a very poor kind of joke. However, the question remained as to whether that worker's father, a simple farmhand, was pleased with his lot? Whatever the answer, logic demanded that the dismissal of Wścieklica's arguments was tantamount to recognizing migration from the countryside to industrial centers as completely irrational.

The rate of industrial growth in the Kingdom had soared after the Russian government started collecting import duties in gold in 1877. An investment boom began and, with the market protected by tariffs, there seemed to be a real chance that the Kingdom, unlike Galicia, would enter a phase of accelerated development. Industry, and with it socialism, suddenly became an object of public interest. But this was still a fledgling capitalism and an industry confined to certain enclaves. The liberals expected that the growth and maturing of capitalism would achieve wonders, and were enthusiastic about the most banal kind of enterprise, such as a new sugar company established by large-scale sugar-beet growers. They knew that such a company would appropriate for itself the "unpaid part" of the workers' labor, but they also realized that the paid part of this labor would occasionally pay for a pound of sugar, which the workers had not previously been able to afford. Świętochowski was aware that the nation's material forces were not distributed in the most desirable and just way, and he did not rule out the socialist solution completely. However, he believed that this solution belonged in the distant future, since "the need for this solution depends on differences in the economic development of societies. In this respect, our society has just left the stage of infancy; the capitalist system has not yet become here a dilapidated building which is in danger of collapsing and must be evacuated as soon as possible. We still have not finished building it, we still have not occupied all its rooms, and in any case, it is the only dwelling we have for the moment."[7]

This did not mean that capital should be allowed to do whatever it wanted in this building. The positivists were not slow to sever their links with the dogmas of economic liberalism. After all, they were not interested in increasing the profits of the capitalists, but in improving the lot of the working people, especially those who were living and suffering in the present, rather than those who had yet to be born. They were becoming more and more insistent about the need for regulations concerning conditions of work—in spite of their distrust of the state and its officials who would have to oversee the implementation of these regulations. In 1891, when the first factory laws had already been introduced in the Russian Empire, Świętochowski wrote: "Just as . . . the factory workers are now safeguarded against exploitation, in a similar way all hired labor will be protected. There is not the slightest glimmer of hope that capitalism will regain its former freedom, or rather license. It is still a beast which can trample on people, but time brings more and more curbs to its power. The legislature of all countries is heading in this direction, though sometimes its progress is very slow."[8]

There was only one thing to be said in favor of the beast—in spite of periodic crises, it was increasing the production capabilities of the country and the purchasing potential of its inhabitants, and by the same token it was increasing the "national wealth." Since the times of Adam Smith, this last term was traditionally understood not as the *enrichissez-vous* of the new rich, but rather as what economic science would later describe as the gross national product. Unless the national wealth were to increase many times over, the advocates of organic work believed, the Polish popular masses had no chance of emerging from the depths of poverty.

The young Polish socialist movement lost no time in denouncing this prognosis as bourgeois ideology. Ludwik Krzywicki, in the *Walka Klas,* did not mince his words, referring to it as the "idealization of social robbery."[9] This was not as illogical as it may seem: since economic growth could not take place without capital and since all capital was obtained from exploitation and led to even more severe exploitation, the strategy of economic growth had to be seen as both immoral and ineffective. And so the "bastardly liberalism"[10] of the positivists immediately became the main ideological target of the pioneers of socialism.

In 1878, a group of young Poles studying in St. Petersburg produced a document entitled *An Appeal on behalf of Polish Socialists . . . to J. I. Kraszewski on the occasion of the jubilee of his literary activity*. This document, which is not widely known and has little historic significance, makes no mention of the idea of the class-based workers' movement. We quote it because it brings out very clearly the opposition between two philosophies of poverty, and consequently, between two recommended paths to prosperity. The authors of the appeal tried to prove the futility of the theory "of the indirect influence of the national wealth:" "We Polish socialists, the successors of the democrats of the 1830s, can see clearly that the accumulation of wealth at the cost of surplus values not only does not eradicate pauperism, but actually causes it to become more durable and widespread . . . Therefore we reject organic work as an objective which strives only towards increasing the absolute mass of wealth . . . Our motto is the most equal division of wealth, power, rights and obligations possible . . . Such equality, which has the genuine makings of happiness and freedom, can only be consolidated through the uniformization of living conditions, which in turn will lead to capital and land being brought under the joint control of social forces."[11]

The question of whether one should be more concerned about the increase of social income or about a more equal and just distribution of this income may, and should, seem absurd to today's readers who know that both objectives should be given equal attention. The fact is, however, that in the last quarter of the nineteenth century this question more than any other divided the two progressive camps. The reason was that the socialists uncritically accepted the theory of the absolute pauperization of the working class, whether in Marx's or Lassalle's formulation—the latter being even more dogmatic than the former. That capitalism breeds and continuously exacerbates poverty became an axiom: anyone who did not recognize this axiom could not be a socialist, or at least a Polish socialist. The following is the opening sentence of the program of the "Proletariat" party (1882): "The cause of poverty and every form of oppression in today's societies is inequality and unfairness in the division of wealth among the different classes of those societies."[12] Ten years later, *The Outline Program* of the Polish Socialist Party voiced this view even more forcefully: "The reason for the destitution of the working masses lies not in insufficient productive forces, but in the fact that the workers are deprived of the ownership of the tools and means of production which have become the exclusive property of a handful of privileged individuals."[13] The same thesis could be found in almost every socialist article at the time.

Increasingly frequently, this thesis was justified by the "absolute, general law of capitalist accumulation" formulated in *Capital*, from which Marx drew the conclusion that "in proportion as capital accumulates, the lot of the laborer, be his payment high or low, must grow worse." And he concluded that "accumulation of wealth at one pole is, therefore, at the same time accumulation of misery, agony of toil, slavery, ignorance, brutality, mental degradation, at the opposite pole, i.e., on the side of the class that produces its own product in the form of capital."[14]

This thesis had far-ranging consequences for socialist thought, of which the author was probably not wholly aware, especially in those countries which were at a low level of industrial development. First, it raised doubts as to whether capitalism could continue to play a civilizing role in the future, a role with which Marx had repeatedly credited it. The second logical conclusion that could be drawn from it was that the living conditions of the working people would gradually deteriorate, or at least would not get any better, as investment and production increased and technology developed. And if this were true, then it was futile to attempt to achieve a permanent improvement in the situation of workers by encouraging them to form trade unions and organize strikes, or by introducing labor legislation. Such measures could produce only a temporary improvement, which would soon be nullified by the merciless capitalist tendency to push the workers' wages down to the level of subsistence. The economic struggle of the workers could be a valuable educational exercise which would give them lessons in solidarity and organization, provided one did not lose sight of the revolutionary objective; as an aim in itself, such a struggle was retrograde since it was conducive to the stratification of the working class, hampered technological progress and the concentration of ownership, and thus pushed the moment of the victory of the class struggle further into the future. "In brief," wrote a young Polish Marxist in 1883, "neither the trade unions nor work-stoppages can bring desirable effects in the economic field. They are necessary only as an educational measure, in the sense of future moral solidarity in the struggle of labor against capital."[15]

The various successes achieved in the struggle for the improvement of the workers' lot inclined the socialists (in practice if not in their ideological programs) to give priority to partial aims. On the other hand, the defeats seemed to reveal the subordinate role, or the entirely illusory nature, of those aims in relation to the revolutionary objective. In despotic states, which included the Russian partition zone where all workers' associations or alliances were illegal and where, when the need came, the factory owner could always count on the police and the Cossacks, defeats came easily and successes, even local successes, were very hard to achieve. In this way, the authoritarian state forced the socialists to take up the political fight and contributed to revolutionary extremism in the fight with capital. Strikes brought paltry gains, and hopes of forcing through labor legislation which would protect the workers proved even more illusory. In this situation, those who advocated the concentration of all forces on economic struggle, drawing hope from the successes of German Social Democracy or the British labor movement, easily became an object of ridicule for the revolutionary avant-garde who called them trade unionists without trade unions. Paradoxically, the thesis that poverty grows in proportion to the accumulation of wealth proved more convincing in backward countries which suffered from rural overpopulation, a low level of education among the workers and a lack of democratic mechanisms—in other words, those countries whose potential for capitalist development was still low. In the countries for which the thesis was originally formulated, it proved less popular.

The theory of the unavoidable pauperization of the working masses fed the impatience of the revolutionaries and strengthened their scientific certainty of ultimate victory. At the same time, however, it entangled in tragic para-doxes the socialist thought of the backward country that Poland was, in that it led people to believe that as the general situation deteriorated, the prospects for the revolution would improve and the moment of liberation would draw closer. Indeed, the experience of the West seemed to indicate that victories scored by the self-organized workers in the economic and parliamentary struggle increased the bargaining power of the movement, but diminished its interest in the ultimate objective. In fact, a sizable number of its ideological leaders eventually chose the path of reform. In the case of the "Vistula Land"[16] one could expect the reverse: many lost battles leading to ultimate victory in the war. In any case, there was a conflict between concern for the immediate improvement of the lot of the oppressed and the socialist concept of the ultimate interests of this class as a whole. By the same token, the moral rebellion against injustice, the impulse which had initially given rise to the revolutionary movement, had to transform itself from compassion for the living into solidarity with class as hypostasis. This class was conceived—just like the "people" of the romanticists—as an unbreakable union of the past, present and future generations, a union entrusted with a mission in the face of which individual fates became immaterial. This included also, or above all, the fates of the Promethean militants for the workers' cause who spared themselves least of all.

It has often been noted that, unlike the Russian revolutionaries, the socialists of the Western school, especially the Marxists, modestly concealed the
ethical motives for their activities, renouncing them in the name of science
and its objective laws.[17] Contemporary Polish socialism was the product of
both these influences, and its adherents assumed ambiguous attitudes in this
respect. Adolf Warski, a leader of the Polish Workers' Union,[18] admitted
under interrogation that his own ideological views had evolved "from a vague
sense of the miseries of the common people, of their degradation and
backwardness, to a more precise awareness of their poverty and needs." One
of his comrades stated that it was only when he had joined the workers in
their activity that he had come to understand better the aim of the struggle:
"Earlier, this was rather a moral impulse of an almost philanthropic nature."[19]

Years later, when Ludwik Krzywicki was describing the Polish intellectual
revolutionaries of his day, he credited them all with a tremendous moral and
emotional sensitivity: "The idea inspired some by its sense of justice, others
were attracted by its aesthetic side, and many saw in it the realization of their
dreams of heroic deeds. The explanation for their presence in the nascent
movement should be sought in their sensitive, emotional, romantic nature.
Their heads were aflame with a belief in the advent of a new social millennium."[20]

In the earliest public declarations of the new ideological movement, no
secret was made of the moral motivation which lay behind it. The criticism
of the capitalist system contained in the first program of the Polish socialists
was not meant as an analysis of its contradictions or its historical direction,
but was intended to reveal the evil it produced. This program was above all
an expression of rebellion against the ethics of competition and against the
dehumanizing effects of the institution of hired labor, which reduced the
worker "to the level of a commodity" and deprived him of "all moral autonomy." "When we also consider the conditions of life of our society, we
come to the conclusion that the triumph of the principles of socialism is an
indispensable prerequisite for the prosperous future of the Polish nation; and
that an active participation in the struggle against the established social system
is the duty of every Pole who is more concerned about the lot of the millions
of the Polish people than about the gentry-capitalist interests of a small part
of our nation." Thus, the socialist objective was formulated here as an
axiological decision and expressed in terms of duty: "In any society, all social,
economic and political instruments . . . should serve the common good of all.
. . . The means and tools of production should pass from the hands of individuals and become the common property of the working people. . . Every individual has the right to benefit from the results of such collective work." The

program ended with the acceptance of the principles proclaimed twelve years earlier by the International Workingmen's Association: Truth, Justice and Morality.[21]

Bolesław Limanowski, warding off the attacks of one of those critics who saw socialism as a symptom of social pathology, had no doubts that "sociology is a natural science which knows only natural laws." In spite of this scientistic declaration, he was anxious clearly to underline the ethical character of his ideas. Socialism, according to him, meant a striving towards social equality for all, without any exploitation or coercion. "It abhors all abuse of power . . . It cannot set itself as its ideal a state which grows in power at the expense of the autonomy of the commune and of civic freedoms. By the nature of things, modern socialism has to be democratic, or even republican. The ravings of those who claim that socialism will bring despotism are not even deserving of our attention. . . . The bond uniting future societies will be love."[22]

However, under the influence of Lassalle, Marx and Engels, this ethic was largely replaced by a completely different type of justification which saw human obligations as determined by social conditions and dialectical contradictions. In this scheme of things, the ideal of a new order was not the consequence of a free choice of values and of the conviction that they had been corrupted by the current social system, but the final product of the economic process, or, more precisely, of the historical and structural analysis of this process. Socialist scientism, however, could not, and probably did not intend to, eliminate moral evaluations completely. A good example of this is the first volume of *Capital*. "My stand-point," the author wrote in the preface, "from which the evolution of the economic formation of society is viewed as a process of natural history, can less than any other make the individual responsible for relations whose creature he socially remains, however much he may subjectively raise himself above them."[23] This methodological declaration contrasts with the moral pathos which pervades the whole book and the frequency with which sentences such as the following occur: "The expropriation of the immediate producers was accomplished with merciless Vandalism, and under the stimulus of passions the most infamous, the most sordid, the pettiest, the most meanly odious."[24] Such statements are most unusual in treatises on natural evolution.

Even the most "natural" interpretation of the economic process left that part of the intelligentsia which had become ideologically conscious with a choice between observing the inexorable course of this process with academic indifference, and actively accelerating its *pereat* and *fiat*. In countries like the Russian Empire, where such attempts at acceleration brought with them the gravest personal hazard, the allegedly scientific decision of the revolutionary was an act of moral heroism of the same caliber as the choice made years earlier by Walerian Łukasiński or Szymon Konarski,[25] whose only support had been their own faith. Nevertheless, the Polish socialists of the 1880s tried as hard as they could, though not always convincingly, to rise above the mass of despised Philistines—not by virtue of their ethical determination, but by virtue of their consciousness, cognition and understanding of the laws of history. The most disinterested of them liked to speak in terms of interests. True, these were not their private interests, but the interests of the class with which they associated themselves, a class which in turn was the mouthpiece of the interests of mankind. This way of speaking changed something, provided a different perspective: ideals can be chosen, but interests are given.

They believed in this, they wanted to believe. They were fond of quoting one particular sentence from Albert Schäffle's *Quintessence of Socialism*: "For there is no doubt whatsoever that this is above all an economic question, that it is above all *the issue of the stomach*."[26] They were also increasingly vocal in proclaiming their descent from the heights of moral philosophy to the hard ground of economics where causality and necessity ruled. An important role in this transformation was played by Engels' *Socialism, Utopian and Scientific* which was the most popular outline of the Marxist doctrine for many years. From this work the Polish socialists learnt that their own moral consciousness was not sovereign, and that their rebellion against injustice, poverty and degradation was merely "the reflex, in thought" of the changes in the modes of production and exchange which no longer fitted in with the existing social system. "From this it also follows that the means of getting rid of the incongruities that have been brought to light, must also be present, in a more or less developed condition, within the changed modes of production themselves."[27] Engels is consistent when he describes future events in the historical present, for in his work the way by which "the historical mission of the modern proletariat" is to be fulfilled is not a goal or a postulate, but the logically obvious continuation of contemporary history, resulting from inner contradictions and transformations of the system that has already been examined.

This scientific guarantee of the fulfillment of the socialist ideal gave its followers a feeling of certainty as regards their victory, even though it might be a posthumous victory. However, in exchange their own Promethean role was diminished. The lives of the Polish socialists in the Russian partition zone contrast particularly sharply with their scientific credo. For they obeyed the moral imperative of the revolutionary who challenges the injustice, oppression and spiritual torpor of society without calculating the forces and means involved. They were the romanticists of socialism who left their homes on a dark night to set out on a voyage of adventure with no guarantee of reaching their destination, but took with them for protection the mantle of scientific economics and its unshakable predictions.

True, all this took place in the climate of an epoch when everything, including morality and faith in the future, had to be scientific, and hence predictable and reducible to the naked struggle of forces and interests. "Those currents that will renounce the political loyalty of the supporters of organic work," Krzywicki wrote, "will sneer at the shallowness of their understanding of social relations, but from the legacy left by positivism they will derive their own free-thinking and their reliance on science as the only jury capable of judging what we should believe and what we should discard."[28]

This handful of people who, with grim determination and an idealism of the highest order, were trying to interrupt the self-propelling motion of the economic process, began to come to the conclusion that they were harnessed to precisely this mechanism. The revolutionary party was only meant to drive on progress consciously and to accelerate it, but it apparently chose neither the route nor the destination of this voyage. It only revealed them. "We do not stand above history, we only succumb to its laws," the leader of the party declared in the court room.[29] These laws, they believed, would ensure that sooner or later the train would reach the station called "revolution." The price to be paid might be higher or lower, but the train would arrive regardless of random historic events and political complications.

This revolution, however, was to be not so much an economic as an institutional upheaval. Since according to the socialists the source of destitution was not want but capital, they concentrated almost all of their attention on the issue of ownership: the private ownership of the means of production which enabled the owner to appropriate the product and value of someone else's work. From the outset, the socialists were interested more in the problem of the equal and fair distribution of the social product than in its growth. Now the question of ownership overshadowed the question of distribution, and the rate of exploitation had proved more important than the standard of living. The development of capitalism, they believed, meant first the expropriation of small producers, and then of small-scale capitalists. Finally, the social revolution would lead to the expropriation of the expropriators in favor of society.

However, socialist thought had the duty of showing how this change was to be engineered and what economic effects it was likely to bring—in other words, how the expropriation of the expropriators would contribute to the liquidation of poverty.

Despite Marx's conviction that only economic changes can be predicted with the precision characteristic of natural sciences, while the form of future public institutions, laws and morality are at best a matter of conjecture, in the utopian visions of the Polish socialists the issue of the organization of society provoked particularly strong emotions and fired the imaginations of the planners of the new system. There were on-going disputes between the "pro-state" and "anti-state" factions, with the latter group elaborating plans for a future federation of territorial communities and manufacturing associations. The writers of the emigré socialist press, which was mainly published in Geneva, painted the picture of a moral utopia, the result of their conviction that human egoism would disappear completely, together with capitalism and the market; from then on, the world would be free of war and usury, "the crime rate will drastically drop, perhaps to zero," the relationship between men and women would be based exclusively on love, and education "would not check the free development of thought," but on the contrary would aim at "the harmonious development of all the faculties of the body and mind, and at creating a whole man capable of using in a versatile way all the forces with which nature and life has gifted him."[30]

In the same journals, one could find much information about the future organization and ethics of work. It was claimed, for example, that both in industry and in farming this would be collective work, but done willingly and eagerly because "in free collective work the forces of each individual increase a hundredfold, since they are awakened by an awareness of social needs and a sense of one's own individual needs, they are enlivened by friendly competition and the presence of one's comrades, who do the same work and are equally concerned about the necessity of this work and the universal benefits it brings. These are no longer slaves driven by a whip to work for someone else, for their tyrants and oppressors. These are free laborers working for themselves and for all." Such work would be done under "the overall supervision of all; the working day will be regulated individually on the basis of medical recommendations; and each worker will be able to have a taste of both physical and mental tasks, the work of the muscles and the work of the nerves, in order to develop his personality fully."[31]

The economic designs of the Polish Marxists of the 1880s had, in principle, a similar ideological and wishful character; in principle, because some elements of economic calculation can be discerned in their programs. Although they could not have known Marx's *Critique of the Gotha Programme*, which was not published during the author's lifetime, the Polish social-revolutionaries were aware of the fact that even under socialism it would be impossible to divide and distribute all the profit obtained from production, that is, to pay the workers the full equivalent of their labor. Szymon Diksztajn explained that the surplus value would remain, only "it would not be spent on luxuries enjoyed by a handful of people, but would be used to improve the lot of all."[32] The journal *Równość (Equality)* argued that "society . . . has to keep a part of the collective product for itself, for its collective needs," in particular for expanding production and for public institutions such as schools, hospitals, etc.[33] The question remained whether with all those deductions from the gross income there would be more left to divide than under capitalism.

The socialists had no doubts whatsoever that the surplus would be much higher from the very outset. Did not Lassalle, who was still quite popular, assure them "of the incredible positive enrichment of the whole of society," which would begin the moment the large manufacturing associations transformed the division of the national product, and, through eliminating competition and waste, "multiplied output to an unheard of degree."[34] Engels, an advocate of the centralized economic system, indicated two sources of reserves which could be utilized immediately after the revolution: "The socialized appropriation of the means of production does away, not only with the present artificial restrictions upon production, but also with the positive waste and devastation of productive forces and products that are at the present time the inevitable concomitants of production, and that reach their height in the crises. Further, it sets free for the community at large a mass of means of production and of products, by doing away with the senseless extravagance of the ruling classes of today, and their political representatives."[35]

Belief in the abundance of both these sources can be discerned over and over again in Polish writings. As to the "senseless extravagance" of the propertied classes, the convictions held were not quite consistent and depended largely on the context. After all, the socialists knew from Marx and from their own observations that capitalism could not survive without reproduction, and so a larger part of the income had to be reinvested. This, however, did not stop the authors of pamphlets and prognoses from showing how the greed of the bourgeoisie had grown to gargantuan proportions. "These individuals," *Równość* wrote, ". . . often grab for their own benefit such quantities of goods as would suffice for thousands." In this particular case the author refers to "magnificent palaces, fine parks, gardens and works of art," all the accumulated treasure which future society was supposed to turn to the benefit of all.[36] It was believed that the equal distribution of this part of social income, which until then had been consumed by the propertied classes, would bring about an immediate rise in the standard of living of the masses.

The second source, that is, the elimination of the crises of overproduction, seemed even more promising. Even the supporters of capitalism regarded such crises as manifest proof of the irrationality of the system. Right from the beginning of socialist thought, from the times of the great utopians, there was a conviction that the system of the future had not only to be more moral, but would also have to utilize human labor and its products more rationally. The absurd waste of goods, which was criminal considering the existence of mass poverty, was caused by the chaos of the free market which, as *Równość* wrote, sent "false signals" to the producers. Only a planned economy would free society of that chaos. "As long as production is run for the speculation of one factory owner who squabbles with another factory owner," Krzywicki said in a lecture to workers in 1884, "crises will continue. If the means of production belong to a free people's state, the crises will disappear, because production will be regulated and not run by people for swindle, as is the case today."[37]

The socialists knew little about economic planning, except that its point of departure should be a scientific, statistical calculation of social needs and the adaptation of the scale and assortment of production to these needs. Hence, the needs were viewed as calculable factors, and it was some time before the realization dawned that the establishment of the level and assortment of basic needs involved a considerable degree of arbitrariness. For the time being, the task was seen as purely statistical. There was also some confusion as to the territorial scope of this planned adjustment of needs and the means of satisfying them: should it be coterminous with a commune, a state, or perhaps the whole of mankind. As we know, the anarchist current of socialism was afraid that any kind of political unification would produce an arbitrary, oppressive bureaucracy; on the other hand, it was not unreasonable to ask how a noncentralized federation of free communes or manufacturing associations could possibly eliminate the market and competition.

In any case, the predicted replacement of the market by planned, controlled distribution of products (whether this was based on the individual contribution of labor or on "essential needs") disposed of the problem of the purchasing power of the working classes in its traditional form, that is, of effective demand. However, it did not dispose of the question of the quantity of goods to be distributed. The answer to this question rested in the conviction that the elimination of the anarchy of the market, and of crises as the gravest symptoms of this anarchy, would make possible the immediate full utilization of the manufacturing potential inherited from capitalism, and would, moreover, set in motion enormous reserves of growth. This conviction was a logical consequence of the thesis concerning the imminent exhaustion of the possibilities available for developing the capitalist economy. In the 1880s, this thesis had yet to acquire the form of the theory of automatic collapse, although it already contained the main elements of that theory. For since capitalism diminishes, or at best maintains in a state of stagnation, the purchasing powers of the working masses, industry is increasingly geared towards satisfying the extravagant needs of the propertied classes. The latter, however, cannot guarantee sufficient demand, as competition forces manufacturers to permanently increase their output. For a time, the proletarianization of small producers and the conquest of foreign markets form a market reserve. "However, foreign markets must become satiated at some stage," argued Adam Sąsiedzki. "Then production stops, economic crisis sets in, hundreds of capitalists go bankrupt, and thousands of workers perish."[38] In other words, periodic crises develop into a structural crisis: the economy chokes on its own products, and the property relations prevent any further development of the productive forces.

Thus, it was not only the ideals of equality, social justice and human dignity that made a social revolution absolutely indispensable; it was first of all the necessity of bringing about a normal functioning of the economy. "The expansive force of the means of production bursts the bonds that the capitalist mode of production had imposed upon them. Their deliverance from these bonds is the one precondition for an unbroken, constantly accelerated development of the productive forces, and therewith for a practically unlimited increase of production itself."[39] The worker, free of coercion and concerned about his own prosperity and the prosperity of society, would work more willingly and efficiently. The machine, when it was no longer a means of exploitation, would become man's ally, would free man from hard labor and multiply the productive forces to an incredible degree.

These prospects were painted graphically in the *Programme of the Galician workers' party* in 1881: "As soon as private capital has become the common property of all working people, social life will take on a different character and direction. The working man will have all the means necessary for a prosperous existence, and will not have to worry about tomorrow and about the lot of his family; moreover, he will become a genuinely free citizen of society, allowed to play a direct part in governing it and shaping its future, and all that makes life more pleasant, better and freer will be open to him. Under the pressure of common fraternal efforts, the poverty that oppresses us will disappear, and ignoble slavery will be replaced by the noble work of all people devoid of exploitation, by liberty, and by the movement and light of the great idea of progress in all dimensions."[40]

Obviously, the nineteenth-century economists knew that the income gained in a factory and in society in general had to be divided between consumption and reinvestment, and that as a result, for a given level of income or earnings, consumption and investment funds were mutually restrictive. However, this simple fact was completely overlooked by the socialist futurologists of the time who seemed to assume that economic growth and technological progress could take place without any expense. The Polish designers of the new economic system did not worry about such problems as poor land productivity which, given the high birthrate, meant that capital-consuming methods were required in agriculture. The commentary on the program of the "Proletariat" party dealt summarily with this matter by giving assurances that the new system "will introduce a rational ratio between the size of the population and alimentary resources, and in this way it will regulate the problem of population,"[41] though the actual methods of this regulation were not mentioned. Nevertheless, this is one of the very few references in contemporary Polish socialist literature to the fact that in the state of the future, needs might have to be adapted to means, and not the other way round.

The socialists were aware of the dynamics of human needs and desires, both material and cultural, which kept growing as people gained a better knowledge of the world outside their parish and of its temptations, and as they began to aspire to a better life. Not only that, they wholeheartedly approved of such aspirations. In their writings, there is not the slightest hint that the victorious revolution could possibly expect the workers to continue in their proletarian poverty and puritanical abstemiousness for any length of time. There is no trace either of any fear that a sudden explosion of hopes for a growth of consumption would not be fulfilled. The belief in the fabulous economic reserves which the revolutionary upheaval was to unleash was so great that the socialists could forecast the harmonic and unrestricted growth of both accumulation and prosperity, without even worrying about the level at which this second phase of development would begin.

However, it is not our aim simply to expose the well-known naivety of this early prognosis, which was, inevitably, immature. Long-term prognoses always appear naive in retrospect. In the second half of the nineteenth century we can observe the characteristic parting of the sociological imagination and the technological imagination which were still united in the visions of Condorcet and Saint-Simon. Later on, prognostications about the future became more specialized: the reformers of the system transformed man's social nature and institutions but left him in the technological landscape of the nineteenth century, while the visionaries of science and technology transported the gentlemen of the Victorian epoch to the fantastic landscapes of the future. Edward Bellamy and Jules Verne, the authors of the most popular utopian visions in the literature of the late nineteenth century, provide a good illustration of these two types of imagination which would come together again in the work of Wells. As it would transpire later, the naiveté of Verne's science fiction lay in the fact that his predictions soon began to lag behind reality; with Bellamy it was the other way round: reality never came any closer to his utopia, and never had any urge to do so.

However, there is another point of more importance to our present argument. A critical reconstruction of socialist model designed by the first generation of Polish Marxists reveals that this model was something it was not supposed to be; it is revealed as a yearning for a more humane world, a projection of the humanistic ideal into the future, an axiological construct whose scientific-economic frame enabled its adherents to rationalize their dreams, but did not provide a genuine foundation for their reasoning. This rationalization, however, forced the Polish socialists not so much to defend the values they cherished, as to defend general laws and "objective" statements which allegedly justified these values, or at least indicated the only road which would lead to their historical fulfillment. For this reason, positivist criticism, which questioned not the values but the very statements, was more troublesome for them than the criticism of the conservatives who regarded socialism as "Asian leprosy," "the propagation of decay," "debauchery of the spirit," or "the Jewish teachings of a sect of Freemasons."[42]

The defense of Marx's economic prognosis put his Polish and Russian disciples in a rather awkward position in view of the considerably lower level of development obtaining in Russia. For Western Marxists, the belief that the expropriation of the expropriators was a sufficient condition for entering the kingdom of freedom and prosperity was based on the conviction that the primary and most unpleasant part of the task of economic growth had already been accomplished, or would soon be accomplished, by capitalism. At the moment of its birth, socialist society was to inherit not only the poverty of the masses, but also an enormous accumulation of wealth: a modern industry and means of transport, a highly productive agriculture, a banking system, universities and laboratories, engineers and a qualified labor force. In view of the above-mentioned deficit of the scientific and technological imagination, it was not unreasonable to assume that the process of modernization, also known as the industrial revolution, was approaching its natural ceiling in the most developed countries, and that the socialist future would only have to ensure the extensive growth of the productive potential of society. This growth, starting from what was regarded as a highly developed economic and cultural infrastructure, would be accompanied by the simultaneous growth of the divided income, that is, of the standard of living of the masses. This is probably why the classics of Marxism paid so little attention to the question of the sources of accumulation in socialist society. In any case, there is no doubt that, as they understood it, the "capitalist revolution" was supposed to complete its task before the bourgeoisie could be considered a "redundant class." "The abolition of classes in society," Engels wrote, "presupposes a degree of historical evolution, at which . . . the existence of class distinction itself has become an obsolete anachronism. It presupposes, therefore, the development of production carried out to a degree at which appropriation of the means of production and of the products, and, with this, of political domination, of the monopoly of culture, and of intellectual leadership by a particular class of society, has become not only superfluous, but economically, politically, intellectually a hindrance to development. This point is now reached."[43]

However, it was not stated clearly enough in which countries, exactly, this point had been reached. For the frequently encountered conviction that Marxist doctrine came face to face with the problem of backwardness only in Eastern Europe cannot be defended. Marxism had lived with the problem of backwardness, or, better, retardation, from the moment it had been born. As its founders emphasized, it was a German intellectual product, but based first and foremost on the observation of English history. Thus, its theory of economic development had a comparative aspect from the very outset. The following much-quoted words from the preface to the first edition of *Capital* compare Germany with England: "the country that is more developed industrially only shows, to the less developed, the image of its own future," and "we, like all the rest of Continental Western Europe, suffer not only from the development of capitalist production, but also from the incompleteness of that development."[44] The limits of this "Continental Western Europe" were not clearly marked; the author definitely included Silesia which was part of the German Reich, but we cannot be sure what he thought of Spain, Italy, Austria or Bohemia. In any case, the expansion of the capitalist continent to include those countries where factory industry had established its outposts did not seem to pose much of a problem for the theory of development in stages, just as it was not a problem for liberal evolutionism. It was quite simple: as Germany's structure gradually approached the model envisaged for developed capitalist countries, new territories afflicted by development and underdevelopment began the same journey. Only Russia presented complications, for two particular reasons. First, a socialist revolutionary party had become established there with practically no links with the nascent industrial working class. Therefore it had to comprehend and explain the different situation, social basis and prospects of the Russian movement. Second, both the Russian and Western theoreticians of the movement were intrigued by the consequences of the preservation, in some areas of Russia, of the ancient form of communal possession of land. These were the main reasons that prompted the Marxists to join issue with the Narodniks on the possibility of peasant Russia entering the epoch of socialized ownership without going through the "phase" of capitalist development.

None of these considerations applied to the Polish Kingdom. By 1880 no one had any doubts that industrial capitalism existed and was developing in the Kingdom, just as in Silesia, and that it was taking root in the remaining Polish provinces. Thus, despite the influence of the Narodniks on Polish revolutionary thought in its earliest period, the focus of Polish disputes on capitalism was basically different. The problem was not whether capitalism could be avoided, but whether Polish capitalism was and would be the same as in the West.

Right from the outset, the Polish socialists took a principled stand in defense of the thesis that there was only one way in which the capitalist economy could function and that the transformations it underwent were governed by universal laws. They only allowed for a time difference, that is, asynchronism in the phases of development, and for secondary differences resulting from different political orders. The program proclamation of the "Proletariat" party claimed that "Against the background of the general development of European societies, our country makes no exception. . . . Our society has within it today all the features of the bourgeois-capitalist system, although the lack of political freedom gives it an impoverished, sickly appearance. This, however, does not alter the gist of the matter."[45] From then on, this thesis would appear in almost all the major texts produced by Polish socialists in the 1880s, since it had a fundamental significance for them. It was expressed even more forcefully by Stanisław Mendelson in the draft program of the Polish Socialist Party (PPS) in 1892: "The upheaval brought about in our country by the events of 1863–64 drew us into the mainstream of international European life. Our country, one of the younger members of this family, is affected by the same diseases as other nations, suffers the same sufferings, witnesses the same social anarchy, and nurtures the same hopes for a better future."[46]

At first glance, it seems surprising that the founders of the PPS should believe that only the January Uprising and the enfranchisement of the peasants had brought Poland into the mainstream of European life—as if it had previously been cut off from this mainstream. But Mendelson was not writing of the Polish national cause or Polish intellectual life; he meant the socioeconomic system, and he also believed that while there had been local differences in feudalism, capitalism was the same the world over. Capitalism could differ only as regarded its age and its degree of maturity, and perhaps also the state of its health, but not as regarded its nature. On this point, there were no differences between the "international" socialists and those who were more nationally oriented. Mendelson had expressed similar sentiments eight years earlier, when he had still been a determined anti-patriot: "The granting of the right of ownership to the peasant, the breaking of the power of the large landowners and the estate whose domination had been based on the possession of land, and finally capitalism, all of these brought Poland closer to Europe. We have become a country like other countries. Admittedly, there are more remnants of the former ascendancy of the gentry, the representation of the bourgeoisie is weaker than elsewhere, and so is the proletariat, but overall our [social] relations have become European. The two strata of owners and non-owners can already be clearly distinguished from each other. There is ground for class struggle, and it is a good thing for society that such a ground exists."[47]

Only the relics of the past, those relics which were doomed to disappear, made one nation different from another. For Mendelson, different problems and local interests belonged to an epoch which was drawing to an end. "The unification of scattered individuals or even tribes into one whole, into a nation, was an extremely important cultural factor. The entire development of mankind would have been impossible without such a bond." But capitalism had moved this process of integration onto a higher rung, creating supranational links and one uniform culture for the whole of mankind. Such was the unavoidable law of development. It left no choice; any attempt at checking the process of integration and refusing to move from the stage of national cultures would be a pathetic gesture because of its ahistorically utopian nature.[48]

While such determined statements were being made by socialist thinkers, the national question was coming to a head in various parts of Europe. The Congress of Berlin (1878) opened the epoch of the disintegration of empires and the multiplication of nations. The Bulgarians, Serbs, Montenegrins, Romanians, Ukrainians, Lithuanians, Jews and others, all began to claim their rights to a separate existence, justifying such rights by the unique nature of their cultures. The shattering of feudal structures liberated and intensified separatist aspirations rather than relegating them to the past, and with the emancipation of the masses local folklore was elevated to the national level. This phenomenon did not lend itself to the kind of rational explanation that was offered by the theory of the growing unification of the world.

Capital, it is true, did not have a national passport and wherever it was invested similar institutions sprang up; cotton mills, railways, commercial law, stock exchange, tenements, and the system of hired labor were similar, irrespective of the country or place. However, the socialist view of the world expanded the semantic field of the notion of "capitalism" endlessly, so that it eventually came to encompass all manifestations of modern civilization: technology, politics, art, law, customs and morals.[49] Hence, wherever new enclaves of the capitalist form of economic organization arose, the socialists were inclined to see all social relations there as capitalist—or else as rapidly drawing towards the capitalist stage and cultural monotony. In this respect, the revolutionary view was characteristically close to the conservative view, for the conservatives had long regarded modern civilization as a mechanical force which deprived the world of all its color. The difference was that what the conservatives saw as an apocalyptical menace, the socialists welcomed with hope, because they believed that the capitalist tendency to uniformity would assure the same happy outcome for all nations.

In this context, the positive civilizational role of capitalism ended the moment it destroyed the remnants of feudal and patriarchal relations and the natural small-scale economy. After that, the only thing left to it was self-destruction. "Capitalism is also only a historical stage in the life of societies and as such it is continuously undergoing a process of development which is also a process of its disintegration, faster or slower, depending on the historical conditions in which it occurs."[50] The faster it developed and reached maturity, the more ruthless it was in subordinating production, commerce and customs to itself, the more indivisible the power it exerted over Europe and the world became, the better, for this made its future gravediggers stronger and brought the moment of revolution closer.

Meanwhile, as described above, Polish capitalism was sickly; it appeared to be the same as in the West, but it lacked the robustness of its Western counterpart. The whole of society, with its leisurely pace of life, lacked such robustness. The Marxists stressed just as strongly as the positivists that, in cultural terms, Poland had become the backwater of Europe. The ideological declaration of the *Walka Klas* admitted in 1884: "Although some of us take pleasure in repeating that we are a western society, and although some of us cite trifling facts in order to claim a role in the development of European relations, when in fact the initiative came from western societies, on closely examining the history of our society and the conditions of our present life we have to admit that only faint traces of the currents of western life have reached us."[51] The point was made even more forcefully in another article in the same journal: "So far, we have been a torpid nation, and civilizational currents have

reached us repeatedly, but deformed and perverted. We have grown attached
to dead memories and thus we have become almost an obstacle to general
European progress. We were the last in Europe to enfranchise our peasants,
we are the last . . . to discard ultramontanian fanaticism . . . we are the last
country of all to learn what genuine knowledge gives the world. It is time to
wake from this torpor, it is time to come alive if we do not wish to vanish forever from the face of the earth as a people that does not deserve to live."[52]

Similar opinions could be found, much earlier, in the writings of the
positivists. Only the conclusions drawn were different. When Bolesław Prus,
in his *Outline of a Programme*, bitterly criticized the weakness of Polish
"national individuality," when he asked the dramatic question: "are we a
nation capable of creating anything for civilization or only capable of inac-
curately adopting other peoples' products?"[53] what he meant was that the
Polish nation had to acquire a modern culture, but a culture that would be
original and not a mere imitation. He imagined the formation of such a culture
as an organic synthesis of civilizational imports, especially in the technological field, and local, popular tradition and its aesthetics. This was yet another
naive attempt at solving the dilemma which had engaged Polish, and not only
Polish, thought for a hundred years: how to modernize the economy and
society without obliterating the marks of national individuality.

The radical students, with their knowledge of the laws of development,
could only smile indulgently at such ideas. "God help you in this battle with
the windmills!" cried the young Ludwik Krzywicki to Prus, while Stanisław
Krusiński, more principled than his colleague, mercilessly jeered at all
"exaggerated claims to native identity and originality." In his criticism of
Supiński's works, Krusiński wrote about the ideas of the author of *The Polish
School of Social Economy*: "He cannot understand that capitalism in its
victorious march is like a storm, and it will break here, like everywhere else,
all dams, tear all knots asunder, and stamp out all marks of nativeness and
separateness."[54] In the face of this storm, the left-wing intellectuals saw the
formation of "Polish schools" and Polish programs as a sentimental idyll.

It did not matter that the storm was late in coming since it had not lost any
of its initial power. "The belated development of capitalism in a given
country," Adam Sąsiedzki argued, "obviously cannot match its earlier maturity. Let us, however, remember that the levers of belated social development
are put in motion by the forces of capitalism in other countries where it has
developed earlier. The hammer of capitalism is knocking down the Chinese
wall and penetrating the Himalayas at an unbelievable speed."[55]

The socialists' faith in the transforming power of capitalism was as great
as that of the most simple-minded bourgeois admirers of this system. Even

Leopold Kronenberg,[56] who was only too aware of the risk involved in capital investment in a country which lacked an elementary economic infrastructure, did not have such faith. This faith blinded the socialists, and prevented them from perceiving the realities of economic backwardness and the structural barriers to economic growth. It also prevented them from understanding the complex tangle of international dependencies. After all, the industry and finance of more developed countries both facilitated and hampered the economic development of backward countries; they facilitated it by supplying capital, technology and skills, and they hampered it by flooding the market with cheaper and better products and often by draining local savings. Cheap labor, which in theory should be so attractive to capitalism, proved not so cheap after all, given its low productivity, and the remaining components of the costs of production were as a rule higher. These interdependencies were already well known and had been much written about. For instance, Józef Hłasko, a half-socialist half-nationalist author, wrote an article about the traps of backwardness. Taking Romania as an example, he demonstrated that the Europeanization of the intellectual elites did not have to result in the Europeanization of the peasantry who were submerged in a state of "Hottentot" primitivism. Moreover, such Europeanization could even hamper the process since a rapid growth in the cultural aspirations of the "leading classes," like the growth of military expenditure, was a burden that exceeded the resources of a poor country and drained potential sources of accumulation by increased taxation.[57]

The model of higher civilization was double-edged at best. Krzywicki, too, came to a similar conclusion in his polemical essay entitled "Democratic illusions," a text which reveals an oscillation between a deduction from the doctrinal assumptions of Marxism and an induction based on comparative observations. "The industrial development of one country," he wrote, "is . . . at the same time the source of stagnation in other countries which have entered the arena of the struggle for profit later." Such countries as Romania or Hungary constitute merely "one huge village for the big metropolis, that is, the foreign country which mercilessly exploits [this village]."[58] When this thesis, known as far back as the times of mercantilism, was transplanted onto the grounds of socialist thought, it forced a revision of views on the strictly imitative character of the processes of economic development, and shook faith in the power of the capitalist cyclone in the territory of the "huge village." However, there was no doubt whatsoever that the fences and barns of the small village could not withstand the force of the hurricane.

The Polish interpreters of scientific socialism were determined to show that Polish capitalism should follow the path of primitive accumulation as described in *Capital*, in its chapters on "the so-called primitive accumulation" with reference to England. They were unable to understand the dialectics of economic development in any other way than by separating the small producer from the ownership of land, tools and the products of his labor. But they failed to take account of the fact that in Eastern Europe this had been accomplished, though only partially, by agrarian feudalism, by serfdom, and that the nineteenth-century reforms had restored to the peasants the ownership of their farms. When studying the genesis of the Western model of capitalism in its "pure form," Marx did not have to take into account the history of the corvée economy; he became interested in it only later. But what about his Polish interpreters? They knew about this system, and they were ready to justify civilizational delay by three centuries of corvée. It was a delay, and nothing more. The primitive accumulation in agriculture was the axiom of their theory; the stratification of the village community and the concentration of property were assumed, and therefore enfranchisement could only be a factor in the process of expropriation, an accelerating factor.[59] We should note that this could only apply, to some extent, to the situation in the Prussian partition zone, that is, that part of Poland which for the time being interested the Polish socialists the least.

There was no agreement among them as to how to evaluate the current stage of the relentless process of expropriation. The issue was important to them for practical reasons: if the farming population of the Kingdom and Galicia was already almost completely proletarianized, then the countryside was a promising area for revolutionary agitation; but if the peasantry was still defending itself against proletarianization, then "it is our most dangerous enemy in its proper strivings."[60]

The leadership of the "Proletariat" party decided that the peasants had been already proletarianized in its appeal "To those who work the land" issued in 1883, in which it promised the land to the peasants after the revolution, "so that everyone would have somewhere to work and earn a living." The appeal was not explicit as to whether landownership was to be granted to individuals or to communes: that the second option was preferred can be deduced from the fact that the giving of the land to the peasants was compared to the giving of the factories to the workers.[61] Some emigré authors also advocated the winning over of the peasants for the socialist movement. For example, the author of the editorial in the *Walka Klas* of December 1885, commenting on the anti-gentry unrest among the Galician peasants, argued that the socialists could not afford to wait until capitalism had removed all remnants of feudalism: "Should we then go to the peasant and tell him: it is necessary that we help the bourgeoisie, which is still in the process of formation, to expropriate you completely; it is necessary for your organism to become wasted working in a factory; it is necessary for you to see the total and lawless domination of the factory owners; and only then shall we think of organizing the working masses, [inculcating in them] the socialist consciousness?" The answer to this question was no, according to the author. To do so would be to succumb to some kind of historical fatalism. Now was the time to agitate the peasants, and for this purpose it was necessary to "discover the issues which are vital to our villagers and which, when raised, are capable of uniting the scattered population into larger masses."[62]

Those who accepted the current views of the Western social-democrats thought it was still too early to be concerned about the peasantry. Thus, in his report to the First Congress of the Social Democratic Party of Galicia (Lwów 1892), Ignacy Daszyński[63] argued that the peasants would "gain consciousness only under the influence of the blows they would receive." Accordingly, the resolution adopted by the congress proclaimed that "the party has no intention of supporting small holdings and regards small-scale production as backward and harmful. In our agitation among the rural proletariat we should appeal to those peasant elements who are not so interested in maintaining small-scale production and whose economic situation allows them to feel solidarity with the modern socialist movement."[64]

This attitude entailed an unpleasant moral dilemma, of which its supporters were fully aware: the necessity to differentiate between progressive suffering and reactionary suffering. But, they replied, "all idealization is unforgivable here." They argued that whatever had to happen for the sake of progress should be allowed to happen. True, the peasant and the craftsman suffered, "but both of them suffer *in defense of antiquated forms* . . . both suffer just as the aristocracy suffered under the guillotine of the great revolution!"[65] This was plain talk indeed, and the peasants, if they had read the *Walka Klas*, could have felt slightly offended that after centuries of serfdom and corvée their struggle to keep their few acres had led to their being compared to their lords and being sentenced to the guillotine of the laws of history. But idealization was unforgivable and even the good-natured Krzywicki wrote the following: "So it is with satisfaction that we observe capitalism carrying away the masses of the rural proletariat. It is creating and organizing fighting crowds for us!" And he further explained that the task of this capitalism was to discipline and educate the country bumpkin.[66]

Irrespective of the different views among the socialists on the existing state of husbandry and the consciousness of the country bumpkin, it was obvious to them that sooner or later the bumpkin would lose his smallholding and that his consciousness would undergo a transformation as a result. Either his primitive farm would not be able to cope with competition from the large landed estates, or he would be destroyed by the merchants, usurers and tax collectors. The division of large estates, the socialists argued, could only be a harmful palliative, unable to reverse the course of the economic process, but bound to have a harmful effect on agriculture and to make it difficult to organize collectivized farming in the future.

All statistics which showed a growth in the number of undersized holdings in Galicia or the Russian zone, and every proof of poverty in the countryside, were seen as supporting the thesis concerning the progress of capitalist stratification, expropriation, and the concentration of land either in the hands of the wealthy nobility or the peasant middle class. "It seems to us," Krusiński wrote, "that very soon a large part of our peasantry will be expropriated and capitalism will gain strong foundations both in the fields and in the factories." "Small property is a thing of the moment," Sąsiedzki added in the same vein.[67] The Polish Marxists of the 1880s would have been immensely surprised if, by some gift of second sight, they had been able to learn that this moment would last a hundred years or more, and that large-scale industry, both private and state-owned, would enjoy a more or less peaceful coexistence with the individual production of peasant farms.

At least Krzywicki openly admitted "a complete lack of familiarity with our agrarian relations" and later on started investigating them in earnest. Others lacked such scruples. Kazimierz Dłuski, who claimed an expert knowledge of agrarian matters, declared authoritatively that Polish agriculture had completely lost its former native features and taken on the shape "that free labor and all-powerful capital had given the Western economy,"[68] although it was known even then that the laws of concentration did not operate in Western agriculture either.

In the course of pointing out the trend of economic transformation, the issue of ownership came once again to overshadow the issue of nutrition. The vital question was how to increase the production of flour, potatoes, milk and meat in a country whose masses suffered from endemic malnutrition and which had almost the lowest soil productivity in Europe—but this question was not considered worthy of investigation by an ideology which, after all, was supposed to be concerned with the "issue of the stomach." Dłuski knew that there was too little arable land and that the agricultural population was too high; the conclusion he drew from this was that even the forced expropriation of large landowners and the division of manorial land would not guarantee a secure existence for the peasants. Therefore, like the majority of the socialists, he was against all agrarian reform, and demanded that in the future all land should be nationalized and large collective farms organized, since only this form of rural management would prevent anarchy in production and increase the productivity of labor. For Bolesław Limanowski, there was only one hope for the starving Galician peasantry: "the organization of socialist agricultural communes and the handing over to them of all the land for cultivation," which, he believed, would be easy, since, unlike in the West, the Polish peasants had not as yet become accustomed to private property and therefore would willingly give up their small fields in the interests of the general welfare.[69]

One of the authors of the socialist journal *Przedświt (The Dawn),* edited in Geneva, had similar views. He advised socialist agitation in the country and argued that the claim of the peasant leaders regarding the alleged attachment of the peasants to private property was "rank nonsense:" "How can someone who either has no land or suffers all his life because he has some be attached to private property? We may rest assured that when, having won power, we pass laws taking away the large landed estates from their owners and giving them for the common cultivation to the smallholders and farm hands living in a given commune, then they will gladly accept our conditions and agree to state control. In any case, all peasants working their own fields will be allowed to keep their plots of land, but all of them, sooner or later, will see the convenience and advantages of large farms and will begin to participate in collective production."[70]

All contemporary socialists were convinced of the advantages of large-scale farming, irrespective of who owned such farms. This was so mostly because they did not believe in the feasibility of applying the methods and inventions of agronomy in smallholdings. But they did not even attempt to address the question of who was supposed to pay for land improvement, machines, buildings and training, and where the money was supposed to come from. The problem of burdening the future social product with the costs of investment in agriculture was lost sight of in this economic program, just like the problem of the cost of investment in industry, transport and other areas. In the context of the late nineteenth century, this matter might seem of little significance in England or the Netherlands, but not on the banks of the Vistula and the San where the prospective revolution would have to inherit lamentably low standards of education and culture in the farming sector.

The Polish Marxists, with their eyes on the common road of all mankind, did not take into consideration this difference in the initial levels and social structures of various countries. "Rather than seeking uncertain separate roads of 'our own'," one of them advised, "rather than losing time and effort on finding in our fourth estate something which can replace the capitalist socialization of labor, we would do better to study in depth the work of the scientific representatives of the theory a part of which was best formulated by the author of *Capital*. We shall not reach the aim quicker if we keep listening at the door of the closed cottage."[71]

However, Adam Zakrzewski, one of the pioneers of the populist current, interpreted the same work differently, and perhaps more closely to the author's intentions, as a description of an "ideal capitalist form" which could be deformed under the impact of various factors, including state interventionism, scientific discoveries and the workers' movement, and also under the impact of local conditions. "In view of all of this," he wrote, "it is doubtful whether any society will develop along the road described by the author of *Capital*; in any case, leaving aside West European societies where the capitalist system has by now struck root deep, this road seems highly improbable in our conditions."[72]

It is irrelevant which ideas taken by Zakrzewski and some contributors to the *Głos*[73] from the Russian Narodniks were original, and how they modified them. The Polish populists were far from any doctrinaire attitudes, at least in the early years of their activity. Their theories were not particularly consistent, and they tended to be eclectic, just as the social realities around them were inconsistent and eclectic. They closely observed these realities, violently attacking all kinds of a priori intellectual constructs. They noted first of all that the crushing and leveling force of capitalism stopped short of invisible territorial and social barriers beyond which different motivations and rules of activity still obtained. They were far from directly contrasting Russia and Europe, or the East and the West, and they discovered in each country various systems of economic organization which coexisted and were mutually linked.

In this way, the democratic eclectics gradually arrived at the idea of an economy with many different sectors, an idea which, much later, would become the foundation stone of the theory of growth. Edward Przewóski, a shrewd Polish observer of European life, made the following contribution to the discussion on the cooperative movement: "Today's society is neither a loose aggregate nor a uniform whole. It is an assemblage of systems and aspirations which as yet do not have the character of a uniform organism. Private ownership, the individual-capitalist system and large-scale production prevail in it, but do not rule exclusively. . . . One should not conceive of capitalism and large-scale production as if they were the cart of the golden calf which can smash to smithereens everything in its path. . . . Other factors live or vegetate side by side with it: minor capital, savings and individual efforts which, instead of allowing the great Moloch to devour them, prefer to unite, to form a collective force and in this way compete with the capitalist colossus. Is such competition possible? The facts prove that it is."[74]

The concept of many sectors had, of course, a particular significance for the evaluation of the prospect of change in agrarian relations. Zakrzewski, who was the first to examine this question, doing so with tremendous perspicacity, admitted that peasant property in the Kingdom was burdened by usurious debts, and even believed that "if it had not been for legal regulations which forbid the Jews and in general people of non-peasant background to buy peasant land designated by the ukase of 1864, then the amount of peasant property in the country would have shrunk at a terrifying rate."[75] However, the country squires were in no better situation. Just like Prus, Zakrzewski maintained that small-scale agricultural production was no less efficient than large-scale production and that it could be successful in opposing the trend towards concentration. The sale and parceling of land since enfranchisement had worked in favor of the peasantry and this, he believed, in time "would lead to a far-reaching peaceful evolution in our agrarian system." Unreliable statistics could be used to draw widely divergent conclusions, and historians were to do this later as well. But this uncertainty was enough to produce the conviction that no obvious process of capitalist stratification was taking place in Polish agriculture. The peasant might suffer a hundred different evils, but he did not give in and often bought more land. Even landless peasants bought up cleared land which once belonged to the manor. "This is no longer 'capitalization' Marx-style. When a farmhand, laborer, forester and tenant buy land, then we have to do with a process which should rather be called 'decapitalization'."[76]

No less important than the establishment of the course of change was the evaluation of that change. Neither Prus nor Zakrzewski and the *Głos* contributors could regard the consolidation of smallholdings as a backward phenomenon. On the contrary: their ideal was for ownership to be as widespread as possible; they supported the development of cheap credit for the purchase of parceled land, the trend towards medium-sized, self-sufficient peasant farms, and at the same time a swing towards more intensive methods of cultivation. Moreover, the populists did not exclude the possibility that in time "higher forms of socialization" might emerge in the country, but only through the voluntary cooperation of smallholders, and not through their ruin and expropriation.[77]

The socialists and the populists could not reconcile their positions on this point: for the former, progress meant the impoverishment and proletarianization of the peasantry: for the latter it meant its increased prosperity.

However, the *Głos* was also vitally interested in the situation of the industrial workers in the Kingdom and in the West. Whether dealing with the peasant or the worker, it always kept to the same principle of evaluating ideological programs and social policies according to their immediate, direct results. "We are akin as to our views on the future of the next generations," wrote Hłasko, taking a principled stand against Krzywicki's views, "but people do not form parties in the name of views of this sort. The bond that unites parties are current issues and activities which take place within the lifespan of one generation."[78] The result of adopting this shorter perspective was, logically, the recognition of the purposefulness of piecemeal rather than radical reforms.

The populists, like the positivists, firmly rejected the dialectical theory which saw progress as taking place through the sharpening of social antagonisms, referring to this theory as "doctrinairism." Thus, when Krzywicki described as "backward" all ideas for improving the lot of farm laborers by giving them land or helping them to purchase land, Hłasko replied: "*Fiat doctrina, pereat mundus!* We hold fundamentally different views concerning this question; . . . we do not think that an improvement, even temporary, of the lot of any part of the working people could be an obstacle to the realization of a better future for the whole of society."[79] Jan Ludwik Popławski[80] urged everybody to remember that economic processes applied to living people, and not to abstract categories. He expected social programs to work towards "decreasing, as far as possible, that sum total of moral suffering and material deficiencies which is the lot of the working masses."[81] For the same reasons, the populists were doubtful about the future "dictatorship of the workers," whose tasks were supposed to include the expropriation of the peasantry from their individual holdings in order that they could become joint owners of the national property. Here Hłasko quoted the opinion of Krzywicki, who himself in his "Democratic illusions" admitted that the peasants were opposed to collectivization. "The result," Hłasko retorted, "would then be fratricidal war compared to which all the gloomy tragedies of the present day would pale." This, he prophesied, would be the enforcement of solidarity among the people with the help of bayonets. "A lofty ideal indeed! The minority coercing the majority into accepting an institution which the latter does not want to accept!"[82] Such were the "democratic illusions" of that time.

A similar controversy between the supporters of the dialectic and the cumulative theories of progress concerned the prospects of industrialization. The populist attitude was ambivalent in this respect. Like the socialists, they considered abhorrent the type of interhuman relations produced by industrial capitalism, and, following the example of the Russian Narodniks, often tended to regard capitalism in general as social regression. In any case, they saw the parallel development of many sectors in the national economy as a real fact, which, moreover, was beneficial and had a chance of being consolidated. One of Zakrzewski's arguments in favor of the superiority of peasant farming over manorial farming was the conviction that the durability and equilibrium of any "economic form" increases the more self-sufficient it is, and decreases in accordance as its dependence on market fluctuations grows.

On the other hand, however, industry, especially if it was evenly distributed throughout a country, provided the only possibility, apart from emigration, for absorbing the flow of surplus population from the countryside; it also increased cash incomes in the countryside and supplied the means necessary for improving the level of agriculture. From then on, this ambivalence was to be a permanent feature of agrarianist ideology.

Analyzing the alignment of interests within the capitalist sector, both the populists and the liberal supporters of organic work had no doubt whatsoever that labor and capital were opposed in one respect, but that in another respect they had common interests. The preservation and the future of industry, argued Hłasko, writing in support of factory laws, "are in the interests of both the workers and the factory owners, since this is an all-national interest."[83]

Using the concepts of the theory of games, we could say that for the liberals and the democrats the development of capitalism was a game in which it paid the players to cooperate in order to increase the total winnings, although there was a conflict of interests when it came to dividing these winnings. However, for the early Polish Marxists this was a zero-sum game, involving only competition and conflict. "Either the capitalists win, and then the whole of the working class loses; or the workers win, and then all the capitalists and industrialists can only lose."[84] In an economy based on class antagonisms, Krusiński claimed, "there is no uniform *social store*, just as there is no store common to the parasite and its host organism." Arguing against the solidaristic views of Supiński and his followers, Krusiński stated unequivocally that "for the time being the development of industry will play into the hands of the capitalists only, while the masses will fall into economic slavery."[85] Wścieklica's argument that the socialists saw industrial development as the curse of mankind was not totally unfounded. He only failed to mention that they regarded it as a curse "for the time being," but a curse which would bear beneficial fruit in the future.

This theory was illustrated by numerous examples in socialist writings. In agricultural Galicia poverty prevailed, but there were also all the conditions required for industrial development: "Only several more years of patience are needed," *Równość* wrote in 1879, "and smoke will be pouring out of chimney stacks, machines will be whirring, and wheels rattling in the hitherto peaceful towns and hamlets of Galicia." The Kingdom already had its industry, but the country still lacked "a capitalist appearance." Poverty had increased with the development of industry, "but the permanent growth of production, the lack of any major crises, and the appearance of ever new factories prove that the development of our industry has not as yet passed the limit beyond which the space becomes too cramped even for factory chimneys." The capitalist ideal, according to *Równość,* was Silesia, whose natural resources and industrial development were "not inferior to any other country in Europe." But even there workers died of hunger or famine fever. This was how the stages of economic growth were graded: "Those who know how quickly the England of workshops turned into the England of factories, and how quickly capitalist production with all its attendant pleasures developed in Germany after 1848, may expect that other districts of Poland will not lag behind Silesia for long. Then we shall have Silesian chimney stacks, Silesian factories and Silesian famine fever in all of Polish lands."[86]

In 1889, Ludwik Krzywicki revised the theory of the zero-sum game. He shifted his position closer to that of the Western social-democrats and reached the conclusion that the well-being of "hired factory hands" depended after all on the favorable situation of the factory owner: "Workers' earnings grow in accordance with the expansion of the market and the feverishness of production, and, as a result, with the incomes of gentlemen 'employers.' It is enough to look at the history of the trade unions in order to understand properly the mutual harmony which exists on the bedrock of contradictory interests."[87] This single statement undermines the entire reasoning of the Polish socialist revolutionaries and signifies the movement of some of them away from the scientistic rationalization of wishful thinking to an observation of real economic processes. Krzywicki, however, needed this new thesis in order to juxtapose more sharply the objective situation of the worker on the one hand and of the peasant and the craftsman on the other. The theory of the absolute opposition of the interests of labor and capital was to be supplanted by an equally absolute opposition between the modern, developing large-scale industrial sector and the obsolete, hidebound sector of the individual economy which was doomed to annihilation. It appeared that the main reactionary opponent of capitalism was, "at the present moment," the craftsman, and the indispensable victim of civilizational progress was the peasant. Krzywicki, a modern city man, wrote about the bestial toil, selfishness and intellectual backwardness of the latter with contempt rather than compassion. "Democratism," he concluded, "which sets up the peasant hamlet as the ultimate and supreme ideal of all aspirations, by the same token passes the death sentence on itself."[88]

The laws of history make impossible either any symbiosis of the oppressed and the oppressors, even one fraught with conflict, or any symbiosis of the modern and the traditional, that is, the coexistence of large-scale and small-scale production. There must be the devourers and the devoured, and to think otherwise has always been reactionary "petty-bourgeois idealization" or "idyllization." Such was, for example, the conviction that small family farms could be modernized and, as in Denmark, could keep going with the help of specialization and cooperative activity. For the idea that class antagonisms and economic rivalry did not necessarily have to lead to the devouring of the weaker rested on two assumptions that the Marxists could hardly accept. Firstly, that it was only rarely that one economic form was superior to another in all respects. Secondly, that there were some values and processes that were advantageous to all classes, although the division of these advantages was not equal: for example, the growth of the gross product and the development of education. In his review of Lafargue's *Mental Work and Machine*, Hłasko quoted the author's view that in the capitalist system the development of public education was dictated exclusively by the interests of the bourgeoisie. Perhaps, the reviewer asked, "the results arising from such selfish motives are after all beneficial to all, if only to a certain extent?"[89]

Such sober-minded convictions, contrary to the views voiced by both the conservatives and the socialists, were shared by the liberal and democratic intelligentsia which defended itself against the label of "bourgeois" imposed on it by its detractors. In fact, the program of economic development propagated by the positivists did not have a clear class character, although some of its variants took into consideration, to a greater or lesser degree, the burdens and advantages which fell to the lot of the country squires or the bourgeoisie, or to the peasants or the workers.

However, the main shortcoming of all variants of the program, admittedly through no fault of their propagators, was the lack of an addressee. All socioeconomic programs, unless they are the direct strategies of those in power or those seeking power, either appeal to the authorities or, in democracies, serve to mobilize public opinion in order to exert some pressure on the authorities. In nineteenth-century Poland, or at least in the Russian partition zone, the channels for such pressure were nonexistent.

Initially, the positivists found that they could manage without them. Classical economics had had a tremendous impact on two generations of Polish intellectuals, convincing them that industrialization would come of its own accord: *pecunia flat ubi vult*, provided no obstacles were put in its way.

Therefore, the program of organic work dealt mainly with things which could not be achieved without some external impulse, that is, education for the people and the inculcation into the upper classes of the spirit of critical and sober rationalism. It took some time for the organicists to become aware of something which had already been known to Minister Lubecki and Friedrich List: that the English model of spontaneous industrialization was not going to materialize in Central and Eastern Europe. Fifty years of Polish experience had proved beyond any doubt that with high interest rates capitalists would avoid risky investments which did not guarantee quick and high returns. Such guarantees could be given only by the state, but appeals to the state encountered understandable psychological barriers. The economy was the only sphere of Polish life relatively free of the heavy hand of the Russian *chinovnik*; besides, those enterprises, National Mining included, which had long been owned and run by the state treasury had been reduced to ruins by inefficient and uneconomical administration, thus discrediting completely the very idea of state management of industry. "No government has ever been a good industrialist, and no government ever will be," claimed Prus,[90] and this view was shared by everybody in the 1870s.

The basic assumption of organic work was the building of the foundations of a modern civilization without any help from the state apparatus of the partitioning power. Making social initiative dependent on the support of ministers in St. Petersburg or, worse still, on the state treasury, would mean crossing the invisible line between legal activity and collaboration with the enemy. This line had to be crossed by men of big business, for example Kronenberg or Bloch;[91] later it was crossed by the founders of the Polish branches of the Society for the Promotion of Russian Industry and Commerce, as well as by such opinion-forming journals as the *Kraj* of St. Petersburg and the *Słowo* of Warsaw. But the ideologues of Polish liberalism stopped short of this line; in any case, though tolerated in Warsaw, they could hardly count on being given a hearing at the imperial court or in government offices. Finally, the question of employment for the Polish intelligentsia, discussed in chapter 4, could not be left out of account. The intelligentsia, driven out of the administration, judiciary, schools, forestry and, finally, the state bank, could find support only in the private sector, especially the railways. No wonder, then, that the prospect of the nationalization of the railways did not arouse much enthusiasm in the Kingdom.

In short, it was not necessary to believe in the gospel of *laissez-faire* to have strong reservations about state-sponsored economic initiatives. On the other hand, it was not possible to do without the state. Due to the increasing size of economic ventures and the enormous attendant expansion in the areas of administrative law and supervision, no joint-stock company could be established without a government permit, no railway company could operate without a treasury guarantee of the dividends of the shareholders, no coal mine could be opened without a license from the mining authority, and no large factory could survive without government orders and customs privileges for importing machines and raw materials. No school of commerce, literary weekly, summer theater, scholarship fund or retirement fund could be established without government permission, and none could survive the loss of government approval. In a bureaucratic state, whether the administration is native or foreign, it is impossible to live, and even more impossible to develop the country without a minimum of day-to-day cooperation with the administration. The existence of this kind of situation in the Russian partition zone meant that movements which took a conciliatory line were bound to be more efficient, while the liberal program of "internal self-dependence" was doomed to an ever growing helplessness, something which was turned to account by both the conservative and the revolutionary camps.

In the late 1870s, the tsarist government finally abandoned liberal economic policies for the sake of protectionism. This new policy proved extremely beneficial for the growth of industry in the Kingdom. However, it promoted only that type of industrialization which, for various reasons, was most disliked by the supporters of internal autonomy. Tsarist protectionism, leading as it did to competition for the patronage of the ministry of finance, favored those groups of capitalists who were able to form the strongest lobby. With its high degree of concentration, foreign capital, especially in the steel and textile industries, was the strongest. Thus, protectionism was a determining factor in putting industrialization in the Kingdom onto a quasi-colonial track. This course was dependent to only a slight extent on local sources of accumulation and had little effect on the petrified social structures. The few oases of industrial agglomeration, such as Warsaw, Łódź or the Dąbrowa Górnicza basin, and an underdeveloped railway network could hardly change the civilizational landscape of the Kingdom, but they succeeded in infecting its life with the virus of *febris aurea*.

The unexpectedly rapid infusion of foreign capital produced a defensive nationalist reaction in Polish society. The landowners and the middle class, or at least those among them who were incapable of entering into industrial competition on a large scale, felt that they were being deprived of the benefits which they hoped to enjoy under tariff protection in the combined market of the Kingdom and the Empire. As discussed above, a similar threat faced the intelligentsia, since foreign capital brought in its wake legions of foreign specialists and managers. The reaction, aggravated by ancient prejudices, was directed above all against the Germans, but also, though not so strongly, against French, Italian and Belgian capitalists who were also eager to invest in the Kingdom, mainly in the mining and steel industries and the railways. Anti-German sentiments were fanned by German agricultural settlement, a process which took advantage of the land-parceling movement. Behind this dual invasion loomed the ominous shadow of Bismarck and his anti-Polish and anti-Catholic policies, subjects on which the whole press in the Kingdom became more vocal the more it was forbidden to write about the growing Russification and the persecution of the Uniates.[92] Anti-German feelings were soon accompanied by aggressive anti-Semitic outbursts, which drew on rich deposits of age-old ethnic and religious prejudice and were intensified by the Russian wave of pogroms in 1880 and 1881, which also spread to Warsaw. This explosion was indirectly linked with industrial revolution: protectionism and the stock exchange intensified the scramble for commercial advantages, and the Jewish capitalists and merchants had much more experience in this field. In the countryside, the old antagonism was exacerbated by the large part played by Jewish capital in the parceling of estates, and the organization of usurious credit for the peasants and the gentry.

This combination of psychological, cultural and economic reasons gave rise to militant nationalism, best personified by the former progressive Jan Jeleński, the founder, in 1883, and editor of the journal *Rola (Soil)*. *Rola* represented a radical right-wing orientation, until then absent on the political scene of the Kingdom, but which would be a permanent component of Polish ideological life from then on. Its program was almost completely negative, and its rousing slogans testify eloquently to the frustration and heavy adaptation trauma suffered by the old social strata, the landowning and lower middle classes in particular, which were incapable both psychologically and financially of adapting to the suddenly accelerated tempo of economic change. Their growing submersion in debt, the real threat of losing their social status, and the feeling of being pushed to the fringe of the developmental process found expression and explanation in the image of the predatory foreign capitalist.

The shunting of economic rivalry onto the tracks of national struggle put the advocates of organic work in a very awkward position. At least since Supiński, the axiom of the liberal intelligentsia had been the conviction that in a country which had a surplus of labor and a dramatic shortage of free money resources all new capital, irrespective of its origin, and all investment in agriculture and industry were levers of development. In addition, a number of observers had pointed out that foreign capital had the advantage of sparing retarded countries the drastic experience of having to go through the process of primitive accumulation. No wonder, then, that the liberal *Ekonomista (The Economist)* argued in the stagnant 1860s that there was nothing to be feared from foreign or Jewish capital, especially if it was invested in agriculture, since this increased the price of land and made it easier for all landowners to obtain investment loans.[93] As fears grew in spite of such efforts to quell them, and as the myth about foreigners buying up the land of the Polish gentry (as if it was not the gentry who sold it) was revived among the country squires, the positivists argued that the best defense would be to acquire the spirit of enterprise and hard work from these foreigners: "We have entrusted almost everything to the hands of foreigners," wrote *Niwa* in 1873, "so today there is nothing to do except to join hands with these foreigners and work together. . . . The Jews and the Germans will not deprive us of our estates, if we forget about their failings and adopt their virtues and talents."[94]

As years passed and as foreign capital continued to flow in, the alarmist tone was heard more and more frequently in the positivist press. The positivists no longer knew whether foreigners helped to develop the national economy or whether, by buying up national assets cheaply, they were depriving Poles of the most valuable institutions of organic work. In 1876, the Bank Steel Mill, which had been closed down, and the state-owned coal mines in the Dąbrowa Górnicza Basin came under the auctioneer's hammer. On the one hand, this was greeted with satisfaction since it brought to an end a notoriously infamous chapter in the history of the administration of the mining industry by the treasury of the Kingdom. But the same decision provoked anxiety when it became known that Kronenberg's mining-metallurgical company had failed to sell out its shares and so could not take part in the bidding. The liberal *Gazeta Handlowa (The Commercial Paper)* and *Przegląd Tygodniowy* demanded from the government that it should give priority to local bidders, and Prus asked: "Who is going to buy Dąbrowa under these circumstances? Poles or foreigners? . . . For generations we have been taught to hold economic laws in contempt, and now these laws are taking their revenge on us!"[95] The Dąbrowa Basin was bought by the French—at a very low price—but within a few years, the completely devastated mines and furnaces had been replaced by a powerful profit-bearing mining and metallurgical combine.

Did the country lose or gain? The question was not an easy one. Prus, who returned to the subject over and over again, could not decide how the situation should be viewed. On principle, he had no objection to foreign capital—but without foreign capitalists, managers, masters and settlers. This, however, was impossible in the Kingdom. A remedy was to be found in assimilation. The influx of German capitalists would lose its dangerous edge provided

Polish crafts and small-scale industries organized themselves, forming a middle-class milieu which would foster assimilation of newcomers.[96] Any hopes for the emergence of a native Polish bourgeoisie capable of taking over the management of the country's economic life seemed to be less and less realistic. In any case, the bourgeoisie did not enjoy a particularly good opinion in the "young press." Just as previously, after the November Rising, Polish emigré democrats had differentiated between the good, patriotically-minded middle gentry and the egoistic, cosmopolitan aristocracy, so now, in the wake of the January Uprising, the progressive camp applied a similar pattern in relation to the middle class. The bankers and industrialists were accused of lacking patriotism and refusing to finance educational and cultural ventures, but the supporters of organic work also pilloried the rich bourgeoisie for its economic timidity and its lack of enterprise.

In 1882, Świętochowski, like many others dazzled by the prospects of "commercial and industrial conquest" opening up before the Kingdom, still seemed to be deluding himself that the Polish bourgeoisie would take advantage of this chance in its own interests and the interests of the country. Later, however, he discovered that the middle class was incapable of achieving anything independently and had only words of contempt for it. When, in 1889, Belgian financiers bought the controlling stock in the Warsaw–Vienna Railway and took over the management of the company, he harangued his compatriot millionaires in the following fashion: "Had Leopold Kronenberg senior been alive, he would have taught you how large national ventures should be protected against exploitation by foreigners. You have no idea how to do this; there are no people among you capable of acting in a grand style; the wealthiest among you know how to sell butter and scrape up pennies, but you lack the understanding and courage to salvage the most important railway company from foreign takeover, despite the dividend of thirteen roubles. Our home-bred Rothschilds, defeated and deprived of their homes, beseech the government to save them by refusing to sign the resolutions taken by the shareholders' meeting. They have shown their true colour in this matter."[97]

Świętochowski was to respond in a similar way several years later when Belgian and German companies won the tender for the electrification of Warsaw: "If Menelik of Abyssinia offers good terms to the municipality and cheap light and cheap tram fares to the public, then I am all for Menelik . . . One might imagine that national capital, always wise when it is already too late, would snatch at the opportunity of electrifying [Warsaw]. With each new economic and financial venture the same myth rises from the ashes. . . The old families of brave, enterprising, energetic people, like the Steinkellers, the Kronenbergs, etc. have died leaving no heirs and . . . our capitalists still dream of extortionate interest rates. For them, five or seven percent interest is *faules Geschäft*; 'decent returns' begin at ten percent. Since lighting and electric trams are not tap-rooms or private pawnshops, which yield secure profits, our capitalists 'need to think things over', that is, they 'need to lie low'."[98]

Considering the disproportion of forces and the above-mentioned principles of calculation, the struggle against foreign capital remained a mere slogan. In fact, as early as 1880, in his response to Jeleński's notorious pamphlet *The Jews, the Germans and Us* which had been reprinted several times, Świętochowski stressed that foreign economic influence could be opposed only by society's own work and activity, and not by propagandist brochures—nor did he change his views on this matter for the next twenty years. The number of brochures grew, and so did the readership of the *Rola*, but despite that the industrial revolution in the Kingdom was carried out by foreign capital and foreign engineers, operating under the protection of a foreign state and producing largely for the Russian market.

The Polish bourgeoisie, together with some of the rich landowners and the intelligentsia, especially the technical intelligentsia, eventually began to take part in this industrial and commercial movement, though they never became its driving force. However, they found moral support not so much in the liberal, as in the conservative press. A genuine breakthrough had taken place in the conservative press with regard to its attitude to business. As late as the early 1880s, the contributors to the *Niwa*, which was addressed to the conservative landowning stratum, were still fulminating against the plutocracy and the stock exchange, and warning their readers not to be too enthusiastic about the growth of "imported" industry. This industry, they claimed, exported goods to the East and profits to the West, and thus only made foreigners rich, while at the same time it cut at the roots of the national economy because it "takes away thousands of able hands from healthy productive work in agriculture and from industry which could otherwise flourish on home soil for the benefit of the country;" as if that were not enough, it also drew on Poland the menacing clouds of the "social question."[99] A completely different note was sounded by the neo-conservative Warsaw daily *Słowo (The Word)*, which, from the moment it was established in 1882, supported economic collaboration with the tsarist administration. One of the reasons for this was that large landowners, threatened by competition from American farmers and the grain crisis, were abandoning their traditional free trade stance in the expectation of benefiting from a protected market. The *Słowo* thus contains much genuine rejoicing at "the forming of cooperative ventures between the West and the East [i.e., between Poland and Russia] in the field of stock breeding and its products," and ardent support for "this idea, born at agricultural shows, which will doubtless have far-reaching consequences."[100] This agricultural-commercial version of the Polish civilizational mission in the East would soon be supplemented by absolute recognition of the benefits flowing from foreign capital "in those branches of industry which do not attract local capital."[101] The interests of exporters were now seen to be mutually beneficial.

The future of these interests was, however, uncertain. The export boom in the Kingdom was not destined to last long, since the industrial revolution had spread to Russia proper and the government in St. Petersburg, pressurized by the Russian industrialists, began to change the tariffs so as to protect Moscow against the competitive ascendancy of Łódź and Sosnowiec. Capital and the intelligentsia moved further east. Both conservative and socialist authors began to prophesy the forthcoming closure of the Eastern markets and a complete crash in industry, which had developed "artificially" under the protection of the customs policy. Jan Ludwik Popławski added a moral warning to this: "These conquests worthy of shopkeepers degrade our intelligentsia . . . Today, we have already begun descending to the level of the Jews, and when it comes to markets and the question of expanding the outlets, we will soon turn completely into a nation of profiteers and traders. Russia and Siberia are full of thousands of despicable 'polacks' . . . shysters and usurers, who are supposed to be leading 'the conquest of the eastern markets'." That was why, the author claimed, the Poles were disliked in Russia. He argued that the industrialists should export whatever they pleased, wherever they pleased, but that this should not be made into a "program."[102] Here, he offers no clue as to whether he means the program of the ideologues of industrial civilization who had become disillusioned with capitalism, or the program of the ideologues of the manorial farms who had gained confidence in capitalism.

After all, the dilemma that faced the liberally-minded organicists was that the colonial-style modernization of the country, which proved the only realistic proposition and the only effective way of obtaining industrial growth, had so little in common with their idea of the development of the national economy. As discussed, their program could be presented neither to the government, nor to the owners of capital. Addressed to "society" at large, it had merely a moralizing and educational character. It is true that time and again the organicists reverted to the idea of a moral government which would design a strategy of collective effort and gain a strong enough foothold to impose this strategy on the enlightened classes. Both the conservatives (who, however, were much less influential in the Russian partition zone than in the Prussian province of Poznań and Austrian Galicia) and the positivists aspired to this role. Prus, for his part, urged the existing camps of public opinion to make mutual concessions and merge into one party which "would envelop the whole of society with knowledge and feeling."[103] However, such a government might have existed for a short while in 1863, but in peacetime it was unrealistic to expect anything of the sort. Hence, various ideas, programs and editorials were to be found in abundance, and only people commanding authority and money were in short supply.

An essential prerequisite for "organic" development was to find out internal sources of accumulation. This did not call for much inventiveness: for the last hundred years, whenever the means for financing economic development were lacking, the press called on its readers to save. After 1864, it returned to this topic with monotonous regularity—particularly the moderately liberal press. The slogan of thriftiness, addressed to the classes in the middle-income bracket, that is, the landowners and the townspeople, had acquired a new economic significance now that joint-stock companies were inviting small investments. The organicists were not concerned to promote the virtue of thrift for thrift's sake. They encouraged the productive utilization of surpluses: "Let all sums of money, small and medium, which are not being put to any use, be brought together, and then we shall see that there is no shortage of capital in the country. Only do something . . . do something and move briskly and boldly, latent capital!"[104] The organicists had high hopes of stock companies, expecting them to bring economic, social and even educational improvement: such companies would be a way of amassing investment resources without concentrating ownership, and at the same time would educate the middle class in running its own affairs.

Small savings, it was argued, would produce middle-sized capital, which in turn would create the kind of small-scale industry suitable for Polish conditions, an industry which would mainly process local raw materials for the needs of the local consumers. These would not be Polish Manchesters or Birminghams, but workshops and small factories scattered throughout the country, requiring more labor than capital, since the masses of village laborers had to be given bread and employment. For each nation, Prus argued, there is a different "maximum" of development and each nation has to decide how high this maximum should be.[105] The Polish maximum, or rather developmental optimum, was to be the economic foundation of middle-class culture, but not of capitalist culture. This distinction had a basic significance for the positivists, and there is also ample evidence for it in contemporary novels.

The difference between those models of middle-class morals and the capitalist economic ethos have been aptly noted by Maria Żmigrodzka in her study on Eliza Orzeszkowa. *Gründerzeit* capitalism meant for contemporary

liberals "the ruthless rivalry of individual egoisms," which led to savage
anarchy on the market and to social chaos. "Orzeszkowa understood and
appreciated the historic role of capitalism in liberating the individual, and in
creating the notion of the value of the human personality . . . However, at the
same time, the religion of individualism and the concept of the sovereignty
of the individual was always alien to her. . . . Both the 'civic' gentry traditions
and the adopted ideals of 'service' led to the subordination of individual
interests to the community and to a conviction of the necessity for the strong
rooting of the individual in the sphere of social notions and values."[106] This
may be applied in principle to the whole positivist current, although none of
its adherents could equal Orzeszkowa in her keen awareness of the moral
consequences and antinomies of the epoch of modernization.

Translated into economic categories, the propaganda of middle-class morality meant a striving towards measured growth without large population
migrations and without a sharp class polarization. Preferably, Poland should
be a country with a numerous, industrious middle class, and not one overrun
by bourgeois sharks and droves of homeless proletarians. Fragmentary and
voluntary parceling of big estates stimulated by cheap loans for peasants (such
loans were still lacking, and the need for an available credit system was
stressed again and again in the press), would contribute to the leveling out of
differences in the countryside and the improvement of farming methods on
peasant farms. The spread of elementary education, hygiene and medicine
would make it possible for the lower classes of society to participate in the
basic benefits of civilization. The assimilation of the Jews would bring them
into the Polish middle class and the intelligentsia. Finally, the democratization
of customs, to which a special importance was attached, would lead to the
abolition of the most durable caste feature of "gentry sociology:" that is, the
strict division into good society on the one hand, and the people on the other.
For this was the country where the starving veterinary student, Stefan
Żeromski, suffered agonies of shame because, having no money to tip the
janitor (who was much better off than himself), he had secretly to carry a
bucket of water at night to his poor garret.[107]

The idea of eliminating the most conspicuous indications of the two
extremes of wealth and poverty and, at the same time, of effecting a gradual
and relative equality in the basic dimensions of the human condition (that is,
ownership, income, education, comforts and lifestyles) was something completely different from the dialectical prospect of reaching perfect equality by
first aggravating the inequalities. The advocates of both these programs
accused one another of utopianism. Prus called socialism a school of sociology "which believes that society can be kneaded like dough." He admitted

that his own program for a more even distribution of land and tools, ownership and wealth was modest, but at least it took account of human nature and social realities: tunnels can be bored through the Alps, he explained, but the Alps cannot be removed from the face of the earth.[108]

Nevertheless, for the advocates of organic work the boring of tunnels in the already existing massif of capitalism was a task which was neither practically nor theoretically feasible. Most of them supported measures for improving the working conditions and earnings of the workers by introducing legal reforms and by solving conflicts between the workers and the owners through negotiation and mediation. They were interested in Western experiences in this field, Western labor legislation, and the plans for social welfare reforms put forward by the spokesmen of "state socialism." These, however, were concepts and experiences completely incompatible with the political conditions of the Russian empire. Paradoxically, it was easier to induce the government to impose restrictions on the liberal arbitrariness of capitalism in liberal countries, where labor and political organizations of the working class were allowed, and public opinion could make itself heard, than in the autocratic tsarist state which permitted associations of employers but not of workers, and the formation of cartels but not of labor unions. Even such state institutions as the factory inspection was introduced there belatedly and enjoyed limited powers.

Although Polish economic thought was clearly evolving from classical liberalism towards a recognition of the mediating role of the state and law, and although it had embraced many ideas of social-democratic reformism, under the conditions prevailing in the Kingdom all of this remained merely a declaration of principles and could not be translated into the language of definite demands. As well as criticizing the German *Reichstag*'s extraordinary legislation against the socialists, Polish authors also wrote scathingly about Bismarck's social reforms, not so much because of their contents as because of their aims and the arbitrary way in which they were introduced. There was, however, a big difference between Bismarck and Pobyedonostsev.[109] Factory owners in Żyrardów and Łódź were quite happy to invite Alexander III, his lawyers and his gendarmes to perform the role of mediators in industrial conflicts, but no respectable publicist would ever do so. The practice of state intervention, that is, intervention in support of capital and the established order, proved the stumbling block of the whole concept of democratic reform; consequently, this was the strongest argument in favor of the idea of social revolution.

Only when the populists from the *Głos* group voiced their violent dislike of the principles of free competition, did the fact that intervention and arbitration by the state, even a state like Russia, could bridle the rapacity and lawlessness of the capitalists gain an acknowledgment. The *Głos* kept a watchful eye on the results of the activities of factory inspectors, and popularized Rodbertus' doctrine of state control of the terms of work contracts which would ensure that wages increased in step with the growth of productivity.[110] For Józef Potocki (Bohusz),[111] the reign of unbridled individualism was tantamount to a return to savagery: competition, he argued, destroyed the human personality, rewarding ruthlessness and cunning rather than courage and skill, and wasted more energy than it released. Any restriction imposed on competition—by monopolies, trade unions or state authorities—meant progress. Potocki was an avid reader and interpreter of British socioeconomic literature in particular. He translated Spencer, but he criticized him for his distrust of authority and his anxiety that the growth of the state's competence could lead to a new kind of slavery and a system of mass forced labor. He preferred the Fabian idea of the rationalization of economic life through the introduction of elements of planning, with the difference that for Potocki the criteria for evaluating any system were the ethical principles of cooperation rather than economic effectiveness.[112]

However, both the populists and the liberal organicists failed to avoid the pitfall into which reception of all Western ideas fell in an autocratic state. Obedient students of the "social science" of that age, they had learnt to neglect in their analyses and programs the force of the realities of the political system, which they believed to be secondary in relation to the system of social organization. As a result, they overlooked the interdependence that existed between freedom of speech and association on the one hand, and the possibility of restricting the freedom to exploit one's fellow man on the other; in any case, they were not allowed to articulate their views on that subject openly under the circumstances. The greatest democratic illusion proved to be something to which Krzywicki never referred: the illusion that the social structure could be democratized in a state which precluded all forms of political democracy.

From 1865 on, the liberal *Ekonomista* published dozens of translations and articles which recommended a variety of associations and companies. It is not always easy to determine when their authors were thinking of capital partnerships, and when they rather meant work cooperatives: for the main idea was to combine the contributions of labor and capital, and not to separate them.[113] Nevertheless, one can trace a progression from the rather nebulous commendation of "partnerships" to the idea of "popular associations," both as an antidote to usury and pauperization and as a means of boosting small-scale production.[114] "Association is the only way of snatching the

lowest social strata from the abyss of poverty and backwardness," wrote
Mścisław Trepka, an economic journalist who recommended forming peasant
credit and commercial associations, and in a more remote future, communities
of ownership and production, provided the individualism which was so
deeply rooted in the character of the country population could be overcome.[115]
For at least twenty years, the projects and cooperatives of Schultze from
Delitsch enjoyed a tremendous popularity in Polish socioeconomic writing.
Józef Kirszrot was indefatigable in his advocacy of work cooperatives and
consumer cooperatives as a means of putting a stop to the preponderance of
big capital in industry and commerce.[116] The financial foundations of the
cooperative movement were to be provided by "people's banks," preferably
also cooperative, which would amass the small savings of the working people
and transform them into low-interest loans which could be used to develop
production.[117] It was just one step from such ideas to bolder economic
fantasies. In the militant years of the "young camp," some authors imagined
that cooperative ownership would enable the workers to take possession of
"all the industrial plants in which they have long been sweating."[118]

Workers' factories, even if they were supposed to be merely small workshops, were a utopia both in Poland and in the West. The situation was
different as regards credit banks and commercial and agricultural cooperatives: in the Kingdom, admittedly, all efforts in this direction had failed, and
the camp of organic work had become disenchanted with the whole cooperative idea, but experiences in this field in many countries in Europe, as well
as in the Poznań region and Galicia, at least deserved some consideration.

Towards the end of the 1880s, the cooperative movement was vigorously
revived in the West and had the support of a number of serious theoreticians,
for example Charles Gide. In the Russian partition zone, after a break of
almost twenty years, hopes for a cooperative coalition of labor and capital
were also revived, and the *Głos* became the main proponent of the movement.
Since cooperatives had proved capable of surviving in competition with
capitalist enterprises, it was argued they would soon be able gradually to
replace the system of hired labor. After all, socialism was supposed to be
nothing more and nothing less than the victory of "the principle of cooperation" over "the principle of competition."[119] The populists found it unthinkable and unacceptable that the passage to a higher social order should take
place at the price of the economic and moral degradation of the peasants and
the workers, and the dehumanization of work.

The vision of general cooperativization was not destined to come true, but
nor did the vision of general stratification materialize either. "Today, one
cannot assume with absolute certainty that small capital will be immediately

devoured by big capital, or that small-scale production will yield to large-scale production," wrote Przewóski in 1889—and he was right.[120] The laws of development proved difficult to decipher. The social economy, even in those countries which were better developed and richer than Poland, continued stubbornly to take on an eclectic multiplicity of forms, and the mutual influences and interdependencies of its various sectors—the state sector, the private capitalist sector, the cooperative sector, the small-producers' sector, and the natural economy sector—were much more complex than the founders of any of the major nineteenth-century systems of political economy believed.

Every hypothetical long-term economic prognosis was constructed on the foundation of some kind of moral utopia. The Polish democratic utopia in both its liberal and populist versions was neither more idyllic nor more unreal than the others. When we consider the history of small countries, such as Denmark or Switzerland, which increased their prosperity by raising the level of peasant culture, by developing the cooperative movement and by aspiring to high standards in the crafts and small-scale industries, we are forced to view the projects designed by the intelligentsia as something more than an illusion reflecting the point of the view of "doomed" classes. The democratic ideologues were sometimes right, sometimes wrong, in their forecasts of the future course of economic processes, but they could not influence them given the state of impotence in which Poland found itself. And in this respect they did not differ from intellectuals representing other orientations.

Their influence on the mode of economic thinking of the intelligentsia was certainly greater, though it cannot be measured. From this point of view, two features of the democratic ideologies of the positivist era seem worthy of particular attention. First, the understanding that the industrialization of the country, which destroyed the routine of settled life, was a traumatic process for many, and that therefore social programs ought to be concerned with facilitating adaptation, or a gradual transfer from one way of life to another. Second, the awareness that the growth of the social product and its distribution were indivisible processes, and that any program which vested all its hopes in only one of them was defective.

Naturally, the program of the Polish democrats at the threshold of the twentieth century was defective in its own way and fraught with many illusions. Perhaps the only people who could be free of illusions, at least in the tsarist partition zone, were the ideologues of the Polish–Russian iron and steel cartel. Even the realism of the conciliatory advocates of "realistic politics," who wanted to gain cultural autonomy for the Poles at the price of political submissiveness to St. Petersburg, was questionable, to say the least.

In a country where the voluntary work and sacrifice of enthusiasts from among the intelligentsia had to replace a non-existent national state and social reforms, where censored articles in weeklies were to substitute for acts of law, where voluntary contributions rather than taxes paid for national projects, and secret workers' cells took the place of trade unions, every attempt to fathom the future and, even more so, the will to create this future, had to feed on illusions. To the authors of programs and manifestos, both overt and conspiratorial, to social workers and political agitators, it may have seemed, indeed must have seemed, that the arguments and conflicts they waged among themselves would decide who would take the helm of the ship of history, what course it would take, what doctrine would guide it. In fact, however, under the watchful eye of the censor, gendarme and police informer, they were arguing fiercely about the hierarchy of values, the sense of sacrifice, and the ethereal glimmer of hope without which a subdued nation stagnates in the humdrum of everyday existence.

Notes to Chapter 6

1. Ludwik Waryński (1856–1889), the first Polish socialist leader, the founder of the "Proletariat" party in 1882, arrested and sentenced, died in the Schlüsselburg prison in St. Petersburg.

2. Alexander II's decree of 2 March 1864 granted the peasants ownership of the plots of land they cultivated; in addition, some landless peasants were allowed to obtain allotments from state demesnes. New land tax was imposed to provide funds for indemnifying the gentry for their loss of peasant rent or corvée.

3. A large number of poor Polish peasants went to Germany as migrant seasonal labor.

4. The names of big factory owners in the textile industry in Żyrardów and Łódź.

5. A. Suligowski, "Kapitały," *Opiekun Domowy*, 1872, pp. 329–31.

6. W. Wścieklica, "Rojenia socjalistów polskich wobec nauki ich mistrza," in *Ognisko* (Warsaw, 1882), pp. 104–5.

7. [A. Świętochowski], "Radosne nowiny," *Prawda*, 1883, pp. 229–30.

8. A. Świętochowski, *Liberum Veto*, vol. 2 (Warsaw, 1976), p. 108.

9. L. Krzywicki, *Dzieła*, vol. 2 (Warsaw, 1958), p. 227. On Krzywicki see note 47 to chapter 4. *Walka Klas* (Class Struggle) was the main Polish socialist journal, edited and published in Geneva in 1884–87.

10. An epithet from an article in *Walka Klas*, see A. Molska (ed.), *Pierwsze pokolenie marksistów polskich: Wybór pism i materiałów źródłowych z lat 1878–1886*, vol. 2 (Warsaw, 1962), p. 631.

11. Ibid., pp. 745–7.

12. F. Tych (ed.), *Polskie programy socjalistyczne 1878–1918* (Warsaw, 1975), p. 186.

13. Ibid., p. 249.

14. K. Marx, *Capital: A Critical Analysis of Capitalist Production*, transl. by S. Moore and E. Aveling, vol. 1 (London, 1887, reprint 1946), pp. 660–61.

15. A. Sąsiedzki, "Polemika," in M. Falkowski and T. Kowalik (eds.), *Początki marksistowskiej myśli ekonomicznej w Polsce: Wybór publicystyki z lat 1880–1885* (Warsaw, 1957), pp. 113–23.

16. See note 73 to chapter 4.

17. A. Molska, *Model ustroju socjalistycznego w polskiej myśli marksistowskiej lat 1878–1886* (Warsaw, 1965), pp. 18–19. See also A. Walicki, *Polska, Rosja, marksizm* (Warsaw, 1983), pp. 46–9, 83–4, et al.

18. Związek Robotników Polskich, an underground party in the Polish Kingdom, 1889–92, mainly organizing industrial workers for economic struggle.

19. Quoted after F. Tych, *Związek Robotników Polskich 1889–1892* (Warsaw, 1974), pp. 92–4.

20. Krzywicki, *Wspomnienia*, vol. 2 (Warsaw, 1958), p. 28.

21. *Polskie programy socjalistyczne*, pp. 65–70.

22. B. Limanowski, *Socyjalizm jako konieczny objaw dziejowego rozwoju* (Lwów, 1879), pp. 15–16, 34. Bolesław Limanowski (1835–1935), a historian and sociologist, the first Polish champion of socialism which he linked with democratic tradition and the drive to win national independence. In 1892, he became a cofounder of the Polish Socialist Party.

23. K. Marx, *Capital*, vol. 1, p. xix.

24. Ibid., p. 788.

25. Szymon Konarski (1808–1839), a courageous leader of Polish clandestine democratic and national organizations in the Lithuanian and Ukrainian lands of the Russian Empire; arrested in 1838, executed in Wilno. On Łukasiński see note 36 to chapter 1.

26. In German: *Magenfrage*, see A. Schäffle, *Die Quintessenz des Sozialismus* (4. Aufl.: Gotha, 1878); cf. A. Molska (ed.), *Pierwsze pokolenie marksistów*, vol. 2, p. 633.

27. F. Engels, *Socialism, Utopian and Scientific*, transl. by E. Aveling (London, 1950), pp. 46–7.

28. Krzywicki, *Wspomnienia*, vol. 2, pp. 40–41.

29. Waryński's speech at the Warsaw trial of "Proletariat" party leaders in 1885, in *Pierwsze pokolenie marksistów*, vol. 2, p. 611.

30. Ibid., vol. 1, pp. 100, 242–3; vol. 2, pp. 91–2.

31. Ibid., vol. 1, pp. 72, 242, 432–4.

32. J. Młot [Sz. Diksztajn], *Kto z czego żyje?* (1st ed.: 1881) (Warsaw, 1952), p. 117.

33. *Pierwsze pokolenie marksistów*, vol. 1, p. 87.

34. F. Lassalle, *Kapitał i praca*, transl. by K.W. (Lwów, 1878), p. 177.

35. Engels, *Socialism*, p. 80.

36. *Pierwsze pokolenie marksistów*, vol. 1, p. 74.

37. Ibid., vol. 2, p. 84.

38. Ibid., vol. 1, p. 475.

39. Engels, *Socialism*, p. 80.

40. *Polskie programy socjalistyczne*, p. 127.

41. *Pierwsze pokolenie marksistów*, vol. 1, p. 96.

42. Epithets from articles in the Kraków daily *Czas* (The Times), commenting on the Kraków trial of socialists in 1880, and from P. Popiel, *Choroba wieku* (Kraków, 1880), p. 18 et al.

43. Engels, *Socialism*, p. 79.

44. Marx, *Capital*, vol. 1, p. xvii.

45. *Polskie programy socjalistyczne*, p. 188.

46. Ibid., p. 247.

47. *Pierwsze pokolenie marksistów*, vol. 2, pp. 292–3.

48. Ibid., p. 271–4.

49. K. Marx, wrote Raymond Aron, "a mis au compte de ce qu'il n'aimait pas, je veux dire le capitalisme, tous les aspects de la societé contemporaine qu'il jugeait fâcheux. Il a rendu le capitalisme responsable de ce qui est imputable à l'industrie moderne, de ce qui est imputable à la pauvreté, de ce qui est imputable aux phases initiales d'industrialisation. . ." R. Aron, *Democratie et totalitarisme* (Paris, 1965), p. 368.

50. *Pierwsze pokolenie marksistów*, vol. 1, p. 590.

51. Ibid., vol. 2, pp. 249–50.

52. Ibid., vol. 2, p. 293.

53. A. Głowacki [B. Prus], *Szkic programu w warunkach obecnego rozwoju społeczeństwa* (Warsaw, 1883), pp. 107, 111.

54. S. Krusiński, *Pisma zebrane* (Warsaw, 1958), pp. 26–7.

55. *Początki marksistowskiej myśli ekonomicznej*, p. 161.

56. See note 66 to chapter 4.

57. *Głos*, 1888, pp. 213–14.

58. Krzywicki, *Dzieła*, vol. 4 (Warsaw, 1960), p. 310.

59. See [K. Dłuski], *Szkice historyczno-społeczne* (Zurich, 1898), p. 108.

60. *Pierwsze pokolenie marksistów*, vol. 2, p. 680.

61. *Archiwum Ruchu Robotniczego*, vol. 8 (Warsaw, 1982), pp. 13–14.

62. Ibid., pp. 16–20.

63. Ignacy Daszyński (1866–1936), a cofounder and leader of the Social Democratic Party of Galicia, the most popular politician of the Polish left.

64. *Archiwum Ruchu Robotniczego*, vol. 8, p. 23.

65. *Pierwsze pokolenie marksistów*, vol. 2, pp. 681–2.

66. Krzywicki, *Dzieła*, vol. 2, p. 227.

67. Dłuski, *Szkice*, pp. 105–8, 202–10; Krusiński, *Pisma zebrane*, p. 47; *Początki marksistowskiej myśli ekonomicznej*, p. 154.

68. Dłuski, *Szkice*, p. 231.

69. Limanowski, *Socyjalizm jako konieczny objaw*, p. 93.

70. *Archiwum Ruchu Robotniczego*, vol. 8, pp. 20–22.

71. *Początki marksistowskiej myśli ekonomicznej*, p. 163.

72. Ibid., p. 139.

73. *Głos* (The Voice), a Warsaw weekly founded in 1886, representing a populist orientation; initial socialist influences were gradually supplanted in its columns with expressions of ethnic nationalism.

74. *Głos*, 1891, p. 510.

75. *Głos*, 1887, p. 333.

76. *Głos*, 1887, p. 269.

77. *Głos*, 1889, p. 13; *Początki marksistowskiej myśli ekonomicznej*, pp. 141–2.

78. *Głos*, 1890, p. 143.

79. *Głos*, 1890, p. 115.

80. Jan Ludwik Popławski (1854–1908), a journalist and political writer, the editor of *Głos*, later a cofounder of the National-Democratic Party (*endecja*), and editor of its main press organ.

81. *Głos*, 1889, p. 13.

82. *Głos*, 1890, p. 142.

83. *Głos*, 1890, p. 114.

84. *Początki marksistowskiej myśli ekonomicznej*, p. 43.

85. Krusiński, *Pisma zebrane*, pp. 16, 47.

86. *Pierwsze pokolenie marksistów*, vol. 1, pp. 112–26, 183.

87. Krzywicki, *Dzieła*, vol. 4, p. 289.

88. Ibid., p. 307.

89. *Głos*, 1891, p. 39.

90. B. Prus, *Kroniki*, vol. 2 (Warsaw, 1953), p. 490. See also J. Jedlicki, *Nieudana próba kapitalistycznej industrializacji* (Warsaw, 1964), pp. 295ff, 349ff.

91. Jan Bloch (1836–1902), one of the biggest financiers and industrialists in the Kingdom, especially active in railway building; widely known also as the author of *The Future War* (1898).

92. The Uniates, i.e. the descendants of those Eastern Orthodox believers who at the end of the sixteenth century had recognized the authority of the Roman Pope, were forcibly "converted" to the Orthodox faith: in the Russian Empire in 1839, in the Kingdom in 1875. The peasants and clergy who resisted were relentlessly persecuted.

93. *Ekonomista*, 1866, I, pp. 34–9.

94. *Niwa*, IV, 1873, p. 50.

95. Prus, *Kroniki*, vol. 2, p. 492.

96. Głowacki [B. Prus], *Szkic programu*, p. 44.

97. Świętochowski, *Liberum Veto*, vol. 2, pp. 23–4.

98. Ibid., vol. 2, p. 226.

99. *Niwa*, XVIII, 1880, pp. 776–7.

100. *Słowo*, 1883, no. 273.

101. *Słowo*, 1889, no. 3.

102. *Głos*, 1887, p. 481.

103. Głowacki [B. Prus], *Szkic programu*, pp. 112–13.

104. *Niwa*, III, 1873, p. 218.

105. Głowacki [B. Prus], *Szkic programu*, p. 123.

106. M. Żmigrodzka, *Orzeszkowa: młodość pozytywizmu* (Warsaw, 1965), pp. 180–81.

107. Stefan Żeromski (1864–1925), a leading novelist of the Polish modernist period; left diaries written in his student days: *Dzienniki*, vol. 4 (Warsaw, 1965), pp. 29–30.

108. *Przegląd Tygodniowy*, 1883, p. 200.

109. Konstantin Pobyedonostsev (1827–1907), a jurist, Alexander III's teacher and advisor, attorney-general in the Holy Synod, principally opposed to any thought of the liberalization of the tsarist regime.

110. Max Schippel, a German economist, close to Social Democracy, advised a similar policy in his *Das moderne Elend und die moderne Übervölkerung*, a book which was translated into Polish and avidly read by Polish socialist theoreticians in the 1880s.

111. Józef Potocki [Marian Bohusz] (1854–1899), an intellectual, sensitive to social and moral issues, co-editor of the *Głos* in which he represented left-wing views.

112. *Głos*, 1891, pp. 195, 210, 244, 269 et al.

113. *Ekonomista*, 1865, IV, pp. 1–12, 24–44 et al. See also K. Libelt, *Koalicja kapitału i pracy* (Poznań, 1868).

114. *Ekonomista*, 1866, I, pp. 241–51, II, pp. 132–9.

115. *Ekonomista*, 1866, II, 1–17.

116. *Ekonomista*, 1866, II, pp. 155–85.

117. *Ekonomista*, 1870, pp. 231–47, 427–55; *Niwa*, IV, 1873, pp. 76–9.

118. *Niwa*, V, 1874, pp. 217–19.

119. *Głos*, 1891, pp. 147–8, 244, 509–10, 520–22 et al.

120. *Głos*, 1889, p. 166.

Selected Bibliography

(lists major historical monographs; for primary sources see notes)

A. In English and French

Albertone M., and Masoero A. (eds.), *Political Economy and National Realities*, Torino 1994.

Berend, T. I., *The European Periphery and Industrialization, 1780–1914*, Cambridge 1982.

Blejwas S.A., *Realism in Polish Politics: Warsaw Positivism and National Survival in Nineteenth Century Poland*, New Haven 1984 (Yale Russian and East European Publications).

Brock P., *Nationalism and Populism in Partitioned Poland*, London 1973.

Chirot, D. (ed.), *The Origins of Backwardness in Eastern Europe: Economics and Politics from the Middle Ages until the Early Twentieth Century*, Berkeley 1989.

Epsztein L., *L'économie et la morale aux débuts du capitalisme industriel en France et en Grande-Bretagne*, Paris 1966.

Fabre J., *Stanislas-Auguste Poniatowski et l'Europe des Lumières: étude de cosmopolitisme*, Paris 1952.

Gerschenkron, A., *Economic Backwardness and Historical Perspective: a Book of Essays,* Cambridge, Mass. 1962.

Hazard P., *European Thought in the Eighteenth Century: from Montesquieu to Lessing*, transl. by J. L. May, Cleveland and New York 1963.

Liebich A., *Between Ideology and Utopia: the Politics and Philosophy of August Cieszkowski*, Dordrecht 1978.

Nisbet R.A., *Social Change and History: Aspects of the Western Theory of Development*, New York 1969.

Okey, R., Eastern Europe 1740–1980: *Feudalism to Communism,* Minneapolis 1982.

Pomian K., *L'Europe et ses nations*, Paris 1990.

Walicki A., *Philosophy and Romantic Nationalism: the Case of Poland*, Oxford 1982, Notre Dame, Ind., 1994.

Walicki A., *The Slavophile Controversy: History of a Conservative Utopia in Nineteenth-century Russian Thought*, transl. by H. Andrews-Rusiecka, Oxford 1975.

Wandycz P., *The Lands of Partitioned Poland, 1795–1918*, Seattle and London 1974 (A History of East Central Europe, ed. P. F. Sugar and D. W. Treadgold, vol. VII).

Williams R., *Culture and Society 1780–1950*, Harmondsworth 1961.

B. In Polish

Baczko B., *Rousseau: samotność i wspólnota* (Rousseau: solitude and community), Warszawa 1964.

Brykalska M., *Aleksander Świętochowski, redaktor "Prawdy"* (Alexander Świętochowski, editor of *Prawda*), Wrocław 1974.

Chałasiński J., *Kultura i naród* (Culture and nation), Warszawa 1968.

Czepulis-Rastenis R., *Myśl społeczna twórców Towarzystwa Rolniczego (1842–1861)* (Social thought of the founders of Agricultural Society, 1842–1861), Wrocław 1964.

Czepulis-Rastenis R. (ed.), *Inteligencja polska pod zaborami* (Polish intelligentsia under partitions), Warszawa 1978.

Górski J., *Polska myśl ekonomiczna a rozwój gospodarczy 1807–1830: studia nad początkami teorii zacofania gospodarczego* (Polish economic thought and economic development, 1807–1830: studies on the beginnings of the theory of economic backwardness), Warszawa 1963.

Grabski, A.F., *Troski i nadzieje: z dziejów polskiej myśli społecznej i politycznej XIX wieku* (Concerns and hopes: essays on the history of Polish social and political thought in the 19th century), Łódź 1981.

Handelsman M., *Rozwój narodowości nowoczesnej* (The development of modern nationality), 2nd ed., Warszawa 1973.

Janowski M., *Polska myśl liberalna do 1918 roku* (Polish liberal thought until 1918), Warszawa–Kraków 1998.

Jedlicki J., *Nieudana próba kapitalistycznej industrializacji: analiza państwowego gospodarstwa przemysłowego w Królestwie Polskim XIX w.* (A failed attempt at industrialization: an analysis of state industrial economy in the Polish Kingdom in the 19th century), Warszawa 1964.

Karpiński W., *Polska a Rosja: z dziejów słowiańskiego sporu* (Poland and Russia: from the history of a Slav dispute), Warszawa 1994.

Kizwalter T., *"Nowatorstwo i rutyny:" społeczeństwo Królestwa Polskiego wobec procesów modernizacji (1840–1863)* ("Innovation and routines:" the society of the Polish Kingdom and the modernization process, 1840–1863), Warszawa 1991.

Klarnerówna Z., *Słowianofilstwo w literaturze polskiej lat 1800 do 1846* (Slavophilism in Polish literature, 1800–1846), Warszawa 1926.

Kłoczowski J. (ed.), *Uniwersalizm i swoistość kultury polskiej* (Universality and individuality of Polish culture), 2 vols., Lublin 1989.

Król M., *Konserwatyści a niepodległość: studia nad polską myślą konserwatywną XIX wieku* (Conservatives and independence: studies on the Polish conservative thought of the 19th century), Warszawa 1985.

Krzemień-Ojak K., *Maurycy Mochnacki: program kulturalny i myśl krytyczno-literacka* (Maurycy Mochnacki: cultural program and literary criticism), Warszawa 1975.

Kula W., *Historia, zacofanie, rozwój* (History, backwardness, development), Warszawa 1983.

Ludwikowski R., *Główne nurty polskiej myśli politycznej 1815–1890* (Main currents of Polish political thought, 1815–1890), Warszawa 1982.

Markiewicz H., *Pozytywizm* (Positivism), Warszawa 1978.

Michalski J., " 'Warszawa' czyli o antystołecznych nastrojach w czasach Stanisława Augusta" ("Warszawa" or on a dislike to the capital city in the times of Stanislaus Augustus), *Studia Warszawskie*, vol. XII, Warszawa 1972.

Modzelewski W., *Naród i postęp: problematyka narodowa w ideologii i myśli społecznej pozytywistów warszawskich* (Nation and progress: the national question in the ideology and social thought of the Warsaw positivists), Warszawa 1977.

Molska A., *Model ustroju socjalistycznego w polskiej myśli marksistowskiej lat 1878–1886* (The model of socialist system in the Polish Marxist thought, 1878–1886), Warszawa 1965.

Pepłowski F., *Słownictwo i frazeologia polskiej publicystyki okresu Oświecenia i Romantyzmu* (Vocabulary and phraseology of the Polish political and social writings of the periods of Enlightenment and Romanticism), Warszawa 1961.

Piątkowski W., *J.C.L. Simonde de Sismondi: teoria ekonomiczna* (J. C. L. Simonde de Sismondi: his economic theory), Warszawa 1978.

Pieróg S., *Maurycy Mochnacki: studium romantycznej świadomości* (Maurycy Mochnacki: a study of Romantic consciousness), Warszawa 1982.

Polska myśl filozoficzna i społeczna (Polish philosophical and social thought), vol. I: 1831–1864, ed. A. Walicki, Warszawa 1973.

Polska myśl filozoficzna i społeczna (Polish philosophical and social thought), vol. II, ed. B. Skarga, Warszawa 1975.

Raszewski Z., *Staroświecczyzna i postęp czasu: o teatrze polskim (1765–1865)* (Old-fashioned ways and progress of time: on Polish theater, 1765–1865), Warszawa 1963.

Rychliński S., "Praca organiczna w Królestwie Polskiem po powstaniu styczniowem" (Organic work in the Polish Kingdom after the January Rising), Ph.D. dissertation [1930], ms. Library of Szkoła Główna Handlowa, Warszawa.

Serejski M.H., *Europa a rozbiory Polski: studium historiograficzne* (Europe and the partitions of Poland: a historiographic study), Warszawa 1970.

Serejski M.H., *Przeszłość a teraźniejszość: szkice i studia historiograficzne* (Past and present: historiographic essays), Wrocław 1965.

Skałkowski A.M., *Aleksander Wielopolski w świetle archiwów rodzinnych* (Aleksander Wielopolski in the light of family archives), 3 vols., Poznań 1947.

Skarga B., *Narodziny pozytywizmu polskiego (1831–1864)* (The birth of Polish positivism, 1831–1864), Warszawa 1964.

Stefanowska Z. (ed.), *Swojskość i cudzoziemszczyzna w dziejach kultury polskiej* (Homeliness and foreignness in the history of Polish culture), Warszawa 1973.

Szacka B., *Teoria i utopia Stanisława Staszica* (Theory and utopia of Stanisław Staszic), Warszawa 1965.

Szacki J., *Ojczyzna, naród, rewolucja: problematyka narodowa w polskiej myśli szlachecko-rewolucyjnej* (Fatherland, nation, revolution: national problems and revolutionary ideas in the Polish gentry thought), Warszawa 1962.

Szacki J. (ed.), *Idea społeczeństwa komunistycznego w pracach klasyków marksizmu* (The idea of a communist society in the works of the founders of Marxism), Warszawa 1977.

Szubert W., *Studia o Fryderyku Skarbku jako ekonomiście* (Studies on Fryderyk Skarbek as an economist), Łódź 1954.

Tazbir J., *Rzeczpospolita i świat: studia z dziejów kultury XVII wieku* (*Res Publica* and the world: studies on the cultural history of the 17th century), Wrocław 1971.

Temkin G., *Karola Marksa obraz gospodarki komunistycznej* (Karl Marx's image of the communist economy), Warszawa 1962.

Tych F., *Socjalistyczna irredenta: szkice z dziejów polskiego ruchu robotniczego pod zaborami* (Socialist *irredenta*: essays from the history of Polish workers' movement under partitions), Kraków 1982.

Ujejski J., *Dzieje polskiego mesjanizmu do powstania listopadowego włącznie* (History of Polish Messianism until the November Rising), Lwów 1931.

Walicki A., *Filozofia a mesjanizm: studia z dziejów filozofii i myśli społeczno-religijnej romantyzmu polskiego* (Philosophy and Messianism: studies from the history of philosophical, social and religious thought of Polish Romanticism), Warszawa 1970.

Walicki A., *Między filozofią, religią i polityką: studia o myśli polskiej epoki romantyzmu* (Between philosophy, religion, and politics: studies on Polish thought in the period of Romanticism), Warszawa 1983.

Walicki A., *Polska, Rosja, marksizm: studia z dziejów marksizmu i jego recepcji* (Poland, Russia, Marxism: studies from the history of Marxism and its reception), Warszawa 1983.

Warzenica E., *Pozytywistyczny "obóz młodych" wobec tradycji wielkiej polskiej poezji romantycznej (lata 1866–1881)* (The positivist "young camp" in the face of tradition of the great Polish romantic poetry, 1866–1881), Warszawa 1968.

Wierzbicki A., *Wschód–Zachód w koncepcjach dziejów Polski: z dziejów polskiej myśli historycznej w dobie porozbiorowej* (East–West in the concepts of Poland's history: Polish historical thought in the post-partitions period), Warszawa 1984.

Witkowska A., *Kazimierz Brodziński* (Kazimierz Brodziński), Warszawa 1968.

Witkowska A., *Słowianie, my lubim sielanki. . .* ("Slavs, we like pastorals . . .), Warszawa 1972.

Wołoszyński R., *Ignacy Krasicki: utopia i rzeczywistość* (Ignacy Krasicki: utopia and reality), Wrocław 1970.

Zieliński A., *Naród i narodowość w polskiej literaturze i publicystyce lat 1815–1831* (Nation and nationality in Polish literature and political writing, 1815–1831), Wrocław 1969.

Żmigrodzka M., *Orzeszkowa: młodość pozytywizmu* (Orzeszkowa: the youth of positivism), Warszawa 1965.

Żmigrodzka M. and Lewinówna Z. (eds.), *Problemy polskiego romantyzmu* (Problems of Polish Romanticism), vol. I, Wrocław 1971.

Żurawicka J., *Inteligencja warszawska w końcu XIX wieku* (Warsaw intelligentsia at the end of the 19th century), Warszawa 1978.

Index